Oculus Rift in Action

Oculus Rift
in Action

BRADLEY AUSTIN DAVIS
KAREN BRYLA
PHILLIPS ALEXANDER BENTON

MANNING

SHELTER ISLAND

For online information and ordering of this and other Manning books, please visit
www.manning.com. The publisher offers discounts on this book when ordered in quantity.
For more information, please contact

> Special Sales Department
> Manning Publications Co.
> 20 Baldwin Road
> PO Box 761
> Shelter Island, NY 11964
> Email: orders@manning.com

Manning Publications Co.
20 Baldwin Road
PO Box 761
Shelter Island, NY 11964

Development editor:	Dan Maharry
Technical development editor	Justin Chase
Copyeditor:	Liz Welch
Proofreader:	Elizabeth Martin
Technical proofreader:	Frederik Vanhoutte
Typesetter:	Dennis Dalinnik
Cover designer:	Marija Tudor

ISBN 9781617292194
Printed in the United States of America
1 2 3 4 5 6 7 8 9 10 – EBM – 20 19 18 17 16 15

brief contents

contents

foreword

Two amazing advances from the smartphone arms race have come together to create the head-mounted display (HMD): light, cheap, high-resolution displays, and a new generation of super accurate and fast-motion sensor chips. Rather than display information or graphics on the surface in front of you, these displays rest on your head and update quickly enough to convince you that what you're seeing is as real as the place you left behind. Although HMDs have existed for decades, they've never worked well enough to be more than aspirational prototypes destined for science museums. But with the Oculus Rift, the sensation of having a stable 3D world surround you as you move your head is a game-changing shift from peering into a 3D space through a desktop screen or handheld device.

Within the next 10 years, improved devices like the Oculus Rift will replace many of the screens we surround ourselves with today as their resolution scales to eclipse our TVs and monitors. Ultimately, we will use them to replace as much or as little of the world around us as we choose, with digital content that is indistinguishable from reality. The impact of these first-generation devices on gaming and virtual worlds will be incredible.

But along this road there are many changes to UI, experience, and computing paradigms that you'll need to understand, and the authors of *Oculus Rift in Action* take you on a comprehensive overview of them. As a developer getting started with the Rift, you get a complete walkthrough of connecting to and rendering to the device.

Beyond this, you'll learn the important differences raised by such devices: How do you type without a keyboard? If Microsoft and the Mac revolutionized computing by putting things in windows, what will we do in an HMD? Why do we get sick using these devices, and how can we fix that? This book gives a complete and grounded overview of the specific technology and operation of the Oculus Rift, as well as the big picture topics that you'll need to survive in a new world without monitors. Finally, it dives into the new and complex design factors around how to correctly control things, navigate, and build in the virtual world as an "avatar" given the capabilities and limitations of these new input devices for the head and body.

PHILIP ROSEDALE
CREATOR OF SECOND LIFE

preface

No matter what people have, they always dream of something more: more power, more influence, more knowledge, but perhaps most importantly, more possibilities. This drive is part of the human condition and is responsible for our going from the Wright brothers to Apollo 11 in a single century.

If you want the future, you have to build it yourself. But the future I want, the one I think many of us want, isn't something we can each build on our own, if only for lack of time and resources.

We've written this book to lend a hand to those who want to help build the future in virtual reality (VR) but perhaps don't know where to start.

BRAD DAVIS
SEATTLE, WA

Virtual reality was not something I'd expected to ever get involved in. As fun as it was to daydream about having my own holodeck to simulate an environment as if I were really there, the technology never seemed to be there, and so I pursued other work. My coauthor Brad, though, paid more attention and spotted the Oculus Rift on Kickstarter. As an early backer, he was very enthusiastic about its potential to create truly commercial VR. Brad made it sound interesting enough that I ordered my own DK1 development kit. While I waited the two months for it to ship, I researched what others were doing and watched YouTube videos. When it finally arrived, nothing I'd seen or read could do justice to the actual experience.

Like many people, my first experience was the *Oculus World* (also known as *Tuscany*) demo. In it you can meander around an old Tuscan villa. The graphics aren't spectacular, and the low resolution on the DK1 made it appear as though I was looking through a screen door, but those things didn't matter one little bit when I tilted my head to look up and the scene changed to match where I was looking. I was overcome by giggly delight, looking up at the wooden rafters of the house. When I moved my avatar outside, I looked up to see the sky. This was immersion as I'd never felt before, and it was amazing.

That first experience sent my mind racing with thoughts about the potential of VR. I could see the Rift being used for gaming, virtual tourism, storytelling, and science. But to me, education was the most interesting, and it's where I first saw the Rift's potential turned into reality. When my younger son came home from school telling me he was learning about Paris and the Eiffel Tower for multicultural day, I downloaded the *Tower Eiffel* demo by Didier Thery and let him see what it's like to stand beneath the tower's impressive metal arches.

When my boys and I watched the *Nova* television series with Neil deGrasse Tyson, I downloaded *Titans of Space* by DrashVR so that they could take their own trip through the solar system and feel how grand and vast the universe truly is. They, of course, now want to visit Paris and work for NASA, and I'm truly excited to see what the future brings.

KAREN BRYLA
TINTON FALLS, NJ

A long time ago, I noticed that people are always looking *around* but they rarely look *up*. I guess it's because there's not usually a lot of stuff overhead to see. I thought that if I could help people learn to look up as often as they look around, then we would go to space sooner, because people would look up at the stars and the moon and think, "Hey, let's go check that out." And I want to go to the moon. Not just as a one-off thing where you leave your lander behind when you go home—I want humans to have real cities in space, with shops and streets and hot dog stands.

So I got into computer graphics because of space. I figured that the best way I can get there (short of becoming an astronaut, which seems too much like real work) is to make virtual reality happen. I want to put people into virtual worlds that train them to expect more from the real one. In VR, there's no reason for the world not to stretch as far above you as it does to either side. In VR, we can make worlds where all the best stuff is overhead, and you'll always have to look up to find it. After a while, looking up will get to be a habit.

And if we can teach people to look up, then someday I'll eat a hot dog on the moon.

ALEX BENTON
LONDON, ENGLAND

acknowledgments

Creating this book was not an isolated effort by the writers. In fact, it took tremendous effort, patience, and support from a great many wonderful and talented people to make this book possible.

Thank you to Dan Maharry, our development editor at Manning, who has the patience of a saint and excellent taste in '90s sci-fi. His guidance throughout this process was invaluable. Thanks to Robin de Jongh for getting the ball rolling for us. And thank you to Mary Piergies, Liz Welch, Elizabeth Martin, Kevin Sullivan, Justin Chase, and Frederik Vanhoutte, and the rest of the team at Manning for all of their help getting this book to completion, something that at times felt like a Sisyphean task. It takes an amazing team to get that rock over the hill.

We need to give special thanks to Iñigo Quilez and Pol Jeremias, authors of Shadertoy.com, for their advice and support on ShadertoyVR. And we also want to thank Philip Rosedale, creator of Second Life, for writing the foreword.

We'd also like to thank our MEAP readers for their comments and corrections to our early draft chapters, and to the following reviewers who read the manuscript at various stages during development: Alex Lucas, Andrew Henderson, Bas van Oerle, Behram Patel, Çağatay Çatal, Daniel Walters, George Freeman, Jan-Jaap Severs, Joaquin Gracia, Jose San Leandro, Kathleen Estrada, Ken Fricklas, Mackenzie Zastrow, Marco Massenzio, and Scott Chaussée.

Finally, none of us could have done this without the support of our families.

BRAD DAVIS wishes to thank Leo and Kesten, for all their understanding and devotion.

KAREN BRYLA wishes to thank her husband Sam Kass and her children, Ted and Max, for their patience and support. She particularly wants to thank them for so willingly testing out early versions of demos to help her better understand what triggers motion sickness in VR. She also needs to thank Sam for taking many of the photos used in this book and for his invaluable feedback on the text and examples.

ALEX BENTON wishes to thank his amazing wife, Dr. Antonia Benton, for her constant support and encouragement, and Verna Coulson for her unwavering enthusiasm.

about this book

Oculus Rift in Action is designed to help you create comfortable and usable virtual reality (VR) applications that run on the Oculus Rift head-mounted display.

How this book is organized

This book is organized into five parts:

- *Part 1: Getting started*—Part 1 introduces you to VR and the Oculus Rift hardware. We'll cover why you'd want to support the Rift in your software and how the Rift works.
- *Part 2: Using the Oculus C API*—Part 2 covers how to develop Rift applications using the Oculus C API. Whether you're looking to write applications using the API directly, to integrate Rift support into your own game engine, or simply to better understand how Rift support works in your game engine of choice (Unity, for example), this part of the book is for you.
- *Part 3: Using Unity*—Part 3 covers how to use Unity, a popular development IDE and 3D graphics engine, to develop Rift applications. Unity is a great way to jump-start creating 3D games as it handles just about every aspect of game development, such as graphics, audio, physics, interaction and networking. With the Unity integration package from Oculus, you can quickly get your application running on the Rift. If you want to use Unity for your VR development, you'll find much value in part 3.
- *Part 4: The VR user experience*—In part 4, we turn our attention to the VR experience. No matter how you've created your VR application, you're going to want

to design your application so that it's comfortable and easy to use in the VR environment. In this part of the book we look at the challenges of creating a usable UI for the VR environment. We cover some of the common pitfalls of designing a UI for VR along with the latest research into the key components to an immersive virtual experience. We also take a look at what you can do to maximize user comfort, including guidelines and examples of how to mitigate motion sickness triggers and other causes of physical discomfort such as fatigue and eyestrain.

- *Part 5: Advanced Rift integrations*—In the final chapters, we provide information and examples for work that goes beyond the core integration of the Rift APIs. Here you'll learn to work with the Oculus C API using Java or Python, along with the basics of how to use the C APIs with any language. We also provide an example of creating a complete VR experience by building a VR version of an existing web application for use on the Rift. Finally, we cover integrating additional inputs into Rift apps, using modern hardware like web cameras and the Leap Motion.

Wondering where to start? Every reader should start with part 1 because it introduces you to the hardware and to the virtual reality concepts we'll be using throughout the book. After that, where you go depends on how you plan to develop your application. C/C++ developers will want to turn to part 2 and Unity developers to part 3. No matter how you're going to develop, your next stop should be part 4, to learn how to ensure your users get the most out of your application. When you're ready to move on to advanced Rift integrations and see a full-fledged VR app in action, turn to part 5.

What this book doesn't do

This book doesn't cover how to use OpenGL, nor does it discuss the basics of 3D programming. It also doesn't cover C or C++ or how to use any particular development environment. If you're unfamiliar with these topics, you'll find some good references listed in appendix C.

Code conventions and downloads

All source code in the book is in a `fixed-width font` like this, which sets it off from the surrounding text. In many listings, the code is annotated to point out the key concepts, and numbered bullets are sometimes used in the text to provide additional information about the code.

We have tried to format the code so that it fits within the available page space in the book by adding line breaks and using indentation carefully. Sometimes, however, very long lines include line-continuation markers. **Bold `fixed-width font`** like this in listings indicates new code.

Source code for all the working examples in this book is available online in our GitHub repository at github.com/OculusRiftInAction/OculusRiftInAction.

If you're using Unity (part 3 of this book), you don't need to download the entire example repository. The scripts and the example scenes for part 3 are in /examples/unity.

If you're using the C API (part 2 of this book), details of how to download and build the C++ and Java example applications are discussed next.

SDK version

All of our C++, Java, and Python examples have been tested against Oculus SDK version 0.5.0. The Oculus SDK will continue to evolve, through the release of the Rift and afterward. As the code in this book gradually drifts further out of date, you should check back on our GitHub repository for updates and improvements.

Unity's Oculus Rift support is updated on a separate track and may be independently maintained.

Required tools: Git, CMake, and a build environment

To access the example source code, you need to use a source control tool called Git. Git binaries for Microsoft Windows, Mac OS X, and Linux are available at git-scm.com.

To make it easier to work with the examples across a variety of platforms, we use a tool called CMake. CMake allows you to create meta-project files that describe how your code is organized into libraries and executables, and it can be used to create project files for a given platform, such as Xcode (on OS X), Visual Studio (on Windows), and Make or Ninja on Linux. CMake binaries are available at cmake.org.

If you plan to run the examples, you'll need to install both CMake and Git.

To build the code, you'll need a build environment on your platform, such as Xcode, Visual Studio, or Make or Ninja. Although the examples listed are the defaults used by CMake, CMake does allow you to specify a different generator if you want to use something other than the default. To see a list of all the generators supported on the current platform, run cmake -h. Note that we don't know if every generator supported will work; we've only tested with the latest free versions of the default for each platform (and Eclipse CDT4 using Ninja, because we like it).

Required libraries

Unless otherwise specified, for the examples we'll be showing throughout the book all of the libraries required are included in the example code repository.

This includes the Oculus VR SDK. Although you may want to get the latest version of the SDK directly from the Oculus website before you start any real-world projects, you don't need it for the example code in the book. The steps we'll describe for setting up your development environment will cover how to download everything you need to get started.

Note that the SDK version here is what we refer to as the "community SDK," because it's a copy of the official SDK with some minor changes and bug fixes. The differences between the community SDK and the official SDK are negligible as of this writing, and intended to remain so. (If any example code hinges on some difference between the official SDK and the community SDK, then we've failed to do our jobs.) Therefore, for the purposes of the code in this book, unless explicitly stated otherwise, please assume the code we're teaching would work just as well with either version.

The libraries on which our example demos depend are connected to the repository as Git submodules. Submodules are a mechanism by which one repository can refer to another, making it easier for the submodules to be updated as needed without disrupting the overall project. For the most part this should all be transparent to you when you do the checkout.

Checking out the example code and creating the project files

To build the example code, you first need to clone the example code repository using Git. After the clone is complete, create the project files using CMake. After you've run CMake successfully, you can go to your development environment of choice (Xcode, Eclipse, Visual Studio, etc.) and open the project files.

CLONING THE REPOSITORY WITH GIT

To clone the repository, complete the following steps:

1 Choose the directory where you want to work. You can select any directory that you want, but keep in mind that when you check out a Git repository, it'll automatically create a folder for it.

2 Open a command prompt[1] and change to your working directory.

To change to your working directory, enter:

```
cd <directory>
```

where <directory> is the path and directory of where you plan to do your work.

3 On the command line, run Git to fetch the files.

```
git clone --recursive
➥ https://github.com/OculusRiftInAction/OculusRiftInAction.git
```

The --recursive flag is very important here. It tells Git to check out not only the specified repository, but all of the Git submodules as well.

By default this will create an OculusRiftInAction folder underneath the current folder. If you want to use a different name, you can add it to the end of the command.

After the clone is complete, the next step is to create the project files using CMake.

---

[1] To open a command prompt on Windows, press Windows-R to open the Run dialog box, type cmd, and press Enter. To open a command prompt on Mac OS X, in the Finder go into Applications, and then Utilities, and start the Terminal application. This should open a console window in your home directory. On Linux, press Ctrl-Alt-T.

CREATING THE PROJECT FILES WITH CMAKE

To create the project files, complete the following steps:

1 Change directories so that you're in the newly checked-out repository.

```
cd OculusRiftInAction
```

2 Create and then change to a build directory:

```
mkdir build
cd build
```

3 Run CMake to create the project files. If you're using the default build environment for your platform, run this command:

```
cmake ..
```

This will create project files for the default build environment on your platform. This is Xcode for OS X, Visual Studio for Windows, and Makefiles for Unix. But you can customize this by telling CMake to use a different generator. Run `cmake -h` to print out a list of command-line switches, as well as the list of generators supported on the current platform. For example, when running in Linux, we use the following command:

```
cmake .. -G "Eclipse CDT4 - Ninja"
```

NOTE Even if a generator is listed as supported, it doesn't mean it'll work. You'll need to have it already installed on your system, at the very least, and we've only tested with the latest free versions of the default for each platform.

Once you've run CMake successfully and it hasn't reported any errors, you can go into your development environment and open the project files. From there, you can use your chosen environment to build the examples.

about the authors

BRAD DAVIS is a software developer for High Fidelity, a startup working on open source, social VR applications. He's an active participant in the Oculus VR developer forums and maintains a set of example Rift applications on GitHub. His ultimate dream is to create a portable VR rig that allows you to watch *Inception* anywhere you want and then to wear it to a theater during a showing of *Inception*.

KAREN BRYLA is a graduate of Carnegie Mellon University and an experienced writer, developer, and usability analyst. Of particular interest to her is how users adapt to new technology and how she can help developers design applications for new mediums that are both functional and intuitive.

ALEX BENTON holds a PhD in applied mathematics from the University of Cambridge, where he is an Associate Lecturer in Advanced Graphics. He was a pioneering author of the original VRML (Virtual Reality Modeling Language) browser for Netscape in 1996. He has since worked at a number of Silicon Valley startups, including multiple 3D gaming companies, and holds patents in three-dimensional orthodontic software. He's currently a Senior Software Engineer at Google in London, England, where he lives with his wife and two cats.

All three authors are contributing writers to Rifty-Business, rifty-business.blogspot .com, a blog focused on Rift software development.

author online

Purchase of *Oculus Rift in Action* includes free access to a private web forum run by Manning Publications where you can make comments about the book, ask technical questions, and receive help from the authors and from other users. To access the forum and subscribe to it, point your web browser to www.manning.com/bdavis. This page provides information on how to get on the forum after you're registered, what kind of help is available, and the rules of conduct on the forum.

Manning's commitment to our readers is to provide a venue where a meaningful dialogue between individual readers and between readers and authors can take place. It's not a commitment to any specific amount of participation on the part of the authors, whose contribution to the Author Online remains voluntary (and unpaid).

The Author Online forum and the archives of previous discussions will be accessible from the publisher's website as long as the book is in print.

about the cover illustration

The caption for the illustration on the cover of *Oculus Rift in Action* is "Veiled Dancer."
The illustration is taken from a collection of costumes of the Ottoman Empire published on January 1, 1802, by William Miller of Old Bond Street, London. The title page is missing from the collection and we have been unable to track it down to date. The book's table of contents identifies the figures in both English and French, and each illustration bears the names of two artists who worked on it, both of whom would no doubt be surprised to find their art gracing the front cover of a computer programming book ... two hundred years later.

The collection was purchased by a Manning editor at an antiquarian flea market in the "Garage" on West 26th Street in Manhattan. The seller was an American based in Ankara, Turkey, and the transaction took place just as he was packing up his stand for the day. The Manning editor didn't have on his person the substantial amount of cash that was required for the purchase, and a credit card and check were both politely turned down. With the seller flying back to Ankara that evening, the situation was getting hopeless. What was the solution? It turned out to be nothing more than an old-fashioned verbal agreement sealed with a handshake. The seller simply proposed that the money be transferred to him by wire, and the editor walked out with the bank information on a piece of paper and the portfolio of images under his arm. Needless to say, we transferred the funds the next day, and we remain grateful and impressed by this unknown person's trust in one of us. It recalls something that might have happened a long time ago.

We at Manning celebrate the inventiveness, the initiative, and, yes, the fun of the computer business with book covers based on the rich diversity of regional life of two centuries ago, brought back to life by the pictures from this collection.

Part 1

Getting started

Part 1 of *Oculus Rift in Action* introduces you to the Oculus Rift hardware and to virtual reality (VR). We begin with an exploration of what VR is and why you'd want to develop for the Rift. From there, we move on to an overview of the Rift hardware and how it works. Next you'll learn about the development paths you can take for creating your Rift application.

One unusual aspect to working with the Rift is that using it can be physically uncomfortable, because it can sometimes trigger symptoms of motion sickness. To help you have a more pleasant working experience, part 1 also includes tips on what you can do to deal with motion sickness.

When you are done with part 1, you'll be ready to start building Rift applications using your chosen development path, either working directly with the C API (part 2) or with Unity (part 3).

Meet the Oculus Rift

Because you picked up this book, you probably already know that the Rift is a virtual reality head-mounted display (VR HMD). You may have one of your own, or perhaps you've tried one out and were, like us, blown away by the intense immersion. Even if you've only read about the Rift in passing, if you watch demo videos and reaction shots you can often see the look of incredulous delight on people's faces the first time they use the Rift.

With its vast field of view (more than double what you get with a typical monitor) and head tracking (the wearer just turns their head to see what they want, with no need to use a mouse or joystick to orient), the Rift represents an opportunity for people to view your work in a way they never could before.

In this book, we'll show you how to build immersive environments that run on the Rift. The first steps are rendering to the device and tracking the user's head movements. After that we'll discuss the unique usability challenges of VR and the steps you can take to avoid causing motion sickness for some users.

Before we get started, let's talk a bit about why you should support the Rift.

1.1 Why support the Rift?

There are really two questions here: whether you should support VR in general and whether you should support the Rift specifically.

1.1.1 The call of virtual reality

If you've ever seen an episode of *Star Trek: The Next Generation* and imagined what you could do with your own personal holodeck, or wished you were the greatest swordfighter in the Metaverse, then this book is for you. Perhaps you've played games where you controlled a giant robot and wished you could look out on the war-torn landscape by turning your head, or maybe you've wished you could build cities with a wave of your hand. If so, you've felt the call of VR, and this book is for you.

Maybe you have more practical interests, such as saving money or increasing safety. For years, VR has been used in specialized niches where immersion in an environment, without actually being *in* the environment, was critical. The canonical example is the flight simulator. When you're training a pilot to operate a piece of machinery that costs tens or hundreds of millions of dollars, spending a few hundred thousand, or even a few million, on creating an artificial environment in which to train without the risks associated with a real aircraft can be a wise investment.

1.1.2 But what about the Rift?

What's special about the Rift is that it can deliver nearly the same level of immersion as existing commercial setups costing orders of magnitude more, but at a price that makes it available, if not to the average consumer, at least to the average consumer who would already have the kind of computing or gaming system that can support the Rift.[1]

---

[1] The first development kit was sold for $300, a price comparable to high-end video cards. Oculus has repeatedly said it's trying to hit the same price point for the consumer version, albeit with vastly improved specifications.

Immersion and presence

Two key terms we use to describe VR are *immersion* and *presence*.

Immersion is the art and technology of surrounding the user with a virtual context, such that there's world above, below, and all around you.

Presence is the visceral reaction to a convincing immersion experience. It's when immersion is so good that the body reacts instinctively to the virtual world as though it's the real one.

When you turn your head to look up at the attacking enemy bombers, that's immersion; when you can't stop yourself from ducking as they roar by overhead, that's presence.

The appeal of applying VR to the field of gaming should be obvious, and indeed gaming is the area that'll almost certainly drive mass-market adoption. But the exciting thing to us is the potential the Rift brings. By democratizing the use and development of VR, it has the potential to radically alter the world in ways we can't yet imagine.

But all this cheerleading might not be assuaging your doubts. Maybe you feel the call of VR, but you (or your manager) don't know whether your project has the budget to include such frivolous features as virtual reality. Well, here's the great part: supporting the Rift is cheap and easy, and we're going to show you how to do it.

Need more inspiration? Let's look at what people are already doing with the Rift.

1.2 How is the Rift being used today?

Developers around the world are taking the Rift and doing amazing things with it, either displacing previous VR solutions at a fraction of the price or creating innovative applications that weren't possible or practical before. The examples that follow are just a small sample of what's going on in VR right now, but we hope they provide some inspiration as you start your own projects.

One obvious application of VR is virtual tourism. In our opinion, no other media comes as close to making you feel like you're somewhere else quite like VR. We'd even say that if a picture is worth a thousand words, a VR experience is worth a million words. One virtual tourism demo that can give you a taste for what VR can do is *Tower Eiffel* (share.oculus.com/app/tower-eiffel) by Didier Thery (figure 1.1). You can look at a picture of the Eiffel Tower or watch a movie, you can read about how tall it is and about how it was constructed, but none of that will convey to you what it feels like to look up and see the metal arches of the tower above you.

Visiting the Eiffel Tower is possible in real life, but visiting outer space is a bit out of reach for most people. That brings us to another one of our favorite demos, *Titans of Space* (share.oculus.com/app/titans-of-space) by DrashVR LLC (figure 1.2). In *Titans of Space*, you can get a feel for the beauty and vastness of space.

Feel like you're
standing here.

Figure 1.1   *Tower Eiffel* by Didier Thery

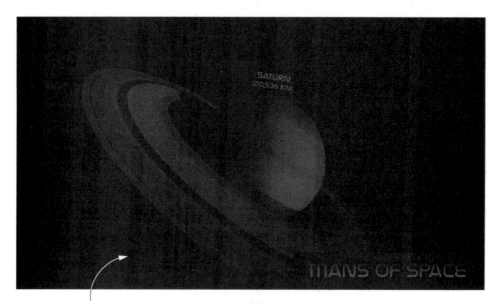

Immersed in this scene, you can
feel the vastness of space.

Figure 1.2   *Titans of Space* by DrashVR LLC

When this spider crawls up "your" arm,
it's a very visceral and creepy feeling.

Figure 1.3 *Don't Let Go!* **by Skydome Studios**

VR can do more than just make you feel what it's like to be someplace else: it can provide an experience so visceral that it'll make you break out in goose bumps, jump with fright, or duck to avoid an oncoming object. *Don't Let Go!* (share.oculus.com/app/dont-let-go) by Skydome Studios, shown in figure 1.3, is a fun example of the chills and thrills of VR.

When you combine a virtual world with thrills and goals, you've got what some consider the ultimate experience: immersive gaming. Valve's *Team Fortress 2* (store.steampowered.com/app/440/), shown in figure 1.4, was one of the first existing games to be updated with Oculus Rift support and is well worth a look.

Of course, not all Rift experiments are fun and games. The Rift has also facilitated some serious work. One of the more interesting experiments we've seen using the Rift is by the research group BeAnotherLab (www.themachinetobeanother.org). Their experiment uses the Rift, multiple cameras, and human actors to allow users to view what it'd be like to be someone else, as shown in figure 1.5. The BeAnotherLab experiment allows researchers to get a view into human empathy that previously wasn't affordable to a lab on a modest budget.

Figure 1.4   *Team Fortress 2*: one of the first games to be updated with Oculus Rift support

Figure 1.5   Two subjects in an experiment by BeAnotherLab look down and see themselves as the other person, thanks to a set of cameras and the Rift as seen in the BeAnotherLab promotional video found on its website (www.themachinetobeanother.org/?page_id=764).

Figure 1.6　An experiment using the Rift to allow tank drivers to drive with the hatch closed, as seen in a report on Norwegian TV station TUTV

In even more practical terms, we think the Norwegian army is taking an intriguing approach to using the Rift (figure 1.6) to increase the safety of soldiers during combat (http://mng.bz/0tzo). In this experimental use of the Rift, cameras are mounted on all sides of the tank. The images are then fed to a driver wearing the Rift inside the tank. The intent is to allow the driver to drive the tank with the hatch closed during combat situations.

Ready to meet the Rift? Let's go!

1.3　Get to know the Rift hardware

So far, two models of the Rift have been made commercially available: the first and second developer kits, known as DK1 and DK2. The DK1 has been discontinued and replaced with the DK2. We'll cover the hardware for both versions.

1.3.1　The DK2

The DK2 kit includes:

- A headset.
- An infrared USB camera for positional tracking.
- Two pairs of lenses, referred to as A and B lenses (plus a cloth to clean them). The A lenses come preinstalled in the headset.

- A paired HDMI/USB cable.
- A positional tracker sync cable.
- A DVI-to-HDMI adapter.
- A 5V DC power adapter for U.S.-style power, with international adapters for other countries.

In addition, the kits include the *Oculus Rift Development Kit Instruction Manual.* This manual covers basic usage of the headset along with important health and safety notes. Please read and observe all precautions before using the Rift. For the most up-to-date health and safety information, check the Oculus VR website (developer.oculus.com/ documentation/).

The following sections provide more information on the bits and pieces that make up the DK2.

THE HEADSET

The headset, shown in figure 1.7, is formed of black molded plastic. It has small adjustment wheels on the left and right sides that allow you to move the display closer to or farther from your face. There's foam padding on the surfaces intended to rest against the skin and straps that secure the Rift to your head. In addition to the normal "around the sides" strap that you might find on any pair of ski goggles, another strap goes over the top of your head. This third strap provides additional support for the headset, which, though light, can be front-heavy enough to cause fatigue during extended use. Perhaps more important, the third strap reduces the need to secure the side straps as tightly, alleviating another potential source of discomfort and fatigue.

The headset's display power button is located on the top edge of the headset next to the power indicator light. The indicator light glows blue when the headset is powered on and receiving a video signal, and it glows orange when the headset is on but not receiving a video signal. (If you're not getting a signal, see the troubleshooting section in appendix A.)

The headset incorporates the following:

- A single 1920 × 1080 display
- An inertial measurement unit (IMU) that reports linear and angular acceleration as well as magnetic field strength and direction
- Several infrared lights that are tracked by the included tracking camera to provide user position data
- A built-in latency tester

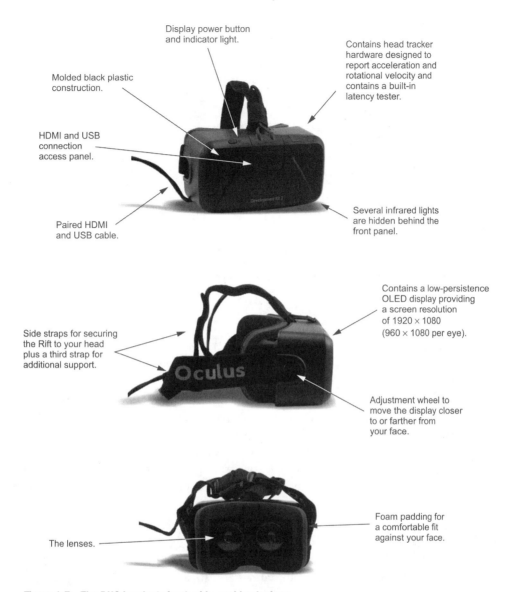

Figure 1.7 The DK2 headset: front, side, and back views

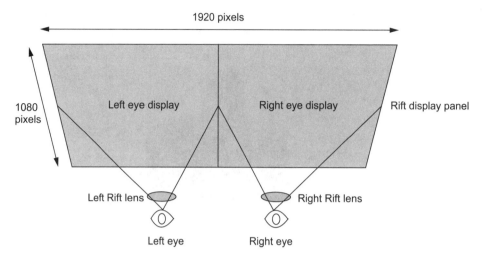

Figure 1.8   **The DK2 display is split between both eyes.**

The display is split between both eyes (each eye can see only half of the display), yielding 960 × 1080 per eye, as shown in figure 1.8.

The display panel itself isn't particularly remarkable, except in the sense that such a lightweight and high-density display would've been remarkable 10 years ago and an astonishing 10 years before that. The mobile computing industry has driven the commodification of small, high-resolution panels at an amazing pace, and the recent rounds of competition between the primary tablet and display manufacturers on the basis of pixels per inch will only drive this trend in a favorable direction.

The head-tracking hardware is somewhat more specialized. It's designed to report both acceleration and rotational velocity at a rate of 1,000 times per second. Even though impressive, this doesn't represent any sort of quantum leap over the commodity hardware found in most modern game controllers and mobile devices.

THE LENSES
The DK2 model includes two pairs of lenses, termed the A and B lenses. The A lenses are for those with 20/20 vision and are installed in the headset by default. The B lenses (shown in figure 1.9) are for those who are very nearsighted.

Figure 1.9   **The DK2 B lenses**

The lens pairs are identical in terms of how they transmit light. How they differ is that they place the lens at slightly different distances from the actual display. Combined with the headset distance-adjustment knobs, this allows the user to vary the distance between the screen and the lenses, as well as between the lenses and the eyes (commonly referred to as "eye relief"), in order to accommodate a wide variety of facial characteristics as well as users who require prescription glasses.

Note that the DK2 doesn't allow you to change the distance between the lenses, which is fixed at 63.5 mm apart, but this isn't as much of an issue as you might expect. The lenses are designed to present the same image to the user regardless of exactly where the eyes are located. If you move an image-capturing device (your eye, for instance) off the center axis of the lens, the image captured doesn't itself move laterally. As long as they're within an area of about 1.5 × 1.5 cm across and 0.5 cm deep, your eyes will perceive the same image from the screen, barring a small amount of distortion at the edges, with the same pixel appearing "directly ahead." This allows the Rift to support a broad swath of users with varying interpupillary distances. This remarkable property is called *collimated light* and will be discussed in detail in chapter 4.

THE POSITIONAL CAMERA

To track the user's head position, the DK2 uses a camera (figure 1.10) to detect infrared lights located in the headset (hidden behind the front of the headset). You'll notice that the lens of the camera is mirrored, because it tracks only infrared light.

The camera is connected to your computer via USB and to the headset using the included camera sync cable. The placement of the camera is critical to how well positional tracking will work. The camera should be placed about 5 feet from the headset, and you should make sure that the camera has an unobstructed view of the headset at all times. The camera can be placed on your desk or on top of your monitor, or because it also includes a standard tripod attachment, you can attach it to a tripod, which gives you more options for placement.

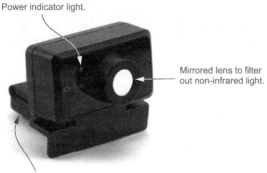

Power indicator light.

Mirrored lens to filter out non-infrared light.

Stand lets you rest the camera on your desk or clip the camera to a monitor. It also has a tripod mount for use with a standard tripod.

Figure 1.10   The DK2 positional camera

It's important that nothing blocks the camera's view of the headset, so you shouldn't place any stickers or other objects on the headset that could block the lights from detection by the positional camera.

Now let's look at the original development kit for those who are still using DK1 hardware.

1.3.2   *The DK1*

The DK1 kit includes the following:

- A headset with an attached control box
- Three pairs of lenses, referred to as A, B, and C lenses (plus a cloth to clean the lenses)
- A USB cable with male A to mini B connectors
- A 5V DC power adapter for U.S.-style power, with international adapters for various other countries
- DVI and/or HDMI cables[2]

Like the DK2, the kit includes an *Oculus Rift Development Kit Instruction Manual* that covers basic usage of the headset, along with health and safety notes. Again, read and observe all precautions before using the Rift. For the most up-to-date health and safety information, please check the Oculus VR website (developer.oculus.com/documentation/).

Now let's take a look at the parts of the DK1.

THE HEADSET

The DK1 headset, shown in figure 1.11, is formed of black molded plastic, has small adjustment wheels on the left and right sides that allow you to move the display closer to or farther from your face, has foam padding on the surfaces intended to rest against the skin, and has straps that secure the Rift to your head. You'll also note that the DK1 adjustment buckles on the straps include a handy gripper for the wire running between the Rift and the control box.

The DK1 headset incorporates a single 1280 × 800 display at the heart of the device, as well as motion-tracking hardware that reports acceleration, rotation rate, and magnetic field strength and direction. The display is split between the two eyes (each eye can see only half of the display), yielding 640 × 800 per eye, as shown in figure 1.12. This resolution does cause what some call the "screen door" effect—that is, it looks like you're looking through a screen door. The grid of individual pixels can become visible to the naked eye, especially when viewing static content. This effect improved dramatically in the DK2 should continue to be less of a problem in later versions of the Rift as screen resolution improves, reducing inter-pixel spacing.

The headset contains the head-tracking hardware that reports both acceleration and rotational velocity at a rate of 1,000 times per second.

---

[2] The number and type of cables shipped with the DK1 varied over time.

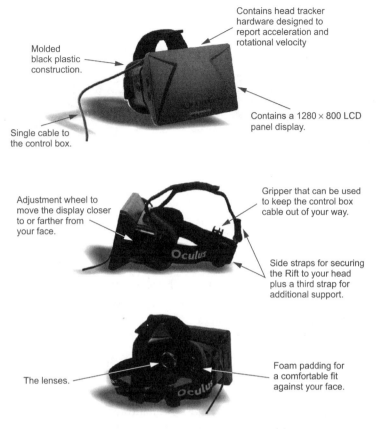

Contains head tracker hardware designed to report acceleration and rotational velocity

Molded black plastic construction.

Contains a 1280 × 800 LCD panel display.

Single cable to the control box.

Adjustment wheel to move the display closer to or farther from your face.

Gripper that can be used to keep the control box cable out of your way.

Side straps for securing the Rift to your head plus a third strap for additional support.

The lenses.

Foam padding for a comfortable fit against your face.

Figure 1.11   The DK1 headset: front, side, and back views

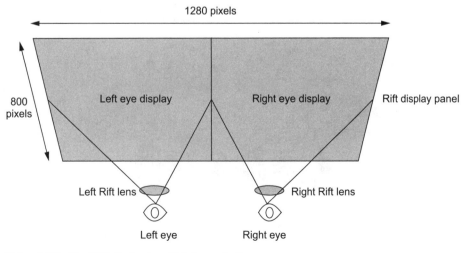

1280 pixels

800 pixels

Left eye display

Right eye display

Rift display panel

Left Rift lens

Right Rift lens

Left eye

Right eye

Figure 1.12   The DK1 display is split between both eyes.

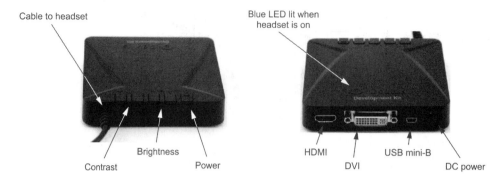

Cable to headset

Blue LED lit when
headset is on

Contrast   Brightness   Power

HDMI   DVI   USB mini-B   DC power

Figure 1.13   The DK1 control box: front and back views

THE CONTROL BOX

In addition to the cable extending to the headset, the control box has a DC power connector, a USB mini-B female port, and DVI and HDMI female ports (see figure 1.13). It has five buttons: one for power, and two each for controlling brightness and contrast on the display. It also has a small blue LED in the center of the Oculus VR logo that glows blue when the Rift display is active.

THE LENSES

The DK1 model includes three pairs of lenses, pictured in figure 1.14. The pairs are all identical in terms of how they transmit light. They differ in placing the lenses at slightly different distances from the LCD display. (You can see this in figure 1.14 by comparing their heights; the C lenses are visibly shallower than the A lenses.) Combined with the headset distance-adjustment knobs, this allows the user to vary the distance between the screen and the lenses, as well as between the lenses and the eyes, in

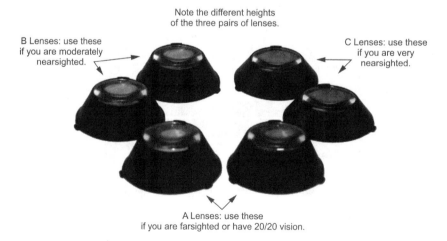

Note the different heights
of the three pairs of lenses.

B Lenses: use these
if you are moderately
nearsighted.

C Lenses: use these
if you are very
nearsighted.

A Lenses: use these
if you are farsighted or have 20/20 vision.

Figure 1.14   The DK1 lenses

order to accommodate a wide variety of facial characteristics as well as users who require prescription glasses.

The DK1 lenses are fixed at 64 mm apart and cannot be adjusted. As with the DK2, not being able to adjust the distance between the lenses does not present a major constraint, because the lenses transmit collimated light. For more on collimated light, see chapter 4.

1.3.3 The GPU

It's worth mentioning one additional component essential to the operation of the Rift that isn't included in either kit: the GPU. Every modern personal computer includes a *graphics processing unit* (GPU) with a programmable pipeline. This remarkable piece of technology is an integral part of what makes the Oculus Rift possible.

1.4 How the Rift works

Virtual reality is about constructing an experience that simulates a user's physical presence in another environment. The Rift accomplishes this by acting both as a specialized input device and a specialized output device.

As an input device, the Rift uses a combination of several sensors to allow an application to query for the current orientation and position of the user's head. This is commonly referred to as the *head pose*. This allows an application to change its output in response to the user's changes in where they're looking or where their head is.

> **Head pose**
>
> In VR applications, a *head pose* is a combination of the orientation and position of the head, relative to some fixed coordinate system.

As an output device, the Rift is a display that creates a deep sense of immersion and presence by attempting to more closely reproduce the sensation of looking at an environment as if you were actually there, compared to viewing it on a monitor. It does this in three ways:

- By providing a much wider field of view than conventional displays
- By providing a different image to each eye
- By blocking out the real environment around you, which would otherwise serve as a contradiction to the rendered environment

On the Rift display, you'll display *frames* that have been generated to conform to this wide field of view and offer a distinct image to each eye.

Generating frames that display properly on the Rift doesn't happen automatically. You can't simply replace your monitor with a Rift and expect to continue to use your computer in the same way. Only applications that have been specifically written to read the Rift input and customize the output to conform to the Rift's display will provide a good experience.

> **Frame**
>
> Because developing for the Rift involves rendering multiple images, it's important to have terminology that makes it clear what image you're talking about at a given moment. When we use the term *frame*, we're referring to the final image that ends up on a screen. In the case of a Rift application, these frame images will be composed of two eye images, one each for the left and right eyes. Each eye image is distorted specifically to account for the lens through which it'll appear, and then the images composited together during the final rendering step before they're displayed on the screen.

To understand how an application running on the Rift is different, it's important to look at how it's distinct from non-Rift applications.

CONVENTIONAL APPLICATIONS

All applications have input and output, and most graphical applications invoke a loop that conceptually looks something like figure 1.15. The details can be abstracted in many ways, but just about any program can be viewed as an implementation of this loop. For as long as the application is running, it responds to user input, renders a frame, and outputs that frame to the display.

RIFT APPLICATIONS

Rift-specific applications embellish this loop, as seen in figure 1.16. In addition to conventional user input, you have another step that fetches the current head pose from

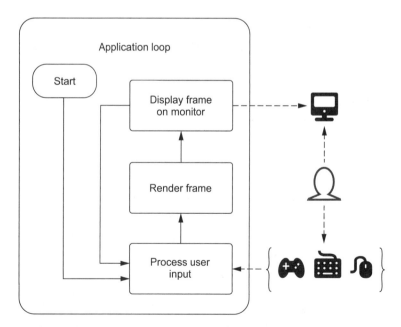

Figure 1.15   The typical loop for conventional applications

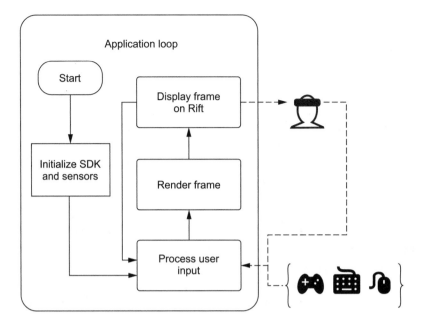

Figure 1.16   A typical loop for a Rift application

the Rift. This is typically used by the application to change how it renders the frame. Specifically, if you're rendering a 3D virtual environment, you'll want the view of the scene to change in response to the user's head movements. You also need to distort the per-eye images to account for the effects of the lenses on the Rift.

Practically speaking, the head pose is a specialized kind of input. We've called it out on its own (the head wearing the Rift) to emphasize the distinction between Rift and non-Rift applications.

You'll note that we didn't put accounting for the effects of the lenses in its own box. This is because it's part of the overall process of rendering and isn't the only specialization required for properly rendering a frame to the Rift.

As we've mentioned, the design of the Rift is such that it shows a different image to each eye by showing each eye only half of the display panel on the device. To generate a single frame of output, you need to render an individual image for each eye and distort that image before moving on to the next eye. Then, after both eye images have been rendered and distorted, you send the resulting output frame to the device.[3]

Let's take a closer look at how the Rift uses these simple pairs of images to give such a strong sense of immersion.

---

[3]   In the early versions of the SDK, distortion and rendering of the final output to the Rift display device had to be done by applications. Since version 0.3.x, the distortion and rendering to the device are typically handled inside the SDK, though you can override this behavior.

1.4.1   *Using head tracking to change the point of view*

The first way the Rift increases immersion is via head tracking, eliminating part of the necessary mental translation when interacting with a computer-generated environment. If you want to see what's to your left, you no longer have to go through the process of calculating how far to move your mouse or how long to hold the joystick. You simply look to your left. This is as much an instance of a natural user interface (NUI) as VR. NUI is all about making the interface for interacting with a computer application or environment so seamless as to essentially be no interface at all. Interacting with a touch-screen surface and dragging a UI element around by literally dragging it is a form of NUI. Changing your perspective within an artificial environment by moving your head is another.

The Rift enables this kind of interaction by integrating sensor hardware that detects spatial acceleration on three axes and rotation rates on three axes. These add up to six degrees of freedom, commonly abbreviated as 6DOF.[4] This kind of sensor hardware is familiar to users of mobile computing devices such as smartphones and tablets. It's also commonly found in some game console hardware, such as controllers for Nintendo's and Sony's lines. Most commodity hardware of this kind is intended to be wielded by hand and doesn't have stringent latency requirements. VR, however, is significantly more demanding; as such, the Rift tracking hardware is a step above what's typically found elsewhere, both in terms of reporting resolution and accuracy.

Even with their high quality, the Rift's sensors alone are insufficiently accurate to track relative changes in position over time periods of more than a second. This means that the DK1 kit is limited to tracking only the orientation of a user's head, unable to determine position. In the DK2, this limitation has been overcome by adding an infrared camera (separate from the Rift itself) as part of the kit. In combination with an array of infrared lights built into the headset itself, this allows the position of the Rift to be tracked, as long as it's within view of the camera.

The Oculus SDK provides methods for retrieving raw sensor messages from the hardware and coalescing them into a single head pose.

The end result is that as you render each frame in your application, you're able to fetch the pose of the user and use that input during the rendering process. That way, you can ensure the viewpoint that appears inside the Rift corresponds with the user's position in 3D space and the direction in which the user is looking (boxes 1, 2, and 3 in figure 1.17).

---

[4] This is a slightly different usage of the term 6DOF than when it's used to describe a system that tracks both position and orientation, because here we're tracking acceleration and angular acceleration, each on three axes.

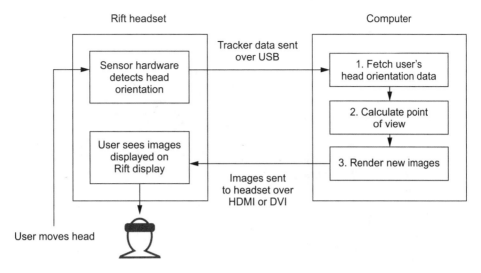

Figure 1.17   The rendering process for each frame: from head movement to new image on the headset

Now let's look at rendering for the Rift.

1.4.2   *Rendering an immersive view*

The second way the Rift increases immersion is by rendering a view that accurately mimics the way vision works, with a wide field of view and different images presented to each eye.

HOW THE RIFT ACHIEVES ITS FIELD OF VIEW

The Rift hardware offers a much wider field of view than a typical monitor (see figure 1.18). Even a 30-inch monitor will usually occupy only about 50 degrees of your field of view, depending on how close you sit to it. Ideally the Rift provides a field of view of over 90 degrees or more vertically and a remarkable 100 degrees or more horizontally. The exact field of view experienced is dependent on a number of factors, including how the Rift hardware is configured and the physical characteristics of the wearer.

The Rift achieves this high field of view through the placement of the display and the use of special lenses. Inside the Rift is a small high-resolution LCD display, and wearing the device places the display directly in front of you at a distance of about 4 cm, as shown in figure 1.19. This alone makes the panel occupy a substantial field of view, but it's far too close to allow a user to easily bring it into focus.

Between your eyes and the display panel are lenses designed to distort light in such a way as to both make the apparent focal depth infinitely far away (resolving the focus

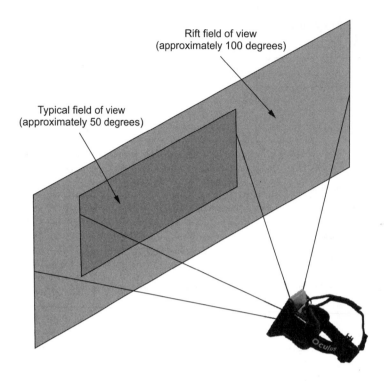

Figure 1.18   Comparison of the field of view of a typical monitor and that of the Rift

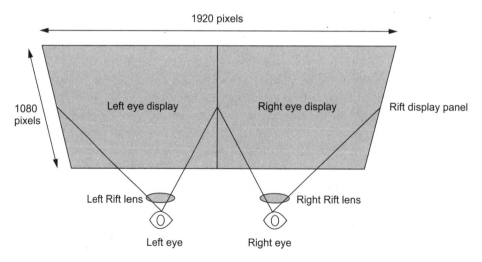

Figure 1.19   Panel and lens positions. The resolution listed is for the DK2.

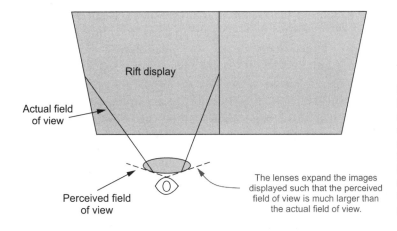

Rift display

Actual field
of view

Perceived field
of view

The lenses expand the images
displayed such that the perceived
field of view is much larger than
the actual field of view.

Figure 1.20   The Rift's lenses and software use collimated light and distortion technology to give a perceived field of view that's wider and sharper than a conventional display.

issue) and to make the panel appear much wider than it is, further increasing the field of view (figure 1.20).

The lenses are also designed to present roughly the same image to the user whether or not your point of view is off the axis of the lens, using collimated light. The effect is similar to a magnifying glass, but with a few important differences.

MAXIMIZING THE RIFT'S FIELD OF VIEW

To understand how you can maximize the Rift's field of view, you need to understand a bit about how the brain interprets the images perceived by the eyes. Each eye covers its own field of view, with the left eye showing more of the world to your left and the right showing more to your right; there's a large amount of crossover at the center, as shown in figure 1.21.

Your brain takes the two images and fuses them into a single panoramic view, which invokes a sense of depth. Even though the actual depth information (parallax)

Field of view

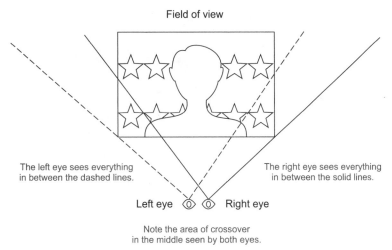

The left eye sees everything
in between the dashed lines.

The right eye sees everything
in between the solid lines.

Left eye   Right eye

Note the area of crossover
in the middle seen by both eyes.

Figure 1.21   Left and right fields of view

is only available for items in the crossover area (see figure 1.22), the overall sense of depth ends up being greater than the sum of the parts. Your brain will also take into account other cues such as lighting, the size of familiar objects, and small object movements relative to one another when the point of view changes, such as when you move your head.

To maximize the field of view in the Rift, the images presented to each eye need to mimic real vision in that more data is presented on the left of the image for the left eye and more data is presented on the right for the right eye.

RENDERING FOR THE RIFT

To render images properly for the Rift, you need to take into account the LCD display, how vision works with separate images for each eye, and the lenses used.

The lenses in the Rift distort the image on the screen (as all lenses do), introducing a fisheye lens effect. This means that images shown on the screen inside the Rift must be adjusted before they appear, inverting that distortion. That way, when viewed

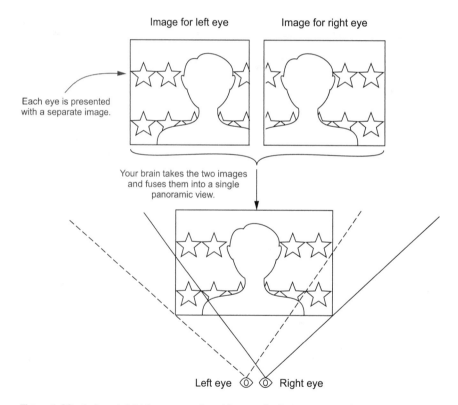

Figure 1.22   Left and right images are fused by your brain to create a single image.

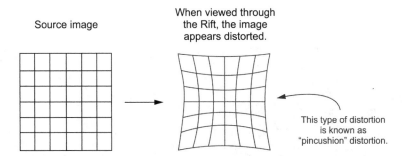

Figure 1.23　A grid of lines as they'd appear on the screen and through the Rift lenses

through the lens, the image distortion and the lens distortion will cancel out, and the resulting picture will look crisp and clear.

As you can see in figure 1.23, a grid of lines, if simply viewed through the Rift as is, would appear distorted inward by the lenses, as though drawn toward the center. This type of distortion is called a "pincushion" distortion.

To counter the pincushion effect, software needs to apply the inverse ("barrel") distortion to the source image before sending it to the Rift, as shown in figure 1.24. Now the image appears as intended in the Rift. We'll cover distortion in more detail in chapter 4.

Now that you know there are two images presenting different data to each eye and that the images are distorted, let's look at a screenshot from a Rift demo to see what it

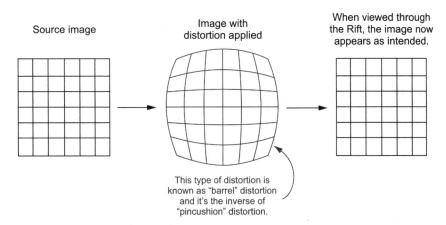

Figure 1.24　The source image, the same image after an inverse distortion has been applied, and then the distorted image as seen through the Rift

The images are distorted and
appear as misshapen ovals.

More data is presented on the
left of the image for the left eye.

There's an image per eye.

More data is presented on
the right for the right eye.

Figure 1.25   A screenshot of the Oculus Tuscany demo as seen on a conventional monitor

looks like when viewed on a traditional monitor (figure 1.25). This two-oval view is often what you'll see when shown a VR application screenshot, and it's one we'll be using in many of the examples in this book.

Now that you understand how the Rift works, it's time to get started developing for it.

1.5   Setting up the Rift for development

Getting the Rift set up for use is pretty well documented in the *Oculus Rift Development Kit Instruction Manual* that comes with the kit, and if you follow those instructions, you should be able to get the Rift up and running. But if you run into issues, or you'd like to spend some time optimizing your setup for development, please see appendix A on hardware setup.

One of the hazards of developing for the Rift is that using it can sometimes trigger symptoms of motion sickness. If you're going to be working with the Rift, it's a good idea to know how to deal with motion sickness to keep it from becoming a serious issue for you.

1.6 *Dealing with motion sickness*

Motion sickness is generally caused by conflicting sensory signals going to the brain, such as a mismatch between the visual appearance of velocity and the inner ear's sensation of motion. It's been known for some time that first-person games alone or 3D vision alone can trigger motion sickness in some people. The Rift provides an incredibly immersive experience, and one of the downsides to such impressive immersion is that even if you're the type of person who never gets motion sickness in real life, you might get motion sickness from using the Rift.

Here are some strategies (for more information see appendix A) to use when you first start working with the Rift that can help with motion sickness:

- *Read and observe all health and safety information included in the Rift documentation.* For the most up-to-date version, please check the Oculus VR website (developer.oculus.com/documentation/).
- *Do not try to power through it.* If you experience nausea or other symptoms of motion sickness, stop and take a break right away. We can't stress enough how important this is. Trying to force yourself to continue will typically make things worse and can even lead to an aversion to using the Rift at all.
- *Learn to recognize it quickly.* The first symptom of motion sickness isn't always nausea. For some people, the first symptom can be headache, flashes of vertigo, or breaking into a cold sweat. The quicker you recognize the issue, the quicker you can take corrective action. Often, waiting until you feel nausea will make it harder to recover.
- *Make sure the Rift has been adjusted to fit correctly on your head.* Be sure to:
  - Use the correct lenses for your vision
  - Set the distance between the lenses and your face—close, but not too close
  - Adjust the straps to ensure a perfect headset fit
  - Read appendix A for more information
- *Create a user profile for yourself.* The Rift takes into account certain physical characteristics of the user, such as height and the distance between the eyes, when rendering content. You can use the Oculus Configuration Utility to create a profile for yourself.
- *Start slowly to get your "VR legs".* Give yourself time to get used to using the Rift. Just like sailors need to get their sea legs, you'll want to get your VR legs. One way to ease into the VR waters is to start by familiarizing yourself with games or demos you want to play on your monitor before using the Rift. Then play on the Rift only in short increments. Give yourself a few days of playing this way before spending extended time using the Rift.
- *Use the Rift sitting down.* Especially when you are just getting started, don't try standing or walking while wearing the Rift. The extra movement from standing or walking can trigger motion sickness, and because the Rift blocks out the real world, there's the added danger of tripping and falling.

- *Turn the brightness level down (DK1 only).* For many people, turning the brightness levels down helps. The brightness and contrast of the headset can be adjusted using the buttons on the top of the control box. Looking from the back of the DK1's control box, the two buttons on the left control the contrast, and the next two control the brightness.

- *Take regular breaks.* Even after you feel like a pro in virtual environments, you should still take breaks to let your mind and eyes rest. Every so often be sure to stop, stretch, take a walk, and get some fresh air. (This is good advice for life in general.)

- *Work in a quiet environment.* Ambient noise can interfere with how your brain perceives the images on screen and can trigger motion sickness. Spatialized sounds that disagree with your virtual environment send conflicting messages that your mind will struggle to contextualize. Try working in a quiet environment or wearing noise-canceling headphones to remove ambient noise.

- *Watch what you eat before strapping on the Rift.* This is common sense. Just as you wouldn't binge on sushi, donuts, beef jerky, and cherry Gatorade right before riding in the back of a speeding minivan going down the Pacific Coast Highway, you should watch what you eat right before using the Rift.

- *Take time to recover.* The disorienting effects of using the Rift can last for some time after taking off the headset. For your safety and the safety of others, you shouldn't operate heavy machinery or drive a car, and so on, if you've just used a VR headset.

There are strategies for mitigating motion sickness from within your application (see chapter 10), and well-designed applications may not cause motion sickness for you. But as you develop, you may find that one of the "bugs" in your software is that it causes motion sickness. It may take many testing iterations before you can fix the problem. In addition, some of the causes of motion sickness are inherent to the Rift itself, and although Oculus has announced improvements (lower-latency devices, higher-resolution screens) that should help in future versions of the Rift, you'll still need to work with the version you have.

You don't need to suffer for your art. If you experience nausea or other motion sickness symptoms and resting isn't enough, here are additional remedies you can try:

- *Eat ginger*—Ginger has long been used as a motion sickness remedy. You can eat it in any form—candied ginger, gingersnap cookies, ginger tea, ginger ale—just make sure that it contains real ginger and not just ginger flavoring. If you don't like how ginger tastes, powdered ginger is available in pill form and can be found in the vitamin aisle of most major drug stores.

- *Eat saltines or other dry crackers*—Nibbling on dry crackers may also help.

- *Try acupressure*—Acupressure uses pressure or other stimulation on specific points of the body to treat ailments. Practitioners of acupressure believe stimulation of the P6 acupressure point, located about two finger-widths from the crease on the underside of the wrist, may help symptoms of motion sickness. You can try applying pressure to this point yourself, or you can use one of the several brands of acupressure bands available.

- *Talk to your doctor about medication*—If you're having persistent issues with motion sickness, there are prescription and nonprescription medicines that may prevent and treat symptoms. Talk to your doctor to learn more.

Using and developing for the Rift should be fun, and we hope these tips help keep any motion sickness issues you might have to a minimum.

1.7 Development paths

This book covers several different approaches to Rift development.

- *Using the C APIs*—If you plan to work directly with the Rift C APIs, head to part 2 and start with chapter 2. It will introduce you to the C API and get you started writing your first Rift programs.
- *Using Java or Python*—If you plan to use a language other than C, such as Java or Python, we recommend reading through part 2, starting with chapter 2 on using the C APIs first, and then reading chapter 11 for examples of building Rift applications with the Python and Java bindings. The methodology discussed in chapter 11 also applies to other languages.
- *Using Unity*—If you plan to use the popular Unity game engine for your development, head to part 3 and read chapters 7 and 8. It's possible to interact with the C API from within Unity, so when you want a better understanding of the C API, you'll find part 2 an interesting read.

No matter which development path you choose, know that you can develop for the Rift even if you don't yet have one, because the Oculus SDK and Unity can be used without a headset. For more information, see appendix A.

1.8 Summary

In this chapter we introduced the Oculus Rift:

- The Oculus Rift is a virtual reality head-mounted display.
- The Rift is immersive, can be used to create presence, and is inexpensive, both in terms of supporting it in your applications, and in terms of hardware cost.
- The Rift is two devices in one: a specialized input device and a specialized output device.
- As an input device, the Rift uses a combination of several sensors to allow an application to query for the current orientation and position of the user's head. An application can change its output in response to where the user is looking or where their head is.
- As an output device, the Rift is a display that creates a deep sense of immersion and presence by attempting to more closely reproduce the sensation of looking at an environment as if you were actually there, compared to viewing it on a monitor.

- Rendering images properly for the Rift means you need to take into account the display, how vision works with separate images for each eye, and the lenses used.

- The lenses in the Rift distort the image on the screen (as all lenses do), introducing a fisheye lens effect. That means that images shown on the screen inside the Rift must be predistorted in software before they are shown.

- Only applications that have been specifically written to read the Rift input and to customize their output to conform to the Rift's display will provide a good experience.

- Using the Rift may cause motion sickness. We provided some simple suggestions that can help you manage any symptoms of motion sickness you might feel when using the Rift.

- When using the Rift, be sure to use the right lenses for your vision, set the distance between the lenses and your face, and adjust the straps to ensure a perfect headset fit. To maximize comfort, be sure to create a user profile using the Oculus Configuration Tool.

- You can develop for the Rift even if you don't yet have one, because the SDK (or the Unity game development environment) can be used without a headset.

Part 2

Using the Oculus C API

In these chapters you'll learn how to develop Rift applications using the Oculus C API. Whether you're looking to write applications using the API directly to integrate Rift support into your own game engine, or to better understand how Rift support was added to your game engine of choice (Unity, for example) so that you can take full advantage of what Rift support offers, this part of the book is for you.

In chapter 2 you'll get your feet wet creating your first Rift applications. We start by introducing you to the software needed for Rift development: the Oculus SDK and runtime. In our first example we cover the first steps in creating every Rift application by showing you the minimal code needed to work with the SDK. The next two examples show the basics of using the SDK to interact with the Rift hardware, demonstrating how to retrieve basic input from the Rift sensors and how to render simple output to the Rift display.

Chapter 3 takes an in-depth look into working with the head tracker by learning how to get reports from the Rift and understanding what it reports and how to apply the data to a rendered scene.

The Rift display is a highly specialized display, and chapter 4 covers the details of what makes rendering to it different from working with a traditional monitor and what you as a developer need to do to account for the differences.

Chapter 5 ties it all together. You'll take a simple demo app from a classic desktop OpenGL program all the way to a full-fledged Rift-based VR application.

Chapter 6 covers performance and quality concerns for VR along with concrete steps for evaluating and improving your application.

Creating your first
Rift interactions

2

This chapter covers

- Initializing the Oculus SDK
- Getting input from the head tracker
- Rendering output to the display

Working with a Rift involves working with two distinct devices: a set of sensors connected via USB (the head tracker), and a monitor device, connected via HDMI or DVI (the display), as seen in figure 2.1.

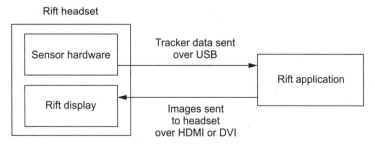

Figure 2.1 Tracker data is taken as input and images are sent as output to the Rift.

Both devices are managed via the Oculus SDK, so the first thing we'll cover is how to initialize the SDK and open the lines of communication. Once you know how to use the SDK, you can begin working with the Rift.

2.1 SDK interfaces

The 0.2.x versions of the Oculus SDK were C++ code that handled the interaction with the Rift hardware directly and required the client application to perform the distortion of the rendered content required by the Rift. The 0.3.x series of the SDK supplanted this with a C API that provided a more streamlined and easier-to-use interface as well as support for having the SDK perform the distortion on rendered content. The 0.4.x version of the SDK made small evolutionary changes to the C API and introduced the concept of the Oculus runtime.

Since the release of the DK2 and version 0.4, the Oculus software can be broken down into two major components: the Oculus runtime and the SDK.

2.1.1 Oculus runtime

The Oculus runtime addresses two limitations of the Rift: concurrent access to the hardware and the inapplicability of the desktop metaphor to the Rift display.

CONCURRENT ACCESS

Prior to the 0.4.x series of the Oculus software, each application was responsible for interacting with the hardware directly in a manner that was necessarily exclusive. This meant that if one application was accessing the Rift's sensors, no other application could do so at the same time. This would preclude the ability for someone to create a launcher application that could operate in VR and subsequently launch other applications that would also operate in VR.[1]

The runtime solves this problem by centralizing access to the hardware to the runtime process. The exclusive hardware functions are now contained within the runtime. Other applications use the SDK to access the tracking information via shared memory. The fine details of this process are abstracted behind the API. From a developer's perspective, you can simply call the function to get the head pose and receive up-to-date information, regardless of how many other applications are accessing the Rift.

DESKTOP METAPHOR

Although the Rift display is essentially a monitor from the perspective of a computer, from the perspective of a user it doesn't have the same functionality as a conventional flat-panel monitor. If you plug it in, your computer is likely to attempt to extend the desktop to this new display. Unfortunately, interacting with OS-created windows that are being rendered to the Rift is problematic at best. Significant portions

---

[1] ...unless they wanted to create an entire separate VR API used by both the launcher application and the launched applications, an approach attempted by Valve with its SteamVR API.

of the display aren't visible to the user unless you remove the lenses and hold the Rift at a distance.

One solution is to clone the Rift display to another of your computer's monitors, but this can have a negative impact on the performance of applications that are rendering to it.

With the 0.4.x series of the Oculus software, the new runtime enables something called *Direct HMD mode*. The intent of this mode is to hide the Rift display from the OS-level interface for working with monitors, thus preventing the problems with the desktop being extended to the display. At the same time, the SDK provides functions that allow applications to continue to target the Rift display with Direct3D or OpenGL rendering systems, in order to allow VR applications to function.

2.1.2 Oculus SDK

The SDK consists of nearly 50 C functions that govern the application's interaction with the Rift hardware and the Oculus runtime. Most times, developers will use only about half of them in a given application, and fewer than half a dozen are typically needed anywhere other than during the setup of your application.

We'll discuss each of the SDK functions as we come to the relevant sections of the text. We'll cover working with the SDK functions from other languages like Java and Python in chapter 11.

2.2 Working with the SDK

Whether you're working with the community SDK provided with the book examples or with the official SDK available on the Oculus VR site, the Oculus libraries require a bit of care during setup and shutdown. Our first example, listing 2.1, covers the minimum amount of code involved in running any code at all that invokes the SDK. The example is disarmingly simple, but it's critically important. In earlier versions of the SDK, failing to properly initialize or shut down the SDK can result in your application crashing, or hanging so that the user has to forcibly terminate it. More recent versions are significantly more forgiving, although this largely means your application simply won't work properly rather than crash.

This example won't generate any output, but then again, if it links and runs, it shouldn't crash either. So without further ado, see the following listing for the absolute minimum you can do to connect to the SDK and disconnect.

Listing 2.1 Basic SDK and HMD usage

```
#include <OVR.h>

int main(int argc, char ** argv) {
  if (!ovr_Initialize()) {            Initializes the SDK.
    return -1;
  }

  int hmdCount = ovrHmd_Detect();     Counts the number
                                      of connected devices.
```

```
for (int i = 0; i < hmdCount; ++i) {          Loops over each device,
  ovrHmd hmd = ovrHmd_Create(i);              opening and closing
  ovrHmd_Destroy(hmd);                        them in turn.
}

ovrHmd hmd = ovrHmd_CreateDebug(ovrHmd_DK2);   ◁──── Creates and destroys
ovrHmd_Destroy(hmd);                                 a "fake" Rift device.

ovr_Shutdown();          ◁──── Shuts down
return 0;                       the SDK.
}
```

As you can see, this listing is only few lines long. Still, it deserves some explanation, especially as we're covering two topics: SDK management and head-mounted display (HMD) management.

2.2.1   SDK management

The function `ovr_Initialize()` *must be called before any other SDK method can be called.* It sets up the SDK's internal mechanisms for logging and memory allocation. Here's what its prototype looks like:

```
OVR_EXPORT ovrBool ovr_Initialize();
```

This function returns an `ovrBool`, which is a typedef for a char type, as C has no built-in Boolean type. You check the return value of `ovr_Initialize()` and fail out of the application if it returns a non-true value.

Similarly, the `ovr_Shutdown()` method should be called when you're finished working with the headset, and you must call no other SDK method afterward. Its prototype looks like this:

```
OVR_EXPORT void ovr_Shutdown();
```

It's critical to ensure that calls to OVR SDK functions are scoped so that they occur inside calls to these "bookend" functions. Bugs related to initialization order can be easy to trigger and hard to diagnose, so it's desirable to place the bookends as close to the top of the call stack as possible, preferably in the `main` function or its equivalent on your platform.

MACROS FOR OUR EXAMPLES

In our examples from this point on, we'll wrap the mechanics of launching our applications with macros. We have two favorites: RUN_APP and RUN_OVR_APP. The former runs a standard OpenGL application in a stable, cross-platform way; the latter does the same but the OpenGL app targets the Rift.

RUN_APP expands to the code in the next listing.

Listing 2.2   `RUN_APP`, our standard run macro for windowed OpenGL (Common.h)

```
#ifdef OS_WIN
  #define MAIN_DECL int __stdcall WinMain(
    HINSTANCE hInstance,
```

```
      HINSTANCE hPrevInstance,
      LPSTR lpCmdLine,
      int nCmdShow)
#else
  #define MAIN_DECL int main(int argc, char ** argv)
#endif

#define RUN_APP(AppClass)
  MAIN_DECL {
    try {
      return AppClass().run();
    } catch (std::exception & error) {
      SAY_ERR(error.what());
    } catch (const std::string & error) {
      SAY_ERR(error.c_str());
    }
    return -1;
  }
```

RUN_OVR_APP expands to the code in this listing.

Listing 2.3   RUN_OVR_APP, our run macro for OpenGL on the Rift (OvrUtils.h)

```
#define RUN_OVR_APP(AppClass)
  MAIN_DECL {
    if (!ovr_Initialize()) {           ◁──  Initializes the SDK
      SAY_ERR("Failed to initialize the Oculus SDK");
      return -1;
    }
    int result = -1;
    try {                                   Runs the example code
      result = ExampleCode().run();    ◁── (we'll use macro parameter
    } catch (std::exception & error) {      substitution here)
      // Do something useful with this error
    }
    ovr_Shutdown();       ◁──  Shuts down the SDK
    return result;
}
```

We have several other macros in our demo library, such as SAY and SAY_ERR, which write to standard output and standard error.

In our RUN_OVR_APP macro, we wrap calls to the ovr_Initialize() and ovr _Shutdown() methods around our example code. This isn't bulletproof, but it suffices for our examples and may provide a design pattern you can follow when developing for the Rift.

We've also taken the opportunity in listings 2.2 and 2.3 to abstract out a few of the more OS-specific irks of running a C++ program by using macros to tuck out of sight the different declarations of main() with a second macro, MAIN_DECL. MAIN_DECL lets us move past whether our entry point method needs to be WinMain() (on Windows systems) or main() (non-Windows).

> ### Delaying ovr_Initialize()
>
> Generally speaking, if you're using the Rift you want to call `ovr_Initialize()` as early as possible to avoid problems. In a number of our examples, though, we want to render to a conventional window on the desktop using information about the orientation of the Rift. As of this writing, there are bugs in the Oculus runtime that sometimes prevent rendering to a normal OpenGL window if you've already run `ovr_Initialize()`. In these cases we'll use the regular `RUN_APP` macro and call `ovr_Initialize()` only after we've created the OpenGL window we want to use.

Again, all of our sample code is online at our GitHub repository (github.com/Oculus-RiftInAction/OculusRiftInAction), so if you haven't downloaded it yet, now's the time. All the code we discuss from here on out will use standard macros declared in our examples.

2.2.2 Managing the HMD

Just initializing the SDK doesn't do anything useful for us as developers, though. You want to interact with the Rift hardware, not the SDK. In order to do that, you need to know how many devices are connected and be able to open a handle to them. Counting the number of connected devices means calling `ovrHmd_Detect()`:

```
OVR_EXPORT int ovrHmd_Detect();
```

This function returns the number of connected devices or zero if no devices are detected. Once you have the number of devices, you can loop over each one, open it, and query it for information about itself using the `ovrHmd_Create()` function:

```
OVR_EXPORT ovrHmd ovrHmd_Create(int index)
```

`ovrHmd_Create()` takes the (zero-based) index of the device you want to open and returns a new type: ovrHmd. This is a new type that serves two roles. First, it acts as a handle to the hardware for making other calls to the SDK. The majority of the SDK C functions take an ovrHmd value as their first argument. Second, the ovrHmd type acts to provide the developer with a description of the connected device. If you look at the C API headers, you'll see that ovrHmd is a typedef for a pointer to another structure, ovrHmdDesc. The members of this structure contain information about the connected hardware as well as its state (for example, whether Direct HMD mode is active). For instance, it contains an ovrHmdType member named Type. ovrHmdType is an enum value that lists all the types supported by the SDK, such as ovrHmd_DK1 or ovrHmd_DK2 (presumably other values will be supported as newer models are released). The special value ovrHmd_Other is used to indicate that a Rift has been detected but the model type isn't understood or supported by the SDK.

Having opened a given device, you should close it again before attempting to shut down the SDK or exit the application; you can use `ovrHmd_Destroy()` to do so. This is the first of the previously mentioned many functions that take an `ovrHmd` value as their first parameter:

```
OVR_EXPORT void     ovrHmd_Destroy(ovrHmd hmd);
```

It's always a good idea to close any resources you've opened before exiting the application to ensure that they aren't locked when other applications come along to use them, although Oculus does a good job of virtualizing access to the hardware so that no one application can gain an exclusive lock on it.

WORKING WITHOUT HARDWARE

Let's say you want to start developing a Rift application but you don't have an actual Rift at hand or you have a Rift but you want to experiment with a different model. Fortunately, developing without a Rift is supported through the use of the `ovrHmd _CreateDebug()` function:

```
OVR_EXPORT ovrHmd    ovrHmd_CreateDebug(ovrHmdType type);
```

This function allows you to create and work with an `ovrHmd` instance exactly as if you'd connected to a device. It lets you specify the model of Rift you want to work with via the `ovrHmdType` parameter. The debug creation function is useful for testing your application's ability to parse the information about the Rift, as well as performing the required rendering distortion. It does have the drawback of not being able to provide head pose tracking, but at the very least it's enough to get you started or to allow for development on the go without having to lug around actual Rift hardware.

Now that you know how to interact with the SDK and headset at a basic level without setting anything on fire, we can move on to more interesting stuff, like setting things on fire.[2]

2.3   *Getting input from the head tracker*

The Rift contains sensor hardware (called an *inertial measurement unit,* or IMU) that detects linear acceleration on three axes and rotation speed on three axes. The three rotation axes and three acceleration axes add up to six degrees of freedom, commonly abbreviated as 6DOF. Additionally, the DK2 (and presumably subsequent models) includes an infrared camera meant to track the orientation and position of an array of infrared LEDs built into the surface of the Rift.

> **Why both an IMU and a camera?**
> The inclusion of multiple different sensing mechanisms may seem puzzling. The camera can determine both the position and orientation of the Rift, as long as the user is within the camera's field of view. In theory you could calculate positional changes along with orientation by using the information from the IMU alone. So why are both mechanisms used?

---

[2] Metaphorically speaking, of course.

(continued)

Well, the theory about determining position from the IMU doesn't work in practice. To turn the IMU acceleration data into velocity, you have to perform a mathematical operation called *integration*, which ends up magnifying the small amounts of error in the data by a significant amount. To turn that velocity data into positional data, you have to integrate again, which amplifies the error. Over a time period as small as a few seconds, you can end up with meters of drift, making the IMU useless for positional data.

The camera, on the other hand, can provide highly accurate positional data, but can't provide information with a high enough time resolution. The IMU reports information at 1000 Hz; the camera reports at a small fraction of that rate.

So the IMU provides the extremely low-latency orientation information and might even provide positional changes over time scales of a few milliseconds. The camera provides accurate positional information that isn't subject to drift in the way the IMU is.

To produce a good VR environment, the view of the scene must be constantly and *accurately* updated based on movement of the Rift. To do this, you first need to fetch the head pose. The Oculus runtime turns the information from the Rift hardware into the requisite accurate pose, and the SDK provides a low-latency mechanism for fetching the most recent pose, as well as providing support to predict information about future poses over short time scales.

In this section we'll cover a minimal example of using the tracker to fetch the current head pose of the Rift. Most of the examples that relate to the display, and the bulk of the code in this book in general, will be creating GUI applications. For working with only the sensor, we find it easier to work with a text-mode console application as shown in figure 2.2.

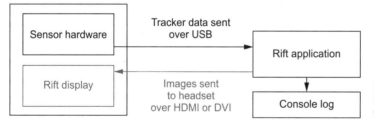

Figure 2.2 Getting input from the head tracker

The example in listing 2.4 should launch and, if it finds the sensor, spend 10 seconds reporting the current orientation of the Rift, expressed as degrees of roll, pitch, and yaw. Assuming the Rift headset is connected, when run you should see output something like this:

```
Current orientation - roll 0.00, pitch 0.00, yaw 0.00
Current orientation - roll -56.48, pitch -50.88, yaw -28.67
Current orientation - roll -56.46, pitch -50.89, yaw -28.65
Current orientation - roll -56.47, pitch -50.88, yaw -28.66
Current orientation - roll -56.48, pitch -50.87, yaw -28.66
```

Roll, pitch, and yaw

There are a number of ways to represent rotations in 3D space. The most common are three-by-three matrices, quaternions, and Euler (rhymes with *oil-er*, not *yule-er*) angles. Euler angles are the easiest to conceptualize, because they can easily be decomposed into roll, pitch, and yaw:

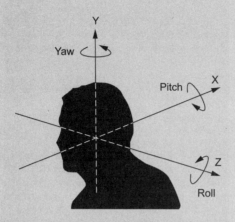

Yaw	Pitch	Roll

Yaw is turning your head to the left or right.	Pitch is tilting your head forward or back.	Roll is tilting your head to the left or right toward one shoulder.
This corresponds to rotation on the Y axis.	This corresponds to rotation on the X axis.	This corresponds to rotation on the Z axis.

Yaw is when you turn your head to your left or right and corresponds to rotation on the Y axis. *Pitch* is when you tilt your head forward (look toward the ground) or back (look to the sky) and corresponds to rotation on the X axis. *Roll* is when you tilt your head to the left or right, toward one shoulder, and corresponds to rotation on the Z axis.

To fetch these values, you need to enable head tracking and fetch the current head pose from the SDK (see listing 2.4). Note that running this example requires a connected Rift. Running it with a "debug" Rift would produce no useful information because the debug mechanism provides no head-tracking data.

Listing 2.4   Getting head tracker data

```
#include "Common.h"

class Tracker {
public:
  int run() {
    ovrHmd hmd = ovrHmd_Create(0);                        Opens the
    if (!hmd) {                                           headset.
      SAY_ERR("Unable to open Rift device");
      return -1;
    }

    if (!ovrHmd_ConfigureTracking(hmd,                    Starts the
        ovrTrackingCap_Orientation, 0)) {                 sensor device.
      SAY_ERR("Unable start Rift head tracker");
      return -1;
    }

    for (int i = 0; i < 10; ++i) {
      ovrTrackingState state =                            Fetches data.
        ovrHmd_GetTrackingState(hmd, 0);

      ovrQuatf orientation = state.HeadPose.ThePose.Orientation;   Converts the
      glm::quat q = glm::make_quat(&orientation.x);               data into a more
      glm::vec3 euler = glm::eulerAngles(q);                      readable format.

      SAY("Current orientation - roll %0.2f, pitch %0.2f, yaw %0.2f",
        euler.z * RADIANS_TO_DEGREES,                     Reports
        euler.x * RADIANS_TO_DEGREES,                     data to the
        euler.y * RADIANS_TO_DEGREES);                    console.
      Platform::sleepMillis(1000);                        Sleeps for a second
    }                                                     before fetching the
    ovrHmd_Destroy(hmd);          Closes the             next value.
    return 0;                     HMD device.
  }
};
                                  We're using the new
RUN_OVR_APP(Tracker);            RUN_OVR_APP macro here.
```

We're using our RUN_OVR_APP macro. This ensures that the ovr_Initialize() and
ovr_Shutdown() functions are called at startup and shutdown. The macro takes care
of it for us. It's important to remember they're being called, but we won't belabor the
point further.

The next sections provide a closer look at what's happening in the code.

2.3.1   *Reserving a pointer to the device manager and locating the headset*

You first use the SDK to acquire a handle to the Rift, similar to the way you did in listing 2.1, although this time you open the first Rift available, rather than attempting to
detect and open a particular one. If no Rift is found, then you emit an error and exit
the application.

As previously mentioned, the ovrHmd type serves as both a description of the basic properties of the Rift and a handle. The client can then go back to the API and say "do something specific with this particular Rift" by passing in the handle. You perform exactly this kind of operation a couple of lines later:

```
if (!ovrHmd_ConfigureTracking(hmd,
    ovrTrackingCap_Orientation, 0)) {
```

This line uses the Rift handle to start the SDK listening to the head-tracking sensors. In addition to a handle, you're passing in two other parameters. These are fields for supported and required capability bits and will be covered in greater detail in chapter 3. You specify the flag for orientation tracking in the supported field and nothing in the required field.

Configuring tracking causes the SDK to start listening to the updates from the Oculus runtime. The runtime in turn is listening to the messages from the head-tracking hardware (the IMU for the DK1, the IMU and camera for the DK2) and aggregating that information via *sensor fusion*, which creates a continuous representation of the current pose of the headset.

2.3.2 *Fetching tracker data*

After you enter the loop, you start fetching data using this function:

```
ovrTrackingState state = ovrHmd_GetTrackingState(hmd, 0);
```

Here ovrTrackingState is a structure that encapsulates quite a bit of data about the current and predicted state of the headset. We'll delve into it more deeply in chapter 3, but for the time being we're focused on a single deeply nested member, state.HeadPose.ThePose.Orientation, which encodes the current orientation as a quaternion.

Quaternions, rotation matrices, and Euler angles

Whenever we discuss the head-tracking capabilities of the Rift, we're going to be talking about rotation. Rotations can be described by *quaternions* (advanced 4-dimensional vectors), *rotation matrices* (3 x 3 or 4 x 4 grids of trigonometric numbers), or *Euler angles* (often expressed as roll, pitch, and yaw). If you're familiar with 3D rendering systems, you've probably already encountered some of these. To learn more, refer to appendix B.

These lines are used to convert the quaternion into a more readable form of rotation known as Euler angles:

```
ovrQuatf orientation = state.HeadPose.ThePose.Orientation;
glm::quat q = glm::make_quat(&orientation.x);
glm::vec3 euler = glm::eulerAngles(q);
```

The glm::quat type[3] is a more fully featured class that represents a quaternion, as opposed to the ovrQuatf struct, which contains only the data and has no methods. Converting from the OVR type to the GLM type allows you to take advantage of the eulerAngles method in GLM. Refer to appendix B on coordinate systems for greater detail.

2.3.3 Reporting tracker data to the console

A program with no output isn't very useful, so you'll use a simple macro to write the angles to the console. The angles are returned in radians, the SI unit for angles, but it's easier to read as degrees, so you do the conversion as you print them.

```
SAY("Current orientation - roll %0.2f, pitch %0.2f, yaw %0.2f",
    euler.z * RADIANS_TO_DEGREES,
    euler.x * RADIANS_TO_DEGREES,
    euler.y * RADIANS_TO_DEGREES);
```

SAY is the printf macro, which writes to stdout; RADIANS_TO_DEGREES is the macro for the conversion from radians to (you guessed it) degrees: $360°/2\pi$.

Finally, you sleep for a second before you fetch the next value:

```
Platform::sleepMillis(1000);
```

Putting this pause in is the only way to make the program reasonably useful. With 10 reports at one-second intervals, you can hold the device in your hands and see the changes in the output as you move it in various ways. If you didn't pause, the output would scroll by so fast that it'd be difficult to make much sense of the output or for the values to change significantly between readings.

2.3.4 Exiting and cleaning up

After you've looped 10 times, you're ready to exit:

```
ovrHmd_Destroy(hmd);
return 0;
```

You call ovrHmd_Destroy(hmd) to release your reference to the headset, allowing it to be deallocated properly.

2.3.5 Understanding the output

Running the application should produce output similar to this:

```
Current orientation - roll 0.00, pitch 0.00, yaw 0.00
Current orientation - roll -56.48, pitch -50.88, yaw -28.67
Current orientation - roll -56.46, pitch -50.89, yaw -28.65
Current orientation - roll -56.47, pitch -50.88, yaw -28.66
Current orientation - roll -56.48, pitch -50.87, yaw -28.66
```

---

[3] Part of the GLM C++ math library at glm.g-truc.net/

The first report has 0 for all the angles. After connecting to the sensor, you don't delay before you report the first value. It's therefore possible for the first item to print before any messages have been received, because data is collected from the device on another thread.

. After that first line, with a device at rest, you'd expect the angles to remain at 0. They don't for two reasons: *drift* and *pitch* correction. Drift is the name for the collection of tiny phenomena that lead to the Rift gradually losing its initial orientation. Pitch correction is the Rift's built-in technology that uses real-world gravity to measure the pitch of the virtual-world camera.

Pitch correction takes at least a few messages to kick in, but once it does, the sensor fusion software reevaluates the reported value, taking the direction of gravity into account. Drift is caused by the random fluctuations in the reported values from the hardware, combining with accumulated floating-point errors. You can see the effect of drift in the tiny fluctuations in the least significant digits.

The sample shown at the beginning of this subsection was captured while the Rift was hanging from a hook, completely still, and even so there's a small random amount of change in the values. The fluctuation here is about 2/100th of a degree, equivalent to about 1.2 minutes of arc, or approximately the width of the International Space Station in the sky as viewed from Earth, and that's just over a period of a few seconds. Because drift is typically random, while the Rift is still it's unlikely to accumulate very quickly. It can be exacerbated by the pattern and order of head movements, so for instance, turning your head left, then looking up, and then moving directly forward can magnify the drift in a particular direction and cause it to accumulate faster.

All good? Then let's move on: now that you know how to talk to the Rift, it's time to lay down a bit of groundwork for bringing up simple OpenGL apps. After that we can get on to the real fun: sending video to the Rift!

2.4 *A framework for demo code: the GlfwApp base class*

One of the downsides to OpenGL (and to programming in general, if we're honest) is that the ratio of "boilerplate" code to the code that actually does the thing you're interested in can be painfully high, especially in little demos. To hide away as many of the OpenGL and platform-dependent issues as possible, we're using the GLFW library (www.glfw.org) and we've written a lightweight wrapper class, GlfwApp, around it. (The acronym GLFW appears to have started life as "[Open]GL FrameWork," but these days everybody calls the project GLFW.)

Like the RUN_OVR_APP macro, GlfwApp is available online (github.com/Oculus-RiftInAction/OculusRiftInAction). Feel free to download it, and we hope it serves you well.

GlfwApp takes care of opening a window, binding an OpenGL context, setting up the rendering frame, and so on. Well, really most of that is taken care of by the underlying GLFW3 C library, and we've just wrapped it in a C++ package. If you look at the example code at the GlfwApp implementation, you'll see that it contains a run() method, which will be called from our OVR_RUN_APP macro. Its core loop is shown next.

> **Listing 2.5 The core loop of GlfwApp, our demo framework base class**

```
int GlfwApp::run() {
  window = createRenderingTarget(windowSize, windowPosition);
  if (!window) {
    FAIL("Unable to create OpenGL window");
  }
  initGl();
  while (!glfwWindowShouldClose(window)) {
    glfwPollEvents();
    update();
    draw();
    finishFrame();
  }
  shutdownGl();
  return 0;
}
```

You launch each of our demo programs with the RUN_APP or RUN_OVER_APP macro, passing in the name of the class you want to run. The RUN macro is responsible for creating an instance of the named class, which implicitly calls the instance's constructor, and then calls its run() method.

GlfwApp is designed to allow you to run both Rift and non-Rift content, so it doesn't have any preconceived concept of the size or position of the OpenGL window. It's up to the derived class to implement the createRenderingTarget() method and specify what the size and position of the window should be, and whether or not it should be a full-screen window. Once this method has been called, the window should've been created, so you test for this and fail out of the program if it hasn't been.

Having created the window, you now need to set up OpenGL, so you call initGl(). This is the place to put any initialization that depends on or interacts with OpenGL. Such initialization can only occur after an OpenGL context has been created, so it can't be done in the constructor. The GlfwApp class has an implementation of this method that does some pretty basic OpenGL setup in its own right. Derived classes are free to override this method but should ensure that they call the base class implementation when they do so.

With all of the setup complete, you enter your primary loop:

```
while (!glfwWindowShouldClose(window)) {
  glfwPollEvents();
  update();
  draw();
  finishFrame();
}
```

`glfwWindowShouldClose()` returns a non-zero value if the window has been closed or requested to be closed by the OS.

`glfwPollEvents()` handles all the pending OS-level events for the window. For our purposes, this refers to input events like mouse and keyboard actions.

`update()` is a virtual `GlfwApp` member function that's called once per frame and is specifically intended for actions that manage the state or affect the output of the application but that are not themselves rendering commands.

It's vitally important to maintain a clean separation between code that does the rendering and code that doesn't. This is critical for the Rift, or for any application that wants to support stereoscopic rendering of any kind. If your state-altering instructions are mixed with your rendering instructions, you may see unpleasant artifacts when you try to render the same scene simultaneously from two different viewpoints.

The heart of the loop is the `GlfwApp::draw()` method. In this method, classes derived from our example framework will make all the OpenGL rendering calls.

Finally, you call `GlfwApp::finishFrame()`. By default, this calls `glfwSwapBuffers()`, triggering OpenGL to update the output device. OpenGL and Direct3D applications, and indeed graphics mechanism in general, are buffered in such a way that the drawing takes place in an offscreen buffer, and pixels are only copied en masse to the actual display output when it's complete. This is typically referred to as *double buffering*, though your video card is free to use more than just two buffers internally.

Once you exit the loop, having been told to do so by the return value of `glfw-WindowShouldClose()`, you destroy the OpenGL window. GLFW automatically cleans up after itself and you return from your run method, thus ending the program.

That's a quick recap of the core of our demo app base class. You'll be using `Glfw-App` and classes derived from it in the rest of the book, so it'll soon become familiar. Now it's time to get some pixels onto the Rift.

2.5 Rendering output to the display

Now that you have input from the tracker and a solid base class for our display demos, let's look at working with the other device in the headset: let's send output to the Rift's display (figure 2.3).

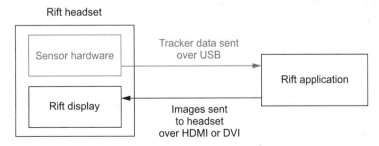

Figure 2.3　Sending output to the display

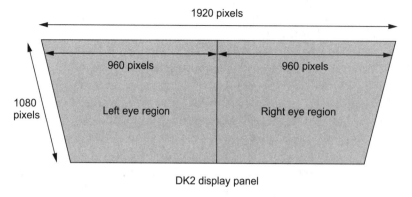

1920 pixels

960 pixels

960 pixels

1080 pixels

Left eye region

Right eye region

DK2 display panel

Figure 2.4   The display panel divided into left and right sections

From the point of view of a computer, the Rift is just another screen; it takes its video input over an HDMI (or DVI) cable and it displays whatever the OS sends it (figure 2.4).

In fact, if you plug your Rift in right now and don't run any targeted software, you'll probably see a portion of your OS desktop glowing at you through the bulbous lenses. You can't really use it like that because the design of the Rift means each eye only sees half of the display panel. The OS doesn't take that into account, so if you look through the Rift you'll see a couple of overlapping views of your own desktop.

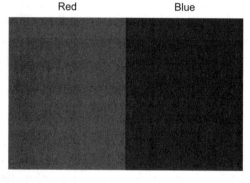

Red   Blue

Figure 2.5   Rendering two rectangles to the Rift, one red (left) and one blue (right)

The challenge that the Rift faces is, of course, the whole "two eyes" thing. We get our stereo vision from the brain's remarkable ability to parse two almost-identical images, separated only by a nose, and turn that into spatial awareness. We'll go into the details of fields of view (with and without noses) in chapter 5.

Let's look at the simple mechanics of showing a unique image to each eye with OpenGL. The example code in the following listing will render two rectangles to the Rift, one red and one blue (figure 2.5).

Listing 2.6   Rendering to the display

```
#include "Common.h"

class RiftDisplay : public GlfwApp {
 ovrHmd hmd;
```

GlfwApp is a wrapper class that abstracts OpenGL platform-specific issues.

```
        public:
          RiftDisplay() {
            hmd = ovrHmd_Create(0);
            if (!hmd) {
              hmd = ovrHmd_CreateDebug(ovrHmd_DK2);
            }
            if (!hmd) {
              FAIL("Unable to detect Rift display");
            }
          }

          virtual GLFWwindow * createRenderingTarget(
              glm::uvec2 & outSize,
              glm::ivec2 & outPosition) {
            GLFWwindow * window;
            bool extendedMode =
                ovrHmdCap_ExtendDesktop & hmd->HmdCaps;

            outPosition = glm::ivec2(
                hmd->WindowsPos.x,
                hmd->WindowsPos.y);
            outSize = glm::uvec2(
                hmd->Resolution.w,
                hmd->Resolution.h);

            if (extendedMode) {
              GLFWmonitor * monitor =
                  glfw::getMonitorAtPosition(outPosition);
              if (nullptr != monitor) {
                const GLFWvidmode * mode =
                    glfwGetVideoMode(monitor);
                outSize = glm::uvec2(mode->width, mode->height);
              }
              glfwWindowHint(GLFW_DECORATED, 0);
              window = glfw::createWindow(outSize, outPosition);
            } else {
              window = glfw::createSecondaryScreenWindow(outSize);
              void * nativeWindowHandle =
                  glfw::getNativeWindowHandle(window);
              if (nullptr != nativeWindowHandle) {
                ovrHmd_AttachToWindow(hmd, nativeWindowHandle,
                    nullptr, nullptr);
              }
            }
            return window;
          }

          void draw() {
            glm::uvec2 eyeSize = getSize();
            eyeSize.x /= 2;

            glEnable(GL_SCISSOR_TEST);

            glScissor(0, 0, eyeSize.x, eyeSize.y);
            glClearColor(1, 0, 0, 1);
            glClear(GL_COLOR_BUFFER_BIT);
```

Locates the headset device.

Detects whether the Rift is running in Direct HMD or Extended mode.

Our parent class calls this virtual method to create the OpenGL window.

You begin by assuming the HMD size and position values are valid for use.

Extended and Direct mode window setup are significantly different.

In extended mode you need to query the resolution of the Rift.

You also need to make sure that the created window doesn't include window decorations.

In direct mode, you create a window wherever you want; use the Rift native resolution for the size.

Direct HMD mode requires that you pass the native window handle you're using into the SDK.

For our drawing method, you want to display the color red on the left eye half of the display, so you set up a scissor region and clear it, with the clear color set to red.

```
    glScissor(eyeSize.x, 0, eyeSize.x, eyeSize.y);
    glClearColor(0, 0, 1, 1);
    glClear(GL_COLOR_BUFFER_BIT);

    glDisable(GL_SCISSOR_TEST);
  }
};
```

> For the right eye, you change the scissor region and the clear color and again clear the display.

```
RUN_OVR_APP(RiftDisplay);
```

This class exposes the complexity of creating an output window for the Rift display. Even this example is significantly smaller than it could be because we're pushing a lot of code into helper methods and the parent class, GlfwApp.

Let's walk through the Rift code now, step by step. After all that setup, it's high time the Rift took center stage.

2.5.1 *The constructor: accessing the Rift*

Our example constructor only does one thing: finds the Rift if one is connected, or returns a debug Rift if one isn't detected.

You locate the headset through the call

```
hmd = ovrHmd_Create(0);
```

This call fetches the first headset it finds. Make sure you check that a headset was actually found, or hilarity will ensue. If users haven't correctly connected their device or don't own a Rift to begin with, hmd will be zero. As in the sensor example, always check your state before continuing, and try to give your users a "friendly" fallback experience in the event of failure.

In this case, because you're only using the Rift for output, it's reasonable for you to fall back on building an instance of the debug Rift device if you can't detect a real one. That's what you do with these lines:

```
if (!hmd) {
  hmd = ovrHmd_CreateDebug(ovrHmd_DK2);
}
```

It's important that you keep your users informed of failures during application launch. There's little in this world more frustrating than working with an application that supposedly supports the Rift but silently ignores it and won't give the user any indication of why. You don't want to be the developer who promises to allow users to enjoy their shiny[4] new hardware and fails to deliver.

---

[4] Well... matte black. But metaphorically speaking, very shiny indeed.

2.5.2 *Creating the OpenGL window*

Now that you've opened the Rift device (or its debug evil twin), you're ready to create the OpenGL window for your output with the `createRenderingTarget()` method. To accomplish that, you're going to let GLFW do all the heavy lifting.

As of SDK version 0.4.4, the Rift can be connected to the PC in one of two modes: *Extended Desktop mode* or *Direct HMD mode.* In Extended mode, the Rift acts like another screen on your computer, so you target it by opening a completely standard OpenGL window. In Direct HMD mode, you have to open a native window and pass the details of that window to the Oculus SDK so that the SDK can handle the rendering for you. We'll come back to the difference between these two modes in chapter 4.

For now, suffice it to say that GLFW has several methods for creating and configuring windows. Choose your setup based on whether the Rift is in Extended or Direct HMD mode, tweaking a few related settings as needed.

For more details about the subtleties of Direct HMD and Extended modes, and how they affect window setup, check out chapter 4.

2.5.3 *Rendering two rectangles, one for each eye*

Finally, there's our `draw()` method. You want to render two rectangles, one for each eye. To do it with close to the minimum amount of code, you'll use the OpenGL *scissor* functionality. OpenGL has two similar mechanisms to limit the output to a given rectangle on the screen: *viewports* and *scissors*. The key difference between the two (for our purposes) is that scissor rectangles limit the area that a `glClear` call will affect; viewports don't. To draw simple rectangles on the screen without going into dealing with geometry and vertices, you just set a scissor region, set the OpenGL clear color to the color you want, and tell OpenGL to clear that region.

This is probably the last time you'll be using the scissor functionality, because most of the time you're going to want to render something more interesting than a colored rectangle.

First, you want to determine the size of the rectangle you'll render for each eye. This is exactly half the window size:

```
void draw() {
 glm::uvec2 eyeSize = getSize();
 eyeSize.x /= 2;
```

You grab the window size from `getSize()`, which the parent class `GlfwApp` provides, and you divide the horizontal distance in two, because the Rift display is bilaterally symmetrical.

Next, you need to enable OpenGL's scissor-testing function, because it's not on by default:

```
 glEnable(GL_SCISSOR_TEST);
```

Now you clear the left eye with the color red:

```
glScissor(0, 0, eyeSize.x, eyeSize.y);
glClearColor(1, 0, 0, 1);
glClear(GL_COLOR_BUFFER_BIT);;
```

The first line establishes the size and position of the rectangle for the left eye. The first two parameters are pixel coordinates for the lower-left corner of the rectangle. The second two parameters are the size of the rectangle. Remember that eyeSize was computed using half the original display width, so this should take up half the screen.

The glClearColor() function is used to specify the color that should be used when clearing the screen, defined as four floating-point values between 0 and 1 that represent the level of the colors red, green, and blue as well as the alpha value. You set red to 1 and blue and green to 0. Alpha doesn't matter for our purposes, but you set it to 1 by convention.

The "drawing" is done by the glClear() call, which erases the contents of the color buffer and replaces them with the clear color.

Next you repeat the process for the right eye with the color blue. The only differences here are the position of the rectangle (now starting halfway across the screen) and the clear color (now setting blue to 1 and red to 0):

```
glScissor(eyeSize.x, 0, eyeSize.x, eyeSize.y);
glClearColor(0, 0, 1, 1);
glClear(GL_COLOR_BUFFER_BIT);
```

Finally you clean up by disabling the scissor test again. This isn't strictly necessary—nothing else is working with the OpenGL state—but it's good practice when working with libraries like the Oculus SDK that might use or affect state to try to manage it effectively.

```
glDisable(GL_SCISSOR_TEST);
}
```

And that's it. If you run the example you should see only red in the left eye and only blue in the right eye, and a general impression of purple if you look through both eyes at the same time.[5]

2.6   *What's next?*

You've seen how to get basic input from the head tracker, and how to render the simplest output to the Rift display panel with information gleaned from the SDK. To create a fully functional Rift application, you'll want to bring these together, creating an interactive scene that responds to the Rift's movements.

Compared to the examples in this chapter, creating a fully functional Rift program pulls in a significant amount of complexity. For one thing, in our output example we

---

[5] Any euphoric or psychedelic effect you experience as a result may be taxable depending on your jurisdiction.

basically cheated. Rendering primary colors to a 2D rectangle by using `glScissor` and `glClearColor` is easily an order of magnitude simpler than doing any real work in OpenGL, like rendering 3D geometry. And, in a real application you'll need to do more than render a scene—you'll need to render it for the Rift headset. That means rendering from two different perspectives and distorting the output image to make the resulting image look correct from within the Rift. And it means you have to start working with 3D geometry, model-view and projection matrices, and OpenGL shaders to render the scene. Don't worry if it's not all clear as crystal yet! In chapters 4 and 5 we'll delve into these issues in greater depth and in an incremental fashion. We'll go deep into the details of what's being done, why it's being done, how you should do it, and how to know you're doing it correctly. We begin in chapter 3 with an in-depth dive into working with the head tracker by looking at not just getting reports from the Rift but also understanding what it reports and how to apply the data to a rendered scene.

But if you just can't wait to start digging into something more substantial, the example code repository also includes an additional example (titled *HelloRift*) alongside the other chapter 2 examples. This application will run with or without a Rift connected and represents a full end-to-end application that both does the required Rift distortion and uses the tracker to detect orientation. You're free to inspect it to see the entire mechanism at work (but we humbly suggest that because you already paid for the rest of this book, you might as well read it).

2.7 Summary

In this chapter, you learned that

- Working with the Rift involves working with two distinct devices: a set of sensors connected via USB (the head tracker), and a monitor device connected via HDMI or DVI (the display).
- Both devices are managed via the Oculus SDK.
- Since the release of DK2 and version 0.4 of the Oculus software, the software is broken down into two major components, the *runtime* and the *SDK*.
- The Oculus runtime serves to address two limitations of the Rift: concurrent access to the hardware and the inapplicability of the desktop metaphor to the Rift display.
- The Oculus SDK is a C API.
- When using the SDK you need to properly initialize and shut down the SDK. Failing to do so can result in your application crashing, or hanging so that the user has to forcibly terminate the application.
- The Rift contains sensor hardware that detects acceleration on three axes and rotation speed on three axes.
- The DK2 includes an infrared camera meant to track the orientation and position of an array of infrared LEDs built into the surface of the Rift.

- The Oculus SDK provides support for taking the raw messages from the hardware and coalescing them into a single orientation in a form that's easily applied to modern rendering systems.
- All of the C++ rendering examples in this book use a set of macros and a lightweight base class called `GlfwApp`, which hides away as many of the OpenGL and platform-dependent issues as possible.
- Because the Rift separates the user's eyes in the headset, to use the Rift a distinct image needs to be rendered for each eye.

Pulling data out of the Rift: working with the head tracker

3

This chapter covers

- Understanding the head tracker
- Using the head tracker API to fetch an orientation
- Applying the new orientation to a rendered scene
- Using gravimetric and magnetic drift correction
- Using prediction to reduce latency

For some users of the Rift, the first impression is, yeah, that's a nice view. They aren't really wowed. Then they move their head, and that's when it hits them. They break into a huge grin and make a 360-degree spin just to take it all in. The sense of immersion they get from having their point of view be consistent with where they're looking completely sells them on the experience.

The Rift includes the hardware that lets you track head movement, but how do you use it to create an immersive experience?

The Oculus Rift includes solid-state circuitry that reports the device's current acceleration and angular velocity as vectors up to a thousand times a second. By combining these individual hardware reports, the Rift SDK is able to provide a continuous representation of the current orientation of the Rift in three dimensions.

3.1 The head tracker API

Access to the head tracker hardware is provided via an `ovrHmd` handle, the acquisition of which we covered in chapter 2.

The C API provided by the SDK masks much of the complexity of interacting with the hardware and software, reducing the interface to a number of supported and required capabilities that you can specify when you activate tracking. Interacting with the sensor hardware boils down to a few simple functions:

- `ovrHmd_ConfigureTracking` allows you to tell the SDK to start tracking the head orientation and position.
- `ovrHmd_RecenterPose` indicates that the internal state of the sensor should be reset so that future readings should be relative to the current position and orientation of the headset.
- `ovrHmd_GetTrackingState` returns the current orientation and position information for the tracker, as well as a variety of other values.
- `ovrHmd_GetEyePose` also returns information about the current orientation and position of the sensor but can be called only at certain times.

The distinction between `ovrHmd_GetTrackingState` and `ovrHmd_GetEyePose` deserves explanation. The latter is typically called twice each frame, once for each eye, and returns a simple `ovrPosef` type. The `ovrPosef` structure contains the information that should be used by the renderer to draw the scene from a particular point of view. The `ovrHmd_GetSensorState` function can be called any time to fetch the current state of the sensor, and it contains quite a bit more information than a simple pose. We'll discuss the distinction and use cases of each function in a bit more detail in a moment.

3.1.1 Enabling and resetting head tracking

To start working with the head tracker, you need to call `ovrHmd_ConfigureTracking`. Typically you'll do this near the start of your application (or near the point when the user activates the Rift mode for your application), shortly after you've acquired your `ovrHmd` handle. The method has the following signature:

```
OVR_EXPORT ovrBool ovrHmd_ConfigureTracking(
    ovrHmd hmd,
    unsigned int supportedSensorCaps,
    unsigned int requiredSensorCaps);
```

As you can see, this function takes two parameters in addition to the `ovrHmd` handle: a supported sensor-capabilities bit field and a required sensor-capabilities bit field. These bit fields are intended to be filled with flags from the `ovrTrackingCaps` enum type. Currently there are three flags:

```
ovrTrackingCap_Orientation        = 0x0010,
ovrTrackingCap_MagYawCorrection   = 0x0020,
ovrTrackingCap_Position           = 0x0040,
```

All present Rift models support orientation, but only the DK2 models[1] and later support position tracking via the camera. Magnetic yaw correction appears to have been dropped from DK2 in favor of using optical yaw correction via the same camera that supports positional tracking. Adding a flag into the `supportedSensorCaps` parameter will have no negative effect if the functionality isn't supported by the hardware.

RESETTING THE TRACKER ORIENTATION

You may be tempted to initialize the sensor during the headset initialization and simply leave it running for the life of the application. But keep in mind that this approach can lead to a problem where the tracker starts its lifetime while the Rift isn't on the user's head or facing in the correct direction.

For this situation, among others, it's desirable to be able to reset the state of the head tracker so that its current orientation and position are reset to identity values. In other words, when the user starts playing they should be able to hit a key and reset what forward means so that it's comfortable. This is done with the `ovrHmd_RecenterPose()` method. This method takes only one parameter: the `ovrHmd` handle to the headset.

When you use the recenter function, it resets the position so that the user's currently reported position is considered the origin for future tracker position data. It also resets the yaw value of the orientation so that the current direction is considered forward, or "no yaw." It doesn't affect the effective pitch and roll values, because those are determined via the direction of the gravitational pull acting on the headset.[2]

We'll discuss at length the need for properly providing a transition from a desktop experience to a VR experience in chapter 9. Ensuring that you give the user an opportunity to become comfortable before starting to use and apply head-tracking data is part of that experience.

3.1.2 Receiving head tracker data

Next we'll look at two functions you'll find useful for fetching information about the current state of the head tracker (including, but not always limited to, its position and orientation). They return different amounts of information and have distinctly different use cases.

ANYTIME TRACKING

The first is `ovrHmd_GetTrackingState`. This method can be called any time in your application, from any thread. It has the following signature:

```
ovrTrackingState ovrHmd_GetTrackingState(ovrHmd hmd, double absTime);
```

The first argument is, as always, the `ovrHmd` handle to the current headset. The second argument represents the time for which you want any predicted data. `ovrHmd_GetTrackingState` returns information about the state of the headset, optionally using current velocities and accelerations to predict the headset's state in the future.

---

[1] The Crystal Cove prototype also supported position tracking, but it was never available to the general public.

[2] Try not to use the recenter function while in a centrifuge, or it may throw off the calculations.

OVRTRACKINGSTATE

The type returned from ovrHmd_GetTrackingState is pretty deep, containing a number of structures, which contain their own structures, and so on. Let's look at all the structures involved (see the following listing; ovrQuatf and ovrVector3f are excluded because they're self-evident).

Listing 3.1 Structures used for head tracking

```
typedef struct ovrPosef_                        Holds the orientation and
{                                               position of a tracked object
    ovrQuatf    Orientation;                    relative to some fixed origin.
    ovrVector3f Position;
} ovrPosef;

typedef struct ovrPoseStatef_                   Holds a pose, speed and
{                                               acceleration informaton, and
    ovrPosef    ThePose;                        the time the sample was taken.
    ovrVector3f AngularVelocity;
    ovrVector3f LinearVelocity;
    ovrVector3f AngularAcceleration;
    ovrVector3f LinearAcceleration;
    double      TimeInSeconds;
} ovrPoseStatef;

typedef struct ovrSensorData_                   Contains the most
{                                               recent raw information
    ovrVector3f Accelerometer;                  from the sensors.
    ovrVector3f Gyro;
    ovrVector3f Magnetometer;
    float       Temperature;
    float       TimeInSeconds;
} ovrSensorData;

typedef struct ovrTrackingState_                Contains a pose state for the
{                                               head, with two variants of a
    ovrPoseStatef HeadPose;                     pose for the camera, some raw
    ovrPosef      CameraPose;                   sensor data, and a bit field for
    ovrPosef      LeveledCameraPose;            status flags.
    ovrSensorData RawSensorData;
    unsigned int  StatusFlags;
} ovrTrackingState;
```

The HeadPose member holds not only the current pose of the tracker (in member field ThePose), but information about the linear and angular accelerations and velocities of the head. The pose is a critical part of our rendering process,[3] although the other values might be useful for triggering effects or rendering changes based on how fast the user was moving or turning their head.

The CameraPose and LeveledCameraPose members can be used to detect the bounds of the camera frustum relative to the head. This information is particularly useful if

---

[3] You'll see this in action in chapter 4.

you want to ensure that as a user approaches the edge of the positional tracking frustum you take some action to prevent or account for the sudden loss of positional tracking when the user moves out of bounds.

HeadPose, CameraPose, and LeveledCameraPose are all of type ovrPosef, a type that encapsulates a particular orientation and position. These are contained in Orientation and Position, which are a quaternion (ovrQuaternionf) and a 3D vector (ovrVector3f), respectively.

Quaternions

Quaternions are one of the three main ways of representing a rotation transformation. More details can be found in appendix B.

So if, for instance, you want to know the exact orientation of the headset right at a given moment, you can do so by calling this:

```
ovrHmd_GetTrackingState(hmd, ovr_GetTimeInSeconds())
  .HeadPose
    .ThePose
      .Orientation;
```

RENDERING TRACKING

The other function that returns head tracker data, ovrHmd_GetEyePoses, is part of the rendering and timing mechanism built into the Oculus SDK. We'll cover this system in more detail in chapter 4, but for now it's important to understand the distinction between what ovrHmd_GetTrackingState and ovrHmd_GetEyePoses are intended to do.

The signature method looks like this:

```
void ovrHmd_GetEyePoses(
    ovrHmd hmd,
    unsigned int frameIndex,
    ovrVector3f hmdToEyeViewOffset[2],
    ovrPosef outEyePoses[2],
    ovrTrackingState* outHmdTrackingState);
```

Unlike the more general-purpose function described earlier, this function is specifically optimized for providing the information required for rendering. As opposed to just the tracking state structure returned by ovrHmd_GetSensorState, this method provides as output a pair of ovrPosef structures, containing a predicted orientation and position for the headset. The exact amount of time used for the prediction is determined inside the SDK based on its knowledge of when the image is likely to be displayed on the Rift panel. You can still get the same tracking state information provided by ovrHmd_GetSensorState by passing in a non-null pointer in the outHmdTrackingState parameter.

USE CASES

Each of these methods has its uses. In the case of ovrHmd_GetEyePoses, there's really only one use case: get the best possible orientation and position of the headset for rendering the scene for an eye, given a good idea of when exactly the rendered pixels will appear on the screen. Because this is, after all, the primary use case for the head tracker, that leaves open the question of what purpose the ovrHmd_GetTrackingState function serves.

For one thing, there may be times when you want to know what the head pose is outside of the rendering loop. If the user leans their head forward or to the side, that movement may need to trigger some event or action within the application. In such cases it'd be advantageous to have a stored pose that's updated once per frame, rather than once per eye, and use that as the aggregate head pose for the user as a whole.

Also, consider an application that includes some sort of head gestural support such as responding to nods or headshakes with programmed behaviors. This sort of interaction would rely much more heavily on the angular velocity data returned by ovrHmd_GetTrackingState than on the actual current head pose. You might even wish to launch a separate thread for sampling the sensor data at a higher rate than the rendering loop might offer in order to provide more accurate gestural detection, or to offload the work onto a separate CPU core.

Finally, in VR applications it may not be uncommon to have additional data injected into the scene that comes from inputs with unstable levels of latency. Consider a camera that might be attached to the Rift. Webcams often have variable frame rates, which are influenced by the amount of light available in the surrounding environment. If you simply inject a webcam image into the scene in a fixed position in the rendered scene, the latency of the webcam will mean that the world inside the camera view will seem to lag behind the rest of the scene. This can be countered by calling ovrHmd_GetTrackingState with an absTime value in the past to determine the orientation the head likely had when the image was captured. The prior orientation can then be compared with the orientation at the time of render (part of the head pose) and the image positioned within the scene appropriately. This kind of integration of external inputs is covered in more detail in chapter 13.

In the following listing, let's look back at some of the code in the run() method from the example in chapter 2, where you fetched an orientation and then printed the orientation to the console. This time around you'll be making much more interesting use of the data by using it to transform the scene.

Listing 3.2 Fetching the Rift's orientation, revisited

```
int run() {
  ovrHmd hmd = ovrHmd_Create(0);
  if (!hmd || !ovrHmd_ConfigureTracking(hmd,
      ovrTrackingCap_Orientation, 0)) {
```
 Opens the headset

```
   SAY_ERR("Unable to detect Rift head tracker");
   return -1;
 }

 // ...

   ovrTrackingState state = ovrHmd_GetTrackingState(hmd, 0);
   ovrQuatf orientation = state.HeadPose.ThePose.Orientation;
   glm::quat q = glm::make_quat(&orientation.x);
   glm::vec3 euler = glm::eulerAngles(q);

   SAY("Current orientation - roll %0.2f, pitch %0.2f, yaw %0.2f",
       euler.z * RADIANS_TO_DEGREES,
       euler.x * RADIANS_TO_DEGREES,
       euler.y * RADIANS_TO_DEGREES);

 // ...

 ovrHmd_Destroy(hmd);
 return 0;
}
```

❷ Fetches the data

❸ Prints orientation in degrees

❹ Closes the headset and releases resources

The listing starts by opening the headset using ovrHmd_Create and then enabling the sensor with ovrHmd_ConfigureTracking ❶. With setup out of the way, you repeatedly fetch the Rift's orientation ❷. The remainder of the inner loop takes the returned orientation, expressed as a quaternion; converts it into a more human-friendly representation of the orientation, Euler angles; and finally prints out the results ❸. Once you've finished with the sensor, you tell the SDK to destroy your handle to the headset ❹. The OVR SDK does its best to clean up on exit, but it may log an error or throw a debug assertion if you fail to do this.

In this example, you printed the orientation data to the console. For Rift applications, you'll want to apply this orientation data to a rendered scene. To do so, you'll convert the orientation quaternion you've read from the Rift into a *basis transform* and transform your scene dynamically. To learn more about the mathematical concepts of basis transforms, please refer to appendix B.

In section 3.2 we'll walk you through some of the mathematical underpinnings that support our use of transforms with the Rift, and we'll introduce the software design pattern called *matrix stacks* as a great way to organize transform data. In the subsequent sections, we'll explore how to build transforms from the Rift's data, how to improve the quality of that data, and even how you can see into the future (for a few dozen milliseconds, anyway).

Ready to go? Read on!

3.2   *Receiving and applying the tracker data: an example*

Using the orientation sensors of the Rift is straightforward. You enable the tracker using one function and read data out using another function for that purpose.

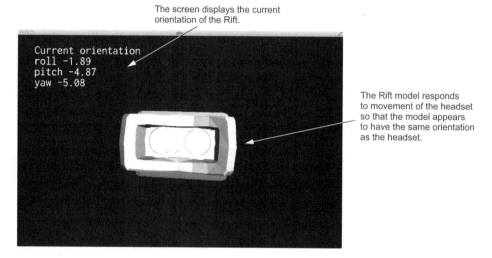

The screen displays the current orientation of the Rift.

The Rift model responds to movement of the headset so that the model appears to have the same orientation as the headset.

Figure 3.1   Output from Example_3_3_Tracker.cpp

Listing 3.3 renders a simple object to your screen that looks like the headset itself (figure 3.1). Note that this example isn't intended for output on the Rift display but rather for rendering to a conventional monitor.

As you move the Rift around, the object responds to the movement. We've abridged this example a bit for print: in the chapter's download files you'll find a slightly cooler version of this demo, which renders the sensor feedback directly to the screen.

Listing 3.3   Example_3_3_Tracker.cpp (Abridged)

```
#include "Common.h"

class SensorFusionExample : public GlfwApp {
  ovrHmd hmd;
  glm::quat orientation;
  glm::vec3 linearA;
  glm::vec3 angularV;

public:

  SensorFusionExample() {
  }

  virtual ~SensorFusionExample() {
    ovrHmd_Destroy(hmd);
    ovr_Shutdown();
  }

  virtual GLFWwindow * createRenderingTarget(
      glm::uvec2 & outSize,
      glm::ivec2 & outPosition) {
```

Ensures you release your resources properly when you're done.

```
        outSize = glm::uvec2(800, 600);
        outPosition = glm::ivec2(100, 100);
        Stacks::projection().top() = glm::perspective(
            PI / 3.0f, aspect(outSize),
            0.01f, 10000.0f);
        Stacks::modelview().top() = glm::lookAt(
            glm::vec3(0.0f, 0.0f, 3.5f),
            Vectors::ORIGIN, Vectors::UP);

        GLFWwindow * result =
            glfw::createWindow(outSize, outPosition);

        ovr_Initialize();                          Acquires the handle
        hmd = ovrHmd_Create(0);                    to the headset.

        if (!hmd
            || !ovrHmd_ConfigureTracking(hmd,        Enables the tracking sensors
                ovrTrackingCap_Orientation, 0)) {    on the headset, requesting
          FAIL("Unable to locate Rift sensor device");   orientation data.
        }
        return result;
    }

    virtual void onKey(int key, int scancode, int action, int mods) {
      // ...
    }

    void update() {
      ovrTrackingState trackingState =          Once each frame, you fetch
          ovrHmd_GetTrackingState(hmd, 0);      the current sensor data.

      ovrPoseStatef & poseState =             poseState holds all the current
          trackingState.HeadPose;             head pose data, including position,
                                              orientation, and motion.

      orientation = ovr::toGlm(              Converts from the OVR C API
          poseState.ThePose.Orientation);    structures to the equivalent GLM
      linearA = ovr::toGlm(                  types, extracting the current
          poseState.LinearAcceleration);     orientation, linear acceleration,
      angularV = ovr::toGlm(                 and angular velocity.
          poseState.AngularVelocity);
    }

    void draw() {
      glClear(GL_COLOR_BUFFER_BIT | GL_DEPTH_BUFFER_BIT);
      MatrixStack & mv = Stacks::modelview();
      mv.withPush([&]{
        mv.rotate(orientation);              Applies the orientation of the
        oria::renderRift();                  Rift to the modelview matrix
      });                                    and then renders your model.
      // ...
    }
};

RUN_OVR_APP(SensorFusionExample)
```

Much of the example is still taken up by OpenGL initialization and rendering support, but you should take note of these three key steps:

- Initially setting up the `ovrHmd` handle and enabling the sensor
- Fetching the sensor data in the update function
- Applying the orientation to the rendered model

These steps are worth examining in detail.

3.2.1 Initial setup and binding

The setup code for this example is nearly identical to previous examples, but we want to cover a few important points.

LOCATING THE HEADSET

First off is the unusual way in which we're initializing the SDK and acquiring the headset. You'll notice that we're only doing this *after* we've created the OpenGL window. This is because when working with the Rift in Direct HMD mode, calling the `ovr_Initialize` function causes the SDK to integrate with the display driver in such a way that if you're working with a window that isn't intended to render to the Rift, you can get unpredictable results.

This has obvious implications for you if you want your applications to support both Rift and non-Rift modes and potentially switch between them. But this behavior is likely due to the relative immaturity of the Direct HMD mode and will, we hope, be resolved in the near future; otherwise we'd make a bigger deal of it.

In this example, you want to use a rendering window to show information from the Rift SDK but display it on a conventional monitor. To avoid problems doing so, you don't initialize the SDK until after you've created the OpenGL window.

The code itself should otherwise look familiar to you. As with all applications that use the SDK, you open a headset handle to grant you access to the rest of the SDK functionality:

```
hmd = ovrHmd_Create(0);
```

ENABLING THE SENSOR AND SELECTING OPTIONS

Having acquired the headset handle, you enable the sensors for it:

```
ovrHmd_ConfigureTracking(hmd, ovrSensorCap_Orientation, 0)
```

You haven't requested yaw correction or position information, so the only thing you can count on from the sensors is the orientation, although in practice, the SDK appears to attempt to provide position data, either using the camera or the head and neck model, even if it hasn't specifically been requested.

No further work is required to get the individual head-tracking readings from the headset; the OVR SDK handles this automatically in a background thread.

3.2.2 *Fetching orientation*

Retrieving the Rift's current orientation from the SDK involves a single method call:

```
ovrTrackingState trackingState = ovrHmd_GetTrackingState(hmd, 0);
ovrPoseStatef & poseState = trackingState.HeadPose;
```

A call to `ovrHmd_GetTrackingState` will return a structure containing the state of the headset. Because you're passing in 0 as the second parameter, you're getting the instantaneous current orientation of the headset at the time of call, rather than a *predicted* value. (That's right—the Rift can predict the future! See section 3.3.2.)

The `poseState` will contain the Rift's best guess of its current orientation and position relative to its last reset and true vertical:

```
orientation = ovr::toGlm(poseState.ThePose.Orientation);
```

`ovrPoseStatef.ThePose.Orientation` is of type `ovrQuatf`. That structure contains the raw values of the quaternion, but because it's a C structure it has no methods to use them or convert them to other types. We're using the GLM math library, so we've written a simple utility function to convert from the OVR type to the equivalent GLM type. You'll see the use of `ovr::toGlm` and `ovr::fromGlm` to convert back and forth between the OVR math structures and the equivalent GLM classes. We're also grabbing the angular velocity and linear acceleration vectors in the same way.

You might be wondering why we put our sensor capture into our `update()` method instead of our `draw()` method. This isn't an example of how you *must* do things—it's an example of good software design patterns. As we'll discuss in chapter 5, there are strong benefits to software design that separates data mutation (such as `update()`) from data display (`draw()`). By keeping a clean and logical separation between these two orthogonal phases of your application, you'll be building a framework that could scale to much greater degrees of complexity down the road.

3.2.3 *Applying the orientation to the rendered scene*

In the `draw()` method we've shown you, you clear the view; then you use a matrix stack implementation to push a temporary change to the local frame of reference. At each call to `draw()` you'll push a new matrix onto the stack, update it to include a rotation based on the inverse of the current orientation of the Rift, render your Rift model, and then pop the local matrix off the stack. The value of `orientation` changes each time you invoke `update()` and our view of the model is re-rendered every `draw()` with the new transformation applied. This causes the model to pivot smoothly on the screen.

```
void draw() {
  glClear(GL_COLOR_BUFFER_BIT | GL_DEPTH_BUFFER_BIT);
  gl::MatrixStack & mv = gl::Stacks::modelview();
  mv.withPush([&]{
    mv.rotate(orientation);
    oria::renderRift();
  });
```

```
   // . . .
}
```

The Rift reports its orientation in world coordinates (figure 3.2). If you were to convert its current orientation into a matrix, it'd form a rotation matrix that, when multiplied against the vectors of the identity basis, would return three orthogonal basis vectors aligning exactly with the orientation of the Rift.

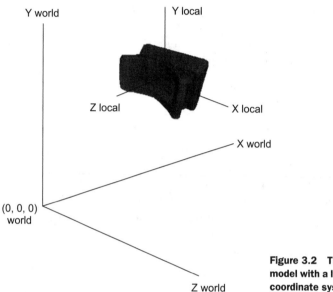

Figure 3.2   **The gray Rift model with a local and a global coordinate system around it**

If you applied the Rift's transform to the world, it would rotate the world into its own frame. But in this example you don't want to convert all other coordinates into Rift coordinates; instead, you want to transform *from* the Rift's frame of reference *into* the world coordinate system. So instead of spinning the world around the Rift, you'll spin the Rift around the world. You invert the world-to-Rift transform to produce the Rift-to-world transform.

That transformation, when applied to geometry already in world coordinates, will rotate the geometry to the Rift's basis in world coordinates; in other words, as you tip the device forward, the model on screen tips forward as well.

Mind you, there's more afoot than we've discussed so far. The SDK is performing a number of tasks internally to ensure it reports the best, most appropriate sensor data for any given request.

3.3   *Additional features: drift correction and prediction*

The SDK tracking system includes two additional bits of functionality that you should be aware of: drift correction and prediction.

3.3.1   *Drift correction*

The sensors in the Rift aren't infinitely precise. As messages are accumulated and the orientation updated, tiny errors will build up. You could be optimistic and hope that the average total of sensor errors would add up to zero and cancel out—but in practice, the various environmental factors that mislead the Rift are invariably asymmetric and errors grow instead of diminish. Drift can occur on any of the three axes of rotation, and must be accounted for and corrected. The SDK does this in a few ways.

For drift on the X and Z axes (pitch and roll), the SDK can use a known vector—gravity—to account for them. Because the headset contains an accelerometer, the SDK can always tell which way is down, because gravity causes the accelerometer to constantly report an acceleration of about 9.8 meters per second squared in the opposite direction. Because the SDK knows which direction is up and which is down, the roll and pitch of the headset can always be found relative to those vectors.

Yaw drift is a little trickier. There's no gravitational force acting on the headset that tells you which direction is forward, so you have to find something else that can provide your drift correction.

For the DK1 Rift, the magnetometer built into the headset was used, but only if it had been calibrated. This tended to be problematic because Earth's magnetic field might not be dominant when you're surrounded by a bunch of computer equipment. In fact, even the DK1's own screen produced a non-negligible magnetic field, which sometimes made performing the calibration difficult.

For the DK2 Rift, yaw correction is accomplished via the tracking camera. The camera can determine the full orientation of the Rift along with its position, making the more temperamental magnetic correction superfluous to the extent that the recent versions of the Oculus configuration software no longer support magnetic calibration for the DK2.

3.3.2   *Prediction*

One of the greatest impediments to presence is latency. If the view doesn't change in response to movement fast enough, then at best the feeling of immersion is lost, and at worst you can make yourself ill. A commonly cited upper limit for acceptable latency in VR applications is 60 ms, but many people can still perceive latency at that level. The lower limit appears to be around 20 ms, but it's subjective. So one of the goals of development is to make sure that the rendered view at any given moment represents the orientation of the Rift at that moment, within (ideally) about 20 ms.

The difficulty lies in the delays imposed by the various steps in the rendering process. Fetching sensor information, rendering the scene, and distorting the image all take time. Double buffering and frame delays by the graphics driver may cost more time. On top of this are the physical limitations inherent in the display panel.

As you turn your head, the image appears
to lag behind where you're looking.

Slow

Fast

The faster you turn your head,
the farther behind the image is.

**Figure 3.3   Bad things
happen when the view
doesn't change in
response to movement
fast enough.**

The end result (figure 3.3) is that if you're turning your head, the image appears to lag behind where you're looking. The faster you turn your head, the further behind the image is.

Fifty degrees per second is a moderate rate of turn for the human head. At that rate, every 20 ms of latency causes 1 degree of error. That's pretty lousy, but things can get a lot worse: it's completely reasonable for a human head to briefly, sharply, turn at a rate of *250* degrees per second. Suddenly as we're moving our heads everything we see is about 5 degrees away from where it should be. It may not seem like much, but your brain is accustomed to seeing things where it expects to see them when you move your head, and defying that expectation can cause distress and motion sickness.

To correct for these issues, the SDK allows you to use *prediction*. Specifically, instead of asking for the pose of the headset *now*, you can ask for the pose of the headset where it *will be* when the image you're rendering actually appears on the screen. Prediction is built into the SDK and will normally be applied without your direct intervention; when you call the ovrHmd_GetEyePoses() function, it's baked in. But if you're interested in seeing prediction in action, you can also query prediction values manually.

The method ovrHmd_GetTrackingState() lets you query for the head pose at any point in time between the present and 0.1 seconds in the future. Thus, if you update your call to ovrHmd_GetTrackingState() as follows:

```
ovrTrackingState trackingState =
    ovrHmd_GetTrackingState(hmd, ovr_GetTimeInSeconds() + X);
```

the call to ovrHmd_GetTrackingState will now return the *predicted* state of the headset, as the Rift believes it will be oriented, X seconds into the future. (Time, in this case, is relative to the start of the application, or more precisely, the initialization of the Oculus SDK.) Predicted pose is computed by integrating the headset's current position, velocities, and accelerations to generate a remarkably good best guess of where the headset will be X seconds (or fractions of a second) from now.

We've written a small demo to illustrate how prediction tries to gauge where your head is going to be. The relevant code appears in the following abridged listing. The full code can be found at github.com/OculusRiftInAction/OculusRiftInAction.

Listing 3.4   Example_3_5_TrackerPrediction.cpp (Abridged)

```cpp
class SensorFusionPredictionExample : public GlfwApp {

    float predictionValue{ 0.030 };
    glm::mat4 actual;
    glm::mat4 predicted;

// ...

    void update() {
        ovrTrackingState recordedState =
            ovrHmd_GetTrackingState(hmd,
            ovr_GetTimeInSeconds());
        ovrTrackingState predictedState =
            ovrHmd_GetTrackingState(hmd,
            ovr_GetTimeInSeconds() + predictionValue);

        actual = glm::mat4_cast(ovr::toGlm(
            recordedState.HeadPose.ThePose.Orientation));
        predicted = glm::mat4_cast(ovr::toGlm(
            predictedState.HeadPose.ThePose.Orientation));
    }

    void draw() {
        oglplus::Context::Clear().ColorBuffer().DepthBuffer();

        MatrixStack & mv = Stacks::modelview();
        mv.withPush([&]{
            mv.transform(actual);
            oria::renderRift();
        });
        mv.withPush([&]{
            mv.transform(predicted).scale(1.25f);
            oria::renderRift(0.3f);
        });
    }
}
```

You'll use the matrix *actual* to store current orientation.

You'll use the matrix *predicted* to store predicted orientation.

Stores a delta in *seconds* of how far into the future you'll ask the Rift to predict its orientation.

① To fetch current state, you call ovrHmd_GetTrackingState() with a timestamp of now.

② To fetch predicted state, you call ovrHmd_GetTrackingState() with a timestamp of now plus predictionValue.

Capture the actual head pose.

Capture the predicted head pose.

Renders a 3D model of a Rift in the current, actual orientation.

Renders a 3D model of a Rift, enlarged and transparent, in the predicted orientation.

In this sample you've doubled up on the data captured in `update()` by capturing both the current, actual pose ❶ and the predicted, integrated pose ❷. You then use the two orientation matrices to render two overlapping models of the Rift: one normal model, showing the current actual orientation, and one slightly larger and transparent, showing the predicted pose (figure 3.4). As the prediction delta grows, this transparent predicted model will begin to wildly overanticipate the motion of its smaller, actual cousin.

Because the predicted pose is computed by integrating current velocities into the future, it should be clear that the further ahead you predict, the lower the probability

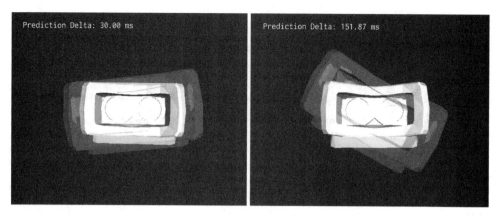

Figure 3.4   Prediction is vital for anticipating the user's head position as they move while a frame is rendered. However, over-predicting can lead to unpredictable results.

of accuracy. That's why prediction is typically limited to a handful of microseconds. When the SDK is handling the prediction gap for you, it uses its knowledge of the current frame rate to gauge how long the current frame is likely to take to render; then it only predicts ahead by that tiny interval (typically less than 20 ms).

In figure 3.4, to emphasize this point, we've sampled at 30 ms and at 150 ms into the future. We rolled the Rift emphatically to the left and right so the prediction integration had a lot of velocity to work with, and you can see that the further ahead we tried to predict, the further apart reality and prediction begin to drift.

Prediction isn't a panacea—clearly our heads can stop, start, change direction, and change speed unpredictably. Still, it provides a better starting point for rendering than simply using the last position retrieved.

3.3.3   *Using drift correction and prediction*

The good news is that you don't have to exert any effort to take advantage of drift correction or prediction. Early versions of the SDK left it up to the developer to enable them and apply them correctly, but as the software has evolved it's been recognized that if their implementation is sufficiently bulletproof, there's no real reason to ever *not* use them.

Drift correction ends up being automatic and invisible. Prediction also ends up being automatic to the extent that you don't need to do any work calculating how far ahead you should be predicting, assuming you're using the `ovrHmd_GetEyePoses()` function for interacting with the tracker. We'll cover its use in chapter 5 which ties the rendering and head-tracking functionality together.

3.4　*Summary*

In this chapter, you learned that

- The C API provided by the SDK masks much of the complexity of interacting with the hardware and software.
- Interacting with the sensor hardware involves four functions: `ovrHmd_Configure-Tracking`, `ovrHmd_RecenterPose`, `ovrHmd_GetTrackingState`, and `ovrHmd_GetEyePose`.
- Using the orientation sensors of the Rift is straightforward. You enable the tracker using one function and read data out using one of two functions (`ovrHmd_GetTrackingState` or `ovrHmd_GetEyePose`) for that purpose.
- `ovrHmd_GetEyePose` is used to get the best possible orientation and position of the headset for rendering the scene for an eye, given a good idea of when exactly the rendered pixels will appear on the screen.
- `ovrHmd_GetTrackingState` is used when you want to know what the head pose is outside of the rendering loop; for example, if you wanted to use head gestures as part of your control scheme (say, allowing the user to nod yes).
- The Rift reports its orientations in world coordinates, which you can convert into a scene transform.
- The sensors in the Rift aren't infinitely precise, but the SDK automatically corrects for drift in all three axes.
- One of the greatest impediments to presence is latency. By using the SDK's prediction functionality, you can reduce the apparent effects of latency.

Sending output to the Rift: working with the display

4

This chapter covers

- Targeting the display in Extended and Direct HMD modes
- Understanding the Rift display
- Performing the required distortion on prerendered images

The Rift contains a specialized display system, consisting of a rectangular LCD or OLED panel typical of standard monitors, paired with lenses that modify your perception of the display. An enclosure mounts the panel in a fixed position relative to your eyes and partitions the panel so that each eye sees only one half of the display. The beauty of this arrangement is that it mimics human vision with a large field of view and different images presented to each eye.

From the perspective of the OS and code-running applications on the Rift, the Rift is just another monitor. But from a 3D-graphics–rendering perspective, it *isn't* just another monitor: when rendering for the Rift you need to account for its unique design. In this chapter we'll take a closer look at what distinguishes the Rift display from a conventional monitor, and we'll show you how to deal with some of those differences. Although we won't be able to address every issue in this chapter, you'll be taking solid first steps toward rendering to the Rift.

Before you take those first steps, let's ensure that the output you create will get rendered to the Rift and not someplace else.

4.1 Targeting the Rift display

As of this writing, there are two ways to connect a Rift headset to your computer: *Extended Desktop mode* and *Direct HMD mode.*

- In Extended Desktop mode, the OS treats the Rift display as just another monitor. It's accessible through the Display control panel and can be resized and repositioned.
- In Direct HMD mode, the host OS does *not* treat the Rift as a conventional monitor. The Rift is hidden from the Display control panel and can't be enabled there. This prevents the user from having to deal with the desktop UI being extended onto a device where it can't properly be used.

There's good news and bad here, for both modes.

4.1.1 Extended vs. Direct HMD mode

Extended mode lets you leverage all the preexisting work that's gone into rendering stuff to monitors over the past few decades—and that's good. But it's a double-edged sword, because the Rift can't be *used* like just another monitor. Many of the assumptions that developers made when writing OSes (that you can see the whole display at once, for example) don't hold for the Rift—and that's bad.

In Direct HMD mode, you can use the Oculus runtime and explicit mechanisms built into the SDK to target your OpenGL or Direct3D rendering output to the Rift display. That's good. But it means that if you want to roll your own display access, you can't reach the display without going through the runtime, which can be a real restriction on developers. That's bad (www.youtube.com/watch?v=r_pqnsKWlpc).

For better or worse, this isn't a choice that you get to make in your Rift software—it'll be a choice that users have made while setting up their system. Many users will favor Direct HMD mode because it doesn't litter your desktop with a new display that you can't access—but as of this writing, Direct HMD isn't supported yet on Linux or Mac OS and it interacts very poorly with DisplayLink USB displays, which are common for laptop users. That means you'll need to expect and plan for a mixed audience.

Your app can always check which mode the user's device is in, of course. Any time after you've acquired an ovrHmd instance, you can query whether the device is running in Direct HMD mode or Extended mode by calling ovrHmd_GetEnabledCaps(). The result is a bit field that can be compared against the bit flag ovrHmdCap_Extend-Desktop to see if the device is operating in Extended mode.

4.1.2   *Creating the OpenGL window: choosing the display mode*

To help isolate the code required for setting up an OpenGL window, we've pulled the code that you first saw in listing 2.6 out into a library method used by many of our upcoming examples: createRiftRenderingWindow() (shown in the following listing). createRiftRenderingWindow() is responsible for detecting whether the user is in Extended mode or in Direct HMD mode and choosing a construction method accordingly.

Listing 4.1   createRiftRenderingWindow() (OvrUtils.cpp)

```
GLFWwindow * createRiftRenderingWindow(          Input parameter: the
    ovrHmd hmd,                                  pointer to the HMD
    glm::uvec2 & outSize,
    glm::ivec2 & outPosition) {                  Output parameter: your
  bool extendedMode = true;                      computed window size

  outPosition = glm::ivec2(
      hmd->WindowsPos.x,                    Defaults to the Rift's own idea of its
      hmd->WindowsPos.y);                   location, but this isn't set in stone.
  outSize = glm::uvec2(
      hmd->Resolution.w,                    Defaults to the Rift's own idea of size
      hmd->Resolution.h);                   as well, but this is also changeable.

  ON_WINDOWS([&] {
    extendedMode =                          ovrHmdCap_ExtendDesktop
        (ovrHmdCap_ExtendDesktop & hmd->HmdCaps);    is currently only reported
  });                                       reliably on Windows.

  return extendedMode
      ? createExtendedModeWindow(outSize, outPosition)     Passes size and/or
      : createDirectHmdModeWindow(hmd, outSize);           position to the
}                                                          appropriate subroutine.
```

Output parameter: your computed window position

The code in listing 4.1 is pretty straightforward, with one exception: as of this writing, Direct HMD mode support on non-Windows systems is still pretty unstable—so much so, in fact, that in our cross-platform experiments we've found that the ovrHmd-Cap_ExtendDesktop flag may not be accurately reported on non-Windows OSes. So our library defaults to assuming that you're in Extended mode, and you only check for Direct HMD if the app is running on Windows.

Presumably, by the time you read these words, that instability has long since been smoothed out; check the book's GitHub repository (github.com/OculusRiftInAction/OculusRiftInAction) and the book's website for updates.

4.1.3   *Creating the OpenGL window: Extended Desktop mode*

In Extended Desktop mode, you'll target the Rift by sending graphical commands to a conventional OpenGL window, positioned to fill a single OS display device. That display device will be (you guessed it) the Rift.

The most stable way to identify the Rift is to examine its current position relative to the OS desktop.

POSITIONING THE WINDOW

In listing 2.6, you saw a simple example of targeting the Rift display and rendering two colors to its left and right halves. We showed you how to use the description of the connected Rift's properties stored in the ovrHmd structure to identify its display. This structure contains information about the device: in particular, it contains a WindowPos member of type ovrVector2i, which contains an X and a Y value representing the 2D integer coordinates of the Rift's display panel relative to the desktop origin.

You'll use this position, in combination with the GLFW functions glfwGetMonitors and glfwGetMonitorPos, to implement your own method, which is able to sift through all the displays on the system looking for the Rift, as shown in the following listing.

Listing 4.2 getMonitorAtPosition() (GlfwUtils.h)

```
GLFWmonitor * getMonitorAtPosition(
    const glm::ivec2 & position) {
  int count;
  GLFWmonitor ** monitors = glfwGetMonitors(&count);      Retrieves the list of all
  for (int i = 0; i < count; ++i) {                        monitors on the system.
    glm::ivec2 candidatePosition;
    glfwGetMonitorPos(
        monitors[i],                                       For each monitor, retrieves
        &candidatePosition.x,                              its current position.
        &candidatePosition.y);
    if (candidatePosition == position) {                   If the position reported
      return monitors[i];                                  matches that of the Rift,
    }                                                      you've found your target.
  }
  return nullptr;
}
```

With this handy method, you can now identify the monitor that's the OS's representation of the Rift.

SIZING THE WINDOW

Having found the monitor to which you'll be rendering your content, you next have to decide how big the window should be.

The ovrHmd structure contains a Resolution member, and at first glance, that might seem to be all the information you need to size the OpenGL window you'll be opening. But this member contains the *native* resolution of the headset. That means you should be cautious in using this value. When running in Extended mode, the Rift may not be running at its native resolution; with this user-controlled display device, the user is free to use the OS control panel to change its resolution at will. Even without user interference, the Rift could be being driven by an older PC or laptop that can't achieve the headset's full resolution.

This was why we hunted up the Rift's monitor: you want the image to fill its screen, and that means sizing the image to the current resolution of the device. So you'll use the `WindowPos` member to identify the Rift display, and then you'll use GLFW method `glfwGetVideoMode()` to retrieve the size of that display.

CREATING THE WINDOW

Once you know the window's target size and place, opening it is comparatively simple (largely because the GLFW library abstracts away virtually all of the OS-specific pain points). Our method for creating an Extended mode OpenGL window is shown next.

Listing 4.3 `createExtendedModeWindow()` **(OvrUtils.cpp)**

```
GLFWwindow * createExtendedModeWindow(
    glm::uvec2 & outSize,
    glm::ivec2 & outPosition) {
  // In Extended Desktop mode, we should be using the
  // current resolution of the Rift.
  GLFWmonitor * monitor =
      glfw::getMonitorAtPosition(outPosition);
  if (nullptr != monitor) {
    auto mode = glfwGetVideoMode(monitor);
    outSize = glm::uvec2(mode->width, mode->height);
  }

  // If we're creating a desktop window, we strip off any window decorations
  // which might change the location of the rendered contents
  // relative to the lenses.
  glfwWindowHint(GLFW_DECORATED, 0);

  GLFWwindow * window = glfwCreateWindow(
      size.x, size.y,
      "glfw", nullptr, nullptr);
  glfwSetWindowPos(window, position.x, position.y);
}
```

Requests that GLFW not apply any chrome to the window you're about to create. ❶

Identifies the Rift's OS monitor and retrieves the current operating resolution.

Uses GLFW to create and size the window.

Uses GLFW to position the window.

The one line here that might seem slightly out of place is where you "hint" to GLFW ❶ that you'd like to create your window without top, bottom, left, or side edges. No scroll bars, please, this code is on a diet; no title bar or close button; just the OpenGL, thanks.

If you failed to remove the window decorations, then the window position you specify would be treated as the upper-left corner of that frame rather than of the OpenGL window itself. This would result in pushing the contents down and to the right by the width of that frame. The midline would shift to the right in the Rift and content meant for the left eye would be visible to the right.

Proper rendering to the Rift requires exact positioning of the OpenGL output on the headset display, so this movement is unacceptable—so you disable the decorations.

4.1.4 *Creating the OpenGL window: Direct HMD mode*

The code for Direct HMD mode is simpler. You'll create a simple OpenGL window. When you bind the Oculus runtime to that window, the window becomes a proxy to the Rift's display screen. Because Direct HMD mode works only with the native resolution of the display, which you've already retrieved in outSize, in Direct HMD mode you can create a window of that size pretty much anywhere.

In theory, you don't even need to match the size of the Rift resolution. You could create a window of half the width and height of the Rift resolution, and then attach it. Your main monitor will display a smaller version of what's on the Rift, but the Rift display will be running at full resolution. Unfortunately, although this works for Direct3D, it doesn't currently work for OpenGL. Creating a window smaller than the Rift resolution results in the content being blurry, because it's using the resolution of the window for the actual Rift display.

To create an OpenGL Direct HMD window, you'll want to create a new window of the correct size, and then, before you take any other action, you'll need to tell the OVR SDK about it. The step where you "bind" the native OS window you've created to the Rift SDK is critical: from there on out, the SDK will use the bound native window as its surface proxy and rendering target. That window will be bound directly to the Oculus runtime and its attendant display pipeline. Our method for constructing a Direct HMD mode OpenGL window is shown in this listing.

Listing 4.4 `createDirectHmdModeWindow()` **(OvrUtils.cpp)**

```
GLFWwindow * createDirectHmdModeWindow(
    ovrHmd hmd, glm::uvec2 & outSize) {

  GLFWwindow * window =
      glfw::createSecondaryScreenWindow(outSize);

  void * nativeWindowHandle =
      glfw::getNativeWindowHandle(window);
  if (nullptr != nativeWindowHandle) {
    ovrHmd_AttachToWindow(
        hmd, nativeWindowHandle, nullptr, nullptr);
  }

  return window;
}
```

You create your proxy window on a screen that isn't the primary monitor, just for ease of use.

Fetches the native window handle from GLFW so you can pass it to the Oculus runtime.

Binds the Oculus runtime to your proxy window's native OS handle. This step is critical in Direct HMD mode.

One nice touch here is that when we got tired of having the Rift ovals open on our main display (which was usually where we were writing our code, and that got pretty annoying pretty fast), we tweaked up a little helper method that would throw the Rift window onto another display. Our helper function, `glfw::createSecondaryScreen-Window()`, takes as input the desired size of the window and attempts to find a monitor that's big enough to place it on that isn't the primary monitor, though it'll fall back to the primary if no other suitable monitors are found. That way, when you're developing using your main screen, the code will find someplace else to open the Rift window.

For Direct HMD mode to function, you must call ovrHmd_AttachToWindow(), an Oculus SDK function, and pass it the native handle to the window:

```
void * nativeWindowHandle = glfw::getNativeWindowHandle(window);
if (nullptr != nativeWindowHandle) {
 ovrHmd_AttachToWindow(hmd, nativeWindowHandle, nullptr, nullptr);
}
```

This uses a second helper function, glfw::getNativeWindowHandle(). It takes a GLFWwindow pointer and returns the native handle. It seems a shame that we've gone through so much trouble to make our code platform-independent only to have to explicitly use special code to get a native handle in this way, but this is simply a limitation of the SDK.

The code for getNativeWindowHandle() is shown in the next listing

Listing 4.5   getNativeWindowHandle() (GlfwUtils.cpp)

```
void * getNativeWindowHandle(GLFWwindow * window) {
  void * nativeWindowHandle = nullptr;
  ON_WINDOWS([&]{
    nativeWindowHandle = (void*) glfwGetWin32Window(window);
  });
  ON_LINUX([&]{
    nativeWindowHandle = (void*) glfwGetX11Window(window);
  });
  ON_MAC([&]{
    nativeWindowHandle = (void*) glfwGetCocoaWindow(window);
  });
  return nativeWindowHandle;
}
```

The listing shows that you can never *quite* get away from platform-specific code in C++, but you can get pretty darned close. Each of the different native methods is its platform's version of how to retrieve a pointer to the native window object.

Caveats: Direct HMD mode in SDK 0.4.4

If you compare the code printed here to the code on *Oculus Rift in Action*'s GitHub repository, you may notice a few differences. As of this writing, there are two small "gotchas" specific to Direct HMD mode that our demo code addresses on the GitHub repository, which we haven't touched on here, because, hopefully, by the time you're reading this they'll have been resolved in the Oculus SDK.

- Direct HMD's Linux support is still nascent, and version 0.4.4 suffers from an alignment glitch. The default orientation of the HMD to the OS will be vertical, not horizontal. We address this by flipping the X and Y dimensions of the window size. Unfortunately, at this time there's no way to detect this inversion in software.

- A bug in the 0.4.4 SDK currently prevents Direct HMD mode from engaging properly unless the `ovrHmd_GetEyePoses` function is called at least once. Although this won't affect normal applications that sample the head pose each frame, it can impact smaller demos if they don't use head tracking.

You'll address these issues with two extra snippets of code in `createDirectHmd-ModeWindow()`.

Before window creation:

```
ON_LINUX([&] {
    std::swap(outSize.x, outSize.y);
});
```

Before returning the attached native window:

```
{
  static ovrVector3f offsets[2];
  static ovrPosef poses[2];
  ovrHmd_GetEyePoses(hmd, 0, offsets, poses, nullptr);
}
```

These resolve both issues silently, making our library clean and portable. After these bugs are addressed in upcoming versions of the SDK, expect this code to change. Keep an eye on the book's GitHub repository for details.

4.1.5 *Full screen vs. windowed: extensions with glfwCreateWindow()*

Most games and fully 3D applications use a mechanism known colloquially as *full screen mode* to get the best possible performance for their application. In full screen mode, all outputs from the GPU except for a targeted display are disabled, and the entire surface of the remaining display is treated as the rendering target for the underlying graphics API (typically OpenGL or Direct3D). This is reasonable because no matter how little computing effort is going into rendering all the other windows on your desktop, it's non-zero, which means that some of the resources that could be going into making your application more responsive are being diverted elsewhere. In many situations those other outputs can be a considerable drag on resources and have a measureable impact on your application's frame rate, though the specifics are subject to the underlying hardware, graphics driver, and OS version.[1] Full screen mode may or may not convey perceptible benefits in terms of your application's performance, but it's unlikely to hurt.

Conversely, when creating an application, ease of development tends to favor windowed mode, where you create a rendering target that exists on the desktop alongside all your other windows. For instance, many OSes are slow to change focus from full screen windows to the desktop, which can seriously impede development. In short, both modes have their selling points; the choice is yours.

---

[1] We're looking at you, Windows 7 "Aero Glass" theme.

If you've decided to create your window in full screen mode, you'll need to identify the Rift in GLFW. If you've chosen to clone the Rift to your primary display while developing, then instead of writing this,

```
glfwCreateWindow(size.x, size.y, "glfw", nullptr, nullptr);
```

you'd write this:

```
glfwCreateWindow(size.x, size.y, "glfw", glfwGetPrimaryMonitor(), nullptr);
```

The second-to-last parameter to `glfwCreateWindow` takes a `GLFWmonitor` pointer. By populating this parameter with a value you've previously fetched from another GLFW function, or our `getMonitorAtPosition()` helper, you're telling GLFW that you wish to create a *full screen* window. The window size parameters are then treated as the resolution you wish to set on the monitor when it goes into full screen mode. Be careful when using this approach—arbitrarily resizing your users' displays can cause chaos on multimonitor desktops. Be sure to always undo any resolution changes you cause.

The final parameter to `glfwCreateWindow()` accepts a `GLFWwindow` pointer, the same type as the function returns. Passing a previously created window in here will cause the new window and the preexisting window to share an OpenGL context, meaning that you could do things like render two views of the same scene without having to copy information like textures and geometry over to each context individually. In theory you could create two GLFW windows, positioned side-by-side on the Rift display, so that each eye has its own dedicated OpenGL window. But we see no advantage to this approach, and we've built no examples that use it.

4.1.6   *Dispensing with the boilerplate*

All this detection and creation code swiftly becomes repetitive, tiresome, and repetitive. For that reason we've created a class in our shared example code called `RiftGlfw-App`, which takes care of calling `createDirectHmdModeWindow()`, creating the window for you, and targeting the Rift display. From this point forward in the book, examples that target the Rift display will be derived from `RiftGlfwApp`.

Now that you can target the Rift display, let's look at the Rift display itself. We know it can't be used like a typical monitor, but what makes it different, and what do those differences mean when rendering to it?

4.2   *How the Rift display is different: why it matters to you*

The Rift display differs from a conventional display in a number of ways, some of which must be accounted for when rendering:

- Each eye sees a distinct half of the display panel.
- The per-eye aspect ratio is 8:9 (4:5 for the DK1).

- Each eye views its half of the display panel through a lens.
- The lenses *are not horizontally centered* above the half of the display that they view.
- The lenses serve two functions:
  - They increase the apparent field of view.
  - They produce collimated light, allowing the eyes to focus on the screen despite its proximity.

The cumulative effect of these differences is, in part, what creates the Rift's impressive field of view, but these differences are also what make rendering for the Rift a challenge. Identifying these differences will make it easier to understand the steps needed to properly render for the Rift.

4.2.1 Each eye sees a distinct half of the display panel

Any system producing stereoscopic content needs to present a different image to each eye. Most commercial systems do this with a single display by generating either superimposed or alternating images and using glasses to divide the two images into a single image for each eye.

The design of the Rift (in the DK2) contains a 16:9 display panel partitioned such that the left eye sees one half of the panel and the right eye sees the other, as shown in figure 4.1.

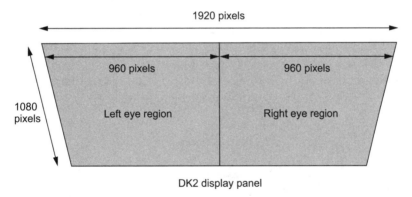

Figure 4.1 The Rift's screen is partitioned into left and right halves, one for each eye. Each eye sees a display with a "portrait" aspect ratio of 8:9.

The Rift's lenses aren't centered directly over their corresponding halves of the display. The distance between the lenses is based on the average human interpupillary distance (IPD; the distance between the pupils of the eyes), whereas the physical size of the display panel isn't exactly twice that value. This means that your eyes aren't likely to be centered behind the midpoints of their respective halves of the display; see figure 4.2.

The panel is wider than twice the distance between your eyes.

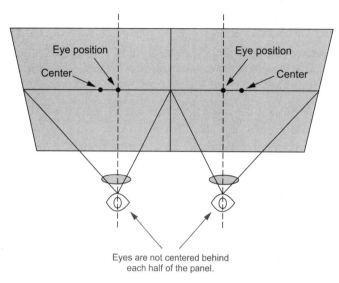

Figure 4.2   The Rift extends out beyond the sides of the head far enough that the eyes can't be centered horizontally.

For the DK1 model the offset between the center pixel and the lens axis was about 7 percent. For the DK2 the offset is actually less than 1 percent. These offsets are part of what the distortion mechanism accounts for.

This offset provides more image data to the outer edge of the per-eye views, which equates to how human vision works (figure 4.3). We see a broad sweep of overlapped image in the center of our field of view, but to either side of the shared viewing cone we also see more to the left and to the right, from only one eye.

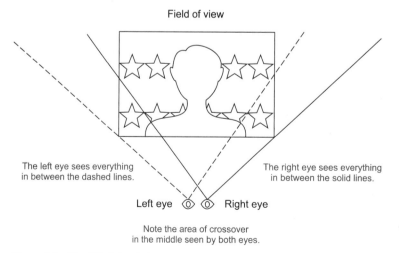

Figure 4.3   The Rift field of view closely reflects how human vision works.

Ultimately, each eye sees a display whose dimensions are 960×1080 on the DK2, which yields an aspect ratio of 8:9.

4.2.2 How the lenses affect the view

The Rift's goal is to present an image that, when viewed through the collimating lenses, will shine light onto the retina in exactly the same manner that natural light would be in a real scene, with depth and perspective. To achieve this, light must reach the eyes from the sides as well as from straight ahead, as it does in real life. To mimic real human vision, the split panel of the Rift's display must be viewed through lenses that expand the image displayed to occupy a much larger field of view (figure 4.4).

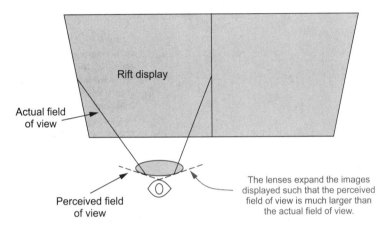

Figure 4.4 The dashed lines represent the *perceived* field of view; the solid lines represent the *actual* field of view. The Rift's lenses ensure that light reaches the eye as though coming from a wider field of view, even though it hasn't. This deceives the eye into perceiving a wider image.

Aside from the increased field of view, the lenses also produce *collimated light*. This is a fancy way of saying that the lenses and the display are set up in such a way as to try to make the display appear as if it were infinitely far away. The upshot of this is twofold. First, it allows the eyes to retain a relaxed status of focus, as if you were looking at a distant landscape. Second, it keeps a fixed relationship between the angle of light hitting the eye and the location on the display panel from which the light was emitted.

Collimated light

Collimated light is light whose rays have been aligned in parallel, such as in a laser. Because it doesn't converge, collimated light is described as "converging at infinity." The Oculus Rift uses high-quality lenses to collimate the light from its screen; similar techniques are sometimes used in smaller laser generators. But the Rift's lenses aren't perfect. Consequently the light in the Rift will still scatter a bit more than the light of a laser would, but all things considered, that's probably for the best.

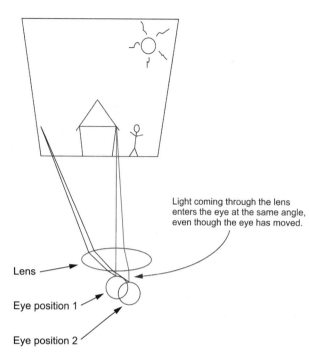

Light coming through the lens enters the eye at the same angle, even though the eye has moved.

Lens

Eye position 1

Eye position 2

Figure 4.5   Even though the eye changes position by small amounts, the collimated light from the individual pixels on the screen enters the eye at the same angle. This holds true through a moderate range of eye motion, up to the point where the eye entirely leaves the central axis of the lens.

These features of collimated light are easy to demonstrate. If you hold the Rift to your head (while it's displaying something static) and wiggle it around a bit, left or right, up or down, the part of the image directly in front of you doesn't change (figure 4.5.) This works in all three dimensions; if you move the Rift directly away from your eye, the image doesn't shrink.

Taking one of the lenses out of the Rift and doing the same experiment shows a remarkable difference. Moving the Rift laterally changes the portion of the image that's "directly ahead," and moving the Rift away from you shrinks the image rapidly.

The lenses can only do so much, so the farther away your eye is from the lens axis, or the greater the distance between your eye and the lens, the more undesirable distortion you'll see. This distortion typically manifests as blurring or warping, increasing in intensity the further from the lens axis you're looking. The Rift design provides an *eye box* (figure 4.6), which is about 1.5 cm across in the vertical and horizontal directions, and slightly less than 1 cm deep. Within this box, barring a small amount of distortion, the image presented to the eye will depend only on the angle between the eye and the lens plane, not the position of the eye relative to the lens.

This also tells us that when the lenses are set up for a perfect image, users with long eyelashes (> 0.5 cm) may feel their eyelashes brushing across the lens.

The use of collimated light reduces the amount of work we have to do to achieve proper display on the Rift, because it removes some of the variables: the exact positioning of the eyes is no longer critical, and the IPD is no longer a factor. Oculus does

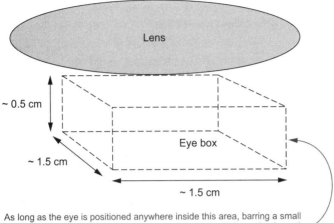

~ 0.5 cm

~ 1.5 cm

~ 1.5 cm

As long as the eye is positioned anywhere inside this area, barring a small amount of distortion, the image presented to the eye will depend only on the angle between the eye and the lens plane and not on the position of the eye relative to the lens.

Figure 4.6   The Rift eye box

offer a configuration utility that allows you to input your actual IPD, but this is only used when rendering a scene in order to produce the proper amount of parallax for a given person. It's not used in the distortion correction mechanism or when displaying nonstereoscopic content.

Collimated light doesn't cure all ills, though; most of the other optical properties we've mentioned (the aspect ratio, the increased field of view, the offset of the lenses from display centers and the distortion) must be accounted for when rendering to the Rift.

Warning: collimated light considered harmful to displays

With collimated light, for any given pixel on the panel, no matter where your eye is, the light from that pixel appears to be coming from the same direction relative to your eye. But lenses work in both directions. That means that all the light from the outside world that's traveling in a given direction ends up getting focused onto a tiny spot on the display. For this reason you must *never* allow sunlight to strike the lenses. All of the sunlight across the surface of the lens would be focused onto a single point on the display and will damage it quite quickly. While being handled or placed onto the head, this may not be a major concern, but the Rift should never be stored in a fashion where the sun might strike the lenses.

Now that you have an understanding of the Rift display, let's look at creating output for the Rift.

4.3   *Generating output for the Rift*

For each frame generated as output for the Rift, the rendering part of the overall workflow for a Rift-enabled application looks like figure 4.7.

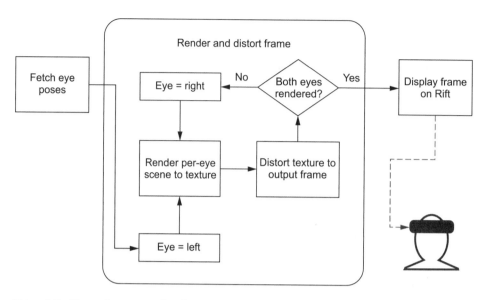

Figure 4.7   The render process flow for each frame displayed on the Rift

We're pretty happy with this image, and ready to call it a day, but we're apparently contractually obligated to go into more detail. Looking at figure 4.7, you might notice that there's a clearly delineated step specifically for distortion (Distort texture to output frame) and that all of the other correction must be going on in the other box, the per-eye rendering of the scene. This is the case. Let's take a more detailed look what exactly is going on in each of those boxes (figure 4.8).

In figure 4.8, you'll see that all the other corrections required for rendering to the Rift are handled by manipulation of the projection and view matrices and that the distortion box only handles the distortion.

Projection and view matrices

When doing 3D rendering there are always (at least) two matrices to deal with.

A projection matrix is responsible for performing the mapping of points in 3D space onto a 2D plane (the display panel). This defines a view frustum that determines the field of view and accounts for the aspect ratio of the output display panel. In addition, manipulation of the projection matrix can move the point on the 2D plane that's the "center" of the image, the point at which the viewpoint is straight ahead.

The view matrix is responsible for determining the position of the virtual camera in 3D space. It controls the position and direction of the point of view. The view matrix is sometimes referred to as the *modelview* matrix because it can also be used to position individual items within the scene relative to the camera.

Manipulation of both these matrices will be covered in more detail in chapter 5. More details about matrices in general and their use in rendering can be found in appendix B.

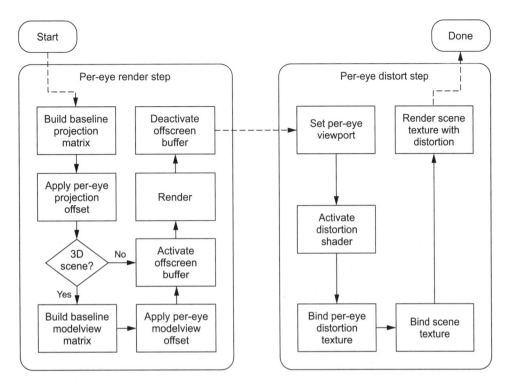

Figure 4.8 The per-eye render step and the per-eye distortion boxes expanded to show the individual steps

Covering both the rendering step and the distortion step is a little much for a single chapter, so we'll be focusing on the distortion mechanism here.

4.4 Correcting for lens distortion

As we discussed earlier, the Rift uses lenses both to increase the apparent field of view (through magnification) and to provide a clear (focused) view of the screen despite its proximity to the viewer. Without the lenses there is no Rift.

But though the lenses are invaluable, they also distort the image by bending it and by introducing chromatic aberration.

Chromatic aberration

Chromatic aberration is a type of visual distortion caused by lenses that fail to bend light of different colors by the same amount. Blue light will be bent at a greater angle than green light, and green at a greater angle than red. This is the property that gives a prism the ability to split a white beam of light into a spectrum. Although this is desirable for spectroscopy and Pink Floyd album covers, it's less desirable for proper image reproduction.

As of SDK version 0.5.0, the Oculus SDK automatically compensates for the distortion induced by chromatic aberration. No intervention is necessary on your part.

In the next section, we discuss the causes of the distortion and why it needs correcting.

4.4.1   The nature of the distortion

The Rift lenses create what is called a *pincushion distortion.* A pincushion distortion is what happens when you magnify an image using a lens. If you apply a magnifying glass to an image, it creates a distortion.

So if you show an undistorted image of a brick wall on the Rift, when you look through the Rift lens, you see it distorted, as in figure 4.9.

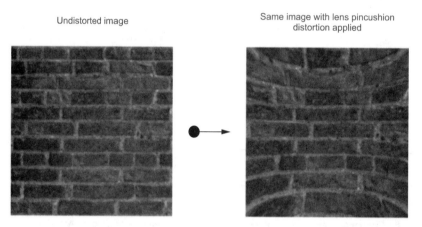

Undistorted image

Same image with lens pincushion distortion applied

Figure 4.9   Undistorted image (left) + lens pincushion distortion = distorted image (right). Some pixels in the source image have been lost, pushed beyond the bounds of the destination image.

HOW WE COUNTERACT THE LENS DISTORTION

Correcting the distortion caused by the lenses is accomplished by applying a different, *inverse* distortion before the frame is sent to the screen. The mathematical inverse of a pincushion distortion is called a *barrel distortion.* In a barrel distortion, the lines that are normally straight curve inward.

This means that for any given pincushion distortion, you can create a specific barrel distortion that exactly counteracts it. That is, if you took a picture of a grid of lines through a barrel lens and you printed it out (resulting in an image where the lines of the grid curved inward) and then took another picture through a pincushion lens that was the exact inverse of the first lens, and printed *that* out, the lines would be straight again.

And that's how distortion correction for the Rift works. You render a scene, with its conventionally straight lines, in memory as a texture. Then you distort the image with a barrel distortion before putting it on the screen. When you view the image through lenses, the lenses impose a pincushion distortion. The distortions cancel each other out, and you're presented with an undistorted view of the screen that retains the magnification effect of the lenses and the wide field of view (see figure 4.10).

You render a scene, with its conventionally straight lines, in memory as a texture.

You distort the image with a barrel distortion before putting it on the screen.

When you view the image through lenses, the lenses impose a pincushion distortion. The distortions cancel each other out, and you are presented with an undistorted view of the screen, but retaining the magnification effect of the lenses and the wide field of view.

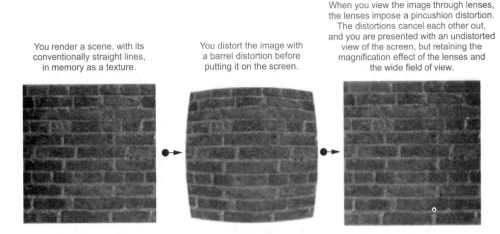

Figure 4.10   How Rift distortion works: Undistorted image (left) + software barrel distortion (center) + pincushion lens distortion = correct image (right). Because the barrel distortion shrank the image inward, no pixels were lost in the subsequent pincushion transformation.

You might be wondering why we distort the image instead of using better lenses. Well, there's a good reason for that.

WHY NOT JUST USE BETTER LENSES?

It *is* possible to create lens *arrays* that introduce the desired properties of magnifying the screen and keeping it in focus without distorting the shape and color. After all, people have been using cameras for many years that produce all sorts of zooming effects without severe distortion. The problem is that such lenses end up being ridiculously complex in design as well as physically heavy and large (figure 4.11).

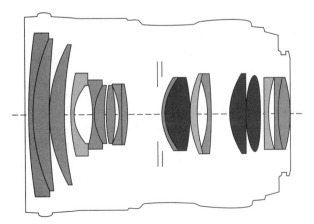

Figure 4.11   There's a reason professional camera lenses are expensive.

These lens arrays can't be made smaller because they're limited by the refraction index of the materials used to create them. Even an array made of diamond or some other exotic material would likely be far too large to place in a head-mounted display, to say nothing of the cost.

On the other hand, the cost of correcting the distortion by applying an inverse distortion to the image before you display it is comparatively negligible. The balance, therefore, leans heavily toward solving the problem with computational power rather than optics. The upside is that the Rift can be made at a consumer price point, rather than costing thousands or tens of thousands of dollars. The downside is that it adds some complexity to applications designed to run on the Rift. Fortunately, the Oculus SDK does most of the heavy lifting.

4.4.2   *SDK distortion correction support*

Early versions of the Oculus SDK provided small example applications that implemented distortion correction using the information made available by the SDK proper. The SDK itself knew nothing about rendering APIs or shaders. The shaders were complex, and the code required to initialize them with the correct data was scattered around the example code, making replicating the distortion correction something of a burden on developers. It also meant that although Oculus could add new features to the distortion correction step, the adoption of those features by applications would be limited by the time required for developers to fully understand the feature and then reimplement it in their own code.

Since the 0.3.x version of the SDK, Oculus VR has undertaken an effort to provide distortion correction support directly within the SDK, referred to as "SDK-side distortion." This means that Oculus can work on optimizing the performance of distortion within the SDK, and they are free to add new features to the distortion mechanism without worrying about whether developers will be able to easily adopt them.

It's still possible to implement the distortion functionality on your own, and the SDK even provides a number of helpful functions to support that. But for this chapter (and most of the others) we'll focus on the use of SDK-side distortion, which is likely to be sufficient to support the needs of most developers.

4.4.3   *Example of distortion correction*

To perform the required distortion for the Rift, you typically render a 3D scene to a set of textures and then pass them to the SDK to perform the distortion and present them to the user. For this example, though, we'll work with prerendered images so that we can focus in isolation on the elements that are required for distortion (listing 4.6; also see Example_4_3_1_Distorted.cpp on the GitHub repository). If you're curious, we've also prepared an undistorted version of listing 4.6. You'll find it on the GitHub repository as Example_4_3_0_Undistorted.cpp.

Listing 4.6 Distorting images with the SDK

```
#include "Common.h"

Resource SCENE_IMAGES_DK1[2] = {
  Resource::IMAGES_TUSCANY_UNDISTORTED_LEFT_DK1_PNG,
  Resource::IMAGES_TUSCANY_UNDISTORTED_RIGHT_DK1_PNG
};

Resource SCENE_IMAGES_DK2[2] = {
  Resource::IMAGES_TUSCANY_UNDISTORTED_LEFT_DK2_PNG,
  Resource::IMAGES_TUSCANY_UNDISTORTED_RIGHT_DK2_PNG
};

class DistortedExample : public RiftGlfwApp {
protected:
  Texture2dPtr sceneTextures[2];
  ovrTexture eyeTextures[2];

public:

  void initGl() {
    RiftGlfwApp::initGl();

    Resource * sceneImages = SCENE_IMAGES_DK2;
    if (hmd->Type == ovrHmd_DK1) {
      sceneImages = SCENE_IMAGES_DK1;
    }

    for_each_eye([&](ovrEyeType eye){

      glm::uvec2 textureSize;
      sceneTextures[eye] = oria::load2dTexture(
          sceneImages[eye], textureSize);

      memset(eyeTextures + eye, 0,
          sizeof(eyeTextures[eye]));
      ovrTextureHeader & eyeTextureHeader =
          eyeTextures[eye].Header;
      eyeTextureHeader.TextureSize =
          ovr::fromGlm(textureSize);
      eyeTextureHeader.RenderViewport.Size =
          eyeTextureHeader.TextureSize;
      eyeTextureHeader.API = ovrRenderAPI_OpenGL;

      ((ovrGLTextureData&)eyeTextures[eye]).TexId =
          sceneTextures[eye]->texture;
    });

    ovrRenderAPIConfig cfg;
    memset(&cfg, 0, sizeof(cfg));
    cfg.Header.API = ovrRenderAPI_OpenGL;
    cfg.Header.RTSize.w = windowSize.x;
    cfg.Header.RTSize.h = windowSize.y;
    cfg.Header.Multisample = 1;
    int distortionCaps = ovrDistortionCap_Vignette
#if defined(OVR_OS_WIN32)
    ((ovrGLConfigData&)config).Window = 0;
```

Undistorted screen grabs from the Tuscany demo, one per eye.

RiftGlfwApp takes care of creating the HMD handle and the OpenGL window.

The OpenGL wrappers for the per-eye texture data

Oculus SDK structures for holding information about the textures

OpenGL setup and SDK configuration.

Uses HMD instances to determine which pair of images to render.

Per-eye setup of the textures

Loads the per-eye image of your resources into OpenGL.

Initializes the SDK texture structure.

Passes TextureID to OpenGL.

Sets up the SDK distortion functionality.

```
#elif defined(OVR_OS_LINUX)
    ((ovrGLConfigData&)config).Disp = 0;
#endif
    ovrEyeRenderDesc eyeRenderDescs[2];
    int configResult = ovrHmd_ConfigureRendering(hmd, &cfg,
        distortionCaps, hmdDesc.DefaultEyeFov, eyeRenderDescs);
    if (0 == configResult) {
        FAIL("Unable to configure rendering");
    }
    ovrhmd_EnableHSWDisplaySDKRender(hmd, false);
}

virtual void finishFrame() {
}

void draw() {
    static ovrPosef eyePoses[2];
    ovrHmd_BeginFrame(hmd, getFrame());
    ovrHmd_EndFrame(hmd, eyePoses, eyeTextures);
}
};
```

Disables the automatic health and safety warning.

Sets up the SDK distortion functionality.

Overrides the finishFrame method of the parent class to prevent your application from performing the OpenGL buffer swapping, because the SDK will be doing it instead.

The per-frame drawing call

The SDK distortion is book-ended by these begin/end frame calls.

RUN_OVR_APP(DistortedExample)

The end result should look something like figure 4.12.

As you can see, listing 4.6 has only two methods. The parent classes handle the work of acquiring an HMD handle and creating the output window on your desktop with the correct size and position. So you only have to worry about two things: setup and frame rendering, as encapsulated in the initGl() and draw() methods, respectively.

Figure 4.12   The image is now distorted.

SETTING UP OPENGL

In initGl() you call the parent class OpenGL initialization, and then immediately enter a per-eye loop. For each eye you must load your texture and then populate an Oculus SDK structure to provide it with information about the texture.

The DK1 and DK2 have different projections, so the choice of texture to load depends on the headset model you are targeting. With that in mind, we've provided sample textures for both headsets. We've encapsulated our texture management in our example code library, so loading the texture is a simple matter of making a call into that library. You'll need to know the texture size for some later operations, though, so store it in a local variable:

```
glm::uvec2 textureSize;
sceneTextures[eye] =
    oria::load2dTexture(sceneImages[eye], textureSize);
```

Your texture handling is done, but you also need to tell the Oculus SDK everything it'll need to know to work with the texture.

OCULUS SDK PLATFORM-SPECIFIC TYPES

The Oculus SDK is designed to be able to work across a variety of platforms, and to work with both Direct3D and OpenGL. Some of the information about textures is common to all platforms. This information is stored in an ovrTextureHeader type, defined in the main OVR C API header: OVR_CAPI.h. The header is then contained in an ovrTexture structure, declared in the same file. ovrTexture also includes an array of values called PlatformData. This isn't meant to be used directly, but rather to reserve space for the platform-specific information to be stored.

To work with platform-specific data, you need to include either the OVR_CAPI_GL.h header or the OVR_CAPI_D3D.h header, depending on the API you're working with. Because we're working with OpenGL we've the chosen the former, although like the OVR_CAPI.h header, it's folded into the common header we include in all our examples.

The OpenGL platform header declares an ovrGLTextureData type that, like ovr-Texture, contains an ovrTextureHeader member. But in place of the PlatformData member it has a TexID member of type GLuint. In OpenGL, a texture ID is all you need to access a texture so that one member provides all the required platform-specific information. The SDK function ovrHmd_EndFrame() requires that we pass in a pointer to ovrTexture, so we've declared the type as such. You'll see how to set the OpenGL-specific data in a moment.

OCULUS SDK TEXTURE SETUP

All the Oculus SDK types are simple C structures, so you have to explicitly zero out their values:

```
memset(eyeTextures + eye, 0, sizeof(eyeTextures[eye]));
```

Next, you grab a reference to the ovrTextureHeader instance to make the subsequent references to it a little cleaner:

```
ovrTextureHeader & eyeTextureHeader = eyeTextures[eye].Header;
```

The SDK needs to know the size of the texture you're working with, and it needs to know the area on to which you've rendered content. You captured the size of the texture as you loaded it, so you just have to copy that information over, converting types appropriately as you go:

```
eyeTextureHeader.TextureSize = ovr::fromGlm(textureSize);
```

You also need to initialize the `RenderViewport` member of the header. `Render-Viewport` is an `ovrRecti` structure, containing both an `ovrSizei Size` member and an `ovrVector2i Pos` member. It tells the SDK where on the texture surface the scene has been drawn. This can be useful in two ways. First, it makes it possible to use a single large texture for both eyes by having the `RenderViewport` point to a different half of the texture for each eye. Second, it makes it possible to dynamically change the size of the `RenderViewport` at runtime in order to respond to lower-than-acceptable frame rates. The latter technique will be covered in chapter 6, when we discuss performance.

For this example you're using two distinct textures and each one has a scene covering the entirety of the image, so you want `RenderViewport.Size` to be equal to the texture size:

```
eyeTextureHeader.RenderViewport.Size = eyeTextureHeader.TextureSize;
```

You don't need to explicitly set the `RenderViewport.Pos` values, because they'll already have the desired position of 0,0 by virtue of the `memset` call you used to zero out the structure as a whole.

Because the relevant SDK functions accept only the non-platform-specific types, those types that do have platform-specific versions also include an API member to specify for which platform they're intended to be used. We're using OpenGL, so populate the API member like so:

```
eyeTextureHeader.API = ovrRenderAPI_OpenGL;
```

Lastly, you need to provide the SDK with the OpenGL identifier for the texture. To access the `TexID` member you need to set, fetch the texture ID from `oglplus`:

```
((ovrGLTextureData&)eyeTextures[eye]).TexId =
    oglplus::GetName(*sceneTextures[eye]);
```

Once you've done this for each eye, your per-eye setup is complete and you can move to configuring the distortion itself.

OCULUS SDK DISTORTION SETUP

Like the texture structures, the baseline-rendering configuration structures are wrapped by platform-specific structures. There's an `ovrRenderAPIConfig`, which contains padding for the platform-specific types, and an `ovrGLConfigData`, which replaces the padding with platform-specific information.

Platform specifics in the rendering configuration

The OVR SDK stored configuration data for OpenGL in `ovrGLConfigData`, but its contents are different depending on what platform you're targeting. The platform-specific members are extra information that the SDK needs in order to perform a buffer swap, making the most recently rendered image on the back buffer visible on the display panel.[2] Buffer swapping isn't part of the OpenGL API but is handled by platform-specific calls, and these calls require platform-specific information.

For a Windows environment an `HWND` value is required, and so the `ovrGLConfigData` structure contains a `Window` member of type `HWND`. For Linux a `Display` pointer and a `Window` are both needed, so the structure contains a `Disp` member of type `Display*` and a `Win` member of type `Window`.[3] For OS X environments, no special value is needed.

This diversity is unfortunate. You use the GLFW library to protect you from the platform specifics involved in using OpenGL, but now the SDK wants you to provide it with the very platform specifics you'd hoped to avoid. It's possible to get GLFW to give you the requested information, but only by including special headers and defining preprocessor values related to the platform on which you're running. Other abstraction layers for OpenGL might not necessarily even provide that.

Happily the most recent version of the SDK does its best to make the parameters optional. If they aren't set, then when the SDK configures its rendering, it'll use the currently active window, which presumably would be the one you've created.

GLFW doesn't normally provide the information you'd use to populate the platform-specific portion of `ovrGlConfigData`, but this isn't the end of the world. On Windows and Linux platforms, the SDK will query the OS to find the active window during startup if the field hasn't been populated. But you need to be sure to initialize the values to 0 for this to work. If you fail to initialize the values, they'll simply be random and the SDK will assume that those random numbers are actually platform-specific window handles, which will likely lead to a crash. On Mac OS X platforms, no special values are required.

Let's take a look at the configuration code. First you declare your configuration structure locally (it won't be of any use to you after configuration) and zero out the memory:

```
ovrRenderAPIConfig config;
memset(&config, 0, sizeof(config));
```

The Oculus SDK only takes the non-platform-specific types, so you need to set the `API` member to indicate that you're using OpenGL:

```
config.Header.API = ovrRenderAPI_OpenGL;
```

---

[2] The reasoning behind this will be discussed in chapter 6 in the section on timewarp.

[3] Yes, Oculus used *Window* as a member name in Win32 environments, even though Window is a type identifier in Linux. Don't look at us; we didn't do it.

The SDK needs to know the size (but not the position) of the output region. Again you use our library function to convert from `glm::uvec2` to `ovrSizei`:

```
config.Header.BackBufferSize = ovr::fromGlm(getSize());
```

The SDK contains a `Multisample` member that's a single int. Currently, this value isn't referenced anywhere in the SDK rendering functions. You're setting it to a value of 1 to indicate that you only want a single sample in the final output image, in the hopes that if the value ever does start being used it doesn't suddenly cause a performance issue:

```
config.Header.Multisample = 1;
```

Finally, you set the platform-specific members by casting to an `ovrGLConfigData` reference and setting the values to 0. Technically this isn't necessary because you've already zeroed out the entire structure, but we want to explicitly call it out here because other platforms might need to take different actions at this point:

```
#if defined(OVR_OS_WIN32)
  ((ovrGLConfigData&)config).Window = 0;
#elif defined(OVR_OS_LINUX)
  ((ovrGLConfigData&)config).Disp = 0;
#endif
```

Now that you have your config data set up, you must call the SDK method that'll initialize distortion rendering:

```
int distortionCaps = ovrDistortionCap_Vignette;
ovrEyeRenderDesc eyeRenderDescs[2];
int configResult = ovrHmd_ConfigureRendering(hmd, &config,
    distortionCaps, hmd->DefaultEyeFov, eyeRenderDescs);
if (0 == configResult) {
 FAIL("Unable to configure rendering");
}
```

The `ovrHmd_ConfigureRendering` call requires five parameters. The first is the Rift headset handle, which is managed by your parent class. The second is your configuration data. Then you specify the distortion capabilities you want (we'll get to these in a moment), with the desired field of view and render settings for each eye—in this case using the default values provided by the SDK in `ovrHmdDesc`. The last parameter is your `ovrEyeRenderDesc` array. This is actually an output member. The fields of your array members will be populated upon the successful return from the configuration call.

"But wait!" you say excitedly. "What are distortion capabilities?" Well, they're flags that let you tell the SDK exactly how you want the distortion to be performed. Currently there are a number of different distortion capabilities you can enable. We'll discuss them all in due course.

With the Vignette flag disabled, the edge of the image is sharply defined.

With the Vignette flag enabled, there is a soft transition at the edge of the image.

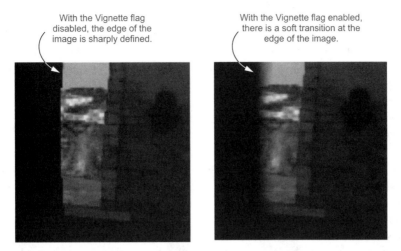

Figure 4.13   Comparison of the image edge with the vignette flag disabled (left) and enabled (right)

The ovrDistortionCap_Vignette flag turns on a fading effect at the borders of the Rift. This helps the sense of presence by smoothing out one of the more apparent indicators that you're looking at a rendered image. The human brain is very good at detecting edges, and depending on how you have your Rift set up and the exact orientation of your eyes at a given moment, it's possible to see the edges of the rendered image. The sharpness of the transition from the rendered scene to the black background makes it more noticeable. If you use the vignette effect to create a transition layer, even one only a few pixels wide, the edge becomes less distracting and the sense of presence is improved (figure 4.13).

We'll cover additional flags in chapter 5.

RENDERING FRAMES

The bulk of the work done in a normal application would be to do the rendering of the scenes to be displayed on the Rift. Because you're working with prerendered images in this example, the draw method ends up being a representation of the minimal loop for working with Oculus' SDK-based distortion.

```
static ovrPosef poses[2];
ovrHmd_BeginFrame(hmd, getFrame());
ovrHmd_EndFrame(hmd, poses, eyeTextures);
```

This "bookend" function marks the boundaries of rendering of the frame as a whole. No rendering should be done prior to the BeginFrame call, and once EndFrame completes, the buffer swap will have already occurred, so no further rendering should be done. These functions also assist the SDK in determining the exact timing of the frame and perform some precondition checking. The SDK will throw an exception if, for instance, they're called out of order or called from different threads.

Between the frame calls, you'd normally perform your rendering. But because you're working with fixed images, you can take a moment here to chill out and relax before moving on to chapter 5.

4.5 Summary

In this chapter, you learned that

- The Rift contains a specialized display system, consisting of a rectangular LCD or OLED panel typical of standard monitors and lenses to modify the perception of that panel. In addition, it provides an enclosure to mount the panel in a fixed position relative to your eyes, as well as to partition the panel so that each eye sees only one half of the panel.

- Applications need to target the Rift display to ensure that the output created will get rendered to the Rift and not someplace else.

- When the Rift is connected to a computer and enabled in the Display control panel, the OS will extend the desktop metaphor to the Rift.

- As of SDK 0.4.x, the Oculus software includes a runtime that provides a display mode called Direct HMD mode. In Direct HMD mode, the host OS does *not* treat the Rift as a conventional monitor.

- For Direct HMD mode, Oculus has provided explicit mechanisms in the SDK to allow you to target your OpenGL or Direct3D rendering output to the Rift display panel.

- The Rift display differs from a conventional display in a number of ways, some of which must be accounted for when rendering.

- The per-eye aspect ratio of the Rift is 8:9 (4:5 for the DK1).

- The lenses aren't horizontally centered above the half of the display that they view.

- The Rift uses lenses both to increase the apparent field of view (through magnification) and to provide a clear (focused) view of the screen despite its proximity to the viewer. The lenses also distort the image by bending it and by introducing chromatic aberration. Chromatic aberration is automatically resolved by the SDK.

- In the workflow for creating images for the Rift, distortion correction is done as a separate step from all other correction (for aspect ratio differences, the lens offset, etc.). Only the distortion correction is covered in this chapter. All of the other corrections required are handled by manipulation of the projection and view matrices and are covered in chapter 5.

- The Rift lenses create what is called a *pincushion distortion*. A pincushion distortion is what happens when you magnify an image using a lens.

- Correcting the distortion caused by the lenses is accomplished by applying a different, *inverse* distortion before the frame is sent to the screen. The mathematical inverse of a pincushion distortion is called a *barrel distortion.*

- When using SDK-side distortion, you can specify the distortion capabilities you want to use. The `ovrDistortionCap_Vignette` flag turns on a fading effect at the borders of the Rift. This helps the sense of presence by smoothing out one of the more apparent indicators that you're looking at a rendered image.

Putting it all together: integrating head tracking and 3D rendering

This chapter covers

- Building a simple scene, displayed on the conventional monitor
- Splitting the scene for stereoscopic viewing, using the Rift's user settings
- Moving your scene to the Rift, targeting the Rift display, and enabling distortion
- Enabling head tracking, producing a fully immersive Rift experience

Let's take stock of all the aspects of computer graphics you've seen so far in this book, because now it's time to put them into play. You'll build a complete example in this chapter, from basic rendering to advanced Riftiness. The scene itself is going to be *very* simple—just a cube on a stick in space—but artistic skill in scene design isn't the focus here.

We'll begin with the basics. To render a 3D scene using Direct3D or OpenGL for a conventional monitor, you need a number of elements:

- A view matrix to position the camera within the scene
- A projection matrix to define the *view frustum*,[1] which contains the field of view and aspect ratio
- Shaders that will transform scene geometry into view geometry, and from there into real pixels
- An actual scene to render

A scene to render typically consists of a set of models, each of which will need the following:

- A *basis*[2] in 3D space, which describes the model's position and orientation with respect to the scene. The basis could also be with respect to the model's parent in a scene graph describing a model hierarchy. The basis is often represented as a 4 × 4 matrix.
- Geometry that defines the shape of the model and perhaps other attributes, such as color, texture coordinates, and normal vectors.

In subsequent examples you'll be adding stereo support. To render the same scene stereoscopically, you'll need all these things, plus the following:

- A per-eye modification to the view matrix, to account for the different positions of the eyes
- A mechanism to subdivide the rendering surface in order to render the two views of the scene, one for each eye

Finally, in order to render a 3D scene for the Rift, you need all of the previous items as well as the following:

- A per-eye projection matrix transform, to account for the different fields of view perceived by each eye (provided by the Oculus SDK)
- An offscreen surface (a "framebuffer" in OpenGL or a "render target" in DirectX) on which to render the undistorted view of the scene
- A distortion mechanism for rendering the offscreen buffer contents to the actual screen, appropriately distorted for the optics of the Rift

Many wheels to set in motion, or so it might seem, but it all slots together quite nicely. To get things rolling, let's start with a modicum of scene design.

---

[1] See en.wikipedia.org/wiki/Frustum for more information.
[2] See appendix B for more about basis transforms and frames of reference.

5.1   *Setting the scene*

This chapter's first example renders to a conventional monitor, *without* distortion or stereoscopic views. This allows you to establish the components required for basic rendering but not specific to any aspect of the Rift.

The scene will consist of a single model: a small cube, supported by a pedestal, colored blue on the front and other colors on each side, as shown in figure 5.1. The cube rests at eye height, initially 0.5 meters directly ahead of the viewer. The floor is overlaid by a wireframe grid, 1 meter square. The scene is surrounded by an infinitely distant skybox, which means that when you get to the Rift you'll have something to look around at.

Figure 5.1   Our sample scene: a cube on a stick

Our small, central cube-on-a-pedestal does have one interesting thing going for it: its width is exactly the distance between the user's eyes (their IPD). We'll come back to why we've chosen such a cubist centerpiece later in the chapter (and no, it's not a nod to Picasso).

Each of the four demos in this chapter will derive from GlfwApp or its child class, RiftGlfwApp. GlfwApp is the core example class in our demo code (github.com/ OculusRiftInAction/OculusRiftInAction). You've seen us using GlfwApp in almost every demo so far. GlfwApp is driven by the core render loop shown in the next listing.

Listing 5.1   GlfwApp::Run(), the heart of our sample app (abridged for clarity)

```
int GlfwApp::run() {
  window = createRenderingTarget(windowSize, windowPosition);
```

```
  if (!window) {
    FAIL("Unable to create OpenGL window");
  }
  initGl();
  while (!glfwWindowShouldClose(window)) {
    glfwPollEvents();
    update();
    draw();
    finishFrame();
  }
  return 0;
}
```

In this render loop, for as long as the window shouldn't close, you'll first call `update()`, and then `draw()`. We separate the two operations in the name of good software design. The intent is that `update()` will be the one-stop shop for all your scene state changes, such as moving the camera; when you call `draw()`, it'll be purely devoted to rendering, with no camera motion or user input handling.

By handling all your camera events in `update()`, you can safely pull changes to your camera position from multiple sources (such as keyboard, mouse, and controller inputs) before rendering begins. This ensures that you won't process a given update more than once per frame, including the per-eye orientation matrices that you'll read from the Rift. More than that, it's a good design pattern and a good idea: your rendering code is isolated from the code that updates your state.

Separating visualization from transformation

A common faux pas among novice 3D coders is to update their app's state in their render loop, usually at the start of their "render my scene" method. It's an easy place to put update code, because you know it gets called once per frame. Typical examples of state changes are updates like "increment a counter," "advance time," or "run the next step of my physics engine."

This is, in general, a Bad Idea. Here's why:

- It introduces a potentially unpredictable delay in your render call, which can cause lag.
- It locks GPU operations and CPU operations together, depriving you of the parallelization benefits of having a GPU with its own processing power.
- Debugging becomes much more difficult, because you've got to wade through rendering code to get to state code (or vice versa).
- Writing unit tests becomes much more difficult as well, because unit tests of your state logic will have to mock out an entire rendering stack, or vice versa.

What's more, it gets worse on the Rift (or any kind of stereoscopic display): an app for the Rift is going to perform two renders for each frame, one for each eye. If you're updating the game state during the render, this means that the displayed state *will be different for each eye*. Worse, your app will behave differently on the

(continued)

Rift than in tests or on a normal screen, which can make debugging subtle bugs terrifically difficult.

You're far better off updating state in a separate event handler. That way, your state and your display are completely isolated from each other.

Each of our examples will render the same scene, albeit in different ways. The scene you need to render has been encapsulated inside a single function, `oria::render-ExampleScene(float ipd, float eyeHeight)`. This function takes care of all the OpenGL-specific work you do to load shaders and geometry and render the contents of the scene.

Two explicit inputs are used—`ipd` and `eyeHeight`—as well as an implicit input, the state of the modelview matrix, which determines the position of the camera. We won't cover the inner workings of `renderExampleScene()` here, because it's largely about the mechanics of OpenGL rendering, and that's not what this book is about; suffice it to say, it renders a scene with a skybox, a floor, and a couple of cubes.

The contents of the scene aren't important; you could be rendering a medical visualization application, or the next *"Medal of Battle Duty"* game. We'll spend the remainder of this chapter fleshing out how you use this method in the context of rendering conventionally, stereoscopically, and finally as a VR scene designed for the Rift. To clearly delineate non-Rift code from Rift code, we'll begin with a minimal, monocular, 3D view of our scene—just the basics, no Rift code.

5.2 Our sample scene in monoscopic 3D

The following listing contains the complete code of our first simple scene rendered with monoscopic rendering.

Listing 5.2 Example_5_1_Monoscopic.cpp, our sample scene in monoscopic rendering

```
#include "Common.h"

static const glm::uvec2 WINDOW_SIZE(1280, 800);
static const glm::ivec2 WINDOW_POS(100, 100);

class CubeScene_Mono : public GlfwApp {
public:
  CubeScene_Mono() {
    Stacks::projection().top() = glm::perspective(
        PI / 2.0f, aspect(WINDOW_SIZE), 0.01f, 100.0f);

    Stacks::modelview().top() = glm::lookAt(
        vec3(0, OVR_DEFAULT_EYE_HEIGHT, 0.5f),
        vec3(0, OVR_DEFAULT_EYE_HEIGHT, 0),
        Vectors::UP);
  }
```

Sets up the camera perspective.

Sets up the camera position. Your camera is 0.5 meters back from the cube.

```
    virtual GLFWwindow * createRenderingTarget(
      glm::uvec2 & outSize, glm::ivec2 & outPosition) {
    outSize = WINDOW_SIZE;
    outPosition = WINDOW_POS;
    return glfw::createWindow(outSize, outPosition);
  }

  virtual void draw() {
    oglplus::Context::Clear().ColorBuffer().DepthBuffer();
    oria::renderExampleScene(
        OVR_DEFAULT_IPD, OVR_DEFAULT_EYE_HEIGHT);
  }
};

RUN_APP(CubeScene_Mono);
```

Creates a simple, decorated GLFW window on the primary monitor.

Clears the screen.

Renders your scene.

RUN_OVR_APP is our standard "launch on any platform" C++ macro.

As you can see, the listing is short! But then, that's object-oriented programming for you. Most of the details of rendering are nicely tucked out of the way for you by your parent classes and helper functions. We want this class to be simple, because what we want you to understand is not *how* this example works, but *what* you need to add to it to get to a fully immersive VR example.

In this example you launch a decorated 1280 × 800 GLFW window, placing its upper-left corner at (100, 100). You use a 90° (expressed in radians as pi / 2) field of view, and you call the parent class's render methods without undue interference. There's really almost nothing to it (figure 5.2).

That's it for monoscopic rendering, so let's spice things up a bit: in Example 2, you'll convert to stereoscopic ("split-screen") rendering.

Figure 5.2 Our sample scene, rendered in basic monoscopic 3D

5.3   *Adding stereoscopy*

Now that you can distinguish the code that renders the scene, you can build on that to create a version that renders the same scene as a stereoscopic view (but *without* distortion).

As we stated, adding stereoscopy requires two things:

- A mechanism to divide the two images in some fashion so that they're perceived by the left and right eyes individually
- The ability to render each eye with a per-eye view transform to provide parallax, which is one mechanism to provide the sense of depth

---

Depth cues

Depth cues are the pieces of information that your brain uses to determine the distance to an object, and four of the main ones are *familiar size*, *binocular parallax*, *motion parallax*, and *oculomotor*.

Familiar size cues are those that come from knowing how big something actually is. If you see a door and have no reason to think you're looking at a dollhouse, then you get a sense of how big the door is, because doors tend to come in roughly the same size. These cues are reasonably accurate out to at least several hundred yards, or to put it in evolutionary terms, "as far as you could sprint if your life depended on it," because determining whether that shelter is a half mile away or a mile away probably doesn't matter when you're trying to outrun a lion.

Binocular parallax cues come from seeing an object at two slightly different angles because your eyes are some distance apart. These are only accurate out to at most a few meters.

Motion parallax cues derive from seeing an object from slightly different angles because of the movement of the observer. This can include both large-scale movement, such as traveling in a vehicle, and small-scale movement, like shifting your head.

Oculomotor cues are based on internal feedback from the muscles controlling your eyes and come in two forms: *accommodation* and *convergence*. Accommodation is the amount to which your muscles are distorting the cornea in order to focus at a given distance. Convergence is the degree to which your eyes are crossing inward to keep both eyes locked on a given target.

One of the shortcomings of VR is that although current-generation consumer HMDs can provide the first three of these kinds of cues, there isn't any way to provide oculomotor cues. This in turn leads to a disparity between what the eye muscles are saying about the distance to an object and what all the other systems are saying. This is likely one of the reasons the Oculus best practices guide recommends against placing objects in a scene very close to the user—the closer an object is, the stronger the oculomotor cues are, and the greater the disparity. This in turn can lead to VR-induced eye fatigue or even sim sickness.

We can introduce the second element easily, but the first component is, in a sense, hardware-dependent. 3D output devices typically take a signal that's in a specific format such as 3D-SBS[3] and then extract the left eye and right eye images and interlace them, either temporally (in the case of active 3D systems involving LCD shutter glasses) or spatially (in the case of passive 3D systems using polarized glasses). The Rift is probably closest in its workings to the 3D-SBS systems, although it's an awful lot more clever.

For Example 2 (listing 5.3) we're not trying to provide you with a 3D experience (yet); we're only demonstrating the additional work it takes to render one. You'll render each eye image and set them next to each other. Note that this example won't look correct in the Rift, because you're not taking the additional steps required for such proper rendering. The goal is to differentiate stereoscopic rendering needs from monoscopic. (New code appears in bold.)

> **Listing 5.3   Example_5_2_Stereoscopic.cpp, adding stereoscopy to the previous listing**

```
#include "Common.h"

static const glm::uvec2 WINDOW_SIZE(1280, 800);
static const glm::ivec2 WINDOW_POS(100, 100);

static const glm::uvec2 EYE_SIZE(                    Describes a single eye's
    WINDOW_SIZE.x / 2, WINDOW_SIZE.y);               viewport as width, height,
                                                     and aspect ratio.
static const float EYE_ASPECT =
    glm::aspect(EYE_SIZE);

struct PerEyeArg {
  glm::ivec2 viewportPosition;
  glm::mat4 modelviewOffset;                         Stores each eye's
};                                                   viewport position and
                                                     camera offset translation.
class CubeScene_Stereo : public GlfwApp {
  PerEyeArg eyes[2];

public:
  CubeScene_Stereo () {
    Stacks::projection().top() = glm::perspective(
        PI / 2.0f, EYE_ASPECT, 0.01f, 100.0f);

    Stacks::modelview().top() = glm::lookAt(
        vec3(0, OVR_DEFAULT_EYE_HEIGHT, 0.5f),
        vec3(0, OVR_DEFAULT_EYE_HEIGHT, 0),
        Vectors::UP);

    glm::vec3 offset(OVR_DEFAULT_IPD / 2.0f, 0, 0);  The left and right eyes
    eyes[ovrEye_Left] = {                            are distinguished by
      glm::ivec2(0, 0),                              distinct viewport
      glm::translate(glm::mat4(), offset)            frames and distinct
    };                                               translations of the
    eyes[ovrEye_Right] = {                           modelview matrix, one
      glm::ivec2(WINDOW_SIZE.x / 2, 0),              positive, one negative.
      glm::translate(glm::mat4(), -offset)
    };
  }
```

---

[3] "3D Side-by-Side," where the two images for the two eyes are compressed into the left and right halves of a single formatted frame.

```
virtual GLFWwindow * createRenderingTarget(
    glm::uvec2 & outSize, glm::ivec2 & outPosition) {
  outSize = WINDOW_SIZE;
  outPosition = WINDOW_POS;
  return glfw::createWindow(outSize, outPosition);
}

virtual void draw() {
  glClear(GL_COLOR_BUFFER_BIT | GL_DEPTH_BUFFER_BIT);
  MatrixStack & mv = gl::Stacks::modelview();

  for (int i = 0; i < ovrEye_Count; ++i) {
    ovrEyeType eye = hmd->EyeRenderOrder[i];
    PerEyeArg & eyeArgs = eyes[eye];
    viewport(eyeArgs.viewportPosition, EYE_SIZE);
    Stacks::with_push(mv, [&]{
      mv.preMultiply(eyeArgs.modelviewOffset);
      oria::renderExampleScene(
          OVR_DEFAULT_IPD, OVR_DEFAULT_EYE_HEIGHT);
    });
  }
}
};
```

> **Updates the camera's position by the eye's modelview matrix and renders to the eye's viewport.**

```
RUN_APP(CubeScene_Stereo);
```

The core of the differences between this example and the last is in the per-eye arguments, which hold the small set of eye-specific values that you use to set OpenGL's rendering viewport and camera position for each eye's point of view:

```
static const glm::uvec2 WINDOW_SIZE(1280, 800);
// ...
static const glm::uvec2 EYE_SIZE(WINDOW_SIZE.x / 2, WINDOW_SIZE.y);
```

The dimensions of the viewports of each eye are fixed, with each viewport at a constant size of (WINDOW_SIZE.x / 2) by (WINDOW_SIZE.y)—that is, 640 × 800. This describes exactly one half of the screen. You then store a per-eye offset of where to place the upper-left corner of the viewport on the display: (0, 0) for the left eye, ((WINDOW_SIZE.x / 2), 0) for the right. The PerEyeArg structure links this offset to a 4 × 4 matrix, the modelviewOffset, which you'll initialize with a small translation along the X axis.

```
struct PerEyeArg {
  glm::ivec2 viewportPosition;
  glm::mat4 modelviewOffset;
};
```

The modelviewOffset matrices represent the displacement of your eyeballs away from the center of your head. Each matrix is an X-axis translation of distance IPD / 2. The IPD is the distance from the central axis of one eye to the central axis of the other, so each eye-specific viewpoint is half the IPD off from the central axis of the head, offset perpendicular to the line of sight:

```
virtual void draw() {
  oglplus::Context::Clear().ColorBuffer().DepthBuffer();
  MatrixStack & mv = Stacks::modelview();
  for (int i = 0; i < 2; ++i) {
    PerEyeArg & eyeArgs = eyes[i];
    viewport(EYE_SIZE, eyeArgs.viewportPosition);
    Stacks::with_push(mv, [&]{
      mv.preMultiply(eyeArgs.modelviewOffset);
      oria::renderExampleScene(
          OVR_DEFAULT_IPD, OVR_DEFAULT_EYE_HEIGHT);
    });
  }
}
```

The `draw()` method has been expanded. Where previously you were calling render-ExampleScene() once, now you call it twice, once per eye. Before you render the scene, for each eye you set the OpenGL viewport,

```
viewport(EYE_SIZE, ivec2(eyeArgs.viewportPosition));
```

after which you push a new frame onto the top of your matrix stack,

```
Stacks::with_push(mv, [&]{
```

which you multiply with the offset of the current eye, effectively shifting the scene to the left or right by half the user's IPD:

```
mv.preMultiply(eyeArgs.modelviewOffset);
```

Finally you render

```
oria::renderExampleScene(
    OVR_DEFAULT_IPD, OVR_DEFAULT_EYE_HEIGHT);
```

and your reward is stereoscopy (figure 5.3)!

5.3.1 Verifying your scene by inspection

Now that you've added the stereo views, it's time to reveal why our sample scene is centered on the IPD cube, a cube whose edges are exactly the user's IPD in length. We've deliberately built a scene that would highlight common mathematical errors in your code, even if they're subtle. The aim is to help you verify that your matrices and perspective transforms are being applied correctly and in the correct order.

When thinking about a cube, the typical assumption is that you can't see two opposing sides at the same time. You can't be looking at the front and back of the

Figure 5.3   Our sample scene, rendered in stereoscopic 3D. The effects of stereoscopy are visible; for example, the convergence point of the lines in the floor grid is different for each side.

cube at the same time. But, for a small enough cube, you can see the left and right sides at the same time.

Consider a very small cube, like a six-sided die,[4] only a centimeter or two across. If you hold it up between your eyes, your left eye can see a sidelong view of the left face of the die, whereas your right eye can see a sidelong view of the right face of the cube.

If the cube size is exactly equal to the distance between your eyes and it's held directly in front of you, you can only see the front of the die. Your line of sight from each eye will be exactly coplanar to the sides. Rotating the cube slightly, or moving your viewpoint slightly, will allow you to see one side or another but never both at the same time, because as soon as one side comes into view, the opposing side has gone out of view (figure 5.4).

For our example we're using a colored cube instead of a die—the high contrast of the different colors makes it pretty apparent if you're seeing even a few pixels of a given side of the cube. The geometry of the setup means that if you move your viewpoint to the right, the right side of the cube (if you run the code, it's bright red) should come into view of the right eye well before the left eye (figure 5.5).

---

[4]   Also known as a d6, if you're hip. Interestingly, this exercise wouldn't work with a d4, d8, or d10, but it would work with a d20 or a d12...not that anybody uses d12s, except barbarians.

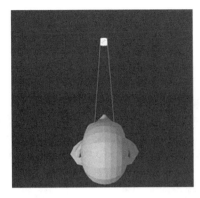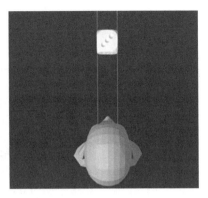

Figure 5.4   When you look at a small die up close, you can see both sides. But if the die is exactly as wide as your IPD, then your eyes are coplanar with the sides of the cube and you can no longer see them.

If you render a scene like this and discover that you *can* see both sides of the cube, then you're likely either applying the modelview offset incorrectly or misapplying the projection matrix.

This may seem like an odd choice of example, but it's a valuable diagnostic tool. Remember that there are two eyes and two matrices (projection and modelview) you

Figure 5.5   The geometry of the setup means that if you move your viewpoint to the right, the right side of the cube should come into view of the right eye well before the left eye.

have to work with. That duality is an easy place for errors to creep into the code. In addition, depending on API design, a common source of error can be confusion as to whether you should be applying a matrix or its inverse, or whether you should be doing premultiplication or postmultiplication of the offset against the existing matrix (whether this is a left- or right-handed coordinate system). That's $2 \times 2 \times 2 \times 2$ ways to botch applying the matrix offsets to the scene, and not all those ways are immediately obvious when you render the application to the screen or even to the Rift. When you start taking into consideration other potential bugs, like failing to initialize one of the matrices, or failing to use the correct scale for your offsets, those 2s can become 3s or more.

If matrices are applied in the wrong order or multiplied incorrectly, or if there's simply a bug in the math, sometimes the bugs aren't too far off from the intended results and can be deceptively close to true. A coder could mistake the double-vision effects that result from accidentally inverting a modelview offset for a more complicated problem with the matrix itself, and attempt to "fix" the problem by adjusting it.

By choosing such a simple sample scene, it should be easy to spot math errors. If you can see both sides of the cube with one eye, then your perspective matrix is probably off. Also, bugs in the order of applying your matrices will often manifest as the left and right sides of the stereo image failing to line up if you tilt the camera. Of course, the easiest way to tilt the camera will be if you're wearing the Rift, so let's move on to that, shall we?

5.4   Rendering to the Rift

The next step in our progression of examples is to take our stereoscopic display and move it to where it will do the most good: the Rift. This will mean targeting the Rift's display as a video output device, and enabling *distortion* in the rendering pipeline. In the following listing you'll use the Rift as a fixed display, and you'll add the orientation and position sensors to fully enable immersion. (New code appears in bold.)

Listing 5.4   Example_5_3_RiftRendered.cpp, moving to the Rift

```
#include "Common.h"

struct PerEyeArg {
  FramebufferWrapperPtr  framebuffer;          Enhanced data for each eye, including
  glm::mat4 projection;                        the use of per-eye projection.
  glm::mat4 modelviewOffset;
};

class CubeScene_Rift: public RiftGlfwApp {      You're now using a Rift-
  PerEyeArg eyes[2];                            specific parent class.
  ovrTexture eyeTextures[2];        The Oculus API requires that
                                    the textures be passed as a
  float ipd, eyeHeight;             single contiguous array.

public:
  CubeScene_Rift() {
```

```
        eyeHeight = ovrHmd_GetFloat(hmd,
            OVR_KEY_EYE_HEIGHT, eyeHeight);
        ipd = ovrHmd_GetFloat(hmd, OVR_KEY_IPD, ipd);
        Stacks::modelview().top() = glm::lookAt(
            vec3(0, eyeHeight, 0.5f),
            vec3(0, eyeHeight, 0),
            Vectors::UP);
    }
```

Now that you're working in VR, it's important to use the user's **IPD** and height.

The Rift requires some extra setup, once you have the OpenGL context.

```
    virtual void initGl() {
        GlfwApp::initGl();

        ovrRenderAPIConfig cfg;
        memset(&cfg, 0, sizeof(cfg));
        cfg.Header.API = ovrRenderAPI_OpenGL;
        cfg.Header.BackBufferSize = ovr::fromGlm(getSize());
        cfg.Header.Multisample = 1;

        int distortionCaps = ovrDistortionCap_Vignette;
        ovrEyeRenderDesc eyeRenderDescs[2];
        int configResult = ovrHmd_ConfigureRendering(hmd, &cfg,
            distortionCaps, hmd->DefaultEyeFov, eyeRenderDescs);

        for_each_eye([&](ovrEyeType eye){
            PerEyeArg & eyeArgs = eyes[eye];
            ovrFovPort fov = hmd->DefaultEyeFov[eye];

            ovrSizei texSize = ovrHmd_GetFovTextureSize(
                hmd, eye, fov, 1.0f);
            eyeArgs.framebuffer = FramebufferWrapperPtr(
                new FramebufferWrapper());
            eyeArgs.framebuffer->init(ovr::toGlm(texSize));

            ovrTextureHeader & textureHeader = eyeTextures[eye].Header;
            textureHeader.API = ovrRenderAPI_OpenGL;
            textureHeader.TextureSize = texSize;
            textureHeader.RenderViewport.Size = texSize;
            textureHeader.RenderViewport.Pos.x = 0;
            textureHeader.RenderViewport.Pos.y = 0;
            ((ovrGLTexture&)eyeTextures[eye]).OGL.TexId =
                oglplus::GetName(eyeArgs.framebuffer->color);

            eyeArgs.modelviewOffset = glm::translate(
                glm::mat4(),
                ovr::toGlm(
                    eyeRenderDescs[eye].HmdToEyeViewOffset));

            ovrMatrix4f projection = ovrMatrix4f_Projection(
                fov, 0.01f, 100, true);
            eyeArgs.projection = ovr::toGlm(projection);
        });
    }

    virtual void finishFrame() {
    }
```

Initialization of the Rift distortion occurs just as it did in chapter 4.

The Oculus SDK provides both a default field of view and a maximum field of view. You're using the default.

Unlike in chapter 4, you're using offscreen rendering areas and frame buffers, rather than static textures.

You need to set up texture details to pass to the SDK.

Your modelview offset and projection matrix are also now provided by the SDK.

Because the Oculus SDK handles the buffer swapping for you, you need to override the parent class method that normally does it, replacing it with a no-op.

Each eye can have a different projection matrix, so you update projection inside the per-eye loop.

Rendering for the Rift must be bookended by these begin/end frame calls, even when you aren't using the eye pose data.

The Rift SDK has a recommended eye order that's related to the refresh rate and direction of the Rift.

You bind your framebuffer so that you can render to an offscreen texture.

You render the example scene, passing in your actual IPD and eye height.

Rendering for the Rift must be bookended by these begin/end frame calls, even when you aren't using the eye pose data.

```
virtual void draw() {
  static ovrPosef eyePoses[2];

  ovrHmd_BeginFrame(hmd, getFrame());
  MatrixStack & mv = Stacks::modelview();
  for (int i = 0; i < ovrEye_Count; ++i) {
    ovrEyeType eye = hmd->EyeRenderOrder[i];
    PerEyeArg & eyeArgs = eyes[eye];
    Stacks::projection().top() = eyeArgs.projection;

    eyeArgs.framebuffer->Bind();
    oglplus::Context::Clear().DepthBuffer();
    Stacks::withPush(mv, [&]{
      mv.preMultiply(eyeArgs.modelviewOffset);
      oria::renderExampleScene(ipd, eyeHeight);
    });
  }
  ovrHmd_EndFrame(hmd, eyePoses, eyeTextures);
  }
};
```

```
RUN_OVR_APP(CubeScene_Rift);
```

We've added some fairly substantial chunks of code, but there shouldn't be any surprises after the previous chapter. The key differences between this listing and its predecessor are as follows:

- The binding and use of an *offscreen rendering target* through our `Framebuffer-Wrapper` class. Because you're rendering offscreen, the framebuffer has replaced the viewport information in the `PerEyeArg` structure.
- Retrieval of the user's actual height and IPD from the Rift's settings.
- Projection matrices that are customized for each eye.
- The `PerEyeArg` structure, which stores these additional components data for each eye.
- The use of the Rift's rendering pipeline and distortion mechanism.

The result is shown in figure 5.6. You now see the Rift's characteristic distortion of the stereoscopic views of the two eyes.

5.4.1   *Enhanced data for each eye*

Now that you're rendering to the Rift, you need to keep track of a bit more information for each eye than you did before. Our per-eye data structures have evolved from

```
glm::mat4 modelviewOffset;
glm::uvec2 viewportPosition;
```

to

```
FramebufferWrapperPtr framebuffer;
glm::mat4 modelviewOffset;
glm::mat4 projection;
```

Figure 5.6 Our sample scene, viewed through the Rift. Notice the clear differences in viewpoint for each eye, introduced by the IPD modelview offset translations.

You still track the `modelviewOffset`, because the user's eyes are still physically separated. But in the previous example you were content for your modelview offset to be a simple lateral shift by IPD / 2. Here, you're being more advanced: you query the Rift for the `eyeRenderDescs[eye].HmdToEyeViewOffset`, a 3D offset whose direction is specific to each eye. This value is based on the IPD the user has entered (if any) and ensures an accurate and more enjoyable experience for each configured user.

You don't need to track the `viewportPosition` explicitly any longer, because you're no longer rendering to a subsection of a larger frame; now you'll be rendering to a framebuffer. (Technically, you now set a viewport for the offscreen buffer, but that's a detail of implementation; see the section on offscreen framebuffer targets later in the chapter.)

For each eye you now also track `projection`. The `projection` field stores a distinct projection matrix for each eye. This matrix, whose values are generated by the SDK, expresses available field of view in each direction. Most conventional applications create a projection matrix from a vertical field of view and an aspect ratio (as well as a near and far clipping plane). The common projection matrix is almost always symmetrical up/down and left/right. The Oculus SDK, on the other hand, constructs an *asymmetrical* projection matrix out of four floating point values that represent the field of view in four directions: up, down, left, and right. The matrix is asymmetrical because each of our eyes has a larger field of view on the outer side of the head (left for the left eye, right for the right eye) than on the inner side, because of the way our skulls are shaped.

Outside of the `PerEyeArgs` structure, you also have an array of `eyeTextures`. These store a reference to the OpenGL texture object to which you'll render, which you then pass to the SDK with `ovrHmd_EndFrame()`. You also track the region within the texture to which you're rendering. The texture is now the offscreen canvas, which the SDK will distort and render to its physical display. Note that although logically it'd make sense to include the texture information in `PerEyeArgs`, the SDK design currently requires that the values for both eyes be passed as a single contiguous array, so you have to declare it as such in the main class.

5.4.2   *Improved user settings*

Two of the lines we've added to the constructor deserve special mention:

```
eyeHeight = ovrHmd_GetFloat(hmd, OVR_KEY_EYE_HEIGHT, eyeHeight);
ipd = ovrHmd_GetFloat(hmd, OVR_KEY_IPD, ipd);
```

These lines fetch the user's IPD and eye height. You'll use these values to position the cube directly ahead of users when the scene first loads, at exactly the height of their eyes if they were standing. You'll also set the width of the cube to exactly their IPD.

Be careful to provide reasonable defaults for these values. If the user hasn't run the setup utility to configure the Rift yet, their IPD and eye height won't be set in the Rift's settings; if so, you'll fall back to `OVR_DEFAULT_IPD` and `OVR_DEFAULT_PLAYER_HEIGHT`.

Reasonable defaults

Oculus VR has provided default values that you should use in your code whenever users haven't configured their Rift properly. Don't try to guess how tall your user is or how far apart their eyes are; let the values in the SDK do that for you. But those values are only averages and human beings tend to differ; your users are sure to have a better experience if your app strongly advises them to configure the Rift and set up their profile.

One tricky angle to the question of "What is default, really?" is that Oculus has chosen to use the average values of IPD and eye height of an adult male as their default constants. This is an interesting choice because the average human isn't, in fact, male. It's been suggested that perhaps the default SDK values, used when no user-specific value has been profiled, should be an average of both male and female adults. When asked, an Oculus representative described their choice of male defaults as "based on common user values," which may be a reflection of the common developers or testers at Oculus.

Because the Rift's "common user values" will align more poorly with the average woman than the average man, it's especially important that your application prompt users to set up their personal profile with the configuration utilities provided by Oculus. In this way you'll ensure that all users, regardless of body type, have a positive experience in VR.

5.4.3 *Setting up the SDK for distortion rendering*

To perform distortion, the SDK needs to initialize one of its rendering subsystems and know exactly what distortion features you'd like enabled. This code is essentially identical to the equivalent code in chapter 4, where we focused exclusively on distortion, but we'll recap it quickly here.

You declare the non-platform-specific configuration type and initialize its memory to 0:

```
ovrRenderAPIConfig cfg;
memset(&cfg, 0, sizeof(cfg));
```

You explicitly specify the rendering API you're using,

```
cfg.Header.API = ovrRenderAPI_OpenGL;
```

and you specify the size of the destination-rendering window, which should generally be the same as the Rift display resolution:

```
cfg.Header.BackBufferSize = ovr::fromGlm(getSize());
cfg.Header.Multisample = 1;
```

You indicate the distortion capabilities you want. Here we've used the vignette effect, which is also nice to have because it improves immersion by reducing the visibility of the transition from the rendered portion of the display to the unrendered portion.

Having prepared these settings, you call the `ovrHmd_ConfigureRendering` method with the desired parameters:

```
int distortionCaps = ovrDistortionCap_Vignette;
ovrEyeRenderDesc eyeRenderDescs[2];
int configResult = ovrHmd_ConfigureRendering(hmd, &cfg,
    distortionCaps, hmd->DefaultEyeFov, eyeRenderDescs);
```

Depending on the rendering API used, you might also want to cast the `ovrRenderAPI-Config` instance to a platform-specific type and populate additional data, but for OpenGL it's not necessary (the SDK will discover the required values on its own if they're set to 0).

5.4.4 *The offscreen framebuffer targets*

For each eye, you build a framebuffer, each of which will contain its own depth and color textures. These framebuffers are where you'll render your scene so that the results of the scene end up in the attached color texture. This example encapsulates the creation of a framebuffer into your wrapper classes, which requires as input only the size of the texture. The size of the texture depends on the field of view being used and the model of the Rift.

Keep in mind that the texture size will generally be higher than the actual per-eye resolution. You fetch the texture size from the SDK by providing the eye, the desired field of view, and another float parameter called `pixelsPerDisplayPixel`, which you hardcode as 1.0 here:

```
ovrSizei texSize = ovrHmd_GetFovTextureSize(hmd, eye, fov, 1.0f);
```

The last parameters specified how many pixels in the texture will map to each pixel at the very center of the view, where the distortion magnification effect is greatest. There's very little reason to ever specify a value other than 1.0 here, unless you're extremely constrained on texture memory. Even if you decide to vary the texture size (and thus the quality and sharpness of the distorted image as it appears on the Rift display), there are easier ways to accomplish this dynamically in the application than to change the value here. This will be discussed in chapter 6.

Given the texture size, this line constructs the framebuffer (including the wrapped depth and color buffers):

```
eyeArgs.framebuffer->init(ovr::toGlm(texSize));
```

`FrameBufferWrapperPtr`, as we've mentioned, is a convenience class that we created to simplify our demo code. Its `init()` method binds an OpenGL framebuffer and builds an OpenGL texture target, which it attaches to the framebuffer. In our demo code on the GitHub repository, we implemented `FrameBufferWrapperPtr` on top of the `oglplus` framebuffer class, which wraps object-oriented design around a self-contained buffer concept.

If you're not using a third-party library, there's nothing stopping you from building your own offscreen framebuffer. The OpenGL code looks roughly like this:

```
GLuint framebuffer, texture;
glGenFramebuffers(1, &frameBuffer);
glGenTextures(1, &texture);
glBindFramebuffer(GL_FRAMEBUFFER, frameBuffer);
glBindTexture(GL_TEXTURE_2D, texture);
glTexStorage2D(GL_TEXTURE_2D, 1, GL_RGBA8, size.x, size.y);
glFramebufferTexture2D(GL_FRAMEBUFFER, GL_COLOR_ATTACHMENT0, GL_TEXTURE_2D,
    texture, 0);
```

This snippet will help you build an offscreen buffer, which you can bind as a render target and render to. This gives you a texture target that you can pass to the SDK for rendering on the Rift.

5.4.5   *The Oculus texture description*

Creating the framebuffer and associated textures isn't enough; you also have to describe them to the Oculus SDK. For this you use the `ovrTexture` type, declared in your class like this:

```
ovrTexture eyeTextures[2];
```

Note that you're declaring the `ovrTexture` member *outside* of the `PerEyeArg` structure, even though you do in fact have one `ovrTexture` per eye. This is because the

Oculus API for accepting the textures for a given frame requires an array of exactly two instances of this type, arranged contiguously in memory:

```
OVR_EXPORT void ovrHmd_EndFrame(ovrHmd hmd,
    const ovrPosef renderPose[2],
    const ovrTexture eyeTexture[2]);
```

If you placed the texture member inside the `PerEyeArg` structure, the two instances wouldn't be contiguous and you'd have to copy them out to another array anyway.

Almost all the data you want to set is in the `Header` member of the `ovrTexture` structure, so create a reference to it and populate the fields:

```
ovrTextureHeader & textureHeader = eyeTextures[eye].Header;
```

You need to let the SDK know what API you're using for rendering. In theory the SDK should be able to deduce this from the rendering configuration you did earlier, but it's also conceivable that a single rendering API might have more than one mechanism for representing textures.

```
textureHeader.API = ovrRenderAPI_OpenGL;
```

You also have to tell the SDK the actual size of the texture you're using, as well as the region on the texture to which you're rendering. The former is done by populating the `TextureSize` parameter. This should always be set to the actual resolution of the texture you've created:

```
textureHeader.TextureSize = texSize;
```

The latter is done by populating the `RenderViewport` member, which has both `Size` and `Pos` members of its own. In most cases you want to render to the entire texture, so `Size` should be set to the same value as the `TextureSize` member of the header, and `Pos` should be set to the origin of the texture at $(0, 0)$:

```
textureHeader.RenderViewport.Size = texSize;
textureHeader.RenderViewport.Pos.x = 0;
textureHeader.RenderViewport.Pos.y = 0;
```

There are a couple of use cases for modifying the values here. The first is that some developers may wish to use a single "double-wide" texture to contain both the left and right images. In this case you'd use a single framebuffer and vary the viewports when rendering. You'd set the `TextureSize`, `RenderViewport.Size`, and `RenderViewport.Pos` values to correspond to your texture size and viewports.

The other use case for varying these values is if you're unable to maintain a suitable frame rate with the specified texture size and you want to trade off image quality for speed. This is discussed in chapter 6, where we explore performance optimizations.

The very last piece of information that you need to provide to the SDK is the identifier of the texture itself. But you can't inject this value directly into the `ovrTexture` or ovrTextureHeader types. These types are intended to be platform-neutral, so they don't contain members for OpenGL- or Direct3D-specific data. If you look at the definition for ovrTexture you'll see something like this:

```
typedef struct ovrTexture_s {
  ovrTextureHeader Header;
  uintptr_ PlatformData[8];
} ovrTexture;
```

Rather than include OpenGL or Direct3D types here, Oculus has reserved room for them by adding an array of integer pointers. To populate the required fields, it's necessary to cast the ovrTexture to a platform-specific type: ovrD3D11TextureData, ovrD3D10TextureData, ovrD3D9TextureData, or ovrGLTextureData, depending on the API being used. This example uses OpenGL, so choose ovrGLTextureData to perform your cast. It looks like this:

```
typedef struct ovrGLTextureData_s {
  ovrTextureHeader Header;
  TexId;
} ovrGLTextureData;
```

You need to populate that TexId member with your OpenGL texture identifier, which is fetched out of the framebuffer's color field:

```
((ovrGLTextureData&)textures[eye]).TexId = eyeArg.frameBuffer.color->texture;
```

5.4.6   *Projection and modelview offset*

Once you've built your offscreen rendering targets, the final piece of the setup puzzle is to build your projection and modelview offset matrices:

```
ovrFovPort fov = hmd->DefaultEyeFov[eye];
//...
eyeArgs.modelviewOffset = glm::translate(glm::mat4(),
    ovr::toGlm(eyeRenderDescs[eye].HmdToEyeViewOffset));

ovrMatrix4f projection = ovrMatrix4f_Projection(fov, 0.01f, 100, true);
eyeArgs.projection = ovr::toGlm(projection);
```

The variable hmd->DefaultEyeFov[eye] stores each field of view for the eyes of the user. This field of view—expressed as functions of angles up, down, left and right—describes the sides of the infinite pyramid representing the user's view through the Rift. You turn this into a projection matrix by providing a near and far clipping plane, turning the pyramid into a frustum that each eye can see. The projection matrix also accounts for the distance between the lens axis and the center of the half of the screen devoted to each eye.

The field of view (FOV) frustum is complemented by the modelviewOffset, which is the translation matrix of the view adjustment for the current eye. This will be a linear translation, exactly half of the user's IPD to the left or right (along the X axis).

5.4.7 *The Rift's rendering loop*

Your use of the Rift's rendering pipeline is bracketed by two key function calls:

```
ovrHmd_BeginFrame(hmd, getFrame());
// ...
ovrHmd_EndFrame(hmd, eyePoses, eyeTextures);
```

These calls, which you first encountered in chapter 4, are the heart of the Rift's distortion and timing pipeline. The function `ovrHmd_BeginFrame` signals that a new frame is beginning, whereas the function `ovrHmd_EndFrame` tells the SDK that rendering has been completed so that it can perform the distortion and the buffer swap to place the rendered image on the Rift display.

The Rift uses "absolute" time to best predict the exact head pose that the sensors should report. That is, it computes the millisecond when the frame that you're beginning now will actually be rendered to the user's eyes. That means, hopefully, reduced latency in user head motion tracking.

This is where the Rift begins sending your rendered imagery to its display. Perceived latency is further improved here by the use of *timewarp,* which corrects for the difference between the estimated position at the time the eye render starts and the actual orientation when the frame is placed on the screen. In fact, the `EndFrame` method blocks until immediately prior to the display's vertical sync (v-sync) so that it can get the most accurate position for the render. Timewarp is discussed in detail in chapter 6.

The `poses` parameter here is a two-element array of `ovrPosef` elements. The parameter can't be null, so you're passing in a local array.

Even though you're populating the array elements using the `ovrHmd_GetEyePoses` function, you're not using them for rendering. The only reason you call `ovrHmd_GetEyePoses` is because in some versions of the SDK, Direct HMD mode doesn't function properly if you don't call it. But you'll need those poses in the very next example, when you turn on the sensors. True VR only comes into play when you're integrating the head-tracking information with the rendering, so let's take a look at that.

5.5 *Enabling sensors*

Now that you can render to the Rift, there's just one more key component and you'll have a fully Rift-enabled application: adding head tracking. We've explored how to use the Rift's sensors in previous chapters, and the SDK makes adding sensor data to your transforms stacks very straightforward; let's take a look. (New code appears in bold.)

> **Listing 5.5 Example_5_4_RiftSensors.cpp (abridged)**

```
// ...
// Everything is the same as the previous example until the constructor and
    destructor:
// ...
```

```
  CubeScene_RiftSensors() {
    if (!ovrHmd_ConfigureTracking(hmd,
        ovrTrackingCap_Orientation | ovrTrackingCap_Position, 0)) {
      SAY("Warning: Unable to configure Rift tracking.");
    }
  }
}

// ...
// And again, nothing changes until the draw method:
// ...

  virtual void draw() {
    ovrPosef eyePoses[2];
    ovrHmd_GetEyePoses(hmd, getFrame(), eyeOffsets, eyePoses, nullptr);

    ovrHmd_BeginFrame(hmd, getFrame());
    MatrixStack & mv = Stacks::modelview();
    for (int i = 0; i < ovrEye_Count; ++i) {
      ovrEyeType eye = hmdDesc.EyeRenderOrder[i];
      PerEyeArg & eyeArgs = eyes[eye];
      Stacks::projection().top() = eyeArgs.projection;

      eyeArgs.framebuffer->Bind();
      oglplus::Context::Clear().DepthBuffer();
      Stacks::with_push(mv, [&]{
        mv.preMultiply(glm::inverse(ovr::toGlm(eyePoses[eye])));
        oria::renderExampleScene(ipd, eyeHeight);
      });
    }
    ovrHmd_EndFrame(hmd, poses, textures);
  }
```

That's all—one new line of setup and two new lines of render loop logic. The Rift's sensors are that easy to access. You only need to call ovrHmd_ConfigureTracking() to start the flow of data.

In your render loop you're now initializing the poses array you've been ignoring, using ovrHmd_GetEyePose(). This function returns the *predicted orientation* of each eye at the time at which this particular frame will be displayed on the Rift.

The method ovr::toGlm() converts the translation and orientation quaternion returned from the Rift into a single 4 × 4 matrix, which you'll be able to pass to the GPU as a complete transform:

```
static inline glm::mat4 fromOvr(const ovrPosef & op) {
  glm::mat4 orientation = glm::mat4_cast(toGlm(op.Orientation));
  glm::mat4 translation = glm::translate(glm::mat4(), toGlm(op.Position));
  return translation * orientation;
}
```

It's important to remember that the Rift returns its sensor data in "user" coordinates. Before you can pass the returned basis transform to the GPU, it must be inverted from player to worldview coordinates:

```
glm::inverse(ovr::toGlm(eyePoses[eye]))
```

You apply the predicted orientation to the *modelview matrix* to reorient the world around yourself.

5.5.1 Implications of prediction

There are a couple of different sensor samples going on during rendering when prediction is enabled: one right before rendering each per-eye view, and (if you've turned on *timewarp*—see chapter 6) another right before the v-sync. The per-eye sensor samples are predicted values, but the shorter the prediction interval, the more accurate the predicted transform is going to be.

If you render the eyes in the wrong order (in the case of DK2, left to right), then the length of the prediction time for the left eye is ((`time to render left frame`) + (`time to render right frame`) + (`time to vsync`) + (`time to display right frame`)). If you render the eyes in the correct order, then the prediction time for the left frame becomes (`time to render left frame + time to vsync + time to display right frame`), and the prediction time for the right frame becomes (`time to render right frame + time to render left frame + time to vsync`). The right eye prediction time becomes longer, but the average prediction length goes down.

As you saw in chapter 4, this means that the Rift cares about rendering order. That's why our code

```
for (int i = 0; i < ovrEye_Count; ++i) {
  ovrEyeType eye = hdm->EyeRenderOrder[i];
  // ...
```

is careful to let the SDK dictate the order of eye update. It gives you better prediction results.

5.5.2 Getting your matrices in order

The modelview matrix is conceptually the collapsing of two individual matrices: the *model* matrix, which represents the position of a given item in the world, and the *view* matrix, which represents the position from which you're viewing the world. They tend to be glued together because generally when rendering a scene, you're not going to change the viewpoint between rendering one object and the next. So there's no point in starting with a blank identity matrix and applying the same view transformation for every single object you render.

You've modified the modelview matrix before, using per-eye translations to displace the camera for each eye. This gave you stereo vision, producing the same kind of stereo depth perception you get in the real world. Adding head tracking is very much the same, and it follows similar logic. As you concatenate the matrices for your modelview transform (perhaps with a Stack metaphor, as we've done here), the order in which you assemble your matrices will look something like this:

```
eye_offset_matrix * view_matrix * model_matrix...
```

Adding in the head tracker transform results in this:

```
eye_offset_matrix * head_pose_matrix * view_matrix * model_matrix...
```

The ordering here is important. The eye offset matrix is specified as a translation on the X coordinate. If you apply it after the head pose and the head pose isn't aligned with the world X axis, then the two eyes won't be positioned appropriately relative to one another.

Remember, matrices are applied from right to left to the vectors that they're multiplied onto: $A \times B \times C \times V = A \times (B \times (C \times V))$.

Fortunately, the Oculus SDK takes some of the risk of error out of the equation if you use their ovrHmd_GetEyePoses() method. When you call ovrHmd_GetEyePoses(), you pass in the eyeOffsets array that you retrieved during initialization, extracted from the headset configuration details retrieved from ovrHmd_ConfigureRendering(). The eyeOffset is an array of two vectors, representing eye separation.

If you dig into the implementation of ovrHmd_GetEyePoses() in the SDK, you'll find this snippet of code:

```
outEyePoses[0] = Posef(hmdPose.Orientation,
    ((Posef)hmdPose).Apply(-((Vector3f)hmdToEyeViewOffset[0])));
outEyePoses[1] = Posef(hmdPose.Orientation,
    ((Posef)hmdPose).Apply(-((Vector3f)hmdToEyeViewOffset[1])));
```

And that is matrix composition in action. The eye poses that are returned to you have the eye offset matrix baked into them so that each eye pose is literally the pose of that eye's view, completely, including IPD.

This means that when you use the existing SDK methods for full pose capture, your odds of accidentally introducing an out-of-order error through your matrix math are significantly reduced.

5.6   *Summary*

In this chapter you learned that

- A complete Rift application is the cumulative product of a series of steps. Our example evolved from mono, to stereo, to stereo distortion, to active use of the Rift sensors.
- The key APIs of the Oculus SDK are easily accessed and each has a logical place in the flow of your application.
- The proper ordering of mathematical matrices is vital to avoid hard-to-spot display bugs.
- With simple scene design, you can set up a virtual environment that makes those bugs easier to catch.

Performance and quality

This chapter covers

- Understanding why performance is so critical to VR applications
- Understanding why performance demands are higher for VR than non-VR
- Using timewarp to deal with poor renderer performance
- Using dynamic framebuffer scaling to improve renderer performance

The performance of your VR app is critical to its success or failure, far more so than in conventional applications. With conventional applications, most of the time poor-quality applications will result in disinterest—a financial disaster perhaps, but generally no one is physically hurt. For VR, the stakes are higher. In VR, poor quality can lead to more than disinterest in your application and financial loss; it may also lead to users feeling physically ill. We'll cover motion sickness in detail in chapter 10, describing its causes and its ill effects; but while those causes can be many and varied, chief among them are poor frame rates and bad software latency. With that in mind, let's take a look at the critical performance criteria for VR applications and what you can do to meet them.

Achieving a given level of performance in VR has a higher cost than doing so in a conventional application because of the need for rendering two views of a given scene rather than one. Another factor is the need to render at a higher resolution than the target display due to the nature of the distortion effect. With these factors in mind, this chapter discusses two technologies available to all Rift applications: *timewarp* and *dynamic framebuffer scaling*:

- Timewarp addresses drops in renderer performance by allowing an application to use data from previously rendered frames if a new frame isn't ready by the time the display is about to refresh.
- Dynamic framebuffer scaling addresses issues with consistently low renderer performance by reducing the workload of rendering a given frame at the cost of quality in the resulting scene.

Before we dig into these techniques, let's see what drives the Rift's performance requirements.

6.1 Understanding VR performance requirements

When building VR apps for the Rift, you're constrained by

- Higher performance requirements
- Stricter performance requirements
- Higher rendering costs

Let's take a closer look at each of these issues.

HIGHER PERFORMANCE REQUIREMENTS

In a standard application rendered on a monitor, low frame rates aren't desirable, but neither are they disastrous. Users may be dissatisfied with only 30 frames per second, but they're unlikely to become physically ill, even if the frame rate drops even further occasionally.

But in VR, the golden rule is, above all else, you must respond to changes in orientation and position instantly.[1] This has consequences for your application. In VR, the *maximum* allowable latency (the interval between the time the user moves their head and the time when the view is updated) is considered to be about 20 ms.

This 20 ms interval puts a floor on your frame rate of about 50 frames per second.[2] Your frame rate must never drop below that point. Lower latency (and consequently higher frame rates) will feel even smoother and provide a greater sense of presence to the user.

Fifty frames per second may not seem so bad, but realistically your requirements are significantly higher. The DK2 headset runs at 75 Hz, and in order to take advantage of

---

[1] "Instantly" here meaning, below the user's level of perception.

[2] You heard it from John Carmack himself (oculusrift-blog.com/john-carmacks-message-of-latency/682/): 1000 ms in a second divided by 20 ms per frame = 50 frames per second, assuming the `SwapBuffer` call is instantaneous.

timewarp, rendering should always be locked to the refresh rate of the device. Subsequent models are likely to push this refresh rate even higher. What's more, this refresh rate isn't currently under the control of the application or available for modification via the SDK. The refresh rate you get is the frame rate you must target.

STRICTER PERFORMANCE REQUIREMENTS

In a standard application, a momentary drop in frame rate can be annoying. In VR, short-term frame rate drops are disastrous. Missing even a single frame of rendering will result in pauses or flickering that's both perceptible to the user and extremely damaging to the sense of presence. Even worse, it can induce motion sickness. Consider the DK2 running at 75 Hz. If a single vertical sync (v-sync) goes by without a new frame being rendered, the effective frame rate is reduced to 38 frames per second, and the latency is pushed above the threshold of perception, even if it's only for one frame.

HIGHER RENDERING COST

Rendering a frame for the Rift is more expensive than rendering one for a 2D monitor. For one, you have to render your entire scene twice, and the increased costs don't stop there.

Due to the nature of the distortion, in order to maintain a high-quality image over the entire distorted scene, the resolution of the offscreen target for predistortion rendering must be significantly higher than that of the screen area on which it'll eventually be displayed. For the DK2, using the default field of view, the optimal offscreen rendering size is 1182 × 1461 pixels, compared to the 960 × 1080 pixel region where the distortion view will be displayed. As newer headsets increase in resolution, the offscreen rendering size will increase as well.[3]

The distortion itself adds a small, but non-negligible, amount of overhead. So you have the overhead of rendering the scene twice, the overhead of rendering over 50 percent more pixels, plus the distortion overhead, and because of the frame rate constraints, you've got much less time in which to accomplish all this work. What's an industrious developer to do?

6.2　*Detecting and preventing performance issues*

Obviously the first thing you should do is make sure you have a well-behaved rendering engine for VR. This means taking advantage of the existing tools that the SDK provides to create a good VR experience.

FOLLOW THE SDK GUIDELINES

In particular, you should ensure that you're using vertical sync to lock the frame rate to the Rift's refresh rate. You should also be using timewarp to ensure that the perceived latency is as low as possible. (More on timewarp in a moment.)

---

[3] Fortunately, the relationship is linear, so a Rift with the same distortion mechanism but twice the resolution will require twice the offscreen rendering size.

OPTIMIZING YOUR RENDERING PIPELINE

Unfortunately, the details of this kind of optimization are largely out of scope for a book on VR development. Rendering performance as a whole is a deep topic. Entire libraries can be written on the topic. But we can make some general basic recommendations.

Take advantage of modern rendering techniques that minimize the number of rendering calls required to draw something.[4]

Where possible, use asynchronous mechanisms to transfer data such as geometry and textures to the GPU. If you're in the middle of your rendering loop and you're suddenly doing extra work to load the new building geometry or character skin onto the GPU, you're doing work you could push to another thread.[5]

Find your bottlenecks so that when the time comes to work on performance in the rendering pipeline, you know where to focus your efforts.[6]

DETECTING PERFORMANCE ISSUES

The first component of addressing performance issues is detecting if (or perhaps admitting) you have one.

"Hi, I'm Crysis, and I have low frame rates."

"Hi, Crysis."

Most games and rendering engines have some mechanism for determining the current frame rate, so this is a good place to start. The frame rate you achieve should be equal to the native refresh rate of the Rift display—60 Hz for the DK1 and 75 Hz for the DK2. Future devices may vary.

The problem with frame rate counters is that they're generally empirical measurements of how many frames you rendered over a given time. By the time you've fetched the counter and found it's not what you want, your users have already suffered the consequences of the dropped frames as a stuttering of their environment.

Ideally you want to discover and resolve performance issues before they happen, or at least before they become apparent to the user. Fortunately, there are some great techniques for doing that.

Two main Rift-specific tools for coping with performance problems are timewarp and dynamic framebuffer scaling. The first, timewarp, helps your application appear to continue rendering smoothly even if the rendering pipeline is falling behind on producing the required number of frames per second. The second, dynamic framebuffer scaling, helps reduce the overall load on your rendering pipeline by reducing the number of pixels you need to render. Both are useful on their own, but they work best if used in conjunction with each other.

---

[4] There's an excellent video on this kind of optimization: www.youtube.com/watch?v=-bCeNzgiJ8I.

[5] See chapter 28 of *OpenGL Insights* (CRC Press, 2012) for an in-depth discussion of the possibilities of asynchronous loading of resources.

[6] See chapter 28 of *GPU Gems* (Addison-Wesley Professional, 2004) for basic guidelines for identifying rendering bottlenecks. This chapter is available online at http.developer.nvidia.com/GPUGems/gpugems_ch28.html.

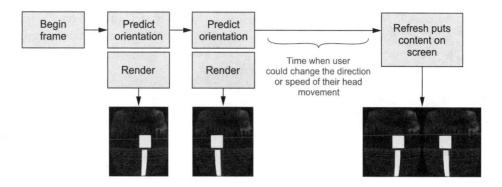

Figure 6.1 There will be a gap between when you sample the predicted orientation of the Rift for each eye and when you display the rendered and distorted frame. In that time a user could change their head movement direction or speed. This is usually perceived as latency.

6.3   *Using timewarp: catching up to the user*

In a Rift application, head pose information is captured before you render the image for each eye. But rendering isn't an instantaneous operation; processing time and v-sync mean that every frame can take a dozen milliseconds to get to the screen. This presents a problem, because the head pose information at the start of the frame probably won't match where the head is when the frame is rendered. So the head pose information has to be predicted for some point in the future, but the prediction is necessarily imperfect. During the rendering of eye views, users could change the speed or direction they're turning their head or start moving from a still position, or otherwise change their current motion vector (figure 6.1).

THE PROBLEM: POSE AND PREDICTION DIVERGE

As a consequence, the predicted head pose used to render an eye view will rarely *exactly* match the actual pose the head has when the image is displayed on the screen. Even though this is typically over a time of less than 13 ms, and the amount of error is very small in the grand scheme of things, the human visual cortex has millions of years of evolution behind it and is perfectly capable of perceiving the discrepancy, even if it can't necessarily nail down what's exactly wrong. Users will perceive it as latency—or worse, they won't be able to say what it is that they perceive, but they'll declare the whole experience "un-immersive." You could even make them ill (see chapter 10 for the relationship between latency and simulation sickness).

THE SOLUTION: TIMEWARP

To attempt to correct for these issues, timewarp was introduced in the 0.3.x versions of the Oculus SDK. The SDK can't actually use time travel to send back head pose information from the future,[7] so it does the next best thing. Immediately before putting the image on the screen, it samples the predicted head pose again. Because this prediction

---

[7]   It's very difficult to accelerate a Rift up to 88 miles per hour.

occurs so close to the time at which the images will be displayed on the screen, it's much more accurate than the earlier poses. The SDK can look at the difference between the timewarp head pose and the original predicted head pose and shift the image slightly to compensate for the difference.

6.3.1 Using timewarp in your code

Because the functionality and implementation of timewarp is part of the overall distortion mechanism inside the SDK, all you need to do to use it (assuming you're using SDK-side distortion) is to pass the relevant flag into the SDK during distortion setup, shown in the next listing.

Listing 6.1 Dynamic framebuffer scaling example

```
int distortionCaps =
    ovrDistortionCap_TimeWarp |
    ovrDistortionCap_Vignette;
ovrEyeRenderDesc eyeRenderDescs[2];
int configResult = ovrHmd_ConfigureRendering(hmd, &cfg,
    distortionCaps, hmd->DefaultEyeFov, eyeRenderDescs);
```

All you need do is add the flag `ovrDistortionCap_TimeWarp` to your call to `ovrHmd_ConfigureRendering()`.

6.3.2 How timewarp works

Consider an application running at 75 frames per second. It has 13.33 milliseconds to render each frame (not to mention do everything else it has to do for each frame). Suppose your "update state" code takes 1 millisecond, each eye render takes 4 milliseconds, and the distortion (handled by the SDK) takes 1 millisecond. Assuming you start your rendering loop immediately after the previous refresh, the sequence of events would look something like figure 6.2.

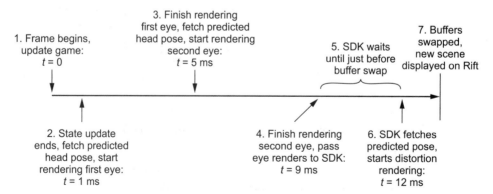

Figure 6.2 A simple timeline for a single frame showing the points at which the (predicted) head pose is fetched. By capturing the head orientation a third time immediately before ending the frame, it's possible to warp the image to adjust for the differences between the predicted and actual orientations. Only a few milliseconds—probably less than 10—have passed since the original orientations were captured, but this penultimate update can still strongly improve the perception of responsiveness in the Rift.

1   Immediately after the previous screen refresh, you begin your game loop, starting by updating any game state you might have.

2   Having updated the game state, you grab the predicted head pose and start rendering the first eye. ~12 ms remain until the screen refresh, so the predicted head pose is for 12 ms in the future.

3   You've finished with the first eye, so you grab the predicted head pose again and start rendering the second eye. This pose is for ~8ms in the future, so it's likely more accurate than the first eye pose, but still imperfect.

4   After rendering has completed for each eye, you pass the rendered offscreen images to the SDK. ~4 ms remain until the screen refresh.

5   The SDK wants to fetch the most accurate head pose it can for timewarp, so it'll wait until the last possible moment to perform the distortion.

6   With just enough time to perform the distortion, the SDK fetches the head pose one last time. This head pose is only predicted about 1 ms into the future, so it's much more accurate than either of the per-eye render predictions. The difference between each per-eye pose and this final pose is computed and sent into the distortion mechanism so that it can correct the rendered image position by rotating it slightly, as if on the inner surface of a sphere centered on the user.

7   The distorted points of view are displayed on the Rift screen.

By capturing the head pose a third time, so close to rendering, the Rift can "catch up" to unexpected motion. When the user's head rotates, the point where the image is projected can be shifted, appearing where it *would have been* rendered if the Rift could've known where the head pose was going to be.

The exact nature of the shifting is similar to if you took the image and painted it on the interior of a sphere that was centered on your eye, and then slightly rotated the sphere. If the predicted head pose was incorrect, and you ended up turning your head further to the right than predicted, the timewarp mechanism would compensate by rotating the image to the left (figure 6.3).

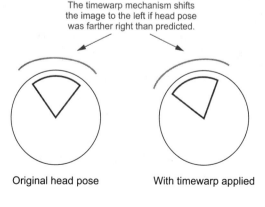

The timewarp mechanism shifts
the image to the left if head pose
was farther right than predicted.

Original head pose   With timewarp applied

Figure 6.3   The rendered image is shifted to compensate for the difference between the predicted head pose at eye render time and the actual head pose at distortion time.

One caveat: when you go adding extra swivel to an image, there'll be some pixels at the edge of the frame that weren't rendered before and now they need to be filled in. How best to handle these uncomputed pixels is a topic of ongoing study, although initial research from Valve and Oculus suggest that simply coloring them black is fine.

6.3.3 Limitations of timewarp

Timewarp isn't a latency panacea. This "rotation on rails" works fine if the user's point of view *only* rotates, but in real life our anatomy isn't so simple. When you turn your head your eyes *translate* as well, swinging around the axis of your neck, producing parallax. If you're looking at a soda can on your desk and you turn your head to the right, you'd expect a little bit more of the desk behind the right side of the can to be visible, because by turning your head you've also moved your eyes a little bit in 3D space. The timewarped view can't do that, because it can't manufacture those previously hidden pixels out of nothing. For that matter, the timewarp code doesn't know where new pixels should appear, because by the time you're doing timewarp, the scene is simply a flat 2D image, devoid of any information about the distance from the eye to a given pixel.

This is especially visible in motion with a strong translation component, but (perhaps fortunately) the human head's range and rate of motion in rotation is much greater than in translation. Translation generally involves large, coarse motions of the upper body that are easily predicted by hardware and difficult for the user to amend faster than the Rift can anticipate.

Oculus recognizes that the lack of parallax in timewarped images is an issue, and they're researching the topic. But all the evidence so far has been that, basically, users just don't notice. It seems probable that parallax timewarp would be a real boost to latency if it were easy, but without it we still get real and significant improvements from rotation alone.

6.4 Advanced uses of timewarp

Beyond the basics, there are a few rather nifty things you can do with timewarp.

6.4.1 When you're running early

One obvious use of timewarp is to fit in extra processing, when you know that you can afford it. The Rift SDK provides access to its timing data through several API functions:

- *ovrHmd_BeginFrame*—Typically used in the render loop
- *ovrHmd_GetFrameTiming*—Typically used for custom timing and optimization
- *ovrHmd_BeginFrameTiming*—Typically used when doing client-side distortion

These methods return an instance of the ovrFrameTiming structure, which stores the absolute time values associated with the frame. The Rift uses system time as an absolute time marker, instead of computing a series of differences from one frame to the next, because doing so reduces the gradual buildup of incremental error. These times are stored as doubles, which is a blessing after all the cross-platform confusion over how to count milliseconds. See table 6.1 for the contents of `ovrFrameTiming`.

Table 6.1 The data members of the `ovrFrameTiming` struct

`float DeltaSeconds`	The amount of time that has passed since the previous frame returned its `BeginFrameSeconds` value; usable for movement scaling. This will be clamped to no more than 0.1 seconds to prevent excessive movement after pauses for loading or initialization.
`double ThisFrameSeconds`	Absolute time value of when rendering of this frame began or is expected to begin; generally equal to `NextFrameSeconds` of the previous frame. Can be used for animation timing.
`double TimewarpPointSeconds`	Absolute point when IMU (timewarp) expects to be sampled for this frame.
`double NextFrameSeconds`	Absolute time when current frame and GPU flush will finish, and the next frame starts.
`double ScanoutMidpointSeconds`	Time when half of the screen will be scanned out. Can be passed as a prediction value to `ovrHmd_GetSensorState()` to get general orientation.
`double EyeScanoutSeconds[2]`	Timing points when each eye will be scanned out to display. Used for rendering each eye.

Generally speaking, it's expected that the following should hold,

```
ThisFrameSeconds
    < TimewarpPointSeconds
        < NextFrameSeconds
            < EyeScanoutSeconds[EyeOrder[0]]
                <= ScanoutMidpointSeconds
                    <= EyeScanoutSeconds[EyeOrder[1]]
```

although actual results may vary during execution.

Knowing when the Rift is going to reach `TimewarpPointSeconds` and `Scanout-MidpointSeconds` gives you a lot of flexibility if you happen to be rendering faster than necessary. There are some interesting possibilities here: if you know that your code will finish generating the current frame before the clock hits `TimewarpPoint-Seconds`, then you effectively have "empty time" to play with in the frame. You could use that time to do almost anything (provided it's quick)—send data to the GPU to prepare for the next frame, compute another million particle positions, prove the Riemann hypothesis—whatever, really (figure 6.4.)

Keep this in mind when using timewarp. It effectively gives your app free license to scale its scene density, graphics level, and just plain awesomeness up or down dynamically as a function of current performance, measured and decided right down to the individual frame.

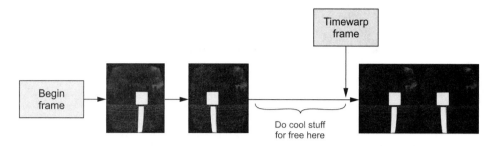

Figure 6.4   Timewarp means you've got a chance to do extra processing for "free" if you know when you're idle.

But it's not a free pass! Remember that there are nasty consequences to overrunning your available frame time: a dropped frame. And if you don't adjust your own timing, you risk the SDK spending a busy-wait cycle for almost all of the following frame, using past data for the next image, which can consume valuable CPU. So you've got a powerful weapon here, but you must be careful not to shoot yourself in the foot with it.

6.4.2   *When you're running late*

Of course, when the flak starts to fly, odds are that you won't be rendering frames ahead of the clock—it's a lot more likely that you'll be scrambling to catch up. Sometimes rendering a single frame costs you longer than the number of milliseconds your target frame rate allows. But timewarp can be useful here too.

Say your engine realizes that it's going to be running late. Instead of continuing to render the current frame, you can send the *previous* frame to the Rift and let the Rift apply timewarp to the images generated a dozen milliseconds ago (figure 6.5). The older images won't be quite right, but if it buys you enough time to get back on top of

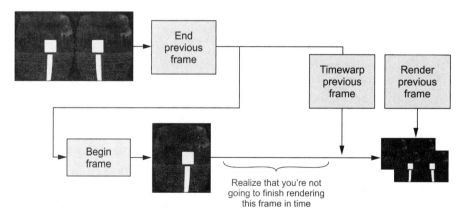

Figure 6.5   If you're squeezed for rendering time, you can occasionally save a few cycles by dropping a frame and re-rendering the previous frame through timewarp.

your rendering load, it'll be worth it, and no human eye will catch it when you occasionally replay one frame out of 75. Far more importantly, the image sent to the Rift will continue to respond to the user's head motions with absolute fidelity; low latency means responsive software, even with the occasional lost frame.

Remember, timewarp can distort any frame, as long as it's clear when that frame was originally generated so that the Rift knows how much distortion to apply.

The assumption here is that your code is sufficiently instrumented and capable of self-analysis that you do more than just render a frame and hope it was fast enough. Carefully instrumented timing code isn't hard to add, especially with such display-bound timing methods as ovrHmd_GetFrameTiming, but it does mean more complexity in the rendering loop. If you're using a commercial graphics engine, the engine may already have the support baked in. This is the sort of monitoring that any 3D app engine that handles large, complicated, variable-density scenes will hopefully be capable of performing.

Dropping frames with timewarp is an advanced technique and probably not worth investing engineering resources into early in a project. This is something that you should only build when your scene has grown so complicated that you anticipate having spikes of rendering time. But if that's you, then timewarp will help.

6.5   *Dynamic framebuffer scaling*

When inspection of your application shows that you're not producing frames quickly enough, it's important to make changes to try to meet your frame rate requirements.

Many rendering engines have multiple options for scaling the rendering load, such as different levels of quality for shadowing or antialiasing, or different levels of texture quality. These options aren't necessarily the kinds of things that are easy to change from frame to frame, though. Even if they were, they tend to have visible effects on the rendered scene and aren't likely to have much fine tuning. If you're only missing your rendering time by 2 percent, ideally you'd want some dial in your rendering engine that could reduce the load by exactly that amount, while maintaining as much quality and stability in the scene as possible.

In fact, there *is* just such a dial. Most high-end rendering systems tend to be bottle-necked in the fragment processing, texture bandwidth, or framebuffer bandwidth portions of the rendering pipeline. Any such bottleneck will be susceptible to rendering fewer overall pixels.

Because the Oculus SDK functions by rendering scenes to offscreen buffer(s), you can easily dial down the load at any time by rendering to a smaller offscreen viewport.

In fact, the SDK appears to have been designed specifically to make this easy. Let's take a look at an example that allows the user to directly control the scaling effect. In this application you'll have two keys, HOME and END, that modify the texture scaling. Each press of the END key will halve the total number of pixels rendered, whereas HOME will double the total number of pixels rendered, up to the maximum of using the full size of the offscreen framebuffer.

Figure 6.6 **Our scene rendered at full resolution**

As with timewarp, the effects of dynamic framebuffer scaling are only perceptible over time, so a static screenshot won't give you any real impression of what's happening. Again, we've created a YouTube video to demonstrate the effect, located here: goo.gl/ KsAFRQ. Because the effect is tied to the resolution of the output, it's best to watch the video at its full 1920 × 1080 resolution.

Still, we can show a bit of the difference in image quality at various levels of scaling. Our basic scene consists of our standard cube, floor, and skybox that we've used before (figure 6.6). This image is captured at the full resolution we've been using up to now.

You can compare a close-up view of the original resolution to one-sixteenth the original resolution (figure 6.7).

Figure 6.7 **When you compare a close-up of the original resolution (left) with a view one-sixteenth of the original resolution (right), you can see that the image quality is significantly degraded.**

The following listing shows the example code required to adjust the "resolution dial."

Listing 6.2 Dynamic framebuffer scaling example: adjusting the "resolution dial"

```
class DynamicFramebufferScaleExample : public RiftApp {     ⟵  The base class
  float ipd{ OVR_DEFAULT_IPD };                                   is RiftApp.
  float eyeHeight{ OVR_DEFAULT_PLAYER_HEIGHT };
  float texRes{ 1.0f };                              ⟵

public:                                               Indicates the percentage
  DynamicFramebufferScaleExample() {                  of the viewport to which
    ipd = ovrHmd_GetFloat(hmd,                        you'll render.
        OVR_KEY_IPD,
        OVR_DEFAULT_IPD);

    eyeHeight = ovrHmd_GetFloat(hmd,
        OVR_KEY_PLAYER_HEIGHT,
        OVR_DEFAULT_PLAYER_HEIGHT);

    resetCamera();
  }

  virtual void onKey(int key, int scancode, int action, int mods) {
    if (!CameraControl::instance().onKey(key, scancode, action, mods)) {
      static const float ROOT_2 = sqrt(2.0f);
      static const float INV_ROOT_2 = 1.0f / ROOT_2;
      if (action == GLFW_PRESS) {
        switch (key) {
        case GLFW_KEY_HOME:                                   HOME and
          if (texRes < 0.95f) {                               END modify
            texRes = std::min(texRes * ROOT_2, 1.0f);         the texture
          }                                                   resolution.
          break;
        case GLFW_KEY_END:
          if (texRes > 0.05f) {
            texRes *= INV_ROOT_2;
          }
          break;
        case GLFW_KEY_R:
          resetCamera();
          break;
        }
      } else {
        RiftApp::onKey(key, scancode, action, mods);
      }
    }
  }

  void resetCamera() {
    player = glm::inverse(glm::lookAt(
        glm::vec3(0, eyeHeight, 0.4),  // Position of the camera
        glm::vec3(0, eyeHeight, 0),    // Where the camera is looking
        GlUtils::Y_AXIS));             // Camera up axis
    ovrHmd_RecenterPose(hmd);
  }
```

```
void renderScene() {
  int currentEye = getCurrentEye();
  ovrTexture & eyeTex = eyeTextures[currentEye];
  ovrRecti & rvp = eyeTex.Header.RenderViewport;
  const ovrSizei & texSize = eyeTex.Header.TextureSize;
  rvp.Size.w = texSize.w * texRes;
  rvp.Size.h = texSize.h * texRes;

  glViewport(
      rvp.Pos.x, rvp.Pos.y,
      rvp.Size.w, rvp.Size.h);

  glEnable(GL_DEPTH_TEST);
  glClear(GL_DEPTH_BUFFER_BIT);
  gl::MatrixStack & mv = gl::Stacks::modelview();
  mv.withPush([&]{
    mv.postMultiply(glm::inverse(player));
    GlUtils::renderCubeScene(ipd, eyeHeight);
  });

  std::string message = Platform::format(
      "Texture Scale %0.2f\nMegapixels per eye: %0.2f", texRes,
      (rvp.Size.w * rvp.Size.h) / 1000000.0f);
  GlfwApp::renderStringAt(message, glm::vec2(-0.5f, 0.5f));
  }
};
```

Here you modify the offscreen texture based on texRes.

You also modify the viewport to which you'll render.

Prints out diagnostic information to the scene.

```
RUN_OVR_APP(DynamicFramebufferScaleExample);
```

The bulk of this example is similar to many of our earlier examples. But you're using a new base class, `RiftApp`, instead of `RiftGlfwApp`:

```
class DynamicFramebufferScaleExample : public RiftApp {
```

`RiftApp` takes care of all of the boilerplate you spent chapters 2 through 5 learning to write. In addition to the functionality that `RiftGlfwApp` and its base classes handle (detecting the Rift hardware, and creating the OpenGL windows in the right place), it handles the configuration of distortion rendering and the handling of the head tracker by applying the head pose to the `player` matrix. Classes deriving from `Rift-App` only need to define what kind of scene they want to render.

In this example you do slightly more than this minimum, because you want to handle user interaction in the form of key presses, and you also want to track your texture resolution:

```
float texRes{ 1.0f };
```

In addition to your usual member variables for eye height and IPD, you have a `texRes` member. This serves as a multiplication factor for the texture dimensions. It should be a number between 1.0 (meaning you're using the entire offscreen texture) and 0.0 (meaning you're rendering no pixels at all). Bear in mind that you use this multiplier with both the X and Y dimensions of the texture, so if you set it to 0.5, you're dividing both the height and width of the texture in half, and thus rendering only a quarter of the pixels, not half.

In your onKey() method, you're looking for presses of the HOME and END keys. The HOME key will increase the texRes value by a constant scale, up to a maximum of 1.0. The END key will decrease the texRes value by the inverse of that constant scale:

```
static const float ROOT_2 = sqrt(2.0f);
static const float INV_ROOT_2 = 1.0f / ROOT_2;
```

Choosing the square root of 2 means that whenever you hit END, you'll halve the total number of pixels rendered, and every time you hit HOME, you'll double the number of pixels (up to the maximum value). This is a bit of a brute-force approach to modifying the resolution and is intended simply to demonstrate the technique. In practice, an application would want to adjust this value by a percentage tied to the gap between their rendering performance target and their current actual performance.

Finally, there's the renderScene() method, which includes the changes required to apply the texture scaling. Here you'll use the value of texRes combined with the size of the offscreen framebuffer to determine the size of the area to which you'll render. The current eye being rendered and the OVR texture types are exposed in the eyeTextures member of the base class, which is an array of type ovrTexture:

```
int currentEye = getCurrentEye();
ovrTexture & eyeTex = eyeTextures[currentEye];
ovrRecti & rvp = eyeTex.Header.RenderViewport;
const ovrSizei & texSize = eyeTex.Header.TextureSize;
rvp.Size.w = texSize.w * texRes;
rvp.Size.h = texSize.h * texRes;
```

By doing this calculation and storing the results in the ovrTexture Header.RenderViewport member, the SDK has implicitly been told the region to which you'll be rendering. The only remaining part is to update your rendering viewport so that you actually target that region of the framebuffer:

```
glViewport(
    rvp.Pos.x, rvp.Pos.y,
    rvp.Size.w, rvp.Size.h);
```

In your applications, you may find it more intuitive to have the scaling factor be a direct percentage, but if you do this, be sure to multiply the texture dimensions by its square root rather than the number itself, or you'll find your image quality degrading faster than you expect.

The final bit of new code is some additional rendering logic, which renders a string containing both the texRes value and the number of megapixels being rendered.

6.6 *Summary*

In this chapter you learned

- The performance of your VR app is a critical component key to its success or failure, far more so than in conventional applications, meaning you have higher performance requirements, stricter performance requirements, and higher rendering costs than for more conventional applications.
- In VR, the *maximum* allowable latency (the interval between the time the user moves their head and the time when the view is updated) is considered to be about 20 ms.
- In VR, short-term frame rate drops are disastrous. Missing even a single frame of rendering will result in a pause or flicker that's both perceptible to the user and extremely damaging to the sense of presence and can even induce motion sickness.
- Your app's frame rate should be equal to the native refresh rate of the Rift display. This is 60 Hz for the DK1 and 75 Hz for the DK2.
- There are two main Rift-specific tools for coping with performance problems: timewarp and dynamic framebuffer scaling:
  - Timewarp helps your application appear to continue smoothly even if the rendering pipeline is falling behind on the required number of frames per second.
  - Dynamic framebuffer scaling helps reduce the overall load on your rendering pipeline by reducing the number of pixels you need to render.
  - Timewarp and dynamic framebuffer scaling, though useful on their own, work best when used in conjunction.

Part 3

Using Unity

In these two chapters, we cover how to use Unity, a popular development IDE and 3D graphics engine, to develop Rift applications. Unity is a great way to jump-start creating 3D games because it handles just about every aspect of game development, such as graphics, audio, physics, interaction, and networking. Along with the Unity Integration package from Oculus, you can quickly get your application running on the Rift. You can even do so without having to write a single script! Unity makes it easy to get an application running on the Rift, and it has the power you need to create fully immersive and playable applications.

Chapter 7 covers obtaining and using the Oculus Integration package to create Unity applications that can run on the Rift.

Chapter 8 covers creating VR applications that take into account some of nuances of being in a VR environment.

Unity: creating applications that run on the Rift

This chapter covers

- Creating scenes that can be run on the Rift
- Adding the Oculus Unity 4 Integration package to your project
- Using the Oculus prefab player controller and prefab stereo camera
- Building your application as a full screen standalone application

Unity is a game development IDE and cross-platform 3D graphics engine developed by Unity Technologies. Unity is a popular game engine and so we're sure that some of you are thinking, "I don't want to parse the head tracker data or do the rendering for the Rift myself in C++. I'm a Unity developer. I want to know how to create Rift applications using Unity." If that sounds like we're reading your mind, this chapter is for you.

Unity handles just about every aspect of game development, such as graphics, audio, physics, interactions, and networking. Developing for the Rift adds two new tasks to the process: using the head tracker data to change the point of view and properly rendering stereo images to the display. That's where the Oculus Unity 4 Integration package comes in. It includes a stereo camera prefab, that, when used in place of the typical single camera in a scene, handles both of those tasks for you.

> **NOTE** Prefabs are reusable game objects stored in your Project view. Prefabs allow you to define an object and reuse it as many times as you want in a scene. When a prefab is added to a scene, the prefab in the scene is an *instance* of the original prefab—essentially a clone of the prefab in your Project view. Any changes you make to the prefab in the Project view will be applied to every instance of the prefab in your scene.

In addition, to give you an example of how to use the stereo camera prefab with a character controller, the Integration package includes a player controller prefab that incorporates the stereo camera prefab with a first-person character controller. With the Oculus player controller prefab, you can even create a navigable Rift application without doing any scripting of your own.

---

[1] As this book was going to press, native VR support was added to Unity 5.1. To use the Oculus Unity 4 Integration package with Unity 5.1, in your project's Player Settings, ensure that the Virtual Reality Supported check box is unchecked.

In this chapter, we'll show you how to use Unity and the Oculus Unity Integration package to create a simple scene that can be run on the Rift. The basic steps are

1 Create a project and scene in Unity.
2 Import the Oculus Unity Integration package into your project's assets.
3 Use the Oculus player controller prefab (OVRPlayerController) or the Oculus stereo camera prefab (OVRCameraRig) with a custom character controller in your scene.

We'll be covering these steps in detail in the following sections along with using data from the user's profile in your application and building your application as a full-screen standalone application for testing and distribution.

Working without a Rift

Using Unity and the Oculus Unity Integration package is a great way to start developing for the Rift, even before you have one. When building your VR application, you should include both a non-Rift player controller (and be sure to include using the mouse to control where the character looks, in both Project view and Y directions) and a Rift player controller. Then, by enabling and disabling the appropriate player controllers, you can easily test-run your application with and without the Rift attached. We'll be pointing out best practices as we go, along with some problems that are only visible when viewed on the Rift, so with good planning you can avoid some unpleasant surprises.

Although our complete example scenes are available on our GitHub repository in the examples/unity directory, we recommend that you create your own project and a similar scene to work with. We'll be going over all of the steps needed to create each scene, and by doing each step as we go, you'll be sure to get a solid grip on using the Oculus Integration package. Start by downloading the Unity 4 Integration package from developer.oculusvr.com. It's not the smallest of downloads (274 MB), so while that download is in progress, you can start creating a scene of your own.

7.1 Creating a basic Unity project for the Rift

You add Rift support to a Unity project from within a scene, so to get started you'll need a project and a scene to work with. If you want to see the Rift in action, for a bare minimum scene all you need is a plane to move around on, a light to see by, and some simple objects to give you something to look at.

An important caveat about creating scenes for the Rift, even for a bare minimum scene, is that virtual size matters!

7.1.1 Use real-life scale for Rift scenes

By default, the units in Unity are meters, and one Unity unit represents one meter in space.[2] When creating a scene for the Rift, you'll find it's best to design the scene to

---

[2] This is a common convention in OpenGL and many other 3D platforms as well.

scale, and there are two excellent reasons for doing so. First, all components in the Oculus Integration package were created to scale, and it'll save you time and customization to already have a world where these components fit. For example, the default character controller in the Oculus Integration package is 2 units (meters) tall and you can't simply stick a 2-meter-tall character into a 10-centimeter-tall world. And, although character size may seem easily adjusted, it's not the only adjustment you'd need to make. You'd also have to update the stereo camera parameters for your one-tenth scale world to look correct. Second, VR worlds designed to scale are more comfortable for players to use and can help curb motion sickness, which is an important issue to consider when creating VR.

> **Creating comfortable virtual environments**
> Designing to scale isn't the only thing you can do to reduce motion sickness. Using darker textures, avoiding objects that flicker (including skinny objects that can flicker unintentionally), and using elevators rather than stairs are all things that can help. For a more complete description of what you can do, see chapter 10.

Now that you know what the bare minimum scene requirements are, let's build a scene to work with.

7.1.2   *Creating an example scene*

For the scenes used in this chapter, we didn't want to be someone who does only the bare minimum. So, for each of the scenes in our example project, we used assets from the Unity 5 Environment asset package to add flair and to create a more pleasant scene[3] to view—a sandy beach with palm trees (figure 7.1).

To create a similar scene, create a new project and new scene. Be sure to include the standard Unity package needed to create your scene (Environment) and to select 3D for the project type. After the project has been created, to create a scene like the one in figure 7.1 complete the following steps:

1   Add a plane[4] for the character to stand on. Use a 10 × 10 plane positioned at the origin point (GameObject > 3D Object > Plane, Transform - Scale – 10 × 1 × 10) to give yourself room to roam around and rename this object Beach.

2   Add a Directional Light set above the scene so you can see where you're going (GameObject > Light > Directional Light). Set the Transform position Y to 30 to move it up and out of the way.

3   Dress the scene up a bit using the sand and palm assets from the Unity standard assets. To add a sky, select Window > Lighting and drag a skybox material onto the Skybox Material slot in the Inspector.

---

[3]   During testing, using darker textures, rather than an all-white scene, caused fewer headaches.

[4]   A plane has no volume and scale doesn't work on the Y axis; therefore, the Y value is typically set to 1. Planes are single-sided objects and the orientation can be changed by setting Y to a negative value (-1).

Figure 7.1   Our sample game scene

With the scene ready, the next step is to import the Oculus Integration package into the project.

7.2   *Importing the Oculus Unity 4 Integration package*

If you haven't already done so, download the Unity 4 Integration ZIP file from developer.oculusvr.com. Extract the contents of the file to a stable location; these are the Oculus resources you'll be using in Unity. While you're there, the download also includes a handy Integration Guide, OculusUnityIntegrationGuide.pdf, that's worth a read.

To import the Oculus Unity Integration package into your project, complete the following steps:

1   From the top menu, under Assets choose Import Package > Custom Package.
2   Find the OculusUnityIntegration folder that you extracted and select Oculus-UnityIntegration.unitypackage.

Alternatively, with Unity already running, you can navigate on your desktop to where you've unzipped the integration package and double-click OculusUnityIntegration.unitypackage directly or drag the package to the asset panel.

You'll now see a list of the items that'll be imported into your project (figure 7.2). For a complete description of these packages, see the OculusUnityIntegrationGuide .pdf that came with the OVR Unity download.

Click Import to add the packages into your project, and then be sure to save the changes.

After importing the Oculus Integration package, you should see an OVR directory and a Plugins directory added to your project's assets (figure 7.3).

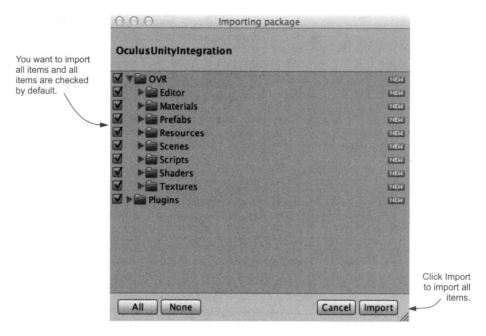

You want to import all items and all items are checked by default.

Click Import to import all items.

Figure 7.2   The Oculus packages to import into your project

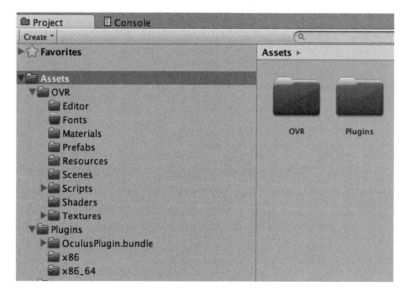

Figure 7.3   The OVR assets and plugins added to your project

If you look in the Assets > OVR > Prefabs folder, you'll see two prefabs: OVRCameraRig and OVRPlayerController:

- The OVRCameraRig prefab is a stereo camera that's used in place of a single Unity camera.
- The OVRPlayerController prefab is an OVRCameraRig prefab attached to a character controller.

These two prefabs are your fast-pass tickets to getting a Unity application running on the Rift.

7.3 Using the Oculus player controller prefab: getting a scene on the Rift, no scripting required

The Oculus player controller prefab, OVRPlayerController, is the easiest way to get a scene running on the Rift because it contains both a character controller and the Rift stereo camera. Let's look at how to use it in a scene, and then we'll take a closer look at the OVRPlayerController prefab itself to give you a better idea of what you can do to customize it for your needs.

7.3.1 Adding the OVRPlayerController prefab to your scene

The OVRPlayerController contains both a stereo camera and a character controller, so all you need to do to have a functioning Rift scene is add it to the scene. In our examples, Beach_OVRPlayerController is the completed scene using this prefab.

To add the OVRPlayerController prefab to your scene, complete the following steps:

1. Drag the OVRPlayerController prefab from the Project view onto the Scene view. The OVRPlayerController prefab can be found in Project view: choose Assets > OVR > Prefabs.
2. Reposition the OVRPlayerController to a good place in the scene. It should be located above the Beach and not colliding with any objects. The OVRPlayer-Controller prefab character controller has a default height of 2 units and a radius of 0.5 units. The position is the center of the capsule, so you should set the Transform Position Y to 1 so that the OVRPlayerController is positioned above the Beach.
3. Remove or disable any other cameras and audio listeners you might have in the scene. Warning! You'll get an error if there's more than one audio listener in the scene. Both the default main camera and the OVRCameraRig prefab contain audio listeners.

You can give this scene a test run.

7.3.2 *Doing a test run: the Unity editor workflow for Rift applications*

For quick iteration, you'll want to be able to run applications in the Unity editor. To run Rift applications in the Unity editor[5] with the Rift attached, do the following:

1 Have your monitors configured for Extended mode.
2 Grab the Game view from the editor and drag it onto the Rift display (the extended portion of your screen).
3 Click the maximize button on the top right of the game window (to the left of the X button) to switch to full screen.

This method can work for quick iteration, but for your comfort, you should build a standalone app for testing. We'll cover how later in this chapter.

Headache warning! Maximize On Play isn't full screen
When testing your game in the Unity editor, using Maximize On Play will maximize the Game view to 100 percent of your editor window, *which isn't quite full screen.* Because the editor window borders are on the game window, you'll still lose a small percentage of the screen to desktop elements. This reduction means the alignment is slightly off, and it also means you aren't seeing the actual scale. Both of these side effects can lead to major headaches. Although using Maximize On Play is a quick way to iterate, for a better and more comfortable testing environment do a standalone build for each test run; see section 7.6.

The first thing you should see when running the application is the Oculus health and safety warning (figure 7.4).

This health and safety warning is automatically included in every Rift application you build. To dismiss this warning, you can press any key. You should now be able to wander the beach and look around (figure 7.5).

Looking down, you'll see that you're a floating head in space—you don't have a body or a static reference point. This can be disorientating for many users, and you can help curb motion sickness in your applications by providing your character with the option to have a body or other static reference point. For more ideas on how to prevent motion sickness, see chapter 10.

You can navigate the scene using the W, A, S, D keys on a QWERTY keyboard and mouse controls, or a connected game controller.[6]

Now that you've seen the OVRPlayerController prefab in action, let's look at the Prefab itself to get a better idea of how it works.

---

[5] This workflow is for Windows development. For Mac users, for quick tests, we found it easiest to run in mirrored mode and select Build And Run from the File menu. Note that there are significant quality issues with mirrored mode, and you may need to build and then launch the application using extended mode to get a usable test run.

[6] XInput-compliant gamepads aren't supported on Mac OS.

Figure 7.4   The Oculus health and safety warning

Figure 7.5   The beach scene on the Rift

7.3.3   *The OVRPlayerController prefab components*

If you look at the OVRPlayerController prefab in Hierarchy view (figure 7.6), you can see that it consists of the OVRPlayerController object and the child objects:[7] ForwardDirection and the OVRCameraRig prefab.

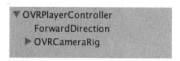

Figure 7.6   The OVRPlayer-Controller prefab hierarchy

The OVRPlayerController object itself is a *character controller* with two C# scripts attached (figure 7.7) that handle character movement.

You can see in the Inspector that the default value for the CharacterController Height is 2 and the Radius is 0.5. This means that the character will take up a capsule-shaped space that's 2 meters high and 1 meter in diameter. When designing your VR world, keep this size in mind so that you can be sure to give your character enough space to comfortably move around without unintentionally colliding with other objects.

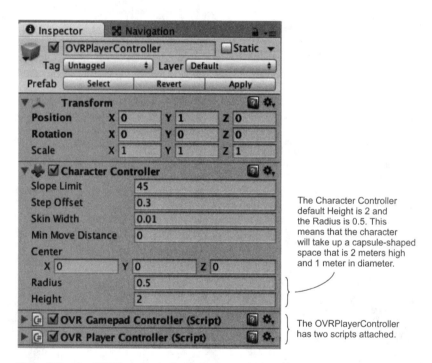

The Character Controller default Height is 2 and the Radius is 0.5. This means that the character will take up a capsule-shaped space that is 2 meters high and 1 meter in diameter.

The OVRPlayerController has two scripts attached.

Figure 7.7   The OVRPlayerController in the Inspector panel

---

[7]   The Unity hierarchy allows you to connect objects with parent-child relationships. To make an object the child of another object, in the Hierarchy view, drag the GameObject you want to be the child onto the GameObject you want to be the parent. This defines the relationship. The parent-child relationship is important because all changes to the parent's Transform (move, scale, or rotate) are applied to its children as well.

The two C# scripts attached to the OVRPlayer-Controller prefab are OVRPlayerController.cs and OVRGamepadController.cs. These two scripts can be found in Project view: choose Assets > OVR > Scripts > Util. The OVRPlayerController.cs and OVRGamepadController.cs scripts allow you to navigate the scene using the W, A, S, D keys and mouse controls or a connected game controller. A complete description of the control layout and supported game controllers can be found in the OculusUnityIntegrationGuide.pdf, which can be found in the Unity 4 Integration package.

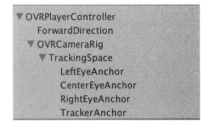

Figure 7.8   The OVRPlayerController prefab hierarchy

Let's now turn our attention to the child objects: ForwardDirection and the OVR-CameraRig prefab (figure 7.8).

The ForwardDirection game object only contains the matrix that determines motor control direction. As we mentioned when testing the OVRPlayerController, when you look down you don't have a body. Being just a floating head in space can be disorienting, and we recommend giving your player the option of having a character body to look at. If you choose to give your character a body, the ForwardDirection game object is a convenient location to put the body geometry.

The OVRCameraRig prefab is the head and eyes of the Oculus Integration package. It includes stereo camera anchor transforms (LeftEyeAnchor and RightEye-Anchor) and a transform for the spot between both eyes (CenterEyeAnchor) all organized under a TrackingSpace object. The attached scripts handle the image processing for proper display on the Rift and using the head tracker data to change the user's point of view. This prefab can be used independently of the OVRPlayerController. We'll cover its use, structure, and attached scripts in the next section.

7.4   Using the Oculus stereo camera prefab: getting a scene on the Rift using your own character controller

If you find that the OVRPlayerController controls don't meet the needs of your application, you can use the OVRCameraRig prefab with your own custom controller to get a scene on the Rift. The OVRCameraRig prefab serves as the head and eyes of the Oculus Integration package. It provides a stereo camera and the scripts for proper display to the Rift, and it handles the head tracker data to change the user's point of view.

First we'll look at how to use the OVRCameraRig prefab with a basic character controller. Then we'll dig into the details of the OVRCameraRig prefab itself to help you get a better idea of what adjustments to the prefab's default values you can make to create a more comfortable experience for your users and to see what options it provides that you can take advantage of to create a better character controller.

To use the OVRCameraRig prefab in your scene, you need to attach it to a moving object, such as a character controller. For our example, you'll take these steps:

1 Create a scene.
2 Add a character controller to the scene.
3 Add the OVRCameraRig prefab to the character controller.
4 Change the MouseLook script for a more comfortable Rift environment.

The next sections will walk you through these steps.

CREATE A SCENE

You can't have two character controllers in the same scene, so you'll need to create a new scene for this example. You can use the same basic scene that you used for the OVRPlayerController; the basic scene requirements are the same. For a simple way to create the new scene, save a copy of the OVRPlayerController scene and then delete the OVRPlayerController prefab from the scene.

ADD A CHARACTER CONTROLLER

In this example you're going to use a character controller capsule with the Character-Motor.js, FPSInputController.js, and MouseLook.cs scripts,[8] which can be obtained from our GitHub repository.

> **Why not use the FirstPersonController.cs script that comes with Unity 5?**
> Unity 5 included a significant refresh of the standard asset packages. These updates included adding a number of options to the first-person controller script, such as footstep sounds, head bob, and FOV kick. These options can be great in traditional games, but for VR they can be rather problematic. Head bob and FOV kick are particularly concerning because these types of motion can be severe motion sickness triggers for some users. For that reason, we've chosen not to use the first-person controller script from Unity 5. For more information about motion sickness and what you can do about it, see chapter 10.

To add this character controller to your scene, complete the following steps:

1 Add an empty GameObject to your scene and rename it `Player` to make it easier to keep track of it.
2 Under the GameObject menu, select Create Empty.
3 Add a character controller to the Player game object and adjust the Transform Position setting of the Player object so that it's located above the Beach plane and not colliding with any objects.

---

[8] These scripts are from the standard Unity 4.6 Character Controller assets package but have been updated for the Unity 5 API.

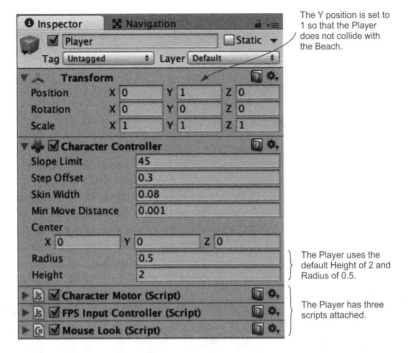

The Y position is set to 1 so that the Player does not collide with the Beach.

The Player uses the default Height of 2 and Radius of 0.5.

The Player has three scripts attached.

Figure 7.9   The Player character controller expanded in the Inspector

4 From the Component menu, select Physics > Character Controller. The default height for the character controller is 2, so for the Transform setting of the Player object, set Y Position to 1 to reposition the Player object so that it's not colliding with the Beach.

5 Add the CharacterMotor.js, FPSInputController.js and MouseLook.cs control scripts to your Player capsule. Simply drag the scripts onto your Player (figure 7.9). If you don't have these assets, these scripts can be found on our GitHub repository.

You now have a character controller, called Player, in your scene (figure 7.9). If you want to test this setup with a single camera, add a camera to the player as a child object and do a test run, but be sure to remove the single camera before adding the OVRCameraRig prefab.

ADD THE OVRCAMERARIG PREFAB TO THE CHARACTER CONTROLLER

With the character controller and scripts in place, you can now add the Rift stereo cameras to the Player. To add the OVRCameraRig to your scene, grab the OVRCamera-Rig prefab from the Project View in Assets > OVR > Prefabs and add it as a child of your Player, as seen in figure 7.10.

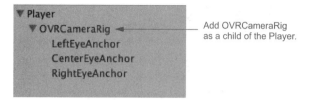

Figure 7.10 The OVRCameraRig added as a child of the Player in the scene hierarchy

If you haven't already done so, you should disable or delete any other character controllers and cameras in the scene, such as the OVRPlayerController we used in the previous section, or the main default camera if you're using a new scene. Go ahead and give the scene a test run. You will see the health and safety warning first. After you press any key to dismiss it, you should see your beach scene (figure 7.11).

Figure 7.11 The scene displayed in the Rift

You should be able to move the character around, but you may notice that using the mouse allows you to look in every direction, which can be very uncomfortable. The mouse cursor is still visible but only to one eye, which can also be quite annoying. To prevent these two issues, you need to make adjustments to the MouseLook.cs script for use with the Rift.

If you're testing with a Rift attached, set Axes to MouseX. If you're testing without a Rift attached, set it to MouseXAndY.

Figure 7.12   The MouseLook script in the Player Inspector

CHANGE THE MOUSELOOK SCRIPT FOR USE WITH THE RIFT

You can make two simple changes to the MouseLook.cs script to create a more comfortable environment on the Rift. First, you should set the axes for the mouse rotation appropriate to your testing environment. If you're testing with a Rift attached, we recommend setting Axes to MouseX because you'll be using the Rift to look in all directions. If testing without a Rift, we recommend setting it to MouseXAndY so that you can use the mouse to look in all directions. Second, you should hide the mouse cursor. To make these changes, complete the following steps:

1   In the Player Inspector for the MouseLook script (figure 7.12), set Axes to MouseX.

2   In the MouseLook.cs script, edit the `Start()` function by adding the following line to hide the mouse cursor:

```
Cursor.lockState = CursorLockMode.Locked;
Cursor.visible = false;
```

3   Give it a test run.

You should now be able to navigate the scene and use the mouse to rotate only on the X axis. The mouse cursor should no longer be visible.

If you tested both the OVRPlayerController and the Unity Standard Player controller, you might have noticed that the default player speeds for OVRPlayerController are much slower than those in the Standard Unity Player controller. Character speed plays a big part in how comfortable the VR environment you're creating is, and in general, you want to use real-world speed and abilities. Again, for more information about motion sickness and what you can do about it, see chapter 10.

Now that you've seen OVRCameraRig in action, let's take a closer look at the OVRCameraRig prefab components to get a better idea of how it works and to see what other options are available.

7.4.1   *The OVRCameraRig prefab components*

If you click the OVRCameraRig prefab in the Hierarchy view, you can see that it consists of an OVRCameraRig object and four child objects: LeftEyeAnchor, CenterEyeAnchor, RightEyeAnchor, and TrackerAnchor (figure 7.13) under a TrackingSpace container object.

Let's start by looking at the OVRCameraRig object and its attached scripts (figure 7.14).

Figure 7.13   The OVRCameraRig hierarchy

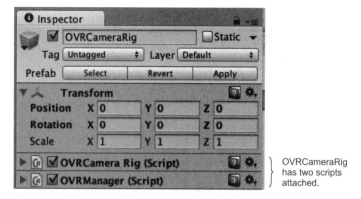

Figure 7.14   OVRCameraRig expanded in the Inspector

As you can see in figure 7.14, OVRCameraRig has two C# scripts attached: OVRCamera-Rig.cs and OVRManager.cs. These scripts can be found in the Project View in Assets > OVR > Scripts.

The OVRManager script is the main interface between Unity and the Rift hardware. It references the low-level C API (Ovrcapi.cs) HMD wrapper, the display manager (OVRDisplay.cs), and the tracker (OVRTracker.cs). Basically, this script performs the heavy lifting of working with the Rift, because it does much of the work detailed in chapters 2 through 5 of this book, including initializing the Oculus SDK, getting an instance of the HMD, getting the tracker data, and properly rendering to the display.

NOTE   This script allows you to change the Rift reset values. It should be declared only once.

Let's take a look at the public values (figure 7.15).

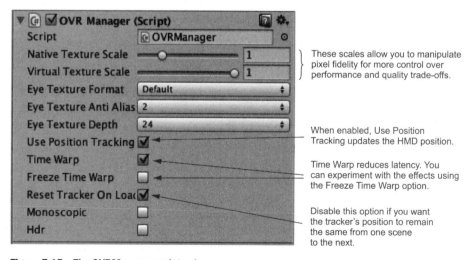

Figure 7.15   The OVRManager script values

Figure 7.16　The OVRCameraRig script expanded in the Inspector

The OVRCameraRig script is the interface between Unity and the cameras, and it's where all camera control should be done. This script has no public values (figure 7.16).

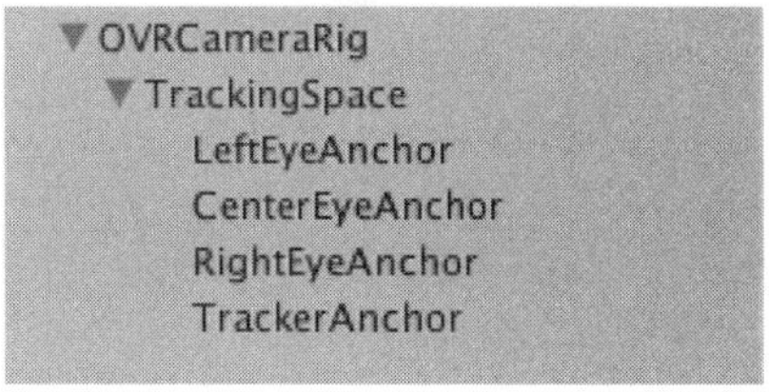

Let's now look at LeftEyeAnchor, CenterEyeAnchor, and RightEyeAnchor, child objects attached to OVRCameraRig in the Tracking-Space container object (figure 7.17).

```
▼ OVRCameraRig
   ▼ TrackingSpace
       LeftEyeAnchor
       CenterEyeAnchor
       RightEyeAnchor
       TrackerAnchor
```

Figure 7.17　The OVRCameraRig hierarchy

These child objects contain transforms for the poses of the left and right eyes, as well as the transform for the pose halfway between the eyes.

As you might surmise, both LeftEyeAnchor and RightEyeAnchor contain Unity camera objects. These are the cameras that provide the views for the left and right eyes (figure 7.18).

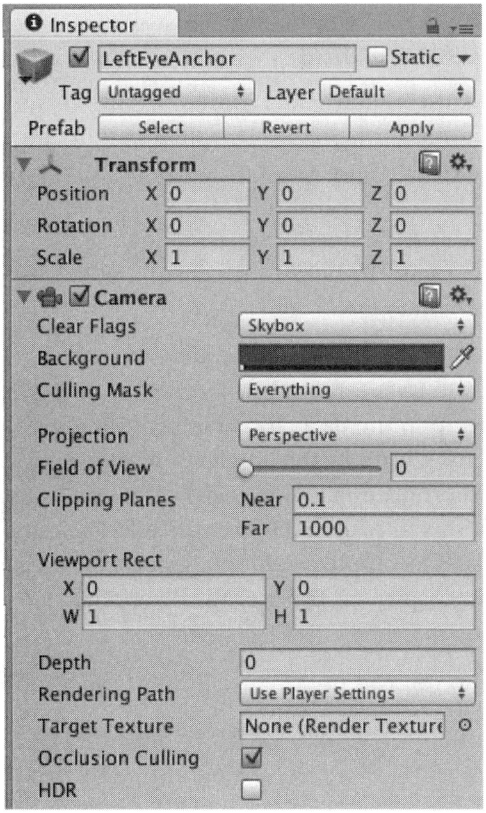

Figure 7.18　LeftEyeAnchor expanded in the Inspector.

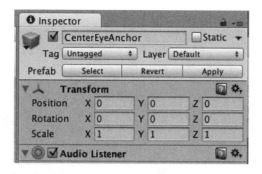

Figure 7.19   CenterEyeAnchor expanded in the Inspector

The CenterEyeAnchor object contains a transform and an audio listener (figure 7.19), but it doesn't contain a camera.

Why have a CenterEyeAnchor? Knowing the exact position between the eyes will make it easier to determine what the user is looking at. That position will come in handy when creating a UI—something we'll cover in the next chapter.

The distance between the cameras (LeftEyeAnchor and RightEyeAnchor) is set by the Oculus scripts to be the user's IPD (the distance between their eyes, as you'll recall). Let's take a closer look at this value and where it comes from.

7.5   Using player data from the user's profile

Included in the Oculus Runtime is the Oculus Configuration tool. This tool allows users to create a personal profile with information such as their height and their IPD. If the user hasn't created a user profile using the Oculus Configuration tool, the default values are used.

Setting the distance between the virtual stereo cameras to the user's actual IPD can help curb motion sickness for your users. To help your users have the best possible experience, you should encourage them to create a profile.

7.5.1   Ensuring the user has created a profile

Creating a user profile is ultimately up to the user. To encourage the user to create a profile, stress the importance of setting it up in the application's documentation. Be sure to cover exactly how to set up a profile and why it needs to be done. Documentation is a good start, but relying on users to read and follow the documentation, something we all know many won't do, isn't a complete solution. You can also check to see if a profile has been created, and if not, prompt the user to create one.

KNOWING WHICH PROFILE IS BEING USED

To learn which profile is being used, you can use the GetString() method found in the OVRManager.cs script:

```
public string GetString(string propertyName, string defaultVal = null)
```

Listing 7.1 shows a simple example of using this method to print the name of the current user profile to the console log. You can test this script by attaching it to an empty game object in a scene that's using the OVRCameraRig or OVRPlayerController prefab. With the Rift attached, run the scene in the Unity editor. If `default` is returned, no user profile has been found.

> **Listing 7.1 report.cs: printing the current user profile name to the console log**

```
using UnityEngine;
using System.Collections;
using Ovr;                                                Prints the name of the
                                                          current user profile to
public class report : MonoBehaviour {                        the console log
    void Start () {
      Debug.Log (OVRManager.capiHmd.GetString(Hmd.OVR_KEY_USER, ""));   ◁─┘
    }
}
```

The `GetString()` method found in the OVRManager.cs script method is used to get the profile values for the current HMD. The OVRManager.cs script gets a reference to the current HMD, `capiHmd`. The `Hmd` class, defined in OvrCapi.cs, provides a number of constants that you can use to get user profile information for the current HMD. This example used `OVR_KEY_USER` to get the profile name. You could also get the user's height (`OVR_KEY_PLAYER_HEIGHT`), IPD (`OVR_KEY_IPD`), or gender (`OVR_KEY_GENDER`).

Knowing which profile is in use is a start, but printing it to the console won't help your users. They won't be able to see it or know what it means. For it to be useful to the user, you need to present this information in a reasonable way—and that means building a UI for your VR application. UI for VR is big topic on its own, and we'll be covering UI design in the next chapter.

7.6 *Building your application as a full screen standalone application*

As we mentioned after the first test run, using Maximize On Play in the Unity editor, though quick and easy, isn't a great way to test the application because it isn't exactly full screen. Because it's less than full screen, the scale is slightly off and the alignment may also be off. Combined, these two issues can make testing uncomfortable. In addition, when using the editor for testing, you'll need to use Extended mode[9] for your monitor setup, which means you won't be able to see what's displayed on the Rift without putting it on. For a better testing environment, you'll want to do a standalone

---

[9] Mac users can use mirrored mode, but application performance suffers significantly. In particular, scene judder—the whole view jittering as you look around—occurs when the application's frame rate falls below 75 FPS. If you want to use mirrored mode, you can try setting your display's refresh rate to 60 Hz. Though this results in screen blur rather than judder, we found this to be less headache inducing and that being able to see what the person on the Rift is doing and the faster workflow were reasonable trade-offs for the performance hit while testing.

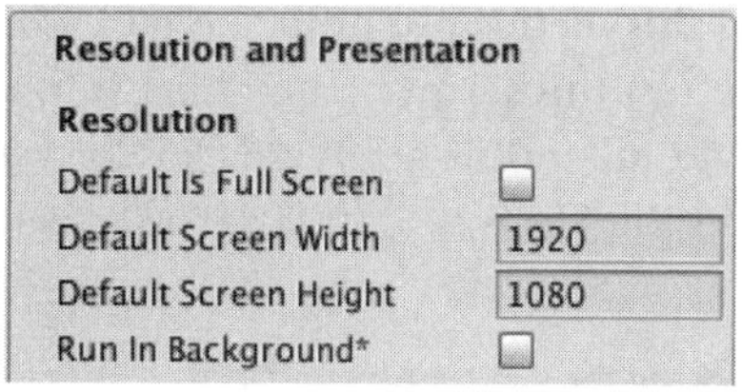

Resolution and Presentation	
Resolution	
Default Is Full Screen	☐
Default Screen Width	1920
Default Screen Height	1080
Run In Background*	☐

Figure 7.20   Player Project Resolution settings for a DK2 Rift in the Inspector

build for each test and you will, of course, also need to package the application as a standalone build for distribution.

To build the project as a standalone application, complete the following steps:

1   In the Project Settings, set the default screen resolution to that of the Rift. For the DK1 use 1280 × 800 and for the DK2 use 1920 × 1080 (see figure 7.20). Setting the screen resolution raises the odds that you'll default to what's present. Select Edit > Project Settings > Player.

2   In the Inspector for Player Settings under Resolution and Presentation, for a DK1 Rift uncheck Default Is Full Screen, and then set Default Screen Width to 1280 and Default Screen Height to 800; for a DK2 Rift, uncheck Default Is Full Screen, and then set Default Screen Width to 1920 and Default Screen Height to 1080, as seen in figure 7.20.

3   Select File > Build Settings from the main menu.

4   In the Build Settings window, select the appropriate Target Platform and Architecture settings for your build.

5   Click Build.

Building the application for Windows will create an <App>_ DirectToRift.exe Rift-specific binary and an <App>_Win.exe standard binary (along with the <App>_Win_Data folder). The <App>_Win_DirectToRift.exe binary produced by the build can be run in Direct to HMD mode. Using Direct to HMD mode will allow you to see what's on the Rift even when you aren't wearing the Rift (a very useful feature when testing). Although <App>_Win_DirectToRift.exe works in both Direct and Extended modes, you should still include the <App>_Win.exe in your final distribution.

When developing on/for Windows, you should avoid using File > Build & Run because it runs the standard binary and not the DirectToRift binary and therefore can't be used in Direct to HMD mode.

When developing on/for a Mac, we've found that File > Build & Run was sometimes a reasonable option. Mac applications can still be run in mirrored mode, although performance suffers. The advantage of being able to see what was on the Rift without wearing it and the turnaround time of simply selecting File > Build & Run to see the results of our changes often outweighed the performance hit.

7.7 *Summary*

In this chapter you learned that

- The OVRPlayerController and OVRCameraRig prefabs handle the Rift-specific development tasks of using the head tracker data to change the point of view and properly render stereo images to the display for you.

- The OVRPlayerController prefab can be used to create Rift-compatible applications without doing any scripting of your own.

- The OVRCameraRig prefab can be used with your own character controllers and scripts to create Rift-compatible applications.

- The OVRCameraRig prefab uses the player data gathered by the Oculus Configuration tool in your Unity applications, allowing you to create a better user experience. Encourage your users to create a profile.

- The OVRManager.cs script is the main interface between Unity and the Rift hardware. Basically, this script performs much of the work detailed in chapters 2 through 5 such as initializing the Oculus SDK, getting an instance of the HMD, getting the tracker data, and properly rendering to the display.

- The distance between the two cameras is set by the Oculus scripts to be the user's IPD—that is, the distance between their eyes.

- To know which profile is being used, you can use the `GetString()` method found in the OVRManager.cs script.

- Using Maximize On Play in the Unity editor isn't full screen, which can make testing uncomfortable. For a better testing environment, create a standalone build for each test.

- Building the application for Windows will create an <App>_ DirectToRift.exe Rift-specific binary and an <App>_Win.exe standard binary (along with the <App>_Win_Data folder). The <App>_Win_DirectToRift.exe binary produced by the build can be run in Direct to HMD mode.

- When developing on/for Windows, don't use File > Build & Run because it runs the standard binary and not the DirectToRift binary and therefore can't be used in Direct to HMD mode.

- When developing on/for a Mac, we've found that File Build & Run might be a reasonable option because Mac applications can be run in mirrored mode (although performance suffers).

Unity: tailoring your application for the Rift

This chapter covers

- Building a UI for VR
- Using Rift head tracking to interact with objects in a scene
- Easing the user into VR
- Improving performance and quality

Creating usable and immersive VR environments takes a lot more than simply getting your application running on the Rift. Being in a VR environment is different than using a traditional monitor, and those differences have some rather far-reaching implications for how you design your application's UI and how you determine performance and quality criteria. They'll even affect how you get the user into the application in the first place!

Looking at things from a Unity perspective

Many of the topics we're covering here are covered more broadly in chapters 9 and 10. This chapter will get you through the basics, but if you want to delve into any of the issues in more depth, we strongly recommend reading those two chapters as well.

Let's start by taking a look at how to create a basic UI for a Rift application.

8.1 Creating a Rift-friendly UI

One of the trickiest things to do in VR is create a GUI. Many of the GUIs we're familiar with are created as 2D overlays of 3D scenes. For a Rift application, a 2D overlay simply doesn't work. To be properly visible on the Rift, the GUI needs to be rendered to both the left and right cameras and it needs to have the Rift distortion applied. As of Unity 4.6, the Unity GUI tools provide the option of rendering the UI as part of the 3D scene (world space)—just what's needed for creating a GUI in VR.

8.1.1 Using the Unity GUI tools to create a UI

Let's say you wanted to have a timer that shows the user the elapsed time since starting the application in your beach scene, as seen in figure 8.1.

This is a simple GUI consisting of just a background box and a text label. To create this GUI, as with all GUIs using the Unity GUI system, you begin by adding a Canvas object to the project.

> **NOTE** A Canvas object is a Unity GameObject with a canvas component attached. All Unity UI elements must be child objects of a canvas. If you create a UI element and there is no existing canvas, a new one will be created. (You may have multiple canvases in a scene, too, which is a neat feature if you want to do something like speech bubbles for characters.)

By default, Canvas objects are rendered as a screen overlay. For the Rift, you need the canvas to be in world space.

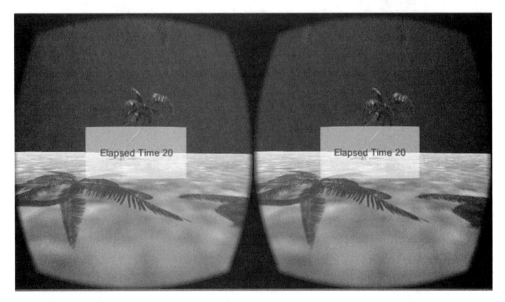

Figure 8.1   A simple GUI showing the elapsed seconds since the start of the application

CREATING A WORLD SPACE CANVAS

To add a canvas to your project, in the Hierarchy window select Create > UI > Canvas. This adds a Canvas object and an EventSystem object to your project (figure 8.2).

To change the Render Mode of a canvas to 3D space, in the Inspector for the canvas, set Render Mode to World Space (figure 8.3).

When you changed the Canvas Render Mode to World Space, you may have noticed that the Rect transform became editable.

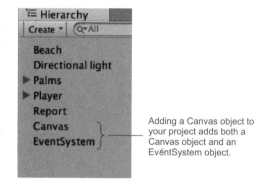

Adding a Canvas object to your project adds both a Canvas object and an EventSystem object.

Figure 8.2   Canvas object and an EventSystem object as seen in the project hierarchy

NOTE   Rect transforms are a special type of transform for GUI elements. In addition to position, rotation, and scale, Rect transforms have a width and height used to specify the dimensions of the rectangle.

The size of a screen space canvas is determined automatically to be the size of the screen, but for a world space canvas you need to set the size manually to something reasonable for your scene by editing the canvas Rect transform.

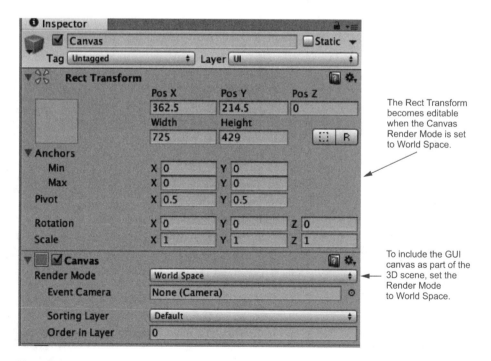

The Rect Transform becomes editable when the Canvas Render Mode is set to World Space.

To include the GUI canvas as part of the 3D scene, set the Render Mode to World Space.

Figure 8.3   Set Render Mode to World Space

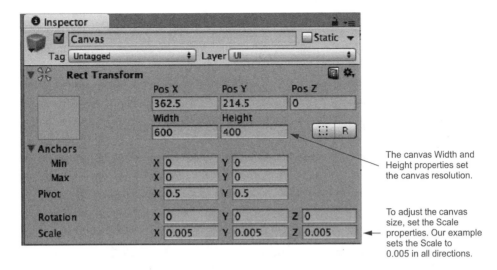

The canvas Width and Height properties set the canvas resolution.

To adjust the canvas size, set the Scale properties. Our example sets the Scale to 0.005 in all directions.

Figure 8.4   To set the canvas size, change the canvas Scale properties.

SETTING THE CANVAS TO A REASONABLE SIZE

Right now, the GUI takes up almost all of the user's view. If you look at the Inspector for the canvas (figure 8.4) you can see there are width and height properties and scale properties.

The height and width properties are pixel sizes and are used to set the canvas resolution. In our example we've set these to 600 and 400. If you're using graphics in your GUI, you'll want to set these to something that works well with your graphics. To change the canvas size, you need to set the canvas scale. You don't need a very large canvas, so set the canvas scale to 0.005 in all directions (figure 8.4).

POSITIONING THE CANVAS

Now that you have a world space canvas of a reasonable size, you need to position the canvas so that the user can see it. For our example, you want the GUI directly centered in front of the player and you want the GUI to move with the player. To do that, grab the Canvas object and make it a child of the CenterEyeAnchor object (figure 8.5).

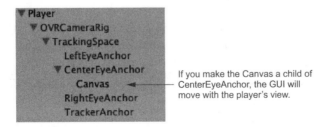

If you make the Canvas a child of CenterEyeAnchor, the GUI will move with the player's view.

Figure 8.5   As a child of the CenterEyeAnchor, the GUI will move with the player's view.

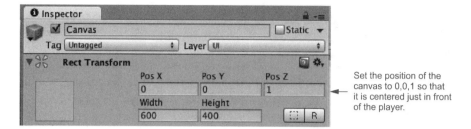

Figure 8.6 Position the Canvas object so that it's centered just in front of the player.

To adjust the position of the canvas so that it's just in front of the player, set the Rect transform for the canvas to 0,0,1 as shown in figure 8.6.

The GUI is now in a position where you should be able to see it. But you haven't added any GUI elements to the canvas, so there's not much to see.

SETTING UP THE GUI ELEMENTS

For this GUI you need a background box and a text label to display the elapsed seconds. To add these objects, in the Hierarchy window select Create > UI > Image and Create > UI > Image > Text. Both objects must be children of the Canvas object (figure 8.7).

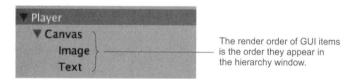

Figure 8.7 The order of UI elements in the Hierarchy window is important because it is the order the elements are rendered.

Note that the hierarchy order is important; the render order of GUI items is the order they appear in the Hierarchy window. If your Text object is above your Image object, when rendered the Image object will obscure your text.

For the Text object to display the elapsed time, you need to attach a script (Update-Timer.cs, shown in the following listing) to the Text object.

Listing 8.1 UpdateTimer.cs: displaying the elapsed time

```
using UnityEngine;
using UnityEngine.UI;          Adds the Unity UI
using System.Collections;      namespace
```

```
public class UpdateTimer : MonoBehaviour {

  Text elapsedTimeText;                    ◁⎯┐  Creates a UI
  private float startTime;                      │  Text variable
  private float elapsedTime;

  void Awake(){                                        ┐  Sets the variable to
    startTime = Time.time;                             │  your UI Text object
    elapsedTimeText = gameObject.GetComponent<Text>();  ◁⎯┘
  }

  void Update () {
    elapsedTime = Time.time - startTime;
    elapsedTimeText.text = "Elapsed Time " + elapsedTime.ToString("N0");   ◁⎯┐
  }                                                                             │  Updates
}                                                                          the UI text
```

If you test the application, you'll see that the UI is a bit messy. You can do a bit of styling in the Inspector for the UI elements to clean it up. In the Inspector for both objects, set the X, Y, Z positions of the Rect transform to 0. The text is aligned top-right by default. You can change the text alignment to center-middle and change the text style in the Inspector for the Text object. To allow the user to see what's behind the GUI, you can set the alpha level of the Image default color to allow some transparency.

GUI styling hints

We haven't done much styling for the GUI and as you can tell, this isn't a very readable GUI. For Rift applications, to help with readability, keep the following tips in mind when creating your own GUIs:

- *Menus can be read most easily when they are at the center of the screen*. When you look through the Rift, you'll notice that the closer the text is to the center of the view, the easier it is to read. The closer you get to the edge of the view, the more the distortion affects the view and the more difficult it is to read. Make sure you either place your menu near the center of the screen or allow the user to look directly at the menu.

- *Text should be readable without having to roll your eyes*. Anything that forces the user to move their eyes in their sockets rather than to move their head to look at something can cause significant eyestrain.

- *The Rift aspect ratio is different than that of a typical monitor*. If your UI assumes that the monitor is wider than it is high, as is the case for most typical monitors, directly porting such menus to the Rift may result in an unreadable menu, because the edges of the menu may no longer fit into the view.

The Unity GUI tools provide some great options for styling including making it easy to include animations. See the online Unity UI tutorials for more information: unity3d.com/learn/tutorials/modules/beginner/ui.

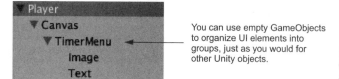

You can use empty GameObjects to organize UI elements into groups, just as you would for other Unity objects.

Figure 8.8   You can use empty GameObjects to organize UI elements in the hierarchy.

Most users would prefer to look at a beach than at a countdown timer, so let's give the user the option of dismissing the GUI.

TOGGLE GUI VISIBILITY

To toggle the GUI visibility, you can make the GUI elements inactive. You want to be able to easily toggle the visibility of both the text and the background, so you'll add an empty GameObject (renamed TimerMenu) to the canvas hierarchy and add both items as children of this object (figure 8.8).

The Unity GUI system allows integration with the Unity animation system. You can use the animation system to create some pretty fancy transitions for GUI elements,[1] but working with the animation system is beyond the scope of this book. So, for our example, you'll take the simple route and change the visibility by setting the container GameObject's active status (shown next). To use this script, attach it to your Canvas object.

Listing 8.2   ToggleMenu.cs

```
using UnityEngine;
using System.Collections;

public class ToggleMenu: MonoBehaviour {

  private bool displayTimer;
  private bool oldTimerKey;
  public GameObject timerMenu;

  void Start () {
      displayTimer = true;
      timerMenu = GameObject.Find("TimerMenu");
  }

  void Update () {
      bool timerKey = Input.GetKey(KeyCode.T);
```

---

[1] If you plan to use the animation system, you also need to add a Canvas group (Component > Layout > Canvas Group) to the GameObjects used for organization to be able to apply the animation effects to all child objects. A Canvas group has an Alpha property, and you can also toggle GUI visibility by changing this Alpha property.

```
    if (timerKey && !oldTimerKey){
        displayTimer = !displayTimer;
    }
    oldTimerKey= timerKey;

    if (displayTimer){
        timerMenu.SetActive (true);
    }else{
        timerMenu.SetActive (false);
    }
  }
}
```

For the timerMenu object used to group your UI elements, set active to true or false to toggle visibility.

The Unity GUI system is a great way to create traditional-style GUIs in VR, and though you'll probably find traditional GUIs very useful, one big drawback is that floating panels simply aren't very immersive. For a more immersive UI, you'll want to build the UI into your world.

8.1.2 Creating an in-world UI

When creating a UI for VR, ask yourself how immersive you want the experience to feel. In general, using conventional menus floating on a plane in between you and the VR world simply isn't very immersive. If immersion isn't a top priority for your application, a conventional-style GUI may work. If immersion is a goal, one way to achieve it is to build the UI into the VR world. For example, the timer GUI shown in the previous example could be a giant clock. Or perhaps for something a little easier to visualize, instead of a level menu, you could use an elevator with buttons (figure 8.9).

If you're getting the idea that you need to redesign your UI from the ground up for VR, you're on the right track. Chapter 9 goes into a lot more detail about what the current research has to say about UI for VR and provides great ideas for what you can do, most of which can be easily applied to applications created in Unity. One excellent technique for creating a more immersive UI for VR is to use the input you get from the Rift.

8.2 Using Rift head tracking to interact with objects

If you think of the head tracker data as one more way to get input from your user, you can take your application in more immersive and interesting directions. For example, the *Trial of the Rift Drifter* (share.oculusvr.com/app/trial-of-the-rift-drifter) game by Aldin Dynamics uses the head tracker data to allow a user to shake their head "yes" or "no" to answer in-game questions. Other games use it to allow you to gaze at an object or menu item to select it, or to use your gaze to aim a weapon.

A level menu on a plane in front of
the user breaks immersion.

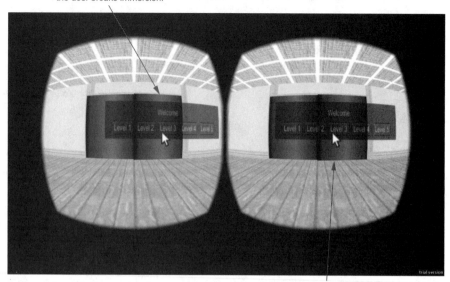

Integrating the menu into the
scene as elevator buttons is
more immersive.

Using the cursor for input requires
the user to use a mouse.

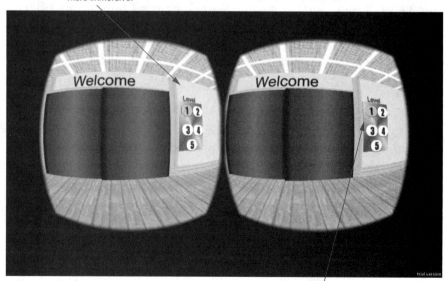

Raycasting can be used to detect which button
the user is looking at. By allowing the user to
select something by looking at it, you don't need
an input device other than the Rift.

Figure 8.9   Building the UI into your VR world creates a more immersive environment for the user.

This block has turned red and moves where you look.

Figure 8.10   Moving crates using input from the Rift

For this next example scene (figure 8.10), we've added several cubes to the scene to give us some objects to play with. Let's call these cubes "crates."[2] When you gaze at a crate, it turns blue. If you keep it in your sight for two seconds, it turns red and then you're able to move the crate to another point on the beach simply by turning your head to look at where you want the crate to go. When the crate collides with the beach or with another crate, it turns white and stays put until you pick it up again.

Let's start by creating the crates and adding them to your scene.

8.2.1   Setting up objects for detection

For the crates, you'll use cubes of various sizes and at various locations. To add a cube, select GameObject > Create Other > Cube. You'll want to add multiple cubes to the beach, so drag the cube to the Asset window to make it a prefab and rename it Crate. Now you can drag as many crates as you want to the scene while only having to update the prefab to properly set up the crates. When adding a crate to the scene, the exact position of the crate isn't important, but you must be sure that it's not *colliding* with the beach.

So you can detect collisions between any two objects, at least one of the objects in the collision must have a *rigidbody* attached. You want the crates to be able to detect collisions with the beach and with other crates, so you attach a rigidbody to the crate. Select the prefab Crate, and then in the Inspector, click the Add Component button and then select Physics > Rigidbody to attach a rigidbody.

Having a rigidbody attached means the crates will act under the control of the physics engine, and the crate's position will be influenced by gravity. You want the crates to fall, so for the rigidbody attached to the crate, check Use Gravity to set it to

---

[2]   Every game needs crates.

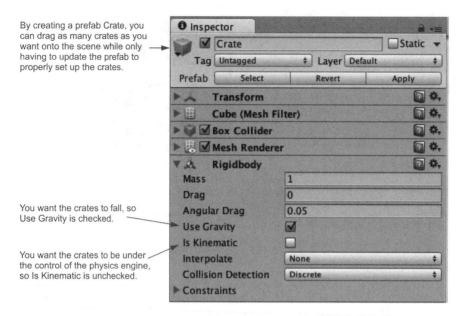

By creating a prefab Crate, you can drag as many crates as you want onto the scene while only having to update the prefab to properly set up the crates.

You want the crates to fall, so Use Gravity is checked.

You want the crates to be under the control of the physics engine, so Is Kinematic is unchecked.

Figure 8.11   The prefab Crate in the Inspector

true. Note that you're leaving Is Kinematic unchecked. This means the crate will be under the control of the physics engine, and if you place a crate hovering in the air, it'll fall to the beach when you run the scene. When you view your prefab Crate in the Inspector, it should look like figure 8.11.

To interact with these objects you'll need two scripts: one to select and move the object, and one to put the object back down.

8.2.2   Selecting and moving objects

Let's start with the script that handles selecting and moving the crates, the Movegaze.cs script in the following listing, which you'll attach to the CenterEyeAnchor object.

Listing 8.3   Movegaze.cs: using Rift head tracking to select and move objects

```
using UnityEngine;
using System.Collections;

public class Movegaze : MonoBehaviour {

  private  float startTime;
  private  GameObject attachedObject = null;
  private  GameObject lookedatObject  = null;

  void Start (){
      startTime = Time.time;
  }
```

```
function Update() {
    Ray ray = new Ray(transform.position, transform.forward);        Casts a ray that
    RaycastHit hit;                                                   originates at the
    float currentTime = Time.time;                                   CenterEyeAnchor.
    if (attachedObject == null) {
        if (Physics.Raycast (ray, out hit, 100)) {               Sets gravity
            if ((currentTime - startTime) > 2) {                 to false.
                attachedObject = lookedatObject;
                attachedObject.GetComponent<Rigidbody>().useGravity = false;
                attachedObject.GetComponent<Rigidbody>().isKinematic = false;
                attachedObject.transform.parent = this.transform;
                attachedObject.GetComponent<Renderer>().material.color = Color.red;
            } else{
                if (lookedatObject == null){
                    lookedatObject = hit.collider.gameObject;
                    lookedatObject.renderer.material.color = Color.blue;
                }
            }
        } else {
            if (lookedatObject != null) {
                lookedatObject. GetComponent<Renderer>().material.color =
                Color.white;
            }
            startTime = currentTime;
            lookedatObject = null;
        }

    } else {
        if (attachedObject. GetComponent<Renderer>().material.color ==
        Color.white){
            startTime = currentTime;
            attachedObject = null;
        }
    }
  }
}
```

Annotations:
- **Sets isKinematic to false.** (points to `attachedObject.GetComponent<Rigidbody>().isKinematic = false;`)
- **Sets gravity to false.** (points to `useGravity = false;`)
- **To move an object in the scene with the Rift, make it the child object of the CenterEyeObject.** (points to `attachedObject.transform.parent = this.transform;`)
- **Sets startTime to currentTime.** (points to `startTime = currentTime;`)

To make sure this script works, you need to do two things. First, attach the script to the CenterEyeAnchor object; then for any objects that you don't want to detect, you need to set them to ignore the raycast.

ATTACHING THE SCRIPT TO CENTEREYEANCHOR

The script must be attached to the CenterEyeAnchor object in the scene for it to work (figure 8.12). The CenterEyeAnchor object in the OVRCameraRig prefab maintains a transform at the pose halfway between the left and right eye cameras. By attaching it to CenterEyeAnchor and by casting a ray that originates from that object, you can find out what's in your line of sight.

To attach the script to CenterEyeAnchor, in the Inspector for CenterEyeAnchor click Add Component and then select the Movegaze.cs script.

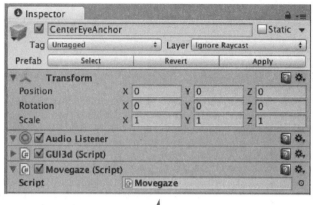

The Movegaze.cs script
is attached to the
CenterEyeAnchor object.

**Figure 8.12   CenterEyeAnchor
in the Inspector with the
Movegaze.cs script attached**

SETTING THE BEACH, THE PALMS AND THE PLAYER TO IGNORE THE RAYCAST

The script changes the renderer color blue for any collider object the raycast hits. To prevent the beach and palm trees from turning blue, in the Inspector for the Beach and Palm tree objects set Layer to Ignore Raycast (figure 8.13).

You also don't want to be able to pick yourself up, so you need to do the same thing for the Player object. In the Inspector for the Player object, set Layer to Ignore Raycast, and when asked "Do you want to set layer to Ignore Raycast for all child objects as well?" select "Yes, change children."

Now that you can pick up the crates, you need a script to put the crates down.

8.2.3   Using collision to put the selected object down

You're moving the crate using input from the headset by attaching the crate to CenterEyeAnchor. When the crate is attached to CenterEyeAnchor, it always stays at the center of your view. This means you can't look away from it to put it down. You have to use some other mechanism to determine when to remove the crate from the parent object, and in our example, the mechanism used is collision.

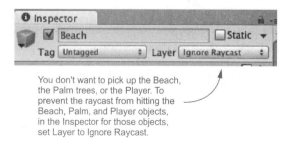

You don't want to pick up the Beach,
the Palm trees, or the Player. To
prevent the raycast from hitting the
Beach, Palm, and Player objects,
in the Inspector for those objects,
set Layer to Ignore Raycast.

**Figure 8.13   Setting Layer to
Ignore Raycast for the Beach
in the Inspector**

To handle the collision, you need a script attached to the object you're moving. The script in the next listing will detect the collision, remove the parent transform, and then reset the crate so that it can be selected again.

Listing 8.4   Cubecollision.cs: Using collision

```
using UnityEngine;
using System.Collections;

public class Cubecollision : MonoBehaviour {

  void OnCollisionEnter (Collision col){
    GetComponent<Renderer>().material.color = Color.white;
    transform.parent = null;
    transform.rotation = Quaternion.Euler(0, 0, 0);
    if(col.gameObject.name == "Beach"){
        Vector3 newPos = transform.position;
        newPos.y = col.gameObject.transform.position.y
          +transform.localScale.y/2.0f + .1f;
        transform.position = newPos;

        GetComponent<Rigidbody>().isKinematic = true;
        GetComponent<Rigidbody>().useGravity = true;
      } else {

        GetComponent<Rigidbody>().useGravity = true;
      }
  }

  void OnCollisionStay() {
     GetComponent<Rigidbody>().AddForce(transform.forward * 20);
  }
}
```

Sets the crate render color to white.

Puts the crate down by setting the transform parent to null.

Positions the crate so it's not intersecting the beach.

Enables gravity and sets isKinematic to true.

Only enables gravity. You want the crate to fall, but you still want it to detect when it has collided with other objects.

Applies force until crates move apart.

For the script to work, it needs to be attached to the crates; we'll show you how in the next section.

ATTACHING THE COLLISION SCRIPT TO THE CRATES

You need to attach the Cubecollision.cs script to the crates. To attach the script, in the Inspector for the prefab Crate click Add Component and then select the Cubecollision.cs script (figure 8.14).

With the crates set up and the script attached, you can give the scene a test run. You should be able to wander around the beach, look at crates, and move them to another spot on the beach.

Whether you're using a UI built into the VR world that uses head tracking as input or a more tradition GUI, the UI won't be of much use if your user can't see it. If you tried out the example timer UI, you may have noticed that by the time you get the Rift on and dismiss the health and safety warning, nine or more seconds may have already gone by. This means that your user won't have seen or been able to interact with your

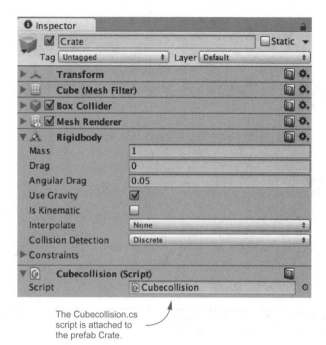

The Cubecollision.cs
script is attached to
the prefab Crate.

**Figure 8.14   The prefab Crate
expanded in the Inspector**

application for those nine seconds. If you want to give your application a chance to
shine, you're going to have to help the user get into the VR experience comfortably
and not start the action until you're sure the user can see it.

8.3   Easing the user into VR

Having the user miss the first few seconds of your application isn't the only issue
with getting the user from a traditional monitor and into VR. You'll also want to
make sure the user is comfortable and that the user's sense of "forward" is the same
as the user's real sense of forward. Doing so will make your users a lot more comfortable. But before we worry about which way users are looking, let's make sure they
can see the application.

8.3.1   Knowing when the health and safety warning has been dismissed

On startup all Rift applications display the health and safety warning (HSW), which
appears as a big rectangle pinned to the user's perspective that largely obscures the
user's view of everything else in the scene.

Let's say you wanted to have your timer not count the elapsed seconds until after
the HSW has been dismissed. There are two small changes you must make to your
UpdateTimer.cs script to do just that, as shown next.

Listing 8.5 Starting the timer after the HSW is dismissed

```
using UnityEngine;
using System.Collections;          Adds the Ovr
using Ovr;                          namespace

public class UpdateTimer : MonoBehaviour {
  <...>
  void Update () {
    if (OVRManager.isHSWDisplayed){       Checks to see if the HSW is
      startTime = Time.time;              displayed, and if it is, resets the
    }                                     start time to the current time
    elapsedTime = Time.time - startTime;
  <...>
}
```

The HSW tells the user to "Press any key to dismiss." You might think that you can simply use the key press as the trigger for starting the timer, but unfortunately, this doesn't quite work. The warning must be displayed for a minimum amount of time before it can be dismissed—15 seconds the first time it's displayed for a given profile and 6 seconds for subsequent times. The result is that often the key will be pressed but the HSW will still be displayed for a few more seconds. Another consideration is whether you want to restart the timer if the scene is reloaded. On reload, the HSW won't be displayed and so the user won't need to press a key.

Fortunately, the Oculus Unity Integration package provides a way to know if the HSW is still being displayed:

```
OVRManager.isHSWDisplayed
```

This code will return true if the HSW is still on screen. Use it in your `Update()` method to wait for the HSW to be dismissed. Once you know users have dismissed the HSW, you can make sure they're facing "forward."

8.3.2 Re-centering the user's avatar

Most users start a VR application and then put on the Rift. Keeping in mind that the Rift DK2 supports positional tracking, if the tracking starts before the user has the headset on, the end result might be that the user's sense of "forward" in the game may not match the user's sense of "forward" in real life, or the user may find themselves standing next to their avatar body, slightly in front of the body, or even sitting *in* the body!

To give the user a good start, you'll want to re-center the user's view when the user first gets the Rift on, and you'll want to provide an option to re-center manually. To re-center the user's avatar, use this:

```
OVRManager.display.RecenterPose();
```

You can ask the user to press a specific key to calibrate, and (ideally) that key will do the same thing in the future.

8.3.3 Creating splash scenes

Many of the best demos we've seen start with a splash scene, and we consider having a splash scene to be a best practice. Splash scenes not only introduce the application, they also allow the user to dismiss the HSW and re-center their view (and learn how to re-center later if needed) without missing a second of critical content. This is also a great place to remind your user to create a profile if they haven't already done so (as we recommended in chapter 7).

8.4 Quality and performance considerations

The user's view matching exactly what the user is doing has an enormous impact on the performance criteria for your application. In chapter 6 we discussed at length the quality and performance requirements for VR and why they're significantly stricter and higher than for many traditional applications. We'd say that failing to meet the quality requirements for VR not only will result in a poor application, but you may also have some physically ill users.

Let's take a look at the performance criteria for VR applications, how you can measure the quality of your VR application, and what you can do to improve the user's perceived sense of quality.

8.4.1 Measuring quality: looking at application frame rates

A good first step in making sure your application is of usable quality is to see what your frame rate is. In the OVR > Scripts > Util folder is the OVRMainMenu.cs script. This script is used to display various diagnostic information, including the frames per second (FPS). To use this script, simply attach it to an object in your scene. Then, when the scene is running, to access the menu, simply press the spacebar (figure 8.15). The top item displayed is the current FPS.

The frame rate should be equal to the native refresh rate of the Rift display. This is 60 Hz for the DK1 and 75 Hz for the DK2.

Not hitting these frame rates can result in missed frames, causing the scene to visibly shake or blink, both of which may induce unwanted physical side effects in your user (headaches, nausea, and so forth). Now that you know there's a problem, what can you do about it?

The next sections will cover techniques for improving the quality of your Unity Rift applications.

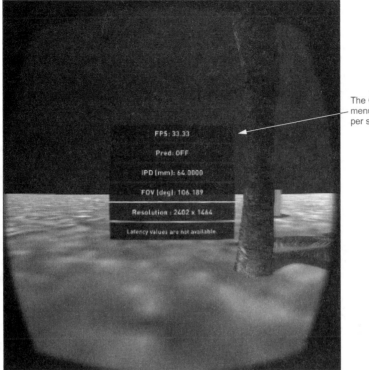

The OVRPlayerController menu displays FPS (frames per second) as the top item.

Figure 8.15   The OVRPlayerController menu displays FPS as the top item.

8.4.2   *Using timewarp*

In the Rift, your view needs to match exactly what you're doing. But as you move your head, the scene being rendered to the Rift display may be a little behind where you're actually looking. One technique used to compensate for that lag is timewarp. We covered timewarp extensively in chapter 6, but here's the gist: timewarp uses the latest tracking pose to adjust the onscreen position of the rendered images to reduce the perceived latency of Rift applications. Given an image, and the head pose for which that image was rendered, the distorted view of the image is adjusted to account for the difference between head pose at the time of render and the head pose at the time the image is displayed on the screen. If we look at the timeline of events, it looks something like figure 8.16.

The head pose is sampled before rendering, allowing the image to be rendered from the point of view of the user, no matter how they've moved or turned their head. But because the head might move between the time the image is rendered and the time the image is displayed (marked as *v-sync* in figure 8.16), timewarp is applied. Immediately before distortion, the head pose is sampled again and the difference

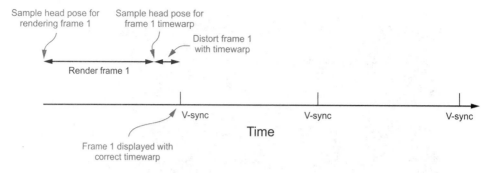

Figure 8.16   A look at when timewarp is applied during the rendering process

between the rendered head pose and the distortion head pose is used to rotate the viewport slightly to match the pose at the time of render. The time taken by distortion in the image here is actually not to scale. It takes an almost negligible amount of time, so the sampled head pose ends up being almost exactly what it'll be at the time of display on the Rift.

Using timewarp is easy because it's enabled by default in the OVRManager script attached to the OVRCameraRig object. We don't expect that you'll need to, but you can disable timewarp in the Inspector for the OVRManager script by unchecking the Time Warp box (figure 8.17).

If you want to experiment with the effects of timewarp, you can use the Freeze Time Warp option.

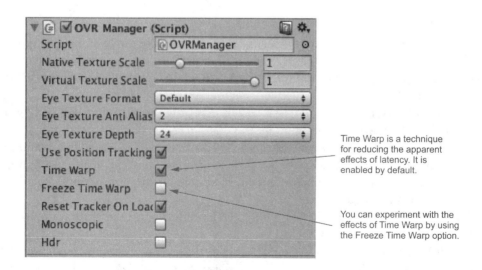

Figure 8.17   Timewarp options are found in the Inspector for the OVRManager script.

8.4.3 *(Not) Mirroring to the display*

Being able to see what the user is seeing can be a very valuable tool when debugging your application, particularly when looking for causes of motion sickness (see chapter 10). Unfortunately, mirroring the Rift display to another monitor can cause significant performance issues.

On a MacBook Pro, running the Tuscany demo from Oculus, we were seeing 75 FPS when running in Extended mode but only 46 FPS when in mirrored mode (in both scenarios the refresh rate was set to 75 Hz).

For Windows applications you have the option of running in Extended mode or of using the Oculus Direct Mode driver. When running in Direct mode, the content is mirrored to a small window on your main monitor. The Direct mode driver was designed as a workaround for the issues of mirroring (cloning) a display, and the performance exchange is less of an issue.

8.4.4 *Using the Unity project quality settings*

The Unity project quality settings provide options for scaling the rendering load, such as different levels of quality for shadowing, or anti-aliasing, or different levels of texture quality, that can help improve your frame rates.

ANTI-ALIASING

The Rift uses stereo rendering, which effectively reduces the horizontal resolution by 50%. One way to compensate for the reduced resolution is to enable or increase anti-aliasing. To change the anti-aliasing settings for your build, select Edit > Project Settings > Quality and look at the setting for Anti Aliasing (figure 8.18).

We suggest starting with a value of 4X Multi Sampling and experimenting to see what works best for your application. Remember to consider your target platform; you may be targeting systems less powerful than your own.

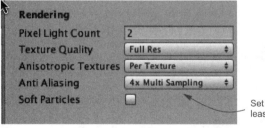

Set Anti Aliasing to at least 4x Multi Sampling.

Figure 8.18   Project quality settings for rendering in the Inspector

8.5   *Summary*

In this chapter we covered

- Rift head-tracking data can be used for more than changing the user's point of view. If you think of the head tracker data as one more way to get input from your user, you can take your application in more immersive and interesting directions.

- When you're creating a UI for the Rift, the UI must be rendered in 3D space. Set the Render Mode to World Space for the UI canvas to have the UI elements rendered in 3D space.

- For a more immersive UI, you should build the UI into the world you're creating.

- Help your user get started right and make the transition from traditional monitor to VR as seamless as possible.

- The user can't see what's going on when the health and safety warning is still displayed. Wait until the user has dismissed the HSW before starting any game action.

- When starting your application you need to think in terms of splash *scenes* and not splash *screens*.

- Performance criteria for VR applications are both higher and stricter than for most traditional applications.

- The frame rate should be equal to (or greater than) the native refresh rate of the Rift display: 60 Hz for the DK1 and 75 Hz for the DK2.

- You can increase the perceived quality of your application by using timewarp.

- The Rift uses stereo rendering, which effectively reduces the horizontal resolution by 50%. This means special attention must be paid to graphics quality.

- Reading chapters 9 and 10 is highly recommended as those chapters cover many of these same topics but in much more depth.

Part 4

The VR user experience

Now we turn our attention to the VR experience. VR gives us the opportunity to visit any world we imagine. As developers, we want the world we create to be one where the user can navigate and interact in a natural and comfortable way. We want the user to feel immersed in the world we've built, to feel like they're really there. We don't want them thinking about how to write an angry email to software support because they can't figure out how to do anything once the application starts. And, of course, we don't want the user to feel ill from using the software.

Chapter 9 looks at the challenges of creating a UI for the VR environment. Many techniques used to create a UI for traditional applications don't work in the VR environment. And the truth is, UI for VR needs to be redesigned from the ground up. This chapter looks at some of the common pitfalls of designing a UI for VR, along with what the latest research says you can do to create an immersive user experience.

Chapter 10 covers what you can do to maximize user comfort. This chapter provides guidelines and examples of how to mitigate motion sickness triggers and other causes of physical discomfort such as fatigue and eyestrain.

Chapter 9 is important if you want your users to have a smooth entry into your world. Chapter 10 is critical if you want them to keep coming back.

UI design for VR

This chapter covers

- Why UI design for the Rift needs to be different from conventional UI
- Ways to move conventional UI elements into VR
- Guidelines for 3D scene and UI design
- Input devices and VR UI design

Hallucinated any big, floating scoreboards lately?

It's funny, but it's true: if we showed you a picture of the world with lots of little floating squares full of words, with numbers and pictures inside funny-shaped symbols all hanging in front of your face (figure 9.1), you'd be totally okay with it. You recognize that all this floating visual noise is the UI of a game, and you recognize the abstract symbols it employs. The big plus symbol in the lower-left corner? Sure, that means health. And behind the pleasantly transparent pop-up, that's your gun, rendered in 3D. 2D and 3D elements coexist on your screen, and that's okay.

Problem is, where is that plus symbol? Is it ahead of you? Is it ahead of your gun? Is it closer than the gun? What about that big "Blue team wins!" in the middle there? It must be between you and your gun, right? But if you can focus on that

Figure 9.1 *Team Fortress 2*, by Valve. The floating scoreboard somewhere in the space between you and your gun, the health and status readouts pinned to the corners of the screen, and the external 2D overlays are all UI conventions that you take for granted in today's computer-generated 3D environments.

temple in the distance, you obviously can't focus on something that's nearer than arm's reach at the same time, can you?

And this is the problem with the UIs of today's non-immersive virtual environments: they blend 2D and 3D in a way that makes sense when the application is running on a flat monitor but that will make very little sense (and very much sim sickness) if you try to copy that same chimeric blend in the Rift. 2D elements overlaid onto a 3D scene can be fine when there's a window or monitor framing them, but VR will strip away that frame, and that's going to cause real issues.

In this chapter we'll explore some of the woes that will arise if you try to use existing 2D and 3D UI conventions in virtual reality. We'll discuss why many of the old UI metaphors from desktop apps and games won't work in VR, how you can adapt your UI so that your user enjoys the experience, and best practices for sound UI development. We'll also touch on some of the ongoing research in this very tricky field.

The bad news is that this isn't yet a "solved" problem, and even this incredibly brilliant book won't have all the answers; the good news is that this isn't yet a "solved" problem, and that means that you're on the forefront of the next generation of UI design. And how cool is that?

9.1 New UI paradigms for VR

A lot of our existing UI design won't work well in the Rift because the Rift is immersive. UIs designed until now have been built for screens, which sat in front of the user and stayed still if the user moved. In the Rift *there is no screen*. The black plastic frame that has enclosed our virtual desktops for so long is just… gone.

Without the screen, there's nothing between us and the virtual environment. This means that UI elements whose utility came from their positions in 2D space on the flat screen are going to be suddenly out of place.

Unfortunately, this isn't an issue limited to the old-style desktop GUIs that run our OSes. Even cutting-edge game UIs today still make broad assumptions about the screen being a static, immobile rectangle.

Consider the non-VR game *EVE Online* (figure 9.2). When you have this kind of heavyweight UI, with dozens, if not hundreds, of potential inputs and outputs, they're usually presented as framing elements surrounding the main presentation area. Broadly speaking, this is a style of UI that simply won't work in VR, because framing elements that build on the "negative space" of the monitor frame no longer have such a negative space to attach to. Actually sticking UI elements to the edge of the rendered image on the Rift would put them, at best, much further away from the center of the view, making it a struggle to flick your eyes back and forth to see them. At worst, they'd become completely invisible because they're actually outside the user's perceived field of view.

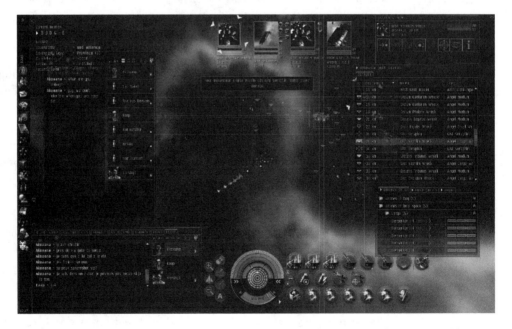

Figure 9.2 *EVE Online*, by CCP. A 3D virtual universe is overlaid by a complex 2D UI. The positions of the many interface elements are driven by the fact that the game is played on a screen, at a fixed distance and position from the player. Skilled players learn where on the screen to look for data at a moment's notice.

Having established that there are classes of conventional UIs that won't "port" well into VR, let's examine a few specific examples.

9.1.1   *UI conventions that won't work in VR and why*

This section explores a few common UI conventions seen in games and nongames alike that don't translate well into VR.

WIDGETS THAT "FLOAT" IN FRONT OF YOUR VIEW OF THE SCENE

Common game examples include health bars, weapon selectors, and ammo counters, such as those shown in figure 9.1.

- *Why they don't work*—By sitting "between" the user and the virtual world, these UI elements break immersion. Their presence creates a barrier, with the player on the wrong side.

- *A better way*—Instead of painting flat symbols onto an invisible plane between the user and the environment, try showing the same information in the game world itself. For example, the *Team Fortress 2* scoreboard in figure 9.1 could've been an *actual* scoreboard, mounted on the wall or projected upward into the sky, *Hunger Games*-style, for all players to see.

WIDGETS THAT ARE "PINNED" TO THE EDGES AND CORNERS OF THE SCREEN

On a Rift headset, the edges of the view lose the most resolution under the distortion function. In *Lessons Learned Porting Team Fortress 2 to Virtual Reality* (media.steampowered.com/apps/valve/2013/Team_Fortress_in_VR_GDC.pdf), Joe Ludwig observes that UI elements glued to the edges will be the least clear and the least often looked at, making them entirely unsuitable for VR UI.

- *Why they don't work*—Those UI elements will be hard to see without rolling your eyes; there's no way for the user to turn their head to look at a widget closely if the widget moves with them.

  Although the edge of the screen is only a few degrees from the center on a normal monitor, on the Rift it's 55 degrees. That's one small step for man, but it's a really long jump for an eyeball. It's stressful to keep the eyes pointed that far off-axis for any length of time.

  Depending on facial structure and eye depth, individual users may see different amounts of content toward the edges, especially if the Rift hasn't been fully calibrated for them. Edge objects could be completely outside their field of view.

- *A better way*—Try to move critical UI elements toward the center of the view whenever possible. Better yet, try to embed critical information into the scene itself instead of onto an interposed UI; build a scene where the user will naturally spend most of their time looking in that direction. A good example is a cockpit *heads-up display* (HUD), where critical information can be shown on in-scene elements at the center of where the user is most likely to be looking, instead of out at the edges.

MAKING ASSUMPTIONS ABOUT THE ASPECT RATIO OF THE SCREEN

Nearly all UIs seem to make assumptions about the aspect ratio of the screen (typically, that it's wider than it is tall) that don't hold in the Rift. Aspect ratios as a whole are a red herring in VR: if there's no width or height to the screen (the user can just turn their head to see more "screen"), then there aren't any ratios between width and height either.

- *Why this doesn't work*—Left unaddressed in a port from a 2D UI to the Rift, these assumptions of ratio can introduce serious bugs, leading to players having to swivel their heads to read portions of their HUD. Several games ported to the Rift in 2013, such as Linden Lab's *Second Life* or Born Ready's *Strike Suit Zero*, suffer from this issue. In the early version of *Strike Suit Zero* shown in figure 9.3, the developers preserved the old wider-than-it-is-tall aspect ratio of their UI, but the player is viewing the game on a Rift, whose display is taller than it is wide. As a result, the status bar and in-game information slide off either side of the player's view.

- *A better way*—Forget about screens! ("Do not try to fit the screen…that's impossible. Instead only realize the truth: there is no screen.") Instead of defining the dimensions of UI elements by the bounds of a rectangle, bind them to the world or the viewing direction of the user. As we suggested earlier, try to move interface elements closer to the center of the user's line of sight.

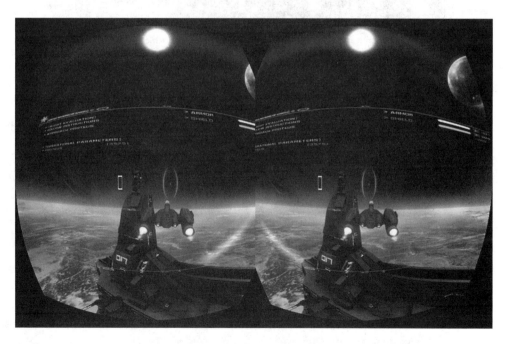

Figure 9.3 *Strike Suit Zero*, **from Born Ready Games. The text and menus describing Armor, Shield, and other stats is sized to the width of a conventional monitor, forcing players to turn their heads to scan the whole line.**

Figure 9.4   *Homeworld*, by Relic. Interaction with in-game entities (here, the user has clicked on a scout fighter ship) will bring up a detailed pop-up menu of commands. If this menu were in the 3D space of the game, it would be a multi-kilometer-tall hanging billboard.

BLENDING "GAME SPACE" WITH "HUD SPACE"

Often, interacting with an element in "game space" will bring up UI elements in "HUD space." In a game like Relic's *Homeworld* (figure 9.4), clicking on a ship brings up a pop-up menu which comes up next to the ship and hovers in space alongside it, although it's not a real 3D object. Rotating the 3D view won't rotate the menu.

- *Why this doesn't work*—If this were in VR, that menu would appear to be hanging in space, a megalithic plank of text kilometers tall, half the height of the *Homeworld* Mothership.

    The user has been using the mouse to select ships in the virtual space. The sudden injection of a flat, planar menu means that the user's mouse control, which was previously moving across the curve of the sphere that implicitly surrounds the user in VR, now suddenly locks to a 2D plane. This change of mouse interaction model can be jarring and disruptive, as well as create an odd sense of distorted perspective.

    Conversely, if the menu were to be integrated into the virtual world, then the game author faces a different sort of problem: spontaneous appearances of massive billboard structures. That sort of thing isn't very good for a game's space fiction.

- *A better way*—This one's tricky. If you can integrate your menu into the virtual world, then that will work well; for example, controls in a cockpit. In a *Homeworld*-style application (any app with an "omniscient" or "god-like" perspective), we suggest placing the user inside a virtual control center whose menus appear outside of the game's space. But such an "augmented reality inside virtual reality" approach won't always be feasible and will require a lot of user experience development work. Finding the smoothest integration between fiction and usability remains an open question.

9.1.2 Can your world tell your story?

> *If you can get away with no HUD at all, that's probably your best bet.*
>
> —Joe Ludwig, 2013

Joe's right. The real world doesn't have a HUD[1] so if you can possibly build your game without one, that's the most surefire path to an immersive VR experience. The best solution to many of the problems we've discussed here is to move as much of the UI as possible into your virtual world. That makes a lot of sense: the very name of the UI element, HUD for heads-up display, came from glass displays first used in aircraft to allow pilots to read data without glancing down. In most games, there's no such glass, so there should be no HUD.

For example, your soldier's gun could show the number of remaining bullets on the clip. (And that's not sci-fi—you can get that for real guns today.) Or your mage's spell-casting energy could manifest as a blue nimbus on its hand that fades as it runs low on power.

COCKPIT HUDS

If you're writing a game and your player is seated in a cockpit or driving seat, then you've got room in-game for as fully detailed a HUD as you might like (figure 9.5). Instead of writing your HUD as a flat 2D graphical UI element, you can build your HUD into your virtual reality so that the content of the HUD augments the virtual scene. Think of this as *augmented virtual reality*.

This is actually an interesting point—the HUDs in games today are unrealistic, but they echo the HUDs of real-world vehicles like fighter planes quite well because the games aren't very realistic either. Think about the difference between the HUD of an F-15 and Tony Stark's HUD in *Iron Man*. In an F-15, when the plane veers away from its target the HUD stays in front of the pilot; in *Iron Man*, when Tony steers away from a target, his in-helmet HUD tracks the target until it's out of his field of view. It does so by enhancing the details about the simulated representation of his

---

[1] Unless you're flying an F-15. Or you're Tony Stark.

Figure 9.5   *Hawken*, **from Meteor Entertainment. Most UI elements, such as speed and heading, are built into the fictional structure of the mech[2] along the lower front of the cockpit, giving them a reason to be in front of the player. It's safe to expect that players will spend most their time in the game looking forward.**

quarry. So where the F-15's HUD augments *actual* reality, Stark's HUD augments *virtual* reality.

So, let's clarify Joe Ludwig's quote. He's right; plastering a flat planar 2D HUD onto the Rift's display is a no-go. But if you can build a virtual HUD in the virtual cockpit of a virtual F-15, that's awesome.

This is an idea that game developers have already begun to use to excellent effect. In Meteor Entertainment's *Hawken* (figure 9.5), their mech's cockpit's controls show all the sorts of stats that your average driver of 80 tons of mechanized death needs to know; the mech's cockpit gives a very natural, immersive place to look for all that data. To the player, the immersive cockpit is enhanced and fleshed out by the flow of live content, and the sense of presence becomes very strong.

DATA ON DEMAND

An even more effective way to provide data to the user is to deliver it on demand, as a function of where the user is looking. We suggested that a soldier's gun could show the number of remaining bullets on the clip, perhaps as a digital readout on the gun. This is an example of contextually relevant content: when players are looking ahead,

---

[2]   Giant mechanical robots, piloted by the player. Ideal for all your building-crushing needs.

spotting enemies is more critical than spotting their ammo count, but if they look down at their gun, it becomes one of the key things players might want to know.

With that in mind, there's no need to try to shoehorn an ammo counter on top of a gun. Instead, use the Rift's orientation sensors to know where the user is looking. When the user looks down and to the right, their gun arm can pivot to show them the side of their rifle, with its ammo count clearly visible; then when they look up again, their gun arm swings back to the ready. The effect for the user would be very immersive; indie projects like *Shadow Projection* (described later in this chapter) already use this technique with great success.

IN-WORLD SCREENS

Another good example of the effective use of flat imagery in a 3D world is the sniper problem. Many first-person shooter (FPS) games have a zoom feature, such as when using a sniper rifle (figure 9.6).

A zoom effect is usually achieved by narrowing the rendered FOV to a small section of arc, often only a few degrees, and filling the screen with the resulting image. The result is flattened and loses 3D convergence cues. (Remember that 3D convergence— the way our eyes point along lines that aren't quite parallel to focus on a distant point—is one of the strongest depth indicators we perceive.) This can be a disruptive experience in the Rift, because in the Rift the viewer's FOV is fixed and must be that of the actual headset or you risk illness (chapter 10), and the sudden lack of convergence

Figure 9.6 *Crysis 3*, from Electronic Arts. The sniper scope zooms up to 10x; if the scope were to track the user's head while wearing a Rift, it would be impossible to control. Consider placing a 2D image of the same zoom level on a small virtual screen at the back of the scope instead.

cues will be disorienting. Plus, it'll no longer be at all clear to wearers what they should expect to see when they turn their head—if the zoomed point tracks their line of sight, they'll lose their target at a glance.

A better solution here would be to fit a virtual screen to the front of the scope, and then lift the scope and its screen up to the user's eye when the user engages the sniper zoom. The virtual screen could fit right into the barrel of the scope. Their heads would remain free to look around, but players would see their weapons lifted in front of them and the image at the base of the scope showing precisely where they were aiming.

BUILDING THE GAME MENU INTO AN IN-WORLD SCREEN

In Activision's *Call of Duty: Black Ops*, the developers use a cleverly immersive way to integrate the game controls into their world. The player menu at the start of the game is shown on a television screen (figure 9.7); user actions change the selection on the TV set. The menu is an integrated part of the game world and avoids the jarring discontinuity of a floating menu pane.

In the sequel, *Call of Duty: Black Ops II*, the storyline begins in 2025, and the main menu sequence is much more advanced: we see the main character don a pair of glasses, presumably some sort of augmented reality or holographic technology, and

Figure 9.7 In Activision's *Call of Duty: Black Ops*, the menu (circled, highlighted) is an integrated part of the game world.

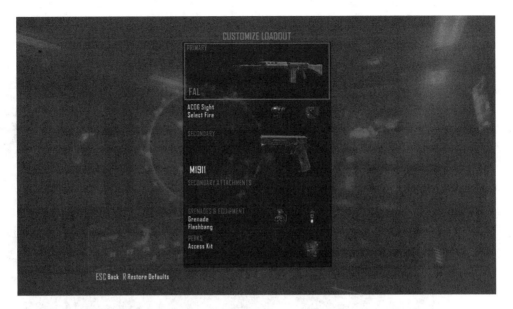

Figure 9.8 In the sequel, *Call of Duty: Black Ops II*, the main character uses augmented-reality glasses to operate the in-game controls (highlighted). Here the player is configuring the weapons loadout of his character before charging into battle.

then manipulate game controls with a futuristic wrist-mounted projected virtual control (figure 9.8).

The idea that the protagonist is the one controlling the TV and virtual console is fascinating. Although the *Black Ops* games aren't Rift games (yet), they demonstrate perfectly that primary, nongame UI elements *can* be integrated seamlessly into the game fiction.

FANTASY SETTINGS

Conversely, if your game is set in a fantasy world where there's no good reason for your number of arrows or hit points to be inscribed on something upon your person, getting away from a HUD UI is going to be a lot harder. Games like Blizzard's *World of Warcraft* (figure 9.9) deliver a tremendous amount of content through the HUD, and it's difficult to conceive of how that gameplay could be delivered in-world.

World of Warcraft demonstrates that there will probably always be use cases where the virtual world can't entirely contain and express the game's content; some sort of abstraction will be necessary. But it's not inconceivable that what today appears as a floating panel of 2D text, tomorrow could hover on a character's shield or perhaps in speech bubbles. There's still a lot of UI experimentation to be done for such games.

Figure 9.9 *World of Warcraft*, by Blizzard. WoW presents the player with a tremendous amount of game data that has no "in-world" context. The UI (highlighted here in multiple rectangles) relies on a mixture of text and iconic widgets to give the user features and feedback.

9.1.3 Getting your user from the desktop to VR

Odds are pretty good that your users are launching your cool VR app from an icon on their desktops, in that old ugly 2D UI we call home. That means when they launch, they're not wearing the Rift. This presents a challenge: swapping between 2D and 3D UIs should be transparently smooth.

Keep these issues in mind:

- You can't assume that the user is wearing the Rift, so you'll need a simple 2D (conventional desktop) UI as well.
- You don't want to stick a flat menu on the screen if users *are* in VR.
- Having to ask users to tell you when they're wearing the Rift (a) requires a UI and (b) feels clumsy. It should be something we already know.
- When they're ready to go to VR mode, you'll want to smoothly transition users from the 2D UI to wearing the Rift.
- Until you know they're wearing their Rift, you can't assume that its current orientation is forward. (It might be on their desk pointing who-knows-where.)

The Rift doesn't (yet) offer a way to programmatically determine whether or not it's being worn. Fortunately, it's not too hard to analyze the accelerometer output of the Rift. Consider this graph of linear accelerations reported by the Rift, averaged over 100 frames per sample.

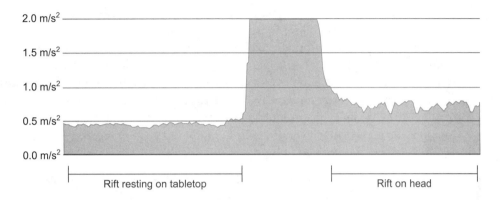

This graph covers an elapsed period of about 20 seconds, sampling at 60 Hz. The vertical axis is the average of a window over 100 samples of the absolute values of the linear acceleration vectors reported by the Rift, so it measures m/s^2. The horizontal axis is elapsed time.

At first, the Rift is at rest on an immobile flat surface. During this time there's noise from the accelerometer, but it's fairly consistent. The user then picks up the Rift, causing a massive spike of accelerometer data (clamped by the graph to $2 \ m/s^2$). After placing the Rift on their head, the user tries to sit as still as they can with, as you can see, less success than the table. The average absolute linear acceleration rises from below $0.5 \ m/s^2$ to roughly $0.75 \ m/s^2$.

As you can see, the accelerometer patterns of a Rift at rest are markedly different from those of a Rift on a human head, no matter how still the wearer tries to be. The Rift detects simple shifts of weight, breathing, and even physiological tremor, the natural built-in twitches and shifts that occur in human muscles at rest. Based on this relatively simple and primitive experiment, it should be possible to determine in code whether or not the Rift is currently in use. You can then switch smoothly between Rift rendering and conventional desktop UI. In fact, that could be an excellent game feature: a Rift game should automatically pause itself when the Rift is removed.

9.1.4   Cutscenes

A *cutscene* is a long-standing device used in games to convey story without direct interaction from the player. In cutscenes the player stops playing and watches a little movie inside the game—maybe a snippet of film with real actors, or a rendered CGI animation, or even prerecorded animations in the engine of the game itself. There are many styles.

Cutscenes are some of the most cinematic elements of video games. Unfortunately, in the Rift they pose a critical problem. When the user is in an environment that has been inducing that sense of presence and immersion, it's not acceptable to suddenly disable head-tracking to lock the player's view to watch a scene. That means many of the classic cinematic tropes based on camera motion can't be used, such as establishing shots, cutaway shots, shot/countershot conversations (where the camera switches between two speakers), following pans, and many more.

Because you can no longer take control of the camera, you're going to have to rethink how you present these cinematics. To begin, you need to refocus on what you want the cutscenes to achieve. Cutscenes are, above all, about the *story*: they exist in a game to move the story forward. Whether it's the flashback to the hero's exploding planet or the villain's final monologue, cutscenes are all about story. You just need to use new techniques to tell your tales in the Rift.

As Neal Stephenson said in his novel *Interface*:

> *It's a new communications medium. What is necessary is to develop a grammar and syntax. [...] It's like film. When film was invented, no one knew how to use it. But gradually, a visual grammar was developed. Filmgoers began to understand how the grammar was used to communicate certain things. We have to do the same thing with this.*

Neal Stephenson, *Interface* (Arrow, 2002), p. 300

CUTSCENES IN CONVENTIONAL VIDEO

Sometimes you've already got a cutscene video ready to go, and it's not feasible to rewrite it from scratch. Games that are targeted at both Rift and non-Rift platforms, for instance, will probably have conventional 2D video cutscenes that can't be migrated into VR. The problem becomes how best to show them there.

One approach, though somewhat jarring to users, is that you can take over their view completely. If you've got a movie cutscene that you *must* show without context, you can show the movie as though the user were in a darkened virtual theater, create a virtual screen a few dozen feet away, and play. But this effect will be unpleasant and disorienting to the user. A movie hanging in space will be just that—a flat 2D movie without context—and it will be very jarring.

Only use this technique as a last resort. Head tracking will have to be restricted and the user won't appreciate being suddenly disembodied. (Most people don't.)

Also, if you must show video instead of your virtual environment, remember to ease the transition. Never just instantaneously replace VR with a movie floating in a black void; instead fade out gently, and then fade back in. This gentler transition is consistent with the familiar fade motif used in movies and will feel much less disruptive to the user.

A far better solution is to borrow an idea that you've already seen: show your cutscene as a flat 2D video inside the 3D virtual environment (figure 9.10).

Figure 9.10 Even cutscene actors who've acted this scene several times before, and would probably claim to be very efficient at it, benefit from embedding 2D video in the 3D virtual world. (*The Matrix Reloaded*, 2003)

Any flat screen in VR can play a flat movie. Perhaps the scientist can explain her evil plan while gesturing—*pointedly*—at the giant monitor playing a video. Perhaps our hero muses over his lost love as misty videos of their times together play on the nearby TV screen. As games like *Call of Duty* show, it's reasonable to break the fourth wall a bit to embed 2D media into a virtual environment.

CUTSCENES WITHIN THE VIRTUAL ENVIRONMENT

An even better approach to cutscenes than prerecorded video is to play out the cutscene in the virtual world itself using the in-world engine. Most virtual reality engines today (such as Unity, discussed in chapters 7 and 8) have more than ample capacity for complex preset animations.

Here you face a different breed of problem: *drawing the user's attention*. In an environment where your users can look around freely, it's not immediately obvious how you can ensure that they're looking at the right part of the scene when the crucial, exciting thing happens. If the mad scientist dramatically throws the switch but the player is looking out the castle window and doesn't notice, then you've lost a lot of storytelling.

- One trick you can use is *audio cues*. Spatialized audio is pretty common in virtual reality engines nowadays. So the scientist doesn't just throw the switch; he makes a speech—a *loud* speech—to draw the player's attention. Perhaps sparks fly as he grasps the switch, casting shadows that point toward him dramatically (and pointedly, for the player distracted by the pretty window).
- Another trick you can use is *responsive triggers*. With the Rift, it's not hard to detect when a particular part of the virtual scene is in the center of the player's view. So, the scientist could launch into his mad monologue, and then you

could pad it out, with multiple bits of optional audio and maybe some cackling, until the player looks around at the madman. By waiting until you know he's on the screen, you're assured that the story won't advance without the player's knowledge.

Avoid distractions in your scenes. This is more important in VR than it was in classic 2D animation, because players can lose track of the action if they're looking at something else, wondering if it's a critical part of the scene too. That means you have to be careful to balance cool, distracting bits of world-building against the demands of keeping the user's attention on the part of the scene that's vital to the story.

Russian playwright Anton Chekhov had the following advice for aspiring word-smiths, commonly called *Chekhov's Gun*:

> *Remove everything that has no relevance to the story. If you say in the first chapter that there is a rifle hanging on the wall, in the second or third chapter it absolutely must go off. If it's not going to be fired, it shouldn't be hanging there.*

> —Anton Chekhov, 1889

In other words, make your scene as simple as possible, but no simpler.

9.2   *Designing 3D user interfaces*

Not too long ago, we were demoing the Oculus Rift at a Maker Faire.[3] We noticed that every so often, we had to tell people to look around. And even when we told them to look around, some people asked, "How?" We had to tell them to just turn their head. It was like a throwback to the 1990s—telling people that underlined text means you can click on it to get to more information on web pages. Of course, nowadays if you see a label that says Click Me after a link, it's annoying; clicking text is so ingrained these days that iOS considers the button graphic to be excessive. Our idea of "good" UI has evolved. But the Rift today is still where web browsers were in the '90s. People won't know what to do; some explicit user instruction has to happen. For now, until the common interface model has become clear, apps are going to have to teach users to interact in VR—and they're going to have to instruct without overwhelming the interface or the user.

In this section we'll explore the following:

- General rules for "good" UI
- Guidelines and ground rules that researchers and experimental developers, as well as hardened game designers like the crew at Valve, have worked out specifically for UIs in VR
- Handling user input for effective immersion, using conventional devices like gamepads and with more novel controllers like the Rift itself

---

[3]   Maker Faires are sort of like mixes of science fairs and county fairs—fun for the whole family, plus electricity.

Most of the material we'll cover here is advice chosen to improve the user's sense of immersion. What we won't cover in this chapter is simulation sickness; make no mistake, that's a topic every bit as critical as UI design, so for an overview of techniques focused on not making your users ill, please see chapter 10.

9.2.1 Criteria for a good UI

If you're just getting started building a 3D UI, it can be helpful to have a set of standards to measure yourself against. In *Usability Engineering* (Morgan Kaufmann, 1993), Jakob Nielsen establishes a set of traits that a good UI should have. Not all of Nielsen's metrics apply in VR, but they remain an effective tool for judging whether your UI is going to work for the majority of your users.

Nielsen wrote that any good UI should do the following:

- *Always display relevant state.* Primary application state should be visible to the user. For an FPS shoot-em-up, this means showing variables like ammo count and health. You don't have to overdo it. If players are fit and healthy, there's no need to tell them that; if they're dying, make sure they know, with visual and audio cues.
- *Use familiar context and imagery.* Don't make your users learn super-specialized custom terms just so they can use your app. If you're writing a surgery interface for medical training, don't force medical students to learn about virtual cameras and FOVs even if you had to think about them a lot as you designed the app.
- *Support undo/redo.* Don't penalize your users for clicking the wrong thing. Where pushing the wrong virtual lever would ignite all the ammo inside your mech, give the user a chance to cancel or revert the command. Wait…why do you even have that lever?
- *Stick with what your users know.* Don't reinvent the wheel, especially if you're unfamiliar with the field. If you're writing that surgery sim, get advice from an actual surgeon—don't invent new names for things.
- *Design to prevent error.* A classic example is a numeric entry field. If you want users to type a value between 1 and 10 in a box, don't ask them to type; they could type 42. Instead, give them a slider that only goes from 1 to 10.
- *Don't require expert understanding.* Visually indicate when an action can be performed, and provide useful data if the action will need context. If a jet fighter pilot can drop a bomb, then somewhere on the UI should be a little indicator of the number of bombs remaining. That tells players that bombs are an option and how many they've got. And better yet, if it takes a key press to drop the bomb, show that key on the UI.
- *Build shortcuts for expert users.* The feeling that you're becoming an expert in a system often comes from learning its shortcuts. Make sure that you offer combos and shortcuts that your users can learn—but don't require them.

- *Keep it simple*. Don't overwhelm your users with useless information; don't compete with yourself for space on the screen. Always keep your UI simple. "If you can't explain it to a six-year-old, you don't understand it yourself" (attributed to Albert Einstein).

- *Make error messages meaningful*. Don't force users to look up arcane error codes (figure 9.11). If something goes wrong, take the time to clearly say what, and more importantly, what the user should do about it.

Figure 9.11   An unhelpful error message

- *Write the manual*. Sure, ideally your UI should be so easy that a child can use it, but that's not always going to be the case. Document how to use your app, both in the app itself and online where people can look it up; these days, wikis are awesome.

In short: always show state; make your UI simple, clean, and clear; don't penalize users if they do the wrong thing, and help them to recover from errors; and don't require expertise, but do reward it.

9.2.2   *Guidelines for 3D scene and UI design*

In the 2008 article "3D User Interfaces—New Directions and Perspectives,"[4] Wolfgang Stuerzlinger lays out guidelines for designing an effective 3D UI for first-person interaction. Although we won't reproduce the full list here, several of Stuerzlinger's points deserve emphasis in the context of designing for the Rift.

Our brains have evolved to do a lot of distance estimation from secondary cues, including the size and occlusion of objects by those around them. That means we see best when things are touching other things. From lions on savannahs to cars on highways, we use relative positioning for context. In the real world, most things don't float untethered in space (excluding balloons, birds, and Death Stars).

Unfortunately, many 3D interfaces show objects floating because it's easy to do. Often for the developer it's easier to have a thing float than to have it rest precisely atop another. If you think about how hard it is to judge just how far away a flying bird is from you, it shouldn't be a surprise that it's difficult to make the same judgment call in virtual reality. (Exhibit A: a VR sequence from the computer game *System Shock* [figure 9.12]. All objects are airborne.)

The key lesson here is simple: your users will have an easier time estimating the size and distance of objects if they're in contact with other objects whose size and distance are already known. For best effect, connect things to the ground.

---

[4] D. A. Bowman, S. Coquillart, B. Froehlich, M. Hirose…and W. Stuerzlinger. (2008). "3D User Interfaces: New Directions and Perspectives," *IEEE Computer Graphics and Applications* 28(6): 20–36.

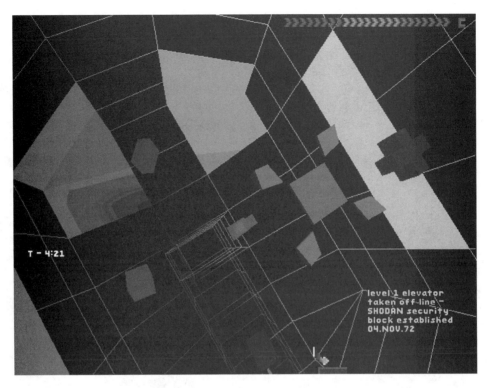

Figure 9.12 *System Shock*, by Looking Glass Technologies. The player has entered "Cyberspace." In this video-game rendition of VR, objects spin, pulse, and float completely without tether or reference to gravity. This makes judging their positions and distances remarkably difficult for the player.

Some applications try to address the disconnected-floating-objects problem with realistic shadows, but you shouldn't depend on shadows for context. Our brains get a lot of 3D data out of shadows, but we intuit more about the objects on which the shadows lie than we do about the objects casting the shadows. It's surprisingly difficult to judge how high something is based on its shadow, because you don't know exactly where the point directly beneath the object should be.

If things in your scene *must* hover, try to give them motion. Even if it's just a subtle bobbing effect, motion dramatically increases the amount of feedback the eyes get from parallax. Parallax signals lend realism. This helps the user estimate distance without other cues.

SOLID THINGS ARE SOLID

In the real world, objects don't (usually) pass through one another. We use this understanding as a visual depth cue. When objects do pass through one another, it can make gauging their relative distance from the viewer quite difficult.

This guideline is less demanding for developers than it once was, because as computing power has risen, implementations of object intersection routines have become

Figure 9.13 *Lego Indiana Jones* from CHAPTER 9 CHAPTERS. Game puzzles often rely on the player positioning objects against others. Here the object to be moved is constrained to the checkerboard tiled path, which greatly simplifies the user's task.

commonplace. Today overlapping objects is almost universally seen as a bug, although some massively multiplayer online role-playing games (MMORPGs) and online FPS games still allow player characters to walk through one another.

Stuerzlinger observes that in a virtual world in which object interpenetration is guaranteed not to occur, the task of moving objects around is much easier. When the user is confident that objects will slide against one another, 3D motion devolves down to 2D motion, a significantly simpler control task. This is well demonstrated by the *LEGO* movie games series, which often contain challenges in which the player must slide some heavy object from one point to another (figure 9.13).

Positioning these game items would be much more difficult for the player if objects' motions were not constrained to sliding in a plane.

ONLY INTERACT WITH WHAT YOU CAN SEE

Studies such as those by Poupyrev and colleagues[5] and by Ware and Lowther[6] have demonstrated conclusively that users find selection with a 2D pointer or control more

---

[5] Poupyrev, I., S. Weghorst, M. Billinghurst, and T. Ichikawa. (1998). "Egocentric Object Manipulation in Virtual Environments: Empirical Evaluation of Interaction Techniques," *Computer Graphics Forum*, 17(3): 41–52.

[6] Ware, C. and K. Lowther. (1997). "Selection Using a One-Eyed Cursor in a Fish Tank VR Environment," *ACM Transactions on Computer-Human Interactions*, 4(4): 309–322.

effective than 3D selection. There's also ample evidence that motion within a 2D plane is easier to control than arbitrary 3D motion. This is corroborated by research showing that using a mouse on a flat surface allows greater precision than using a mouse in the air.

There's a strong intuitive sense to these results. If we accept the premise that users are less adept at selecting and manipulating objects that lie behind something else in the scene (a reasonable assumption), then the set of manipulable objects in any scene becomes the set whose geometry is immediately visible to the user. This set maps to a 2D plane and is therefore easily accessible with a mouse. Note, though, that Poupyrev and colleagues did observe a clear loss of 2D accuracy as 3D distance increased.

Poupyrev and colleagues also note the long-understood UI design phenomenon that test subjects performed better when the experiment included visual feedback. Whenever your user interacts with anything, give that user some feedback. Users love feedback.

Stuerzlinger draws the conclusion that if the primary interface to manipulation in a virtual world is to be through 2D controls such as the mouse, then the user's viewpoint becomes critically important and therefore ease of navigation is essential. Unfortunately, this conclusion is at odds with Rift-specific research showing that navigation should be avoided if possible (see chapter 10). An acceptable middle ground appears to be to try to design virtual scenes to reduce occlusion, thereby reducing the need for motion.

THE STRONGEST DEPTH CUES ARE PERSPECTIVE AND OCCLUSION

Stuerzlinger states that for manipulation of objects beyond arm's length in a virtual space, perspective and occlusion are the strongest signals of depth to the brain. This conclusion is supported by the fact that 3D FPS video games such as *Doom* and *Quake* were so successful long before stereo 3D technologies were readily available for the home.

The best signals for perspective in a scene come from objects' *relationship to other objects*. If an item in a virtual environment rests against another, larger object whose scale is intuitively known (such as the ground, a building, or a starship), then perspective cues will quickly kick in to inform the user's understanding of the scene.

When one object occludes another, their relative scale helps us sense their relative distance; by the same token, failure to occlude can make such judgments quite difficult. In figure 9.14, stills from the 1982 movie *Tron* demonstrate how a lack of occlusion can make judging the size and distance of a virtual object difficult. This is a scene where Flynn (Jeff Bridges) meets Bit, a floating binary life form. It's difficult to judge Bit's size—comparable to an apple, perhaps, or maybe about the size of a basketball. Had the scene shown Bit behind Flynn or ahead of him, we'd have had significantly stronger visual cues, because we have a sense of the size of a human. Unfortunately in 1982 it was difficult to occlude a virtual object with a real person, or vice versa. To compensate, in this scene Bridges acts with exaggerated physical motions and looks pointedly at Bit, yanking his head dramatically back as Bit flies past him; the human

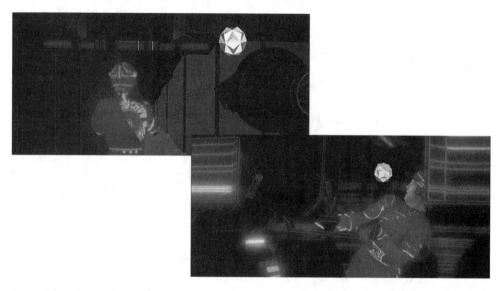

Figure 9.14   Scenes from the movie *Tron*: Flynn meets Bit, a floating character. Because Bit never occludes or touches or is occluded by another object, its size is difficult to judge; we're forced to guess its size from the direction of Flynn's startled look.

actor lends realism (and scale) to the virtual actor by using body language to fix it in the scene.

If you can, give your users better cues to gauge size and distance. (Or hire Jeff Bridges. That works too).

It's also worth noting that although occlusion and perspective are very strong signals to the brain, others are at play as well:

- One of the strongest *secondary* signals we use is *parallax*, the apparent change in an object's size when viewed from two different positions (such as when the object, or the viewer, is in motion).
- A secondary signal we use to determine depth is *shape-from-shading*. Our eyes shift constantly, even when at rest, and the subtle changes in shading that we see from these very slightly separated viewpoints are used by the brain to reconstruct the shape and depth of an object.

The Rift easily supports parallax, but not shape-from-shading.

9.2.3   *The mouse is mightier than the sword*

Gestural interfaces may or may not be the future of virtual reality UIs, but until the hardware is more widely available, UIs for the Rift are going to have to assume more primitive forms of input.

MOUSE AND GAMEPAD

One open question is the age-old gamepad versus mouse debate: which is better for exploring and playing in virtual environments, a gamepad or a mouse and keyboard?

Gamers have been arguing this one since FPS first came to consoles, and despite ad hoc surveys and vast reams of anecdotal evidence, we don't seem to be any closer to an actual answer. Even Microsoft, whose Xbox and PC games would stand the most to gain from a final answer, has categorically denied ever having run such a study. The best conclusion from the gaming world has been that games can be designed for mouse and keyboard or for controller, and that the game design makes all the difference.

The Oculus Best Practices Guide (static.oculus.com/sdk-downloads/documents/Oculus_Best_Practices_Guide.pdf) suggests that, for the simple reason that players can't see a keyboard when they're wearing the Rift, a gamepad could be easier for most people to use in VR. Admittedly, not everybody has a gamepad, but for those who do, they're far easier to use "blind" than typing on a keyboard. Gamepads are also much easier to learn to use than traditional mouse-and-keyboard FPS controls, which will make learning a new app much less of a barrier for novice Rift users. And, of course, the fumble factor is dramatically lower with a gamepad. Nothing breaks immersion faster than having to lift the Rift off your face to peer down at your keyboard and hunt for the right key to press.

That said, the mouse is an incredibly effective pointing tool, and the modern user is intimately familiar with mouse UI semantics. Most modern users are very accurate with the mouse.

So our advice is to support both, and let your users use whichever works best for them.

THE GAMEPAD OR MOUSE AS INTERMEDIARY

A number of studies have been conducted on the most effective type of mouse action for a 3D virtual environment and how best to represent the pointer visually. Researchers have explored the effectiveness of presenting the pointer in stereo or to only one eye (Ware and Lowther, Schemali and Eisemann[7]), of using virtual hand or virtual ray pointer metaphors (Poupyrev and colleagues, Schemali and Eisemann), and of presenting the pointer in 2D on the screen plane or in 3D in the scene (Ludwig, *Lessons Learned*).

With any mouse or gamepad, the device is an intermediary between the user and the scene. In *New Directions and Perspectives*, Stuerzlinger discusses the aspects of 3D UI design that must be considered in light of this mediation.

- *We look at the entire tool, not just the pointy end.* Research indicates that when we manipulate an object, we're aware of the whole object, not just of the point of

---

[7] Schemali, L. and E. Eisemann. (2014). "Design and Evaluation of Mouse Cursors in a Stereoscopic Desktop Environment," available at vimeo.com/91489021.

collision. When we reach for something, proprioception ensures that we're aware of our hand and entire arm, not just the fingertip about to make contact. This implies that in a virtual experience, the user is aware of the virtual mouse as a whole, not just the single pixel at the pointer's tip that's the point of interaction.

- *Arbitrary manipulation can be too much; restrict motion to what's natural.* Truly free-form manipulation systems can be difficult to use, compared to manipulating objects that have natural constraints. For example, chairs have a natural direction of up; a good UI won't overwhelm the user by offering tools to spin and flip a chair unless there's a strong reason in the virtual world to do so.

- *Many tasks are really 2D or 2.5D.* Many motions that we execute in the real world are intrinsically one-dimensional (pulling or pushing, lifting or lowering) or two-dimensional (cleaning a surface, scooping and raising food). In fact it's fairly rare for our motions to be truly three-dimensional (martial arts is probably a good example). This means that the challenge for a good UI design isn't in the execution of the *motion*, but rather in the smooth *transition* between planes of motion (figure 9.15).

Although further research is warranted, Stuerzlinger's conclusions appear to be supported by Schemali and Eisemann's work on optimal types of mouse cursor in virtual environments. Schemali and Eisemann explored how quickly users could select and manipulate an object in 3D using conventional mouse cursors, cursors with 3D form that existed "in" the scene, and cursors with 3D form that pivoted smoothly around the interaction point to always be pointing away from the surface of the object (effectively colliding with the shape of the object and "feeling" it). They concluded that flat 2D cursors were ill suited to VR, but that their rotating cursor took longer to use than a simpler 3D cursor in the scene.

The observation that most objects have a natural interaction (chairs aren't usually flipped upside-down) tells us that although someday holodecks may offer us truly arbitrary interactions with all elements of our scene, for now a good UI in the Rift should focus on presenting clean, simple, minimalist interactions in only dimensions appropriate to the object and its environment.

THE CROSSHAIR IN TEAM FORTRESS 2

In *Lessons Learned*, author Joe Ludwig discusses the issues that Valve faced in bringing the game *Team Fortress 2* to the Rift. It's an excellent talk and the slides are available online (media.steampowered.com/apps/valve/2013/Team_Fortress_in_VR _GDC.pdf).

One problem that Valve solved was where to put the HUD; in TF2, you can't live without it. (Pun intended.) For the most part in VR the TF2 HUD elements are rendered onto a transparent pane about 10 meters ahead of the player.

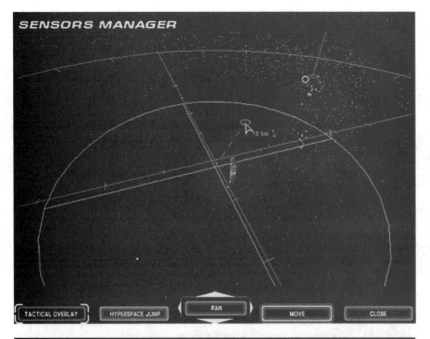

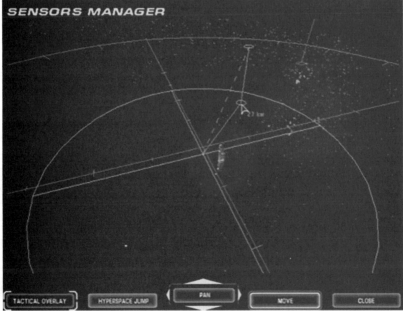

Figure 9.15 *Homeworld*, from Relic. Tactical view for ship commands. (Left) The user drags in the 3D plane to instruct a fighter ship to travel laterally in space. (Right) With a key press, the user changes control mode to dragging in a vertical plane, setting the target height of the fighter. This allows players to easily instruct their spaceships to move in three dimensions.

Figure 9.16   *Team Fortress 2*, from Valve. Note how the HUD elements are in different places for the two eyes, causing them to float between the user and the scene, but the crosshair is deeper in the scene, projected to the middle of the dark wooden cabinet to the left.

The crosshair is handled differently (figure 9.16). In VR *Team Fortress 2*, the crosshair is projected out to the point where the ray from the midline of the player intersects the scene. This means that the crosshair *changes depth* as the player turns their head and mouse. Ludwig describes the effect as "a little odd" but effective. This is akin to making the crosshair into a laser sight.

Valve's design choice is supported by research results such as Teather and Stuerzlinger's 2013 paper[8] on how the choice of 3D pointer influences human ability to point at an object, and by Schemali and Eisemann's work on mouse cursors. But both papers report that user accuracy decreased with depth in the scene. Teather and Stuerzlinger also observed that when tasked with selecting a point atop one of a set of virtual stone columns all pointing toward the camera, the speed with which subjects were able to accurately respond diminished both with the depth of the column and the perceived height of the column, implying that subjects were less confident in their accuracy as they traced the cursor along the column.

[8]   Teather, R. J. and W. Stuerzlinger. (2013). "Pointing at 3D Target Projections with One-Eyed and Stereo Cursors," in *Proceedings of the SIGCHI Conference on Human Factors in Computing Systems* (CHI '13), 159–168. ACM, New York, NY.

Valve explored a number of ways to map the user's head and mouse control to character behavior. They experimented with several options, including the following:[9]

- Aiming and steering coupled on the Rift. The mouse steers as well.
- Aiming with the Rift, steering with the mouse.
- Steering has a dead zone. Inside the dead zone you aim with the Rift and the mouse aims and steers simultaneously. Outside the dead zone, aiming and steering are coupled for both the Rift and mouse. This is the default in TF2.
- Steering with the Rift, aiming with the mouse inside a dead zone. Outside the dead zone, the mouse steers as well.
- Relative camera control with the Rift (no influence on aiming or steering, relative to your character's facing direction).
- Absolute camera control with the Rift. Your reference isn't tied to your character's orientation, so steering with the mouse doesn't influence the direction in which you look. You must actually turn around to see where you're going if your character turns around. Aiming and steering is coupled and controlled with the mouse.

In user testing, Ludwig reported that their best results came from the third option: a blend of Rift and mouse. If the player turns their head, the Rift's rotation turns their character in the game. Conventional FPS mouse and keyboard controls still work, but the mouse has a "dead zone" within which the crosshairs can move freely (the shaded rectangle in the center of figure 9.17) that doesn't affect which way the character is facing. As the mouse leaves this central area, it swings the camera and the character.

Figure 9.17 A rough approximation of the mouse's dead zone (no pun intended) in *Team Fortress 2*. Inside the dead zone you aim with the Rift and the mouse aims and steers simultaneously. Outside the dead zone, aiming and steering are coupled for both the Rift and mouse.

---

[9] Source: from the online game documentation at wiki.teamfortress.com/

In play, this feels like a reasonable balance of inputs, and hand and head seem to quickly blend well. There's a bit less of the uncanny valley feeling of turning the camera with just the mouse and more control of gameplay than turning the character with just the Rift. Still, Ludwig emphasizes that these control schemes are an ongoing area of research and that further exploration is required.

9.2.4   *Using the Rift as an input device*

In several of the modes, Valve effectively made the Rift itself into an input device. By turning their heads, users turned themselves in the game, just like with the mouse. This raises an intriguing prospect: could we do away with the mouse entirely and just use the Rift?

When they're wearing a Rift, it's easy to tell roughly what users are looking at. We can't be pixel-precise, of course, because we're relying on gross head motion, but even without the classic gaze-tracking signals (fluctuation of the pupil, involuntary dilation of the iris), we can still get a pretty good estimate of what part of a scene has caught the user's attention.

One excellent demo of this technique is *Shadow Projection*, an early Oculus Rift demo developed by Kent Bye, Jesse Falleur, and Yori Kvitchko. In *Shadow Projection* you take on the role of a crystalline sci-fi energy being, recognizing and assembling the pieces of a 3D puzzle. As you play the game, you "click" on virtual pieces by examining them each in turn and then looking directly at a cloud of lights above your choice; the cloud shrinks down and winks out, indicating selection.

Wisely, *Shadow Projection* teaches the user how to play right from the start: when you launch the game, you appear in the virtual environment facing the large, clear words "WATCH HERE TO START." Many users will surely look around to visually explore their

Figure 9.18   In *Shadow Projection*, red sparkles appear on the words "WATCH HERE TO START," but only when the user turns to look directly at them.

new surroundings, and in the game, nothing happens for as long as you do. But when you pause and turn to look directly at "WATCH HERE," a cloud of red sparkles appears to indicate that you've successfully "clicked" (figure 9.18).

Once you, the user, have figured out how to "click," the game interface is quite simple and the same effective visual metaphor is used consistently from then on. You're given a choice of three puzzle pieces, with a cloud of sparkles above each; when you look directly at a cloud, the sparkles gradually all turn red over the course of about 2 seconds, and then collapse down (figure 9.19).

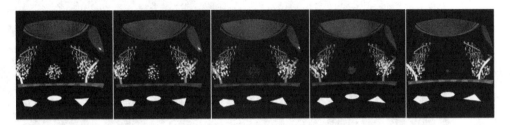

Figure 9.19 *Shadow Projection*'s "click" animation, triggered by the user gazing at a particle cloud. The condensing particles take about 2 seconds to shrink to full density; looking away during that time will immediately cancel the click.

This shows several excellent UI features:

- Selection regions are clearly delineated and distinct, but they're not square buttons.
- You have time to look away again if this wasn't the cloud of points you were looking for.
- The condensing cloud goes "down," evoking a downward mouse click.

When designing the interface, you need to think about the context for each element you present.

9.3   *Animations and avatars*

One of the best ways to promote immersion is *context*. If the day ever comes that we look down and discover that we've turned invisible, that'll be more than a little disturbing.

Problem is, many apps being written for the Rift seem perfectly willing to cast the user in the role of the Invisible Man (or Woman). Even the canonical demo, *Tuscany* from Oculus VR, is guilty. In the *Tuscany* demo, when you tilt your head and look down, there's nothing there (figure 9.20.) That'll break your sense of immersion faster than a guillotine.

What's going on here is a conflict of proprioception. *Proprioception* is our instinctive awareness and understanding of where our limbs are and what they're doing.

Where are your hands and feet?

Figure 9.20   The Oculus VR *Tuscany* demo. The camera is as close as can be to the railing and you're looking down, so you should see your feet (and ideally your hands on the balcony as well). You don't, and that immediately breaks the sense of immersion.

Proprioception is easy to demonstrate: close your eyes and clap. Your brain automatically tracks your arms and knows where they should be.

In the Rift, we run into a major problem: proprioception tells us that our hands are on a keyboard and mouse and that our thighs are at right angles to the floor as we sit in our chair. But in the Rift we look down and we don't see anything of the sort. So, how can we help our users feel like they're really there?

9.3.1   Cockpits and torsos: context in the first person

To counter the lack of in-world presence, some demos provide better context. Most users of the Rift are going to be in a chair, so if your virtual environment centers the user's point of view above a chair, that will help significantly for context and immersion.

In the tech demo *Spaceflight VR*, the player is seated in a high-tech fighter cockpit (figure 9.21), and the chair is empty. (Perhaps the player is invisible?) Although the fiction of the cockpit is believable, it's still jarring to glance down and not see your own legs and body flying the ship.

One of the most effective demos we've tried recently was *Don't Let Go!*, by Yorick van Vliet of Skydome Studios (figure 9.22). In *Don't Let Go!*, the player must struggle to

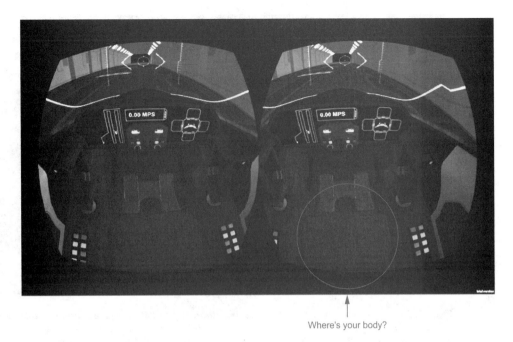

Where's your body?

Figure 9.21 *Spaceflight VR*, a demo for the Rift. The player is sitting in a chair, but the chair appears to be empty.

Figure 9.22 Yorick's *Don't Let Go!* demo. The goal of the game is to sit with your hands on a keyboard, exactly like your in-game avatar. Seeing your in-game body hold the same pose as your real body makes the sense of immersion very strong.

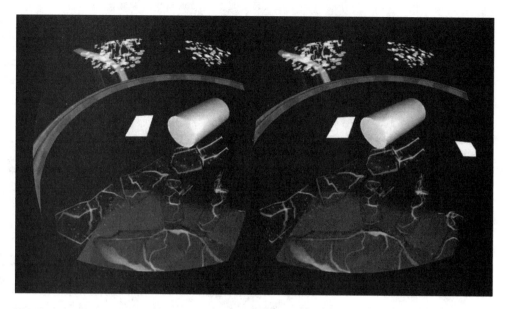

Figure 9.23   In *Shadow Projection*, when you look down at your left hand, the avatar naturally raises its arm so that you can look more closely at what you're holding.

sit in a chair. That makes the immersion very believable: after all, you're already *in* a chair. Best of all, when you look down in *Don't Let Go!*, you see an upper body and arms, with hands in almost the same position as your real hands; it's not hard at all to fool yourself into thinking that you're really in the game.

Shadow Projection uses a similar design, with its seated crystalline avatar (figure 9.23). *Shadow Projection* takes the proprioception benefits of a seated avatar one step further by binding natural body language to the Rift's gaze direction. When you look down at your left hand, your avatar raises that hand up so you can examine whatever's in it more closely. The avatar's animation is limited and simple, but fluid and natural; it feels incredibly realistic to glance down at your hand and see it lift up, even if your real hands are still idle on the keyboard.

The lesson here is clear: the more closely you can match the virtual avatar to the player's proprioception, the more immersive your experience becomes.

9.3.2   *Character animations*

This raises a tricky question: when avatars in the game move their heads, what happens to the camera?

Let's say your character has to defuse a bomb on the ground. You move your avatar up to the bomb; then your character kneels to disarm it. Tension builds as you lean in over the ticking fuse. You peer closer, searching for that one red wire…this is an example of a *preprogrammed character animation*. Users won't explicitly instruct their avatar to kneel or lean forward, but realism and cinematography will call for it.

Unfortunately, it's not a good idea to pin the camera to the moving avatar, for several reasons:

- The canonical rule of VR is *don't move the user's point of view unexpectedly.* Moving the camera without direct action from users, or without setting the scene so they anticipate motion, is far too likely to cause simulation sickness. See chapter 10 for details.
- When the avatar kneels or stands up, it will badly violate the proprioception of a sitting player.
- If you allow the user to continue to look around, you risk users turning away from the bomb. But if you lock their view to the avatar, users will feel that they've lost control as the Rift ceases to respond.
- If your animation rotates users (the character turns as they kneel at the bomb), you risk breaking the game's sense of forward.

The right solution for avatar animations that move the avatar probably hasn't been discovered yet. If your game is heavily geared for the Rift, it may be best to sidestep the issue and avoid animations when you can.

If your animation is designed to move the character, it's okay for users to see a quick fade-to-black and then a fade-back-in and see the character has moved. In his 2014 GDC talk *Developing VR Experiences with the Oculus Rift* (gdcvault.com/play/1020714), Tom Forsyth gives the simple examples of getting into a car, getting out of bed, and getting up after being knocked down—all seemingly innocuous animations that would swing the user's head through a nauseating series of angles and turns. For these cases, Forsyth reports that it's okay just to fade out and fade quickly back in again with your character in the new pose; the viewer's brain adapts pretty readily. But, he cautions, keep head tracking turned on throughout the cut-and-fade; even as you fade out and back, let your users turn their heads—otherwise it'll leave them feeling like they've lost control.

For animations that don't move the user, the "right" answer is open for debate. Forsyth suggests that perhaps it's best to show a "ghostly" version of the player's avatar performing the animation and then return to match with the eyes of the player; for something like leaning over to pick up a fallen weapon, it might be acceptable to the user if the character avatar peeled away from the Rift viewpoint, leaned down, picked up the weapon, and then stood up again until the avatar's eyes lined up with the Rift again. Of course, that approach is fraught with complexity—you'll have to turn the avatar's head to match the Rift at the same time as you're running the animation, which will be a real technical animation challenge. In addition, it'll probably be pretty weird to see a ghost view of your own face peel away from you and then come back. But it could work.

THE MEATHOOK AVATARS OF *TEAM FORTRESS 2*

In *Team Fortress 2*, each of the characters has a lot of wacky personality. When you play the game in VR mode, you really *are* that character, and the effect is great. The Heavy lumbers about, the Scout sprints like a maniac, and all the character animations—the lumbering gait, the swinging bat—happen like you're really there. Forsyth describes how "ridiculously fun" these engaging animations are and how much they add to the experience of gameplay.

When a character animation plays, often the character's feet are firmly planted on the ground, or if they aren't, it's part of the animation. Characters may bob or duck, lifting and lowering their heads as they move. And here, Forsyth observes, there's a problem: moving the avatar's head without tracking it with the Rift is bad, and moving the Rift view is much worse. So Valve needed a way to run complex animations without moving the avatar's head.

The solution that Valve adopted for *TF2* is what Forsyth calls "meathook avatars." The idea is that by anchoring the animation to the observer's neck and head, instead of to the ground, an animation can play and move the avatar's limbs without bobbing the head about. Of course, this means that the avatar's feet *will* leave the ground, but unless players are looking straight down and watching for it, they won't notice the disconnect.

Forsyth explains that they used the word *meathook* because if you hang an avatar's body from the neck and head and animate it below that so the feet dance in the air, it looks like it's been hung on a hook. As long as you're careful to play the Rift variant only to the Rift itself, this works well. Of course, don't play the same animation in third-person view or to other players online—that would look more than a little odd.

9.4 Tracking devices and gestural interfaces

So far we've looked at all the ways you can help your users feel as immersed as can be while they navigate in the Rift with a gamepad or mouse. But no VR UI will be complete until you can reach out in the real world and reach out inside the Rift as well.

9.4.1 Beyond the gamepad

In this section we're going to sum up a few of the VR tracking devices that are commercially available today, or will be available soon. These are devices whose sensors offer a much higher potential of immersion than a gamepad or mouse. The presence of a particular product in this section doesn't mean that we endorse it; we've chosen just a few devices out of the many that are beginning to spring up. (Thank you, Kickstarter!)

3DCONNEXION SPACEMOUSE

3Dconnexion's SpaceMouse (www.3dconnexion.com) is a 6DOF joystick designed for animators and 3D modelers (figure 9.24).

The SpaceMouse transmits translations and rotations, and it claims to offer a smooth and intuitive mapping from the user's hand motion to in-app manipulation. The Space-Mouse has highly precise variable pressure sensors. This allows a trained user to twist, pull, and push with anything

Figure 9.24   3Dconnexion's SpaceMouse

from fine shades of pressure up to broad, coarse motions. In 2013, 3Dconnexion introduced a wireless version of the SpaceMouse.

3Dconnexion works closely with application developers to integrate the SpaceMouse, and their site boasts a long list of integrated platforms. They don't position their product as a gaming peripheral; this is a precision pointer, not a tough piece of gaming hardware. Developers can sign up for the free 3Dconnexion SDK at www.3dconnexion.com.

LEAP MOTION

The Leap Motion (www.leapmotion.com) is a small, oblong peripheral that sits beside your keyboard or mouse and watches the airspace above it (figure 9.25).

Figure 9.25   The Leap Motion

The Leap Motion detects a human hand or hands hovering overhead and transmits the hand's position to the PC. With the Leap Motion a user can send swipe, pinch, wave, and grab motions to the PC, which can then be captured by software for gestural UI. Leap offers an impressive array of software apps that integrate its gesture controls.

Leap has a robust developer support program and offers their SDK for free download (developer.leapmotion.com). They've also recently announced "The Leap Fund, a $25 million investment initiative focused on entrepreneurs that use Leap Motion technology to develop breakthrough experiences" to encourage small and medium-sized developers building the next killer app or integrating the Leap into existing software. Leap's clear commitment to applications beyond the games industry is good news for VR developers who aren't sticking to the entertainment space.

MICROSOFT KINECT

The Microsoft Kinect (www.xbox.com/xbox-one/accessories/kinect-for-xbox-one) is an oblong bar designed to be mounted above or below a video display (figure 9.26).

Figure 9.26   The Microsoft Kinect for the Xbox One

The device comprises a suite of sensors, including a conventional webcam-style camera, an infrared laser-projection depth sensor, and an array of microphones for spatialized audio. The Kinect is able to provide full-body 3D motion capture, allowing software to "see" where a human body is in space. The Kinect is also suitable for facial recognition, although its resolution isn't typically sufficient for resolving hand gestures. Microsoft continues to evolve the Kinect; the version shipped with the Xbox One is significantly more advanced than the original, and the Kinect 2 for Windows began shipping in summer 2014.

For developers, Microsoft's SDK (www.microsoft.com/en-us/kinectforwindowsdev) is freely available for download. Ample resources from Microsoft are supplemented nowadays by a cornucopia of third-party community projects on the web; curious people

Figure 9.27   The Virtuix Omni

with screwdrivers have reverse-engineered a large number of the Kinect's features. Ask your favorite search engine for details.

Many feel that the Kinect is the last piece in the gesture UI puzzle; all that's needed now is the software. By helping applications to detect waves, swipes, and other common gesture UI motions, the Kinect sensors seem well positioned as a mainstay for future VR UI. A team at MIT has built a JavaScript plug-in to Google Chrome that allows users to control their browser by gestures; another MIT group has used a Kinect to re-create the *Minority Report* UI. A number of other academic and research-driven projects have emerged.

VIRTUIX OMNI

Unlike the examples cited so far, the Virtuix Omni (www.virtuix.com) is a VR support device for the rest of us…literally: it's not for your hands, it's for your feet (figure 9.27).

Players stand inside a 20-inch-diameter ring of restraining plastic wearing special shoes; to move yourself forward in a game, you simply walk forward in the Omni. The developers of the Omni claim that the device allows for "running, jumping, backwards stepping, strafing (sideways stepping), and even sitting." High-precision sensors in the Omni track the player's body motion and translate human motion into keyboard and gamepad controls, theoretically allowing intuitive control of almost any first-person game.

Virtuix have suggested that the Omni could also be used for nongame activities, such as fitness and exercise programs. This has interesting implications for the couch potatoes among us. The Virtuix Omni SDK is available from Virtuix's developer website at www.virtuix.com/resource-center/.

RAZER HYDRA

The Razer Hydra (www.razerzone.com) is a pair of 6DOF joysticks, comparable to those of a Nintendo Wii (figure 9.28).

Figure 9.28   The Razer Hydra

The central base station allows the joysticks to report not only their orientations and rotations but also absolute position relative to the base station. This means that users can lift and twist a Razer Hydra controller and watch their hands lift and twist in VR. The Hydra is a computer games controller and has been successfully integrated into a number of best-selling titles, such as Bethesda Software's *Skyrim.*

The Razer Hydra began its commercial life as the Sixense TrueMotion. An SDK for programming the controller is offered by Sixense at sixense.com/hardware/sixensesdk.

STEM SYSTEM

The STEM System (sixense.com/hardware/wireless) is developer Sixense's next-generation sequel to the Razer Hydra (figure 9.29).

According to the website, the STEM System is "a wireless, motion tracking platform for video games, virtual reality (VR), and more. It enables players to interact naturally and intuitively with games by tracking full position and orientation at all times, whether at the desktop or throughout the entire living room."

The STEM System consists of up to five wireless tracking beacons and a central base station, echoing the design of the older Razer Hydra. Each of the five beacons transmits its location and orientation with (according to the developers) sub–10 ms latency. By

Figure 9.29   The STEM System

attaching a beacon to each arm and leg and another to the torso or spine of the user, the STEM System can compute a remarkably accurate projection of where a human body must be (figure 9.30). Beacons in the hand are held in Razer Hydra–style game controllers.

Figure 9.30   Still from the video "Five-Tracker Demo: STEM System Prototype," on YouTube

Using the inverse kinematic support already available through Unity, developers have reported being able to integrate the STEM's data into virtual worlds remarkably easily. For more advanced integrations, the Sixense SDK (sixense.com/hardware/sixensesdk) is available.

In early prototypes of the STEM system, Sixense suggested that the fifth sensor could alternatively be attached to the user's head rather than the torso. But with the addition of high-resolution head tracking to the Crystal Cove, this now seems like a less likely configuration. The flexibility of the system is clear: with the ability to place each sensor almost anywhere, a remarkable degree of immersion can be achieved.

9.4.2 *Gestural interfaces*

With such a panoply of high-potential devices becoming available, the end could well be in sight for the gamepad and mouse. As immersive hardware becomes more commonplace, we can expect to see paradigms for UI design shift even further than they already have.

That said, it's possible that the UI of the future has already been designed. There's been a strong trend in the movies lately toward what researchers have begun to call *gestural UIs*. With waves of their hands, actors can give crisp, clear instruction to their computers and data flows around them.

Today dozens of science-fiction movies have used gestural UIs, among them

- *Minority Report* (2002)—Detective Anderton (Tom Cruise) waves scores of images across his screen, pauses the stream with an outthrust hand, spreads his fingers apart to zoom, and more.
- *World Builder* (2007, short)—A romantic artist uses simple hand gestures to stretch, translate, rotate, and clone primitive objects into a virtual city street.
- *Iron Man* (2008)—Tony Stark (Robert Downey Jr.) redesigns his eponymous armor by grasping a hologram, tapping to select, grabbing and dragging to discard, and spinning the model with a wave of his hand.

  The same hologram interface was later spoofed in an episode of *Marvel's Agents of S.H.I.E.L.D.* TV series (2014), in which Agents Coulson and Ward can't figure out the gestural UI and are unable to zoom the mystery device they've captured (figure 9.31).
- *Ender's Game* (2013)—Video playback is paused with an outthrust hand and rewound with a gesture from right to left; later, Ender Wiggin (Asa Butterfield) pivots the cameras of a massive 3D virtual battlespace by tilting his arms to tip the scene forward.

The best part is these UIs aren't entirely fictional. The *Minority Report* interface, as we mentioned earlier, was re-created in the real world in 2010 by researchers at MIT (video.mit.edu/watch/kinect-hand-detection-12073/) using a Kinect and the open source `libfreenect` library for Linux (figure 9.32). The hand detection software, which is publicly available, is said to be able to distinguish hands and fingers in a

Figure 9.31 *Marvel's Agents of S.H.I.E.L.D.* Coulson and Ward struggle to convince their holographic table to "zoom in" on a mysterious device. (Episode 1x13, "T.R.A.C.K.S.," 2014)

Figure 9.32 The *Minority Report* UI running on a Kinect, by researchers at CSAIL, MIT's Computer Science and Artificial Intelligence Laboratory (image and video by Garratt Gallagher).

cloud of more than 60,000 points at 30 frames per second. The developers claim that this enables natural, real-time interaction.

The work at MIT is clearly only the beginning, and we expect many more innovations to come along, especially now that tracking devices and the Rift make things like holographic tables a realistic possibility. What's interesting is that this new field of UI design has already been designed, sort of, by Hollywood: a sort of informal consensus is growing across recent films that already defines many of our gestural preconceptions.

To learn more about this growing new interface field, we encourage you to read the book *Make It So: Interaction Design Lessons from Science Fiction* by Nathan Shedroff and Christopher Noessel (Rosenfeld Media, 2012). Their chapter on the gesture UI summarizes a few of the key concepts that Hollywood has now taught us to expect:

- *Wave to activate*—To engage something's primary function, just wave at it. Modern-day faucets already do this.
- *Push to move*—Virtual objects can be pushed and pulled in space, with collision but without gravity or friction. Mobile web browsers echo this today as we navigate up and down a web page on our phones by dragging a finger.
- *Turn to rotate*—Grasping opposing points on a virtual model and twisting around a central axis will rotate an object. We see a similar metaphor again on mobile devices, where a two-finger rotation can often rotate images or game cameras.
- *Swipe to dismiss*—The most natural of motions, flinging our hand through a virtual object dismisses it from view. This is the virtual equivalent of shoving everything off a table.
- *Point or touch to select*—The mouse without the mouse: the user reaches out naturally to a virtual object, and the object responds to the contact.
- *Extend the hand to shoot*—When wearing a device with a single distance function (such as a glove that fires repulsor beams), it's enough to thrust out your arm with the hand in a specific pose to fire the weapon.
- *Pinch and spread to scale*—Like rotation, users can grab arbitrary points in the virtual model and collapse their hands down or fling them open, expanding or contracting their view of the entire model.

Shedroff and Noessel emphasize that their catalog of the gestures UI of Hollywood requires the computer to understand subtleties of human intent and context; actor Tom Cruise can page quickly through *Minority Report* images by waving both hands, but when he *really* sweeps his arms, he clears the screen. They also remind their reader that the set of gestures is not yet complete; Hollywood—or perhaps the gaming industry—will uncover more.

In the meantime, with the Rift and Kinect and body trackers like the STEM System all coming on line, the gestural interface of the future may well be much closer than we think.

9.5   *Summary*

In this chapter you learned

- Because the frame of the screen has been removed and the user is now immersed in a virtual environment, conventional UI practices must be rethought from the ground up for the Rift.
- By following well-researched guidelines, you can produce clear, easy-to-use, and above all simple UIs that work smoothly in VR.
- Giving your user a strong sense of context is key to immersion and can help reduce simulation sickness.
- Don't move the camera without the user's direct command.
- VR interfaces are already being influenced by Hollywood science fiction, such as gestural interfaces, but there's still a lot of experimentation left to be done.
- Remember the guidelines of good UI design:
  - Always show state
  - Make your UI simple, clean, and clear
  - Don't penalize users for errors, and help them recover
  - Don't require expertise, but do reward it.

Reducing motion sickness and discomfort

This chapter covers

- Why the Rift can cause user discomfort, including motion sickness
- Creating a comfortable VR environment
- Testing your VR application for motion sickness potential

You've created the first version of your software. The graphics are stunning and the software is responding to every head movement. For the first few minutes, your new test subjects are impressed and smiling but pretty quickly their smiles fade and they start to look a little green. One test subject even pulls off the Rift and asks if there's someplace he can lie down for a bit. You wanted to create an immersive experience that gave your users the feeling they'd been transported somewhere else, but instead they ended up feeling like they had been on a bad trip to nowhere. This reaction wasn't at all what you expected. You tested the software yourself many times and never had this reaction. So, what happened? And more important, what can you do about it? As your users graphically demonstrated, motion sickness is one of the biggest challenges to creating a usable, comfortable, and immersive VR environment.

10.1 What does causing motion sickness and discomfort mean?

Motion sickness, VR sickness, or simulator sickness—whatever you call it, what we're talking about are the symptoms of discomfort people feel when experiencing a mismatch between actual motion and what their body expects. In traditional motion sickness, such as you might get from riding in a car or airplane, motion is felt but not seen. You may feel fine riding in a car looking out the window and watching the world go by, but the minute you look down to read a book and you've focused on a stationary object, you feel sick. Simulator sickness and VR sickness from using the Rift can arise in the same way. With the Rift on, you can feel that you've moved your head but the view hasn't changed, or illness can be triggered from the inverse situation where motion is seen but not felt; that is, the view changes but you're sitting still. No matter the trigger, the symptoms of discomfort are similar: headache, drowsiness, nausea, dizziness, and sweating.

> **Migraine headaches and motion sickness**
>
> People who get migraine headaches are more prone to motion sickness.[1] There's a wide range of migraine triggers (among them, food, stress, and weather), most of which aren't relevant to Rift use. But eyestrain, lights (bright or flickering), and movie viewing are all part of the experience of using a Rift and all are possible migraine triggers.

It is also important to note that with the Rift, motion sickness symptoms aren't the only discomfort users might feel. The Rift is a device worn on the head and over the eyes. Although it isn't heavy or particularly uncomfortable, using it can cause fatigue, eyestrain, and neck strain.

Finding and addressing the specific cause of motion sickness or other discomfort in your software may not be simple or easy to do by yourself. It'll take testing, iteration, and intuition. For testing, you're going to need to get help from others, because what might cause one person severe discomfort may not be noticed by another. Just because you felt no symptoms using the software doesn't mean no one else will. You'll need to test carefully, in stages, and with a variety of people, so that you can get the feedback you need to create comfortable software. But before you even get to testing, you're going to need your intuition to get a prototype worth testing. Fortunately, you don't have to rely on your intuition alone. As more and more VR applications are being created, some general design guidelines for increasing comfort are taking shape.

---

[1] Cuomo-Granston, A., and P. D. Drummond. (2010). "Migraine and Motion Sickness: What Is the Link?" Progress in Neurobiology 91: 300–312.

10.2 Strategies and guidelines for creating a comfortable VR environment

Motion sickness from VR isn't a solved problem, nor do we expect it to be in the near future. The good news is that everyone working on VR is also working on this problem.

Limitation of 3D display and the Rift

The Rift, like many 3D devices, uses stereoscopic images to create the illusion of 3D. With stereoscopic 3D there's a disparity between focus depth and *vergence* (the simultaneous movement of both eyes in opposite directions to obtain or maintain binocular vision), and this disparity can lead to eyestrain. When we perceive a real object coming toward us, our eyes refocus to ensure clarity. But with 3D displays like the Rift, our brain is tricked into thinking an object is coming at us when in reality the screen is at a fixed position. As our eyes constantly readjust to fight our natural tendency to focus on the closer object, we get eyestrain.

In addition to our own observations,[2] the ongoing discussions on the Rift Forums on this topic, and the information in the *Oculus Best Practices Guide* (developer.oculusvr.com/; a must-read for anyone doing VR), we found the postmortems published by Valve about *Team Fortress 2* (media.steampowered.com/apps/valve/2013/Team_Fortress_in_ VR_GDC.pdf) and by Marauder Interactive about *Enemy StarFighter* (enemystarfighter .com/blog/2013/9/5/vr-lessons-learned) very helpful.

In this section, we'll look at some of the best advice currently available. We'll be covering the following topics:

- Starting with a solid foundation
- Giving the user a comfortable start
- Following the golden rule of VR comfort: the user is in control of the camera
- Rethinking your camera work to use new approaches for favorite techniques
- Making navigation as comfortable as possible
- Designing the world with VR constraints in mind
- Paying attention to ergonomic issues such as eyestrain, neck strain, and fatigue
- Using sound to orient the user and increase immersion
- Giving your player the option of an avatar body
- Accounting for human variation
- Helping your users help themselves

---

[2] We've done both formal and informal testing of the Rift using various demos. We've posted some of our testing results on our blog at rifty-business.blogspot.com/search/label/usability-test-results.

- Evaluating your content for use in VR
- Experimenting as much as possible

As you develop your application, keep in mind that any time someone is using the Rift there's the potential for discomfort. You'll want to pay attention to these guidelines for everything you create, including menus and loading scenes, not just for gameplay.

10.2.1 Start with a solid foundation for your VR application

Building a comfortable VR environment starts with building a solid foundation. Almost everything we've talked about prior to this chapter goes into creating a comfortable VR environment. And if you do nothing else, at the very least make sure you get the foundation right:

- Make certain your users are aware of the health and safety issues of using the Rift.
- Use the correct distortion for the Rift lenses (covered in chapter 4 for using the C API or done for you by using the Unity Integration package).
- Use the correct projection matrix and model view matrix (covered in chapter 5 for using the C API or done for you by using the Unity Integration package).
- Have latency down to a reasonable level (covered in chapter 6 for using the C API or chapter 8 for using Unity).
- Use a UI intended for VR (covered in chapter 9).

Displaying a safety warning is easy. Oculus has taken care of that for you—all applications built with the 0.4 SDK and later automatically display a safety warning on startup. For the rest, as you can see, just by reading and following the development process in this book you're on the right track. But there's more you can do.

10.2.2 Give your user a comfortable start

The Oculus Health and Safety Warnings found in the *Oculus Best Practices Guide* tell the user to "remain seated whenever possible." Oculus has stated that they're targeting a seated experience at this time. When using the Rift, users will typically be seated and they'll naturally get themselves into a comfortable position. You want the user to be able to remain in that comfortable position even after putting on the Rift. But when observing people using the Rift, we've seen them put the Rift on, then twist around to get a better view, and then spend the entire time trying to navigate a demo with their head turned toward their shoulder. When they take off the Rift, they complain that their neck hurts (figure 10.1).

We've also observed people who, instead of turning their head to look, used the gamepad to turn around and then groaned and said, "I did not like that, at all."

The user has turned his head over his shoulder for a better view of the game. Playing for long periods in this position can lead to neck strain.

Let the user get into a comfortable position before the game starts and then orient the player in the direction they need to be.

Figure 10.1   Don't force your user to look over a shoulder to get a good view.

You can prevent both of these scenarios by

- Making it clear to the user when to put on the Rift
- Letting the user indicate when to start tracking head position
- Orienting a user's avatar in the direction they need to look/move at the start of the game

We covered how you can help the user move from the desktop environment to the Rift environment in chapter 9. By analyzing the head tracker data (the data from a Rift sitting on a desk shows a very different pattern compared to the data from a Rift being worn by a person), you can know when to start head tracking and when you can assume the current orientation is forward. After the user has the Rift on, you'll also want to give the user an option to re-center the view if drift has occurred or if the user wasn't facing forward.

Now that the user is off to a good start and head tracking has been enabled, the first rule of head tracking is that the user needs to be in control.

10.2.3   *The golden rule of VR comfort: the user is in control of the camera*

If there's a golden rule for VR comfort, it's that the user is in control of the camera. Looking around in the VR world needs to feel to the user as much as possible like looking around in the real world. This means that head tracking must exactly match what the user is doing and it means you can't change the FOV.

HEAD TRACKING MUST EXACTLY MATCH WHAT THE USER IS DOING

You want to make sure that head tracking exactly matches what the user is doing. As the Team Fortress folks put it, "If the user turns their head 27 degrees to the right and rolls it 3 degrees, their view in the game needs to turn 27 degrees to the right and roll 3 degrees. Anything else is going to make people sick."

Usurping control of the camera's orientation is pretty much a recipe for motion sickness. That said, there might be times for judiciously breaking this rule, and as you'll see later in this chapter, there are places where compromises need to be made.

DON'T CHANGE CAMERA POSITION IN AN UNEXPECTED WAY

Moving the camera's position in a way that the user doesn't expect can be a motion sickness trigger for some people. When changing the camera's position, do so in a way that puts the user in control of the change, such as using the gamepad for navigation. If you're moving the camera for the user, we suggest moving in the direction the user (or the vehicle the user is in) is facing and that you make sure the user expects the change. If the user is inside a cockpit or car, the user expects the scene outside of the vehicle to change and the movement is more comfortable.

DON'T CHANGE THE FIELD OF VIEW

In the Rift, the FOV is fixed because it must be the same as the actual headset. The *Oculus Best Practices Guide* puts this rule in very strong terms: "You should not change any of the default settings related to FOV or scale under any circumstances, and care must be taken to get the view scaling exactly the same way the SDK specifies."

So, why is changing the FOV such a big deal? No matter how still you think you might be sitting, your head is always moving a tiny amount. You naturally adjust to this movement by moving your eyes to preserve the image at the center of the visual field. For example, when you turn your head to the left, your eyes move to the right. This reflexive movement is called the *vestibulo-ocular reflex* and it's what allows you to have a stable view of any object.

If the rendered FOV doesn't match the perceived FOV, those small head movements and the reflexive eye movements will no longer correspond one to one. This mismatch can make it appear as though stationary objects gain sudden motion when you turn your head, leading to severe motion sickness. It may also lead to maladaptation of the vestibulo-ocular reflex, diminishing the user's ability to maintain a stable view of an object.

10.2.4 Rethink your camera work: new approaches for favorite techniques

Many modern games borrow heavily from cinema for storytelling techniques, such as using cutscenes for flashbacks to provide the required background information to play the game or zooming in on an important element in the story. Unfortunately, many of those techniques violate the golden rule of VR comfort by taking control of the camera. If you want to incorporate some of these techniques into your application, you need to take a new approach. The exciting thing is, in some cases, using a new approach won't just make the experience more comfortable; it can also make the experience more immersive.

DON'T TURN THE CAMERA VIEW: GET THE USER'S ATTENTION INSTEAD

Users are going to look at what they want to see. It may be tempting to turn their view for them to get their attention, but that's a surefire way to make the user sick.

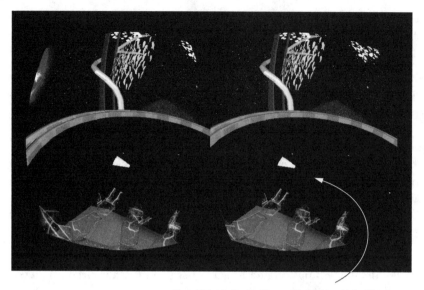

To get the user's attention and have them look at the
object in the avatar's hand, the first object in the game
(a triangle) flies across the user's view and into the
avatar's hand.

Figure 10.2 *Shadow Projection* **uses a flying object to get the user's attention.**

As discussed in chapter 9, if you need to get a user to change their head orientation, you must do it by getting their attention and having them change where they're looking on their own. Motion, color changes, and sound cues are all ways to get the user's attention. In the Oculus Rift demo *Shadow Projection* users have to look at the avatar's hand to see the shape they're searching for (figure 10.2).

Users are free to look anywhere they please, but as the game begins an object flies in and down into the avatar's hand to get users' attention, showing them where to look.

DON'T SIMPLY ZOOM THE CAMERA: PROVIDE CONTEXT, GIVE THE USER CONTROL, AND USE A SUBSCREEN FOR THE ZOOMED-IN IMAGE

You can zoom in on an object comfortably if the user has the proper context to understand it and you use a subscreen for the zoomed-in image so that you're not changing the Rift FOV. Context comes from the storytelling in your game; for example, using a scope on a gun for targeting. Or, as in *Private Eye* (privateeyevr.com/), you're a 1950s New York detective, and one of your tools is a pair of binoculars (figure 10.3).

The binoculars give the user context for the zoom, and because players must choose to bring the binoculars to their eyes, they're in control. More critical than context and control in this case is using a subscreen for the zoomed-in image. If you try out this application, you'll notice that the head tracking remains relative to the Rift FOV, but the FOV you see in the subscreen is a much smaller portion of the screen. This results in an experience similar to looking through binoculars.

The player has binoculars that are raised to the eyes before the scene is zoomed in. This gives the user both control over the zoom and context.

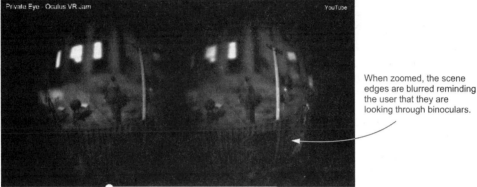

When zoomed, the scene edges are blurred reminding the user that they are looking through binoculars.

Figure 10.3   An example of giving the user control and context for a camera zoom

DON'T FREEZE THE CAMERA: USE OTHER METAPHORS TO SHOW THAT THE WORLD HAS STOPPED

Suddenly stopping the head tracking is disorienting and you don't want to do it for any reason. Many games freeze the camera when a character dies as a cinematic way of expressing that the world has stopped. If your character dies, you need to use a different metaphor to express death, such as a slow fade to black (or try to be a bit more creative).

PAY SPECIAL ATTENTION TO CUTSCENES

We wrote at length about cutscenes in chapter 9, but because it's going to be one of the major hurdles in getting high-quality cinematic-style games on the Rift, we want to discuss them here as well. Cutscenes are one of the great tools in cinema for story-telling; the director can show you what's going on somewhere else and can focus the camera on what's important. As a software developer, you're used to being in the role of director. You choose where the user looks and where to focus the camera, but the golden rule of VR comfort is that the user is in control of the camera. So, as the developer/director of the story, how do you move the story forward if you don't

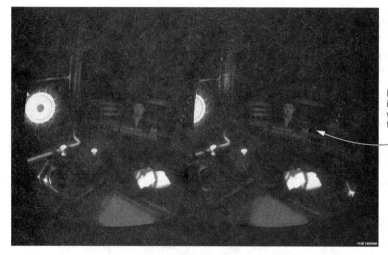

Background information is presented on a screen within the game rather than as a cutscene.

Figure 10.4 **Background content that might have been a cutscene in other media is shown on a computer screen that's part of the environment, as in *Technolust*, by Iris Productions.**

have control of the camera? And how do you do it without breaking the user's feeling of immersion?

For background content or other content that the user is simply viewing and not part of, the easiest solution is to find a way to transition to a more screen-like experience for the duration of the non-interaction. For example, there could be some kind of actual screen or display in the environment to which the user's attention is somehow drawn (figure 10.4), as in *Technolust* (irisproductions.ca/technolust/).

Incorporating scene changes into the story can also be very effective. As you can see in figure 10.5, one example is *Trial of the Rift Drifter*, created by Aldin Dynamics (share.oculusvr.com/app/trial-of-the-rift-drifter).

In *Trial*, you're a prisoner and for a scene change, a sack is placed over your head and when it's pulled off, you're in the new scene. Both the visual and audio cues make for a believable transition.

No matter which technique you use, the content needs to serve the story you're telling. A sack over your head works great for a dystopian prison scene or an oak barrel over your head works well for a pirate pub brawl, but throwing something over the user's head won't work for every scene. The point is, you've got to be creative in your storytelling (and quite honestly, that creativity is something we can't wait to see).

Scene changes built seamlessly into the story provide
greater immersion and are less likely to cause motion sickness.

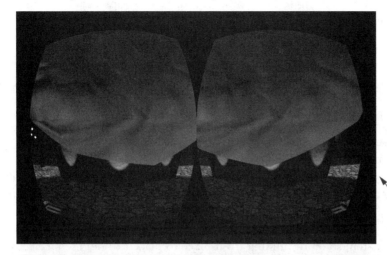

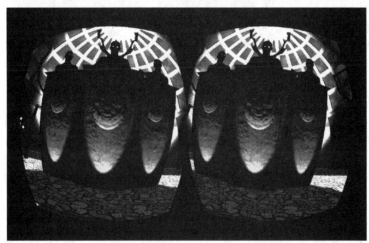

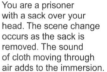

You are a prisoner
with a sack over your
head. The scene change
occurs as the sack is
removed. The sound
of cloth moving through
air adds to the immersion.

Figure 10.5   In *Trial of the Rift Drifter*, the scene change is part of the story.

10.2.5 Make navigation as comfortable as possible: character movement and speed

You can avoid most motion sickness by providing a stationary experience for the user. Depending on the story you're telling, this can be a good solution to the problem. For example, *Private Eye*, a film noir detective game with more than a nod to Hitchcock's *Rear Window*, cleverly limits movement in the game by giving the player character a broken leg. Of course, that won't always work; you can't break the leg of every player character, and simply saying "don't let the player move" is about as practical as telling someone who gets car sick to just stay home. Balancing the trade-off between navigation and comfort is going to be a difficult job, so let's look at ways you can tip the scales in your favor.

USE REAL-WORLD SPEEDS

Whenever possible, use real-world speeds for your characters. The *Oculus Best Practices Guide* lists a walking rate of 1.4 m/s and a jogging rate of 3 m/s as most comfortable. In general, the more natural the interaction, the more comfortable the user experience will be.

DON'T USE HEAD BOB

Head bob, the slight up and down movement used to simulate human movement in some first-person games, doesn't work well on the Rift. Each of those small movements adds a bit of discomfort for most users. We want the user to be in control of as much motion as possible, and any added motion not initiated by the user, no matter how small, is a source of discomfort.

Unfortunately, smoothly gliding from place to place can be disconcerting as well, and more research needs to be done in this area. Solutions may come from using input devices that take into account more body movement. We've been experimenting with using the Wii Fit board as a controller to allow walking by putting pressure alternately onto each foot, because this will naturally cause the body to shift and the view to move with it.

LIMIT BACKSTEPPING, SIDESTEPPING (STRAFING), TURNING AROUND, AND SPINNING

Try to limit situations that require backstepping, sidestepping (strafing), and turning around. Spinning the user around is just cruel.

When we talk about spinning, we mean both actively making users turn themselves around, and having objects rotating around the user or using stripes (of light or texture) streaming around users to make it appear as though they're inside a rotating object. We've even heard complaints from some users that moving along a curved wall was too much.

You don't want to eliminate these situations completely—it can make moving around in your virtual world too cumbersome—but be cognizant of the cumulative effects these actions can have on your users.

TRY USING "VR COMFORT MODE" FOR TURNING

Users are typically sitting in a chair where they're not able to easily turn 180 degrees around and face the opposite direction. For turning around, users are going to need to use the mouse or gamepad (or other input device), and for many people this type of movement is very uncomfortable. The main problem with turning via controllers is that it's a sudden transition from a match to a mismatch between eye/head motion and the world.

The team at Cloudhead Games (www.thegallerygame.com) has shared their ideas on how to make turning in VR more comfortable, and they've called their method VR

Comfort Mode. In it, turning isn't continuous, but rather turns happen in rapid chunks. For example, you're looking forward and then in an instant you're looking 15 degrees to the left of the former view.

Both types of turns are examples of taking control of the camera, but in order to give users a full world to explore, and without requiring them to be able to turn their actual heads and face every direction (and do so without getting tangled up in cables), this is unavoidable.

According to the Cloudhead Games team, their tests show that turning ends up being less distressing if the change in orientation is sudden, without any actual perceived motion, rather than constant transitions between modes where the inner ear matches the motion and those where it doesn't.

Turning is one of the most common complaints that we've heard from users in terms of comfort. Because it's difficult to design a fully immersive world without being able to turn around, we expect that there will be a lot more research done in this area. And because what's best practice today may easily change by tomorrow, techniques for turning is an area to watch in the VR development community.

USE CAUTION WHEN ADDING FLYING OR OTHER EXTREME ACTIONS

Even though your users can be faster than a speeding bullet, more powerful than a locomotive, and able to leap tall buildings in a single bound inside a virtual world, extreme actions in VR are still extreme actions. And unless your user is Superman, they probably aren't used to being able to do these things. Learning to handle new superpowers will take time. Even Superman was probably a little queasy the first time he flew.

Be kind to your users (who probably aren't Superman or Wonder Woman) and do the following:

- Provide some orientation to them up front about what they need to do or about what they're about to experience.
- Provide multiple play paths that are more and less extreme. Doing so gives your users the chance to participate or decline, and if they choose the more extreme path, be sure to give them time to get used to the VR experience before actions become extreme.
- Build in rest time between extreme actions even after users have had time to get used to the experience. Most people don't want to ride the roller coaster nonstop for the entire day at the fun park.

Even with these precautions, extreme actions in VR may still cause motion sickness just as they would in real life. But don't let motion sickness dissuade you from trying out extreme actions in VR. In VR, you aren't risking broken bones, so it can be an awesome opportunity to safely be a bit of a daredevil.

10.2.6   *Design your world with VR constraints in mind*

VR gives you the opportunity to visit any world you imagine. But some of those worlds will be more comfortable to visit than others, and in this section we're going to look at some points to consider when designing your world.

DESIGN TO SCALE

The scale of the world and the player is an important part of the immersive VR experience. By default, the Rift SDK uses meters as the reference unit and, to keep things simple, you should use meters too. In addition, objects should be sized based on real-world sizes when the scale of the objects isn't part of the game.

Real-world architects know that the size and scale of everything contributes to how comfortable and navigable the building they've designed is. Many books are available on architectural graphics standards that provide examples of properly scaled rooms, doorways, stairs, and kitchens. You can leverage what real-world architects already know about design and scale as a starting point for creating comfortable VR spaces.

Using real-life scale is part of what makes it feel natural to be on the set of a famous TV show in the demo *Jerry's Place* (jerrysplacevr.com) by Greg Miller (figure 10.6).

We also love the artwork and attention to detail that went into this demo.

LIMIT STAIRS AND OTHER UNEVEN SURFACES

The *Tuscany* demo included with the Oculus SDK contains stairs that a user can go up and then look out at the sea from a balcony. In a fair number of the Rift demos we've

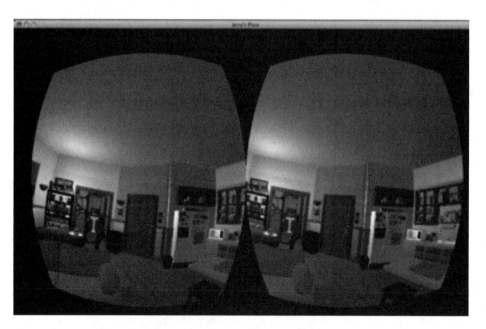

Figure 10.6   Using real-life scale is part of what makes it feel natural to be on the set of a famous TV show in the demo *Jerry's Place*.

given, the moment users got hit with motion sickness for the first time was going up or down these stairs.

We suggest, if possible, that you use flat walking surfaces and elevators/lifts. Invisible ramps can be placed over stairs to create a smoother experience. Also, remember that if users enter an elevator, have them exit the elevator on the opposite side, so they don't need to turn around to continue.

DON'T CHANGE THE USER'S HORIZON LINE

One piece of advice given to people who experience motion sickness while traveling in a car or on a boat is to focus on the horizon line. This advice is so common that we can imagine many users who start experiencing motion sickness do just that. Now, imagine that the horizon line moves.

DON'T LEAVE THE USER FLOATING IN A VOID: ADD STATIC REFERENCE POINTS WHENEVER POSSIBLE

Having static reference points, such as a cockpit, can help. This makes driving games a natural fit for VR. A cockpit, though, isn't a suitable solution for many scenarios. One suggestion for first-person scenarios is to use an indicator on the ground to show which way the user's body is facing in relation to the head, although we suspect that would break immersion rather quickly.

If you choose to provide an on-rails experience where users don't control where they go, a static reference point is almost essential. Additional cues to help orient the user are also quite welcome. The demo *Titans of Space* (www.crunchywood.com) by DrashVR displays the words "Auto Pilot" in the cockpit when you're moving, as seen in figure 10.7.

DON'T ADD LARGE MOVING OBJECTS THAT TAKE UP THE MAJORITY OF THE USER'S VIEW

If a moving object takes up the majority of the user's view, they may interpret the situation as self-movement that they didn't initiate. This type of self-movement illusion is

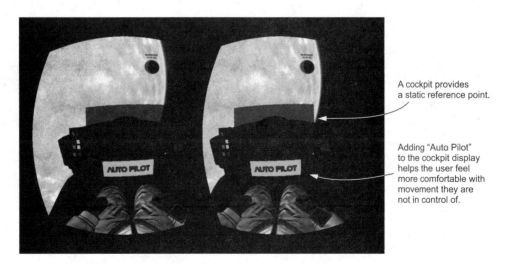

A cockpit provides a static reference point.

Adding "Auto Pilot" to the cockpit display helps the user feel more comfortable with movement they are not in control of.

Figure 10.7 *Titans of Space* **uses a cockpit (set on "Auto Pilot") as a static reference point.**

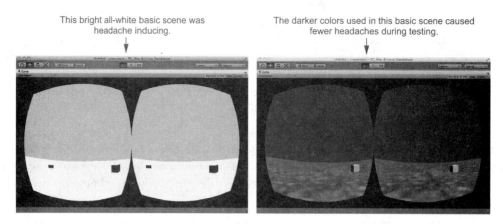

Figure 10.8 A basic scene created in Unity for this book

called *vection*, and it can lead to disorientation and motion sickness. A classic example of vection is when someone is at a train station and a nearby train moves. They see the train move and interpret that as though they're moving.

In VR, a specific scenario regarding vection to look out for is when the user's view is very close to the ground plane and the user moves the avatar's position. Remember, the user is not actually physically moving, they are only pressing buttons. If the ground plane entirely fills their view, when the user moves the avatar's position it creates an illusion similar to the train pulling away from the station, causing a feeling of motion sickness.

USE DARKER TEXTURES

Some people are sensitive to bright white light, so using darker textures can help them feel more comfortable. In addition, the darker textures can help with the sense of immersion.

When we were creating the example scene used in chapters 7 and 8 (figure 10.8), we'd initially used a plain white scene. During testing, we found that the white scene induced headaches. After adding darker textures to the scene, we had fewer headaches.

DON'T INTRODUCE INTENTIONAL FLICKERING OR USE HIGH-CONTRAST FLASHING

Pay attention to small and thin objects as well. These objects can cause unintentional flickering, because they can sometime seem to appear and disappear. Flickering and flashing, aside from contributing to motion sickness and user eyestrain, can cause seizures in photosensitive people, and so is best avoided.

10.2.7 *Pay attention to ergonomics: eyestrain, neck strain, and fatigue*

When playing a game or watching media on a traditional monitor, the user can look straight ahead at the monitor. With the Rift, the user has a device on their head and they're moving their head around and looking in all directions. Though slight, the added weight of the Rift itself can contribute to user discomfort. With that in mind, let's look at things you can do to limit eyestrain, neck strain, and fatigue.

LIMIT HOW MUCH THE USER NEEDS TO MOVE THEIR HEAD AROUND

As we mentioned in chapter 9, head motion can be used as a control scheme. In *Proton Pulse* (share.oculusvr.com/app/proton-pulse-rift) by Justin Moravetz, you control the transparent panel that the "ball" bounces off of with your head. In *Chicken Walk* (share.oculusvr.com/app/chicken-walk) by Mechabit Ltd. you're the chicken and you need to "peck" the ground to eat and drink (figure 10.9).

Using head motion as part of the control scheme can increase immersion. You really do feel more like a chicken by pecking for food. Like real-life chickens, the *Chicken Walk* chicken doesn't need to eat and drink constantly, so pecking for food adds to the immersion but doesn't give the user a workout. If you force your user to turn their head constantly or to rotate the head further than is comfortable, you do risk tiring them and causing neck strain.

This is one of those situations where carefully breaking the rules can pay off. Dejobaan Games and Owlchemy Labs, the makers of *AaaaaAAaaaAAAaaAAAAaCULUS!!!* (share.oculusvr.com/app/aaaaaaaaaaaaaaaaaaaaculus), found that by slightly over-rotating the camera, users had the illusion of looking straight down, even though they weren't (www.youtube.com/watch?v=DqZZKi4UHuo). By using this illusion, they were able to reduce fatigue from being hunched over.

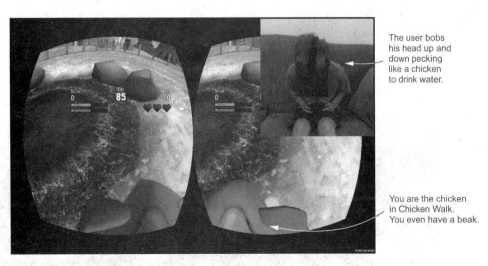

The user bobs his head up and down pecking like a chicken to drink water.

You are the chicken in Chicken Walk. You even have a beak.

Figure 10.9   In *Chicken Walk* the user needs to peck like a chicken to drink water.

Items "pinned" to the edge of your view are hard to see
without rolling your eyes in their sockets, causing eyestrain.

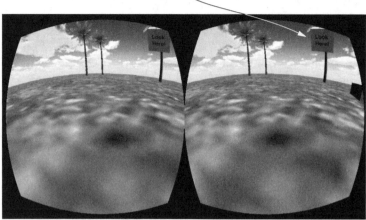

**Figure 10.10   The "Look Here" box in this example scene is hard for the user to
look at without rolling their eyes.**

DON'T MAKE THE USER ROLL THEIR EYES TO SEE SOMETHING

If the user needs to see something, make sure that it's comfortable look at it. Don't pin it
to the edge of the screen and force the user to roll their eyes to look at it (figure 10.10).

Even if the user does roll their eyes to see an item pinned to the edge, the item
may simply be too difficult to read because the Rift's distortion is greatest at the edges
of its display and can make items appear blurry.

Instead, let the user move their head to place the object or text in the center of the
screen where it's easily seen (figure 10.11).

The user can look at the text to get it in the center   And the user can look around at the scenery
of the screen where it is easily read.   without the text blocking their view.

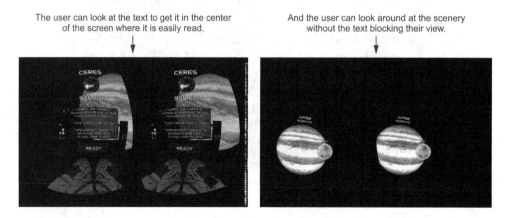

**Figure 10.11   In *Titans of Space* the user can look down at the console to read the text, but also look
up to see the planets.**

Even if the user can get the text into a position where it can be seen, take special care to make sure the text is easily readable on the Rift screen.

MAKE SURE ANY DISPLAYED TEXT IS EASILY READABLE

You want to make sure any displayed text is easily readable. Eyestrain from reading text that's too small or lacks contrast is no less of a problem in VR than it is anywhere else.

If your users are able to move about in the game, you may not be able to control how close or how far away they are from certain textural elements in your applications. But if it's something you can control, such as the depth plane of a HUD, the *Oculus Best Practice Guide* recommends that it be rendered at least 50 cm from the camera. Ideally, if you choose to use a HUD, you should give users the ability to adjust the depth of the HUD to what feels most comfortable for them.

Speaking of HUDs, remember that if you port a game to the Rift and you used a 2D overlay for the HUD or for floating text, you need to make sure the UI overlay is also properly rendered in 3D. If not, you'll end up with text appearing doubled, which, aside from being unreadable, can be headache inducing at the least.

Floating text and HUDs, even when very readable, can break immersion for the user, especially if they are out of place for the story you're telling. We suggest that you try to avoid floating text interfaces as much as possible and use other cues to move the story forward. See chapter 9 for more details.

10.2.8 Use sound to increase immersion and orient the user to action

The Rift covers your eyes, blocking out the real world, but it doesn't block out sound. Sound cues can orient the user to the action, and more important, sound can help with the sense of overall immersion. The *Shadow Projection* team noted, "The sound design proved to be a crucial element to the overall immersion. It wasn't until we added the music that people really started to feel like they were being taken to another place."

For many users, outside sound can be a distraction and cause disorientation, so some may choose to wear headphones. Your sound design should take into account the audio output: headphones or speakers. For both speakers and headphones, the soundscape should follow the player's position, but if the person is wearing headphones, the audio output can also follow the user's ears (via head movement).

10.2.9 Don't forget your user: give the player the option of an avatar body

Give your character a body (figure 10.12). Many of the people we've seen test out the Rift weren't bothered by not having a body, but for some, it was very disorienting to look down and not see arms, a body, and legs. Some users, discovering that they didn't have a body, could no longer pay attention to the rest of the demo. They kept looking down and exclaiming "I have no body!" and missed out on anything else that was happening around them. And even for those who were comfortable with being a floating

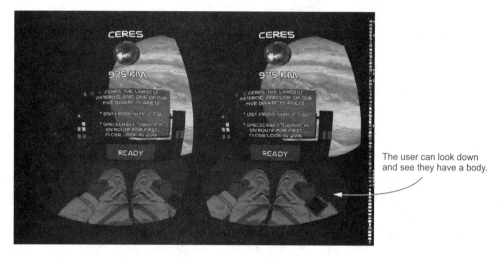

The user can look down and see they have a body.

Figure 10.12   In *Titans of Space* users can look down and see that they have a body.

head, it broke the sense of immersion. One user described it as feeling like he was "watching video from a drone," whereas when he played a demo that included an avatar body, he felt like he was really there.

The downside of an avatar body is that without additional hardware, the user's hand movements and the avatar's hand movements don't match. Some users find the lack of control over the avatar's hand movements more disconcerting than having no avatar at all. You may want to give users the option of not having an avatar body.

Don't forget that if your VR world has a mirror, you should include a head in the reflection. Seeing yourself headless might not make you sick but it'd be a little creepy.

10.2.10 Account for human variation

We're sure it isn't news to you that not all humans look alike or are the same size. But how do those differences affect the VR experience? Physical differences can affect the VR experience in two important ways: comfort and immersion. The good news is that you can account for this variation in your software and create a better experience for your users.

We'll first look at the profile data collected by the Oculus Configuration Utility and how that data is used. Then, because there are also additional human-variation issues that aren't covered by the Oculus Configuration Utility that we think also need to be addressed, we'll cover those as well.

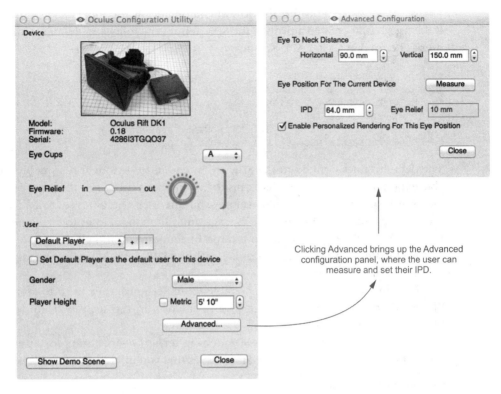

Figure 10.13   The Oculus Configuration Utility

USE THE PROFILE DATA GATHERED BY THE OCULUS CONFIGURATION UTILITY

The Oculus Configuration Utility is included with the Rift and allows users to create personal user profiles (figure 10.13).

The data stored for each user's profile includes gender, player height, eye-to-neck distance (horizontal and vertical), and IPD. It also includes a handy utility for measuring the user's IPD. Let's look at what these values are and how they're used:

- *Gender*—The SDK uses this value to calculate the distance from the top of the skull to the eye using average head size values. This value can also be used to determine avatar generation.
- *Player height*—This value is used to calculate the player's eye height to set the location of the point of view.
- *IPD*—This is the distance between the pupils, used to determine the separation of the stereo cameras.
- *Eye-to-neck distance (horizontal and vertical)*—The horizontal and vertical distances between the eyes and the neck pivot. These values are used by the SDK to determine the pivot point around which the point of view moves.

If a user has created a profile, the SDK will automatically use the data from the profile. If the user hasn't created a profile, the SDK defines the following default values for the user as defined in OVR_CAPI_Keys.h:

```
#define OVR_DEFAULT_GENDER                 "Unknown"
#define OVR_DEFAULT_PLAYER_HEIGHT          1.778f
#define OVR_DEFAULT_EYE_HEIGHT             1.675f
#define OVR_DEFAULT_IPD                    0.064f
#define OVR_DEFAULT_NECK_TO_EYE_HORIZONTAL 0.0805f
#define OVR_DEFAULT_NECK_TO_EYE_VERTICAL   0.075f
```

The default values defined in the SDK are intended to provide a reasonably comfortable experience for what Oculus terms their "common user." For the most part, these values are based on adult human averages, but the user's height is set to 1.778 meters, the average adult male height. The average adult human is closer to 1.692 meters[3] tall (in the United States). And, not to put too fine a point on it, half the world's population isn't male. Although you can tinker with the SDK default values, making changes to the SDK isn't recommended.

For your user to have the best possible VR experience, they need to create a profile. We'll cover ways to encourage profile creation in the section "Help your users help themselves."

Now that you've seen what the SDK does in terms of accounting for human variation, let's look at other human variation issues that you might want to address.

CORRECT FOR STRABISMUS

Strabismus (also known as being cross-eyed or wall-eyed) is a disorder in which your eyes don't line up; this misalignment can result in stereoblindness (the inability to see in 3D using stereo vision) or double vision. Prismatic lenses are sometimes used to correct for this disorder, and though it's possible to wear glasses while using the Rift, doing so isn't ideal.

This disorder can be compensated for in the software by calibrating a per-eye offset, and we've included the sample StrabismusCorrection application (figure 10.14) in our GitHub repository to show you how that can be done. We'd like to see this as an addition to the user profile created by the Oculus Configuration Utility.

CREATE AVATARS FOR EVERYONE

We covered how avatars provide context for the user—looking down and seeing a body with arms and legs can help with the sense of immersion. And we also covered how the sense of proprioception helps with immersion—the closer the avatar's position matches your own physical position, the greater the immersion. The avatar's appearance can also increase immersion the more the user can identify with the avatar.

---

[3] The average height listed here is an average of male and female heights. The average height for men over age 20 in the U.S. is 1.763 meters (5 feet, 9 inches) and for women over age 20 the average height is 1.622 meters (5 feet, 4 inches). Children are, of course, shorter. (Source: en.wikipedia.org/wiki/Human_height.)

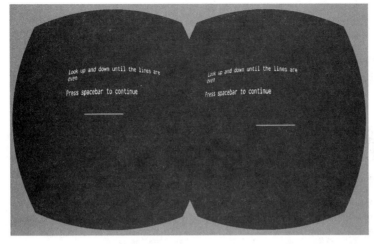

Strabismus, a disorder in which the two eyes do not line up, can result in stereoblindness.

It can be compensated for by calibrating a per-eye offset as is done in the StrabismusCorrection example application.

Figure 10.14   Strabismus correction

Karen's hands are not *that* masculine (thank you very much)

Karen: When I played the *Titans of Space* demo and looked down at the gloved hands and I sat exactly as the avatar was portrayed, I thought "those are my hands." In the *Don't Let Go!* demo, even with my hands positioned exactly like the avatar's hands, I didn't quite get the same sense that those were my hands. They were just too masculine to be mine. It wasn't until the spider reached the avatar's shoulder that it really felt like the spider was on me (and then, I admit, I let go).

Being able to *feel like yourself* in the story means being able to *see yourself* in the story. To give your users a more immersive experience, you should create male, female, and androgynous avatars in a range of skin tones, ages, and physiques, and then allow users to choose the avatar they most identify with. Yes, we know this is a seriously large amount of work to do, but it's the kind of inclusiveness we'd like to see for the future of gaming, and avatar skin tone is another profile option we'd like to see in the Oculus Configuration Utility.

Not every story is about giving your users the opportunity to see themselves in a new environment. Your story may hinge on giving the user the experience of feeling what it's like to be someone else. For example, the artists and researchers at BeAnotherLab (www.themachinetobeanother.org) have been experimenting with using VR to create an environment that offers users the experience of seeing themselves in the body of another person. Their *Machine to Be Another* uses a human performer as the avatar. The performer's job is to replicate the user's movements as accurately as possible, thereby providing the illusion that the user is the performer. One of the conclusions they reached from this project based on statements from the users and performers was that "the system has great potential as a social tool to stimulate empathy among different groups."

10.2.11 Help your users help themselves

When it comes to making the Rift a comfortable experience, it isn't entirely up to you, the developer. Users have to do their part as well. The good news is you can help them help themselves.

ENCOURAGE USERS TO SET AND USE THEIR USER PROFILE

Creating a user profile is ultimately up to the user, and if a profile hasn't been set up, the default profile is automatically used. To help your users have the best possible experience, you should encourage them to create a profile:

- *Stress the importance of setting up a profile in the application's documentation.* Be sure to cover exactly how to set up a profile and why it needs to be done. Documentation is a good start, but relying on users to read and follow the documentation, something we all know many users won't do, isn't a complete solution.
- *Provide the user with a way to select and update the profile from within your application.* You can display the current profile settings and prompt the user to either use those settings or create another profile. To get the name of the current profile, use the following:

```
ovr.Hmd_GetString(hmd, OVR_KEY_USER, "")
```

If `default` is returned, prompt the user to create a profile.

A profile will help users have the best possible VR experience while they're playing. Another thing to consider when thinking about creating a comfortable user experience is that users are going to get tired and will need to take breaks.

ENCOURAGE USERS TO TAKE BREAKS

Make it easy for users to suspend the game and return to where they left off. You want to create content so engaging that your users can't tear themselves away from it, but users are human and they must take breaks. In addition, if users try to push themselves through symptoms of motion sickness, those symptoms might get worse and can result in such an unpleasant experience that users could develop an aversion to your software, no matter how much they initially enjoyed it. You don't want that to happen. Give your users the ability to pause and take a break whenever they need it and you'll have happier users.

By making it easy for your users to do the right thing, you can make the experience one they will enjoy.

10.2.12 Evaluate your content for use in the VR environment

Goals and other engaging content help keep users immersed in the experience and can provide an excellent distraction from any motion sickness they might be feeling. Users can forgive some discomfort if they're getting an exceptional experience in

The T-rex is not scary on the page, but viewing it on the Rift is a different story.

Figure 10.15 The T-Rex in the *GiganotosaurusVR* demo by Meld Media isn't very scary on a traditional screen, but seeing it on the Rift is a different experience entirely.

exchange. But be wary of relying too heavily on your content to distract your users. At a certain level, no amount of engagement can overcome the discomfort.

VR EXPERIENCES CAN BE MORE INTENSE THAN TRADITIONAL MEDIA

Be aware that immersive experiences can feel much more intense than viewing the same content on a traditional screen. What seems not that scary on a traditional screen can be terrifying in VR (figure 10.15).

For example, the silent T-Rex in the *GiganotosaurusVR* demo by Meld Media (share.oculusvr.com/app/meld-media–giganotosaurusvr) is not at all frightening on the screen, but what a difference viewing it on the Rift makes! When the dinosaur's teeth are bared over your head, it can make you flinch and it can give kids nightmares.[4]

You might not realize it, but vision and hearing aren't the only senses you have contributing to the feeling of immersion and presence you get with VR—proprioception is also at work. Proprioception, as we explained earlier, is the sense of the relative position of neighboring parts of the body and the strength of effort being employed in movement. In our personal experience, when the sense of where our body was happened to match up exactly with the position of the avatar, it was a very visceral feeling.

---

[4] Karen regrets letting her younger son view this demo.

Seeing a spider crawl up "your" arm is a very visceral and creepy experience when viewed through a Rift.

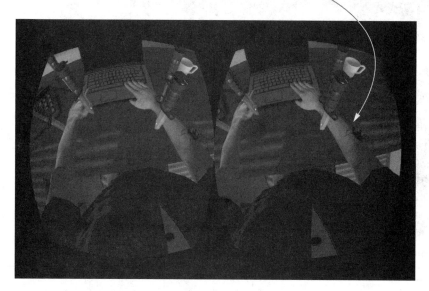

Figure 10.16 *Don't Let Go!*

The demo *Don't Let Go!*, created by Yorick van Vliet for the Oculus VR and IndieCade VR Jam (figure 10.16), demonstrates this phenomenon in a terrifying way using a very large spider.

Knowing that the immersive experiences can feel much more intense than viewing the same scene on a traditional screen, you need to ask yourself two questions: Does the experience create an appropriate emotional response? And how intense is too intense?

RESPONSIBILITY TO CONSIDER THE IMPACT OF YOUR WORK

The first-person perspective along with the sense of presence provided by VR can result in intense psychological responses in users. We've observed users getting goose bumps and flinching in fear when using the Rift, as well as having nightmares from what first appeared to be mild content. We've also seen many very happy users (intense responses haven't all been negative).

When testing your software, you need to take your users' emotional response seriously. And if the response is too intense or not appropriate to the experience you want to provide, you should reevaluate inclusion of that content.

Intense emotional responses, including being scared silly, can be part of the fun. But for those suffering from phobias or other psychological trauma, the virtually real experience the Rift provides may be too real. We suggest that for intense content, warn your users ahead of time and allow them to make an informed choice about continuing. For example, White Door Games, maker of the horror game

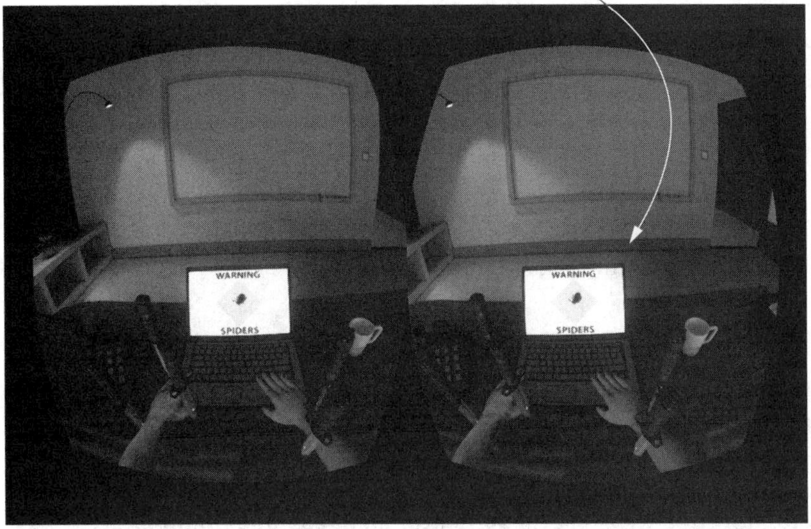

A spider crawling up your arm is an intense experience in the Rift.
A helpful spider warning lets those with arachnophobia
opt out before the spider appears.

Figure 10.17 *Don't Let Go!* **does a great job of warning you that a spider is coming.**

Dreadhalls (www.dreadhalls.com), rightly claims on their website that the game "is an intense and scary experience, not for the faint of heart." And the demo *Don't Let Go!* we referenced earlier does a great job of warning you that a spider is coming (figure 10.17).

One of the authors (not saying who)[5] really doesn't like spiders, and despite the fact that the demo is a great example of how proprioception affects the sense of presence, the spider-fearing author chose not to try it out.

10.2.13 Experiment as much as possible

You probably noticed that we've posted screenshots from a number of our favorite demos in this section. Although we've gained a lot of knowledge working on our own projects, we've also learned a great deal simply by keeping an eye on what others are doing and by trying out their demos. We suggest that if you haven't already, check out the demos at Oculus Share (share.oculusvr.com), which is basically a developer portal where you can upload games, tech demos, and experiments. It's a great place to find new ideas, and you can upload your own demo to get feedback from others.

---

[5] It's Brad.

10.3 *Testing your VR application for motion sickness potential*

Before you bring your application to mass market, you'll want to be sure you're providing a reasonably comfortable experience for your users. To help you get the most out of your user testing, we suggest that you follow these recommendations:

- Use standardized motion sickness and simulator sickness questionnaires.
- Test with as many users as you can, and be sure to test with users of various heights, ages, and susceptibility to motion sickness.
- Test with new users.
- Test with users who have set their personal profile; using the default profile will introduce bias into your results.
- Test in stages.
- Test using different display modes if Direct HMD mode doesn't work for you.

Motion sickness can be a truly unpleasant experience.[6] We cannot stress that enough. We strongly advise you to ensure that any test subjects you work with are fully aware of the risks involved with testing and have the ability to opt out of testing.

10.3.1 *Use standardized motion and simulator sickness questionnaires*

There are a number of ways to assess motion sickness caused by VR, but the most popular is the Simulator Sickness Questionnaire (SSQ) published by R.S. Kennedy, N.E. Lane, K.S. Berbaum, and M.G. Lilienthal in 1993. This questionnaire uses a list of 27 symptoms, such as fatigue, headache, nausea and difficulty focusing, all commonly experienced by users of VR. Users report the degree to which they experienced each symptom and scores can then be calculated and compared. A copy of this questionnaire can be found on page 294 in the *Oxford Textbook of Vertigo and Imbalance* (http://bit.ly/1Q8eTYe). Another option is the much simplified Fast MS Scale (FMS), created by Behrang Keshavarz and Heiko Hecht. In that scale scores range from 0 (no sickness at all) to 20 (frank sickness).

10.3.2 *Test with a variety of users and as many as you can*

What doesn't make four people sick might make a fifth person violently ill. You'll need to test with a fairly large group. Be sure to use a group of people of different heights and ages. Motion sickness may also have a genetic component (www.ncbi.nlm.nih.gov/pubmed/17086768), so try to have testers who are unrelated.

If you've used a standardized motion sickness questionnaire, try to get a variety in susceptibility and triggers. Again, use a standardized questionnaire designed to find out how susceptible to motion sickness your users are, and to get an understanding of what has caused them motion sickness in the past.

---

[6] The authors are neither doctors nor lawyers and therefore can't give medical or legal advice. It's your responsibility to ensure that any testing you perform meets with all ethical, medical, and legal requirements.

10.3.3   Test with new users

If you've been at this for a while, you've got your VR legs, and just like it takes some pretty rough seas for an old sea dog to take notice, you may not be as sensitive to the issue as your users. Think about who your users are. If they aren't hard-core VR gamers (and who is at this point?), be sure to test your software using people who are not only new to your software but are also new to VR.

10.3.4   Test with users who have set their personal profile

The closer your users' profile values are to their physical measurements, the better experience they'll have in VR. To ensure that each tester is evaluating your software from the same baseline experience, you want to make sure your testers have set up a personal user profile. If a user profile hasn't been set, the Rift will use the default values set by the SDK. The default values in the SDK aren't for the average human, but they're set to what Oculus terms the "common user." Because these values favor a specific demographic of users, if your testing is done using the default values, your results will be biased.

10.3.5   Test in stages

To minimize bad experiences causing negative associations, you should stage testing. Don't just go to beta because you didn't get sick. Try testing with yourself, then 5–10 people, then 50–100 people, and so on. And give yourself time to respond to feedback before you go to beta.

10.3.6   Test in different display modes

If you're unable to use Direct HMD Access From Apps as your display mode, your display setup is an important consideration while testing.

TESTING IN EXTENDED OR CLONED MODE

If you aren't running in Direct HMD mode, the Rift can be configured to be run as a cloned display or as an extended display. In appendix A, we list the advantages and disadvantages of each setup, and these differences are an important consideration during testing. Table 10.1 shows the pros and cons of each setup.

Table 10.1   Extended vs. cloned: pros and cons

Display configuration	Advantages	Disadvantages
Extended	Better performance Resolution can be optimized for the Rift without affecting your primary display.	There's a portion of the desktop where you can "lose" windows or your mouse. On some systems, when selecting Extended, the Rift is set by default as the primary display, making your system almost impossible to use.

Table 10.1 Extended vs. cloned: pros and cons *(continued)*

Display configuration	Advantages	Disadvantages
Cloned (Mirrored)	You can see your entire desktop. There's no portion of the desktop where you can "lose" windows or your mouse. You can preview Rift graphics and show them to others, in the iconic "two ovals" view.	Performance can suffer. *Screen tearing* (visual artifacts in the display caused by showing information from two or more frames in a single screen draw) may occur. You may see significant apparent shaking, particularly if the frame rate falls below 70 FPS. You can set the refresh rate to 60 Hz to minimize this issue, but you'll then see blurring.

The big advantage of Extended mode is performance. Using the latency testing hardware available from Oculus VR on a DK1, we found that the latency between rendering a frame on the computer and having the pixels on the display panel change in response was about 20 milliseconds when running in Extended mode versus 50 milliseconds when running in cloned mode. If you're measuring performance to fight motion sickness, that kind of latency differential can have a significant impact. You'll also note that screen tearing won't be an issue and screen shaking is less likely to be an issue. Because screen tearing, shaking, and blur can all be causes of discomfort, when testing you may want to eliminate them as a possible causes of motion sickness for a particular scene.

The disadvantage of Extended mode is that you can't see what the players are seeing and doing. You need to rely on the users telling you what they're doing to know what's happening in the game that might have provoked an unwanted physical reaction. If you run in cloned mode, you can see your users' physical reaction and see what they're doing at the same time, and that can give you a lot of insight into what might be the cause of motion sickness.

You may need to run the same tests in each mode to help narrow down the cause of motion sickness in a scene. Running in Extended mode can remove variables that could affect your results, and running in cloned mode can provide better insight into what's happening at the moment.

10.4 Summary

In this chapter you learned

- Using the Rift can cause symptoms of motion sickness and discomfort such as headache, drowsiness, nausea, dizziness, vomiting, sweating, eyestrain, neck strain, and fatigue.
- You can minimize the possibility of motion sickness by making sure the user is in control of the camera.
- The user being in control of the camera means that head tracking must exactly match the view, and it means that you can't change the field of view.

- You need to use new approaches to camera work for telling your story because many current popular techniques (zooming the camera, freezing the camera, using motion blur, turning the camera, using cutscenes) take control of the camera away from the user and can result in motion sickness.

- World design—what the world looks like and how the character can move around—affects user comfort.

- You can minimize some causes of neck strain, eyestrain, and fatigue by paying attention to how much the user needs to move their head and eyes to use your application.

- Your software can account for human variation to create a better experience for your users.

- The VR experience can be more intense than what's experienced with traditional media. You need to be aware of the emotional impact of your work.

- Testing your application for potential motion sickness and discomfort needs to be done in stages, with a varied group of people, and with people new to your software.

- Using the default user profile can introduce bias into your testing results. You need to make sure your testers have set a personal profile.

- Motion sickness from using the Rift isn't a solved problem. New techniques are being discovered all the time.

Part 5

Advanced Rift integrations

Building complete Rift applications typically involves more than using the Rift APIs. Often you'll need to integrate with other libraries, perhaps for UI creation. Or maybe you've got a preexisting library of awesomeness, legacy code written in a language other than C. In these final chapters, we provide information and examples for work that goes beyond the core integration of the Rift APIs.

In chapter 11 we show you how to work with the Oculus C API using Java or Python. We also discuss the basics of how to use the C APIs with any language.

In chapter 12 we cover creating a complete VR experience by building a VR version of an existing web application for use on the Rift. ShadertoyVR is a complete Rift-based VR editor.

In chapter 13 we explore creating Rift applications using additional inputs such as web cameras and the Leap Motion. ´

Using the Rift
with Java and Python

This chapter covers

- Working with the Rift in Java with JOVR
- Using the Rift in Python using PyOVR
- Developing Rift applications in other languages

The Rift is often seen as a gaming device, and gaming will likely be a big driver for its initial market. Because of this, and because of the backgrounds of some of the original developers[1] working at Oculus, the initial SDK for interacting with the Rift was exclusively in C++. Most big gaming engines are developed in C++, most triple-A games are written in C++, and so on. Similarly, early development focused on delivering features first for Windows and Direct3D, with the OpenGL API and platforms like Mac OS X and Linux lagging in feature support and stability. There were some attempts by developers to create non-C++ mechanisms for interacting with the Rift, either attempting to wrap the Oculus libraries or interacting with the hardware directly and attempting to reproduce the same functionality in another language. To our knowledge, none of these have gained widespread adoption thus far.

---

[1] Many of the Oculus crew came from Scaleform (later purchased by Autodesk), a middleware company for game development.

Mainstream VR will need to include applications written in languages other than C and C++. Many current-day applications and games would benefit from a VR overhaul, and not all of them are C++ apps. Minecraft is a popular game written entirely in Java. PyMOL is a molecular modeling application written in Python. In this chapter we'll discuss how to leverage the power of the Rift using bindings and examples in Python and Java.

The examples presented here will build on the basics and theory covered in chapters 2 through 5. Even if you prefer to develop strictly in Python and/or Java, we strongly recommend you review those chapters before jumping directly into this one. Although the examples in those chapters are in C++, they provide an in-depth discussion of the basic concepts involved; this chapter will, of necessity, be comparatively truncated.

That said, this book isn't intended to be an introduction to either Java or Python, and some level of proficiency with the language in question is assumed in the following sections.

11.1 Using the Java bindings

Your goal for the Java bindings is to get the same level of functionality that you've achieved in the chapter 5 examples. In this example, you'll render a familiar colored cube with a cityscape background (figure 11.1).

The application should respond to head movement in a realistic fashion, and once you're done, the output should look very much like the output from chapter 5's later examples.

Figure 11.1 The example scene as rendered to the Rift from your Java application

REQUIREMENTS

For this Java example, you have two basic requirements worth noting:

- Java 7 or higher
- Maven (maven.apache.org/)

You don't need to download the Oculus SDK to use the Java example code. The binaries for the standard platforms are built into the JAR file that contains the Java bindings, the JAR files are automatically fetched by the Maven build system (see the accompanying sidebar), along with all other dependencies.

Maven

Maven is a tool used for declaratively specifying a number of things about your project, probably the most significant being the libraries your project depends on. It's also network aware, so you don't have to download your dependencies. Maven does that for you, either from the central Maven repository or from another repository you've declared in your project file.

Maven project files (POM files) can be used as the exclusive management mechanism for a project, but that's only effective if you're planning on doing most of your development from the command line or a standalone editor. If you're more comfortable with an IDE such as Eclipse, you'll be happy to know that most Java development environments have Maven integration available or built in.

When using Maven to work with native libraries, such as those used here, you may prefer to manually configure native library paths and use Maven's command-line tools. If you do so, remember to add `-Djava.library.path=target/native` to the VM arguments so that Java can find the Rift native binaries. Alternatively, you may prefer using *mavennatives* (code.google.com/p/mavennatives/), an Eclipse plug-in that automates native binary management, which obviates all need for manual configuration of native library paths. But be warned that the mavennatives project is open source and is no longer actively supported.

JNA VS. JNI VS. HOMEBREW

Working with the Rift in Java still requires interaction with the Rift hardware at some level. Fortunately, Java has mechanisms that allow applications to interact with libraries written in other languages. The existing Oculus SDK C API can be accessed through either JNI or JNA.

JNI (*Java Native Interface*) is a framework built into Java that allows Java code running inside the JVM to call code in external libraries, such as Windows' DLL files. JNI is often used for direct access to OS-specific feature implementations; hardware accelerated graphics, for instance, are often implemented through native libraries accessed via JNI.

JNA (*Java Native Access*) is an open source project that provides similar access to native libraries but aims to do so through a simpler and easier-to-use API compared to JNI.

JNI tends to be faster, but it requires you to write your binding code with both a Java portion and a C portion that wraps whatever native code you want to run. By contrast, JNA isn't as fast (developers.opengamma.com/blog/2012/05/25/jna-jni-and-raw-java-performance), but it's easier to work with, requiring only that you declare functions in Java with method signatures that match those in the library you wish to use.

Although JNA is slower than JNI, both mechanisms are measured in milliseconds (if not microseconds) per call, and the performance difference tends to be a function of how much information is being passed per function call. Because the number of calls to the SDK tends to be less than a dozen per frame, each passing only a tiny amount of data, we've opted for JNA for its ease of use.

Mind you, for your own project nobody's forcing you to use either solution. Technically, you *could* use the Rift in Java without going to the C API at all by reproducing the SDK functions in native Java. But this approach would present an enormous maintenance burden—you'd be reinventing the wheel, the cart, and the horse that pulls it. And even then you wouldn't entirely escape from the need to use JNI or JNA: reading data from the Rift requires reading the head tracker hardware using the HID (a hardware specification for interacting with human interface devices, such as mice, keyboards, and in this case, head-tracking hardware) via platform-specific APIs. Because calling C code ends up being on the critical path, it's simpler to accept that you'll be using the C SDK through native access, rather than try to reimplement all the subtle features like sensor fusion.

11.1.1 *Meet our Java binding: JOVR*

To communicate with the Rift in Java, we've built a native binding library called *JOVR*.[2] JOVR was written by the authors of this book, but unlike most of the code in this book it's not meant to be merely illustrative. Instead it's a fully usable tool designed to allow *any* Java application to integrate with the SDK and support the Rift. Indeed, it's being used to integrate Oculus Rift support into the Java Monkey Engine renderer as we write.

Our examples use JOVR, so you'll get to see it in action here.

JOVR

JOVR is nearly 2,000 lines of code, but most of that was automatically generated by the tool we've used to create the bindings based on the Oculus SDK C headers.

JOVR declares Java versions of all of the structures and functions in the Oculus C API header. For instance, in the Oculus C API there's a structure for encoding a quaternion defined like this:

```
typedef struct ovrQuatf_
{
    float x, y, z, w;
} ovrQuatf;
```

---

[2] Decoding this clever acronym is left as an exercise for the reader.

There's a corresponding Java type in the JOVR project that looks (something) like this:

```
package com.oculusvr.capi;

public class OvrQuaternionf extends Structure {
  public float x;
  public float y;
  public float z;
  public float w;

  public OvrQuaternionf () {
    super();
  }

  public OvrQuaternionf (float x, float y, float z, float w) {
    super();
    this.x = x;
    this.y = y;
    this.z = z;
    this.w = w;
  }
}
```

That may look overly verbose compared to the C definition, but the upside is that you don't have to write it—you just use it. Actually, we should confess: we didn't write it either. Instead we used a tool called JNAerator (code.google.com/p/jnaerator/) to automatically parse the Oculus C API header files and generate the corresponding Java classes. JNAerator did 90 percent of the required work for us.

That said, JNAerator's output wasn't optimal. For instance, originally the Java class it produced was named `ovrQuatf_`, exactly like the C structure definition. Fortunately, Eclipse has powerful refactoring tools that allowed us to easily rename the classes to be more Java-like.

In addition to the few dozen classes created for the C structures, there's a single `com.oculusvr.capi.OvrLibrary` class that was generated to encapsulate the C API functions and constants. This is the heart of the JOVR bindings. Each function that's exposed by the OVR C API is converted into a method in the `OvrLibrary` class. There's one instance of the class that's created when the library is loaded; this happens automatically when `OvrLibrary` is loaded by the Java class loader.

Here's a small sample of the `OvrLibrary` class that demonstrates how the constants and functions from the C API have been mapped to Java. Note that constant values are encapsulated into interfaces, whereas C functions become method members of the `OvrLibrary` interface:

```
public interface OvrLibrary extends Library {
  public static final String JNA_LIBRARY_NAME = "OVR_C";
  public static final NativeLibrary JNA_NATIVE_LIB =
      NativeLibrary.getInstance(OvrLibrary.JNA_LIBRARY_NAME);
  public static final OvrLibrary INSTANCE =
      (OvrLibrary) Native.loadLibrary(
          OvrLibrary.JNA_LIBRARY_NAME, OvrLibrary.class);
```

```
public static interface ovrHmdType {
  public static final int ovrHmd_None = 0;
  public static final int ovrHmd_DK1 = 3;
  public static final int ovrHmd_DK2 = 6;
  ...
};

byte ovr_Initialize();
void ovr_Shutdown();
int ovrHmd_Detect();
```

JOVR has a class to represent the HMD abstraction that the SDK declares: ovrHmd, now renamed to the more Java-like Hmd. The ovrHmd type in the Oculus SDK serves both as a description of a particular device as well as a handle for interacting with it. Most of the functions in the C API take it as their first parameter. But in JOVR we've turned the structure into a more fully featured class. This class contains members that map to the C API methods. Internally, Hmd still calls the C API methods, passing itself as the first parameter where appropriate. The few methods in the SDK that don't take an ovrHmd parameter have been converted into static methods on our Hmd type, again for convenience.

The Hmd class ends up being the primary mechanism through which clients can most easily access the SDK functionality, as shown in the following listing.

Listing 11.1   Hmd.java

```
public class Hmd extends PointerType {

  public static void initialize() {
    if (0 == OvrLibrary.INSTANCE.ovr_Initialize()) {
      throw new IllegalStateException(
          "Unable to initialize Oculus SDK");
    }
  }

  public static Hmd create(int index) {
    return OvrLibrary.INSTANCE.ovrHmd_Create(index);
  }

  public void destroy() {
    OvrLibrary.INSTANCE.ovrHmd_Destroy(this);
  }

  public boolean configureTracking (
      int supportedCaps, int requiredCaps) {
    return 0 != OvrLibrary.INSTANCE.ovrHmd_ConfigureTracking(this,
        supportedCaps, requiredCaps);
  }

  public void recenterPose () {
    OvrLibrary.INSTANCE.ovrHmd_RecenterPose(this);
  }

  ...
```

Functions from the C API that don't take an ovrHmd parameter are exposed as static members on the Hmd class.

INSTANCE is a singleton, akin to the library handle you'd receive from LoadLibrary() on windows or dlopen() on Linux.

Allows you to create instances of the Hmd type.

Static functions from the C API that take an ovrHmd parameter are exposed as nonstatic members on the Hmd class.

And so on. You'll see how this benefits you later on, when we look at the actual example code.

API DIFFERENCES BETWEEN JOVR AND THE OCULUS C API

In a very few cases the C API has been tweaked slightly for ease of use. For instance, C methods can't return more than one type, and if a method can reasonably fail and needs to be able to return an error indicator, then there's no way to return other data the function normally would've produced. Typically if a C function must have complex output and needs to return error states, then it declares an output variable as part of its parameter list. Consider the following function from the mapped C API that's used to construct a distortion mesh:

```
ovrBool ovrHmd_CreateDistortionMesh(
    ovrHmd hmd,
    ovrEyeType eyeType,
    ovrFovPort fov,
    unsigned int distortionCaps,
    ovrDistortionMesh *meshData );
```

Here's its corresponding Java mapping in the OvrLibrary class:

```
byte ovrHmd_CreateDistortionMesh(
    Hmd hmd,
    int eyeType,
    FovPort.ByValue fov,
    int distortionCaps,
    DistortionMesh meshData);
```

In both of these cases the final parameter, meshData, is an output variable, the piece of information that you want when you call the function. The return value is simply an error indicator that returns a nonzero value if the function succeeded. But most object-oriented (OO) languages include exception handling, meaning that methods should return the type of information that's most natural for them to return (in this case, an instance of DistortionMesh) and errors should be handled by raising an exception.

Therefore, the Hmd wrapper method that JOVR builds around such functions hides some of the gory details of checking for a return value and converting it to an exception:

```
public DistortionMesh createDistortionMesh(
    int eyeType, FovPort fov, int distortionCaps) {
  Preconditions.checkNotNull(fov);
  DistortionMesh meshData = new DistortionMesh();
  if (0 == OvrLibrary.INSTANCE.ovrHmd_CreateDistortionMesh(
      this, eyeType, byValue(fov), distortionCaps, meshData)) {
    throw new IllegalStateException("Unable to create distortion mesh");
  }
  return meshData;
}
```

Additionally, the methods `ovrMatrix4f_Projection` and `ovrMatrix4f_OrthoSub-Projection` have been renamed to `getPerspectiveProjection` and `getOrthographicProjection`, respectively, but still take the same arguments and provide the same results.

BINARY FILES

In addition to the Java classes, the JOVR JAR contains binary files for each of the supported platforms. This means a DLL for 64-bit Windows, another DLL for 32-bit Windows, a shared library file for 64-bit Linux, and so on.

These binaries are stored in the JAR in such a fashion that JNA is able to automatically extract and load the shared library. This removes the need to download and install a driver or SDK or to have the binary in a special location on the disk, making it much easier to get up and running.

MOVING ON

We're not going to delve any deeper into the inner workings of JOVR. As stated, it's intended to be used as is. Whether you're working with our examples or developing your own set of demos or even a full-fledged game, JOVR can simply be treated as an upstream dependency.

> ### JOVR development
> If you're interested in following or participating in the development of the JOVR wrapper, or submitting bugs or just hurling abuse, it's maintained on Github at github.com/jherico/jovr.

We'll focus on showing an example of such usage in our sample project, the unimaginatively titled *Jocular-examples*.

11.1.2 *The Jocular-examples project*

If you downloaded a zip file containing the examples for the book, or if you recursively cloned the example repository on GitHub, then the Jocular-examples project should be available in the examples/java folder of the main example code. If you're only interested in the Java examples, they're available as an independent repository at github.com/jherico/jocular-examples.

If you're using Eclipse, you can create a project for the example code by selecting File > Import, selecting Existing Maven Projects, and then selecting the directory where the POM file resides. Eclipse will handle the rest.

THE PROJECT FILE

We begin by looking at the Maven project file for the Java example project. Maven project files are called POMs (Project Object Models). The following listing shows the complete POM file for the example.

Listing 11.2 pom.xml

```
<project ... >
  <parent>
    <groupId>org.saintandreas</groupId>
    <artifactId>parent</artifactId>
    <version>1.0.0</version>
  </parent>
  <artifactId>jocular-examples</artifactId>
  <version>1.0-SNAPSHOT</version>

  <dependencies>
    <dependency>
      <groupId>org.saintandreas</groupId>
      <artifactId>jovr</artifactId>
      <version>0.4.0.0</version>
    </dependency>
    <dependency>
      <groupId>org.saintandreas</groupId>
      <artifactId>math</artifactId>
      <version>[1.0.4, 2)</version>
    </dependency>
    <dependency>
      <groupId>org.saintandreas</groupId>
      <artifactId>oria-resources</artifactId>
      <version>[1.0.2, 2)</version>
    </dependency>
    <dependency>
      <groupId>org.saintandreas</groupId>
      <artifactId>glamour-lwjgl</artifactId>
      <version>[1.0.3, 2)</version>
    </dependency>
  </dependencies>
</project>
```

Annotations:
- **Uniquely identifies this Maven project and its output.**
- **A dependency on JOVR for access to the Oculus SDK.**
- **A math library to perform matrix, vector, and quaternion manipulations.**
- **Holds shaders, textures, and models.**
- **The Java-based OpenGL wrapper library. Depends on LWJGL for low-level OpenGL bindings.**

In the POM file you declare a number of things. The most critical from the point of view of you, the reader, are probably the dependencies.

EXAMPLE DEPENDENCIES

You declare a dependency on the JOVR library, first and foremost. This will allow you to access the Rift API and is equivalent to linking your application to the SDK in a C or C++ application.

We (the authors) maintain the JOVR library and have released versions of it for each version of the SDK since the CAPI was introduced in 0.3.1. The JOVR library includes an additional version-number field so that bug fixes and enhancements may be released for JOVR while still tracking a given Oculus SDK version. For example, the 0.3.2.x version of JOVR corresponds to the 0.3.2 version of the Oculus SDK.

For JOVR, we've declared that we're using 0.4.0.0 specifically, but for each of our other dependencies we've declared a *version range* rather than a specific version. For instance, we've declared the glamour-lwjgl dependency as [1.0.3, 2). The first value, 1.0.3, is the minimum version that Maven is allowed to use. The square bracket at the beginning marks it as *inclusive*, meaning that Maven can use the exact version number listed. The second number is a maximum version and uses a parenthesis instead of a square bracket. That marks the maximum as *exclusive*, meaning that Maven's allowed to use anything up to but not including that version. So 1.0.3 is okay, as is 1.0.4 or 1.10, but 2.0 isn't allowed, and 2.1 or anything higher is right out. Using a version range tells Maven to use the most recent version available within limits. This lets us pick up newer versions automatically, while hopefully avoiding compatibility breaking changes.

For the Oculus SDK, because we're actively tracking a library whose version number is out of our control, we have to append an additional point version onto the existing Oculus version number, and because that library is in active development, we can't allow a version range at all.

The `oria-resources` dependency brings in a JAR file that contains all the images, models, and shaders used for the example code. In previous C++ demos, on Windows, this content was compiled into a resource DLL from which it was loaded. Building it into a JAR file accomplishes the same purpose in Java.

The Oculus API can use OpenGL to do distortion, but it doesn't expose the OpenGL API to you. For that you use the `glamour-lwjgl` dependency. The Glamour project serves a function similar to the OpenGL header library you've used in the C++ examples. It provides class wrappers around some of the commonly used OpenGL concepts like vertex and index buffers, textures, and shaders. Glamour in turn depends on the Lightweight Java OpenGL Library (LWJGL for short; available from lwjgl.org) for the actual low-level OpenGL bindings. It'd be just as easy to use the other popular Java OpenGL library, JOGL (jogamp.org/jogl), if you so desired.

11.1.3 *The RiftApp class*

In our C++ examples, as we became familiar with certain concepts we moved portions of the per-application work into base classes—first into `GlfwApp`, then later `RiftApp`. This was done in order to reduce the amount of boilerplate code in each example. We don't have space to go through the same series of examples we did in chapters 2 through 5 here, but we still want to distinguish between the example-specific code and the common base code you might see in any Java-based Rift application.

In our examples we follow a basic pattern of pushing functionality out of the example code itself and into utility classes and parent classes to reflect good Rift-oriented design. So you'll see a recurring pattern of developing a class to handle the basics of interacting with the rendering and input systems (`GlfwApp` in C++, `LfwJglApp` in Java). From there you derive a class that knows how to interact with the Oculus SDK, create a window on the Rift display, and perform a rendering loop that includes distortion (called `RiftApp` in both C++ and Java). Finally, from `RiftApp` you derive an example-specific class that knows how to draw something interesting.

Now we'll look at the contents of the Java version of `RiftApp` and briefly cover, in the following listing, exactly how each component relates to the examples from earlier chapters. Once the base class is sorted out, you'll move on to the actual example and render a simple scene.

Listing 11.3 RiftApp.java, a Java equivalent to our C++ `RiftApp` class

```java
package org.saintandreas.vr;

// (imports not shown for brevity)

public abstract class RiftApp extends LwjglApp {

    protected abstract void renderScene();

    protected final Hmd hmd;                           // Gives an entry point into
                                                       // all the Oculus C API
                                                       // functionality.

    private EyeRenderDesc eyeRenderDescs[];

    private final FovPort fovPorts[] =
        (FovPort[])new FovPort().toArray(2);

    private final Texture eyeTextures[] =
        (Texture[])new Texture().toArray(2);           // Everything we need
                                                       // for perspective and
    private final Posef poses[] =                      // distortion.
        (Posef[])new Posef().toArray(2);

    private final FrameBuffer frameBuffers[] =
        new FrameBuffer[2];
    private final Matrix4f projections[] =
        new Matrix4f[2];

    private int frameCount = -1;

    private static Hmd openFirstHmd() {                // Finds the right
        Hmd hmd = Hmd.create(0);                       // Hmd instance.
        if (null == hmd) {
            hmd = Hmd.createDebug(
                OvrLibrary.ovrHmdType.ovrHmd_DK1);
        }
        return hmd;
    }
                                                       // Gives a place to initialize
    public RiftApp() {                                 // everything that isn't dependent
        Hmd.initialize();                              // on having an OpenGL context.

        hmd = openFirstHmd();
        if (null == hmd) {
            throw new IllegalStateException(
                "Unable to initialize HMD");
        }

        hmdDesc = hmd.getDesc();
        if (0 == hmd.configureTracking(
            ovrTrackingCap_Orientation |
            ovrTrackingCap_Position, 0)) {
            throw new IllegalStateException(
                "Unable to start the sensor");
        }
```

```java
      for (int eye = 0; eye < 2; ++eye) {
        fovPorts[eye] = hmd.DefaultEyeFov[eye];
        projections[eye] = RiftUtils.toMatrix4f(
            Hmd.getPerspectiveProjection(
                fovPorts[eye], 0.1f, 1000000f, true));

        Texture texture = eyeTextures[eye] = new Texture();
        TextureHeader header = texture.Header;
        header.TextureSize = hmd.getFovTextureSize(
            eye, fovPort, 1.0f);

        header.RenderViewport.Size = header.TextureSize;
        header.RenderViewport.Pos = new OvrVector2i(0, 0);
      }
    }

    @Override
    protected void onDestroy() {
      hmd.destroy();
      Hmd.shutdown();
    }

    @Override
    protected void setupContext() {
      contextAttributes = new ContextAttribs(3, 3)
          .withProfileCore(true)
          .withDebug(true);
    }

    @Override
    protected final void setupDisplay() {
      System.setProperty(
          "org.lwjgl.opengl.Window.undecorated", "true");

      Rectangle targetRect = new Rectangle(
          hmd.WindowsPos.x, hmd.WindowsPos.y,
          hmd.Resolution.w, hmd.Resolution.h);
      setupDisplay(targetRect);
    }

    @Override
    protected void initGl() {
      super.initGl();
      for (int eye = 0; eye < 2; ++eye) {
        TextureHeader eth = eyeTextures[eye].ogl.Header;
        frameBuffers[eye] = new FrameBuffer(
            eth.TextureSize.w, eth.TextureSize.h);
        eyeTextures[eye].TextureId =
            frameBuffers[eye].getTexture().id;
      }

      RenderAPIConfig rc = new RenderAPIConfig();
      rc.Header.BackBufferSize = hmd.Resolution;
      rc.Header.Multisample = 1;

      int distortionCaps =
          ovrDistortionCap_TimeWarp |
          ovrDistortionCap_Vignette;
```

Cleans up on application shutdown.

Specifies the specific version and profile of OpenGL requested.

Determines the exact size and position of the Rift display.

Finishes initialization of items that need an active OpenGL context.

```
      for (int i = 0; i < rc.PlatformData.length; ++i) {
        rc.PlatformData[i] = Pointer.createConstant(0);
      }

      eyeRenderDescs = hmd.configureRendering(
          rc, distortionCaps, fovPorts);

      for (int eye = 0; eye < 2; ++eye) {
        this.eyeOffsets[eye].x = eyeRenderDescs[eye].HmdToEyeViewOffset.x;
        this.eyeOffsets[eye].y = eyeRenderDescs[eye].HmdToEyeViewOffset.y;
        this.eyeOffsets[eye].z = eyeRenderDescs[eye].HmdToEyeViewOffset.z;
      }
    }

    @Override                                           ◁─┐  Called by the main
    public final void drawFrame() {                        │  application loop.
      hmd.beginFrame(++frameCount);
      Posef eyePoses[] = hmd.getEyePoses(frameCount, eyeOffsets);
      for (int i = 0; i < 2; ++i) {
        int eye = hmd.EyeRenderOrder[i];
        Posef pose = eyePoses[eye];
        MatrixStack.PROJECTION.set(projections[eye]);
        poses[eye].Orientation = pose.Orientation;
        poses[eye].Position = pose.Position;

        MatrixStack mv = MatrixStack.MODELVIEW;
        mv.push();
        mv.preTranslate(RiftUtils.toVector3f(
            poses[eye].Position).mult(-1));
        mv.preRotate(RiftUtils.toQuaternion(
            poses[eye].Orientation).inverse());
        frameBuffers[eye].activate();
        renderScene();
        frameBuffers[eye].deactivate();
        mv.pop();
      }
      hmd.endFrame(poses, eyeTextures);
    }

    @Override                                           ◁─┐  Signals the SDK
    protected void finishFrame() {                         │  to swap buffers.
      Display.processMessages();
    }
}
```

Wow, that's oodles of code. If you've dug into the C++ examples, then this code should look somewhat familiar. If you've jumped directly into this chapter, we'll do our best to accommodate you and cover the gist of what's going on in terms of interaction with the SDK.

Let's skip past the package declaration and imports. These are standard concepts; they shouldn't need illumination to a Java developer and are outside the scope of this book.

CLASS DECLARATION

The base class for our applications is declared like this:

```
public abstract class RiftApp extends LwjglApp {
```

It's declared as an abstract class, meaning it can't be instantiated because it's missing some piece of implementation. In this case the portion it's missing is an actual scene to render. To render a scene you're going to create a new class that declares RiftApp as its parent class and provides an implementation for our only abstract function:

```
protected abstract void renderScene();
```

We'll get to just such an implementation after we've discussed the entire RiftApp base class.

You also declare a parent class of your own, LwjglApp, which is equivalent to the GlfwApp base class in our C++ examples. LwjglApp handles the interaction with the OpenGL library you're using to initialize and use OpenGL from Java. The methods within RiftApp that are tagged with @Override are overriding LwjglApp methods in order to implement missing functionality or to augment default behaviors.

> ### The LwjglApp base class
>
> As with C++, our OpenGL base class declares your primary game loop, which looks something like this:
>
> ```
> while (!Display.isCloseRequested()) {
>   update();
>   drawFrame();
>   finishFrame();
> }
> ```
>
> The first method, update(), is meant as a placeholder for updating the game state and handling user input. If a user presses a key that should move their position forward, or if a particle system needs to have its positions recalculated, it would happen inside the update() method. The second method, drawFrame(), is where the rendering should occur. The third, finishFrame(), typically serves the purpose of moving the rendered pixels to the screen.
>
> In LwjglApp, finishFrame() is implemented as a call to Display.update() which is LWJGL's way of performing a buffer swap. Oftentimes applications won't push this into a method; they'll simply call the appropriate buffer-swap function or method directly in the main loop. This approach isn't suitable for applications using the Oculus SDK's built-in distortion rendering, because the SDK depends on being able to do the buffer swap itself.[3]

---

[3] See chapter 5 for a discussion of why the SDK needs to control the buffer-swapping mechanism.

MEMBER VARIABLE DECLARATIONS

After the class declaration and the abstraction function we've declared, we get into the member variables. There are quite a few of them and some have unusual patterns in their declarations, so we'll cover them piecemeal.

```
protected final Hmd hmd;
```

The Hmd type has a direct equivalent in the Oculus C API in the form of ovrHmd. It has two roles. First, it acts as a handle that provides access to much of the headset functionality via functions in the SDK. Second, it provides a basic description of a given HMD's properties and capabilities.

In the JOVR library the Hmd type has been augmented to include member functions providing access to virtually all of the SDK C API functionality. Rather than calling a (wrapped) C function and passing an Hmd instance as the first parameter, you can call a member of the Hmd class, which in turn calls the C function and passes itself as the first parameter. Many error values returned from the C library are converted to exceptions as control passes back to Java.

Unlike most of the member variables, which are declared private, the member variable hmd is declared protected. The hmd has less restrictive access controls because derived classes will have legitimate reasons to use hmd. Access to the active user profile's settings is all done through functions that require the hmd instance to be passed in as a variable. These settings, which include things like the height, gender, and IPD for a user, can be valuable in setting up the scene and the user's viewpoint in it. As such, we must make the hmd protected and not private so that derived classes can access this information as needed.

```
FovPort fovPorts[] = (FovPort[]) new FovPort().toArray(2);
```

If you haven't worked with JNA before, this declaration (and the corresponding ones for eyeTextures and poses) is likely to look a little odd. The reason can be traced back to the Oculus SDK C API declarations. Many of the declarations look something like this:

```
ovrBool ovrHmd_ConfigureRendering( Hmd hmd,
    const ovrRenderAPIConfig* apiConfig,
    unsigned int distortionCaps,
    const ovrFovPort eyeFovIn[2],
    ovrEyeRenderDesc eyeRenderDescOut[2] );
```

As you can see, the C API calls for fixed-size arrays of values to be passed in. In C terms this means that the two structures must be contiguous in memory. Java arrays are entirely different from C arrays and the elements aren't necessarily contiguous in memory. To rectify this, the JNA library provides a base class, Structure, from which you must derive all the types you use in calling C methods. Structure has a toArray() method that returns precisely what you need: a Java array in which the items in the array are contiguous in memory. Because the base class can only return the base type, we must explicitly cast the returned arrays to the types you're interested in.

The remaining member declarations are pretty vanilla. We're allocating space we'll need to initialize and then perform distortion rendering.

HMD HANDLE HELPER METHOD

You've declared you Hmd instance as final. You assign a value to it exactly once in the constructor of you class and thereafter it can never be altered for the lifetime of the RiftApp instance.

There are two different functions in the SDK that can return a valid HMD, so you've pushed the creation of the Hmd instance out into a static method. This method uses a local Hmd type that can be assigned to multiple times, and then returns the final result:

```
private static Hmd openFirstHmd() {
  Hmd hmd = Hmd.create(0);
  if (null == hmd) {
    hmd = Hmd.createDebug(OvrLibrary.ovrHmdType.ovrHmd_DK1);
  }
  return hmd;
}
```

A real application might wish to do something more complicated than this, such as first determining how many HMD devices are connected to the system and then iterating over them to open the first available device.

CONSTRUCTOR

The constructor is quite lengthy, so we'll break it down for you.

As with any Rift application, the first thing we must do before calling any other SDK methods is to initialize the SDK itself:

```
public RiftApp() {
  Hmd.initialize();
```

We're using our friendly Hmd wrapper class static method here, but we could just as easily have called the C API binding directly like this: OvrLibrary.INSTANCE.ovr _Initialize(). This is pretty much the case throughout the application, so we won't mention it again.

Next, we'll use another static method, create(), to open the first HMD we can find. If we fail to get a reference to any Rift device, we'll throw an exception. This should never occur, because if there's no physical Rift connected to the system, the ovrHmd.createDebug() method should *always* return a fake Rift for us to work with.

```
hmd = openFirstHmd();
if (null == hmd) {
  throw new IllegalStateException("Unable to initialize HMD");
}
```

We'll want our application to respond to head orientation and position changes, so we need to start the sensor devices and raise an exception if we're unable to do so. The first parameter is the supported sensor capabilities, and the second is the required capabilities. Both are bit-field flags that accept the constants defined in the type OvrLibrary.ovrTrackingCaps. We're passing in ovrTrackingCap_Orientation and ovrTrackingCap_Position to indicate that we're ready to receive orientation and position data and the method shouldn't fail if it can't configure the sensors:

```
if (0 == hmd.configureTracking(
    ovrTrackingCap_Orientation |
    ovrTrackingCap_Position, 0)) {
  throw new IllegalStateException(
      "Unable to start the sensor");
}
```

Finally, we want to determine the correct projection matrices to use for each eye and the ideal texture sizes in preparation for when we're actually ready to set up and then perform rendering:

```
for (int eye = 0; eye < 2; ++eye) {
  fovPorts[eye] = hmd.DefaultEyeFov[eye];
  projections[eye] = RiftUtils.toMatrix4f(
      Hmd.getPerspectiveProjection(
          fovPorts[eye], 0.1f, 1000000f, true));

  Texture texture = eyeTextures[eye] = new Texture();
  TextureHeader header = texture.Header;
  header.TextureSize = hmd.getFovTextureSize(
      eye, fovPort, 1.0f);

  header.RenderViewport.Size = header.TextureSize;
  header.RenderViewport.Pos = new OvrVector2i(0, 0);
}
```

Note that the TextureHeader type also contains a member variable named API, which we're *not* initializing. This is because that member is used to distinguish between Direct3D versions and OpenGL. In Java we can only reasonably be expected to be rendering via OpenGL, so the JOVR library defaults that member to the value for OpenGL, and there's no need to set it.

The most interesting thing to note here is the existence of a RenderViewport member on the texture header. This allows you to specify the size and position of the portion of the texture to which you've rendered your scene. You may ask why you'd ever *not* use the entire texture. There are a variety of reasons.

A developer might wish to use a single texture allocation for both eyes, devoting half of the texture to each eye. In this case, the Size member of RenderViewport would be half the size of the full texture and the Pos member would be different for each eye.

Or a developer might have a well-established system for allocating textures, but it's constrained to produce only textures from a certain fixed set of sizes. In this case, it'd be desirable to grab a texture of the smallest size into which the recommended texture size will fit, and then render only to a subsection of that texture that matches the recommended size.

Finally, because the Texture header is passed into the distortion function on every single frame, it's possible to respond to low frame rates by reducing the amount of pixels being rendered, using a combination of glViewport manipulation during the scene rendering and `RenderViewport` manipulation during the distortion. This is covered in greater detail in chapter 6, in which we focus on performance.

DESTRUCTION

If you're a Java developer, you know that Java doesn't have the same concept of a destructor as C++. There's a concept known as a *finalize* method that appears roughly analogous, but every Java resource since the dawn of time[4] tells you in no uncertain terms not to rely on it, ever. That's because finalizers aren't guaranteed to be called in any given timeframe.

What you have instead is an `onDestroy()` method, which your parent class guarantees will be called once your OpenGL window has been destroyed and you're about to shut down:

```
@Override
protected void onDestroy() {
  hmd.destroy();
  Hmd.shutdown();
}
```

In our `onDestroy` method you release your hold on the HMD, and then shut down the SDK. It's important to notice that the first method is nonstatic but the second is being called in a static context, using the type `Hmd`, not the instance variable `hmd`, because the instance variable `hmd` has now been destroyed. Practically speaking, failing to do these things probably won't have any impact on your application, but failing to clean up after yourself should be considered playing with fire. It's possible that not shutting down properly could leave your Rift in an unusable state, requiring a reset of the device or even the host system before you can resume development.

OPENGL CONTEXT AND WINDOW CREATION

Just as with the C++ `GlfwApp` base class, the Java `LwjglApp` base class expects its derived classes to determine where and how to create the output rendering window:

```
@Override
protected void setupContext() {
  contextAttributes = new ContextAttribs(3, 3)
    .withProfileCore(true)
    .withDebug(true);
}

@Override
protected final void setupDisplay() {
  System.setProperty(
      "org.lwjgl.opengl.Window.undecorated", "true");

  Rectangle targetRect = new Rectangle(
      hmd.WindowsPos.x, hmd.WindowsPos.y,
      hmd.Resolution.w, hmd.Resolution.h);
  setupDisplay(targetRect);
}
```

---

[4] Well, 1997 or so...

Just as we do in our GlfwApp class, we take special steps here to ensure that we will create an OpenGL 3.3 Core profile context. The contextAttributes member is actually a base class member that we're replacing, which would otherwise have simply provided us with the default OpenGL context, whatever that might happen to be for the version of LWJGL that we're using.

Additionally, we set a system property that indicates that we want no window decorations. Such decorations are the bane of proper positioning of the rendered imagery relative to the lenses on the Rift and should never be allowed when using windowed OpenGL. Most applications will probably be using full-screen rendering anyway. See chapter 4 for more details on the distinction.

Finally, we're using the information from the Hmd structure to set the position and resolution of the window itself. This is something of a cheat. If you refer to the chapter 2 example on using the display, you'll see that we point out that the resolution provided in the Hmd structure is the native resolution of the device, not necessarily the *current* resolution of the signal that is being sent to the device. What we should be doing is iterating across all the displays and finding the one whose desktop position matches that of the Rift, and then detecting the current resolution of that display.

For the sake of brevity, though, we're omitting that step. *Caveat coder.*

OPENGL INITIALIZATION

Next we come to the OpenGL setup method, initGl(). As mentioned in the sections on C++, the work done in this method has to be distinct from the work done in the constructor because it uses methods that won't do anything until an OpenGL context has been created.

```
protected void initGl() {
  super.initGl();
  for (int eye = 0; eye < 2; ++eye) {
    TextureHeader eth = eyeTextures[eye].ogl.Header;
    frameBuffers[eye] = new FrameBuffer(
        eth.TextureSize.w, eth.TextureSize.h);
    eyeTextures[eye].ogl.TextureId =
        frameBuffers[eye].getTexture().id;
  }
```

The Oculus SDK examples tend to favor the creation of a single offscreen rendering target, with each eye rendering to half of it. We prefer to create two distinct rendering targets (framebuffers in OpenGL parlance). We haven't found any particular advantage to one approach over the other, so far. We prefer ours because it means we don't have to do any additional math to create the single combined texture size from the recommended per-eye texture sizes.

After you've created your framebuffers, you can assign the actual texture ID to the Oculus SDK TextureHeader type, which will be used to let the distortion mechanism know exactly from where it should pull the undistorted view of the scene.

Finally, you're ready to initialize the SDK distortion mechanism:

```
RenderAPIConfig rc = new RenderAPIConfig();
rc.Header.RTSize = hmdDesc.Resolution;
rc.Header.Multisample = 1;

int distortionCaps =
    ovrDistortionCap_TimeWarp |
    ovrDistortionCap_Vignette;

for (int i = 0; i < rc.PlatformData.length; ++i) {
  rc.PlatformData[i] = Pointer.createConstant(0);
}

eyeRenderDescs = hmd.configureRendering(
    rc, distortionCaps, fovPorts,);

for (int eye = 0; eye < 2; ++eye) {
  this.eyeOffsets[eye].x = eyeRenderDescs[eye]
      .HmdToEyeViewOffset.x;
  this.eyeOffsets[eye].y = eyeRenderDescs[eye]
      .HmdToEyeViewOffset.y;
  this.eyeOffsets[eye].z = eyeRenderDescs[eye]
      .HmdToEyeViewOffset.z;
}
}
```

The bulk of this code is pretty unremarkable and is directly equivalent to the corresponding C++ code that would be used to perform the same action. One unusual point is worth noting: the current Oculus SDK is designed around the idea that the SDK performs the buffer-swapping operation that takes the rendered pixels on the back buffer and actually causes them to appear on the screen.

Buffer swapping is a platform-specific operation that correspondingly requires platform-specific information. For instance, on Windows a Microsoft-specific HWND for the window (or an HDC for the window's drawing surface) is required. These platform-specific details are the kinds of things Java is supposed to insulate you from. The LWJGL library provides a mechanism for swapping the buffers, just as it provides a platform-neutral way of creating an OpenGL window. It doesn't expose the low-level platform-specific information about the windows that have been created and makes it impossible to provide the information normally required by the SDK.

Although the Oculus SDK wants these platform-specific values to be set, if they aren't set the SDK does its best to derive them from the current state of the system, essentially looking at the currently active window, which is presumably the one you've just created.

As with the TextureHeader type we described earlier, RenderAPIConfig has an additional parameter API that we don't bother setting, because JOVR kindly defaults it to the OpenGL value for us.

BUFFER SWAPPING AND MESSAGE PROCESSING

As we mentioned earlier, our parent LwjglApp class uses the finishFrame() method to perform buffer swapping, and we need to disable that behavior because the SDK will handle it instead. As such, we have an overridden version of that method:

```
@Override
protected void finishFrame() {
  Display.processMessages();
}
```

The parent class calls Display.update() in this method to perform the buffer swapping, but the function does more than that. It also interacts with the input system, allowing applications to receive events relating to keyboard and mouse input. Because we still want these aspects to function, we have to replace the missing call with another method that performs the same actions but that doesn't perform a buffer swap: Display.processMessages().

FRAME RENDERING

Having set up OpenGL, the only remaining task for the RiftApp parent class is to encapsulate the per-frame actions that will result in output to the headset:

```
@Override
public final void drawFrame() {
  hmd.beginFrame(++framecount);
  Posef eyePoses[] = hmd.getEyePoses(frameCount, eyeOffsets);
  for (int i = 0; i < 2; ++i) {
    int eye = hmdDesc.EyeRenderOrder[i];
    Posef pose = hmd.beginEyeRender(eye);
    MatrixStack.PROJECTION.set(projections[eye]);

    poses[eye].Orientation = pose.Orientation;
    poses[eye].Position = pose.Position;

    MatrixStack mv = MatrixStack.MODELVIEW;
    mv.push();
    mv.preTranslate(
        RiftUtils.toVector3f(poses[eye].Position).mult(-1));
    mv.preRotate(
        RiftUtils.toQuaternion(poses[eye].Orientation).inverse());
    frameBuffers[eye].activate();
    renderScene();
    frameBuffers[eye].deactivate();
    mv.pop();
  }
  hmd.endFrame(poses, eyeTextures);
}
```

This function is in itself somewhat complex. This isn't surprising because it's the heart of the Oculus SDK–based distortion mechanism. So let's break it down further, piece by piece.

First, note that we've declared the function final so that it can't be overridden in child classes. This is because we want to ensure that any child classes don't try to override this method, mistakenly thinking that it's intended to contain scene-rendering logic. Although that's broadly the intent for classes derived from `LwjglApp`, for classes derived from `RiftApp` that purpose is served by the `renderScene()` method.

Our first call lets the SDK know that we're rendering a new frame so that it can set up state. `beginFrame()` returns a type called `FrameTiming` (equivalent to `ovrFrameTiming` from the C API) that includes specific information about things like the delta time between frames and the midpoint render time. We're not using this information in our example, so we don't bother to capture it:

```
hmd.beginFrame(++frameCount);
```

Next we come to the per-eye loop:

```
Posef eyePoses[] = hmd.getEyePoses(frameCount, eyeOffsets);
for (int i = 0; i < 2; ++i) {
  int eye = hmdDesc.EyeRenderOrder[i];
```

You may note that in most places where we iterate over the eyes we do so in strictly ascending order, but that here we fetch which eye we're working on from the `HmdDesc` structure. This is because the SDK itself knows the order in which the pixels will be illuminated.

Most displays light up their pixels row by row, meaning that each row will be divided half and half between the eyes. But the DK2 HMD illuminates pixels column by column, starting at the right side of the display.

If a user renders the eyes in the order specified in the `EyeRenderOrder` member of `HmdDesc`, the SDK is able to provide better prediction of the head position for each eye, because it's able to empirically measure the time required to perform the first eye render and can typically assume a similar amount of time will be required for the second.

Next, we need to inject the projection for the eye. As discussed in chapter 4, the projection matrices must account for the asymmetrical FOV of each eye, as described by the FOV port, and also account for the offset between the physical center of the per-eye half of the screen and the lens axis for that eye. Fortunately, the SDK takes care of all of this for the user, so all we need to do is ensure that whatever mechanism we're using for matrix stacks has the correct value set at the start of the render:

```
MatrixStack.PROJECTION.set(projections[eye]);
```

Our `MatrixStack` class is analogous to the `gl::Stacks` type in our C++ examples. Both fill the role previously provided by the now deprecated OpenGL matrix stack functions. Like that class, it has static members for both projection and modelview matrix stacks. This is handy, because it's time to start manipulating the latter.

For each eye we want to do several things. First we want to apply the head pose to the matrix. The head pose represents the orientation and position of the user's head. We get the current pose information as a return value whenever we begin the render for a given eye, like so:

```
Posef pose = hmd.getEyePose(eye);
```

Now we're going to pass this pose in to the SDK as part of an array. Unfortunately we can't simply say poses[eye] = pose, because that would break the contiguous memory nature of the array. Instead we have a small hoop to jump through, which is assigning the values from pose to the members of the array entry:

```
poses[eye].Orientation = pose.Orientation;
poses[eye].Position = pose.Position;
```

Now that we have the pose information, we want to apply it to the modelview matrix. In a typical game or application, the modelview stack might already be populated with information about the current viewpoint of the user. We don't want to disrupt that information, so we need to push the modelview stack before we manipulate it:

```
MatrixStack mv = MatrixStack.MODELVIEW;
mv.push();
```

For each eye we want to do several things:

- Apply the head pose to the modelview matrix.
- Apply the eye offset to the modelview matrix.
- Activate an offscreen framebuffer and render our scene to it.

First we want to apply the head pose to the matrix. The head pose represents the orientation and position of the user's head. We got the current pose information as a return value when we called beginEyeRender() previously. But the pose we've received is given as the coordinates and orientation of where the player actually is, similar to if they were the coordinates of a camera for rendering the scene. A modelview transform is the inverse of a camera transform, so we need to apply the inverse of the orientation and position.

Additionally, we need to apply them in the correct order, applying the position first and then the rotation, doing both as pre-multiplications of the modelview matrix. Details of why this is the case can be found in chapter 5.

Note that because the CAPI structures provided by the Oculus SDK don't have the kind of functionality that we'd expect from vector, matrix, or quaternion classes, we're using a RiftUtils class to convert from the CAPI types to the equivalent types in our own math library (which in turn is based on the jMonkeyEngine [jmonkeyengine.org/] math library). These classes have member functions like inverse, which allow us to perform the required transformations:

```
mv.preTranslate(RiftUtils.toVector3f(pose.Position).mult(-1));
mv.preRotate(RiftUtils.toQuaternion(pose.Orientation).inverse());
```

Finally, having set up our matrices, we're now ready to activate the framebuffer and render the scene to an offscreen texture:

```
frameBuffers[eye].activate();
renderScene();
frameBuffers[eye].deactivate();
```

As described earlier, our `renderScene()` method doesn't do anything. It's up to a derived class to implement drawing something of interest, which we'll get to in a moment.

Having done the rendering for our eye, we pop our changes to the modelview matrix off the stack and close the per-eye loop:

```
    mv.pop();
}
```

Once we've rendered both eyes, we let the SDK know we're done with the scene itself, providing it the poses we used and the textures that contain our rendering:

```
hmd.endFrame(poses, eyeTextures);
```

It's at this point that the Oculus SDK takes the scene information and performs the distortion, rendering to the OpenGL back buffer.

11.1.4 *The RiftDemo class*

The Java `RiftApp` class is abstract, so it doesn't make for a terrifically engaging demonstration. Rather, it's the Java analog to the `RiftApp` class in our C++ example code: the end result of putting together all the pieces of code that are required for rendering to the Rift, *sans* an actual scene to render.

To that end we've re-created our original sample demo scene from chapter 5, now in Java. This fully armed and operational demo class is shown next.

Listing 11.4   RiftDemo.java, extending `RiftApp` to render our demo scene

```
// Import statements
public class RiftDemo extends RiftApp {
  private float ipd = OvrLibrary.OVR_DEFAULT_IPD;
  private float eyeHeight = OvrLibrary.OVR_DEFAULT_EYE_HEIGHT;      │ Fetches the IPD
                                                                     │ and eye height
  public RiftDemo() {
    ipd = hmd.getFloat(OvrLibrary.OVR_KEY_IPD, ipd);
    eyeHeight = hmd.getFloat(OvrLibrary.OVR_KEY_EYE_HEIGHT, ipd);
    recenterView();
  }
                                                                     │ Positions the camera
  private void recenterView() {                                      │ five steps out from
    Vector3f center = Vector3f.UNIT_Y.mult(eyeHeight);               │ the central cube
    Vector3f eye = new Vector3f(0, eyeHeight, ipd * 5.0f);
    MatrixStack.MODELVIEW.lookat(eye, center, Vector3f.UNIT_Y);
    hmd.recenterPose();
  }

  @Override
  protected void onKeyboardEvent() {
    if (Keyboard.getEventKeyState()
        && Keyboard.getEventKey() == Keyboard.KEY_R) {
      recenterView();
    }
  }
```

```
@Override
public void renderScene() {                    ◁──┐  Renders a cube on
  glClear(GL_DEPTH_BUFFER_BIT);                    │  a pedestal, with a
  SceneHelpers.renderSkybox();                     │  background scene
  SceneHelpers.renderFloor();

  MatrixStack mv = MatrixStack.MODELVIEW;
  mv.push();
  mv.translate(new Vector3f(0, eyeHeight, 0 ))
      .scale(ipd);
  SceneHelpers.renderColorCube();
  mv.pop();
  mv.push();
  mv.translate(new Vector3f(0, eyeHeight / 2, 0 ))
      .scale(new Vector3f(ipd / 2, eyeHeight, ipd / 2));
  SceneHelpers.renderColorCube();
  mv.pop();
}

public static void main(String[] args) {   ◁──┤  Runs the
  new RiftDemo().run();                          │  example
}
}
```

The results of rendering should look something like figure 11.2.

The Rift demo code isn't terribly interesting, and it has only a couple of interactions with the Oculus SDK worth mentioning. The first is that it uses the user profile eye height (the distance in meters from the ground to the user's eyes) and IPD (the distance in meters between the user's pupils). These are used to construct the scene where the viewpoint is a reasonable distance above the rendered ground,

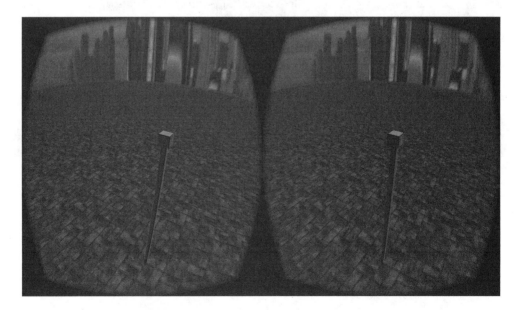

Figure 11.2 The Java demo in action

and to render a cube on a pedestal that's exactly as wide as the distance between the user's eyes.

The justification for this is established in chapter 5, on 3D rendering. Succinctly, having the cubes be exactly as wide as the distance between the pupils and positioned a small distance ahead of the user makes it easy to detect a large number of potential mistakes in setting up the modelview and projection matrices.

The second point of interaction with the Oculus SDK is that we use the `recenter-Pose()` method on the `Hmd` type both during initialization and if the user presses the R key. This allows the user to put on the headset, get seated comfortably, and then inform the SDK that they're in their starting position, from which all movement and orientation changes should be considered relative.

The remainder of the code is mostly interaction with helper classes for rendering various scene entities. In our `renderScene()` method, we draw our skybox and a floor, and then we render a color cube in front of the user at a distance of five times the distance between the pupils. This puts it close enough that you can get a sense of depth even if you're completely still, yet far enough that it doesn't feel like it's invading your personal space or forcing you to cross your eyes.

11.2 Using the Python bindings

Our Python example returns once more to our simple color cube, although this example is somewhat more primitive, dropping the skybox and pedestal for a simple gray background (figure 11.3).

Integration of Python with C code is even easier than with Java. Python includes a foreign language library called ctypes. This library provides the same functionality as the JNA/JNI mechanisms in Java: access to methods defined in C-style libraries. There

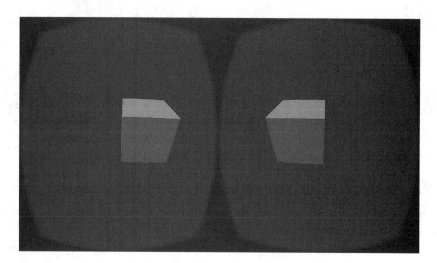

Figure 11.3 Our Python example scene, a simple cube

are a number of open source projects designed to allow you to generate code bindings. For our application, we used ctypesgen (code.google.com/p/ctypesgen/).

11.2.1 Meet our Python binding: PyOVR

The Python bindings we're working with are called PyOVR, based on code generated by ctypesgen, and then supplemented with custom Python code intended to provide a more Python-like façade on the exposed functionality.

11.2.2 Development environment

Our Python 2.7 example depends on the libraries PyOpenGL, cgkit, Numpy, and Pygame. Please note that although it shouldn't be hard to update the example from version 2.7 to the latest build of Python, the four supporting libraries don't all have support for the latest version of the language.

In order to use the demo sample, you'll need to add the Oculus SDK Python bindings directory to your PYTHONPATH system variable.

If you've checked out all of the demo code on our GitHub repository, you'll find the bindings in OculusRiftInAction/libraries/OculusSDK/Bindings/Python. The oculusvr module is in this path. This is the directory you should add to your PYTHONPATH.

Alternatively, you can check out the Python demo and bindings directly, on their own, from GitHub:

- *Bindings*: github.com/jherico/python-ovrsdk
- *Demo*: github.com/OculusRiftInAction/pyovr-examples

11.2.3 The pyovr-examples project

The Python examples are less sophisticated than the C++ and Java ones. We've developed libraries to encapsulate much of the OpenGL boilerplate and heavy lifting for our work in Java and C++, but we didn't find any such tools in Python and weren't well positioned to write them. As such, the Python example provides only the bare minimum in terms of scene content: the colored cube. A skybox and floor representation are both absent.

11.2.4 The RiftApp class

As with C++ and Java, we've created a base class that encapsulates the boilerplate of working with the Oculus Rift and OpenGL.

Because OpenGL only defines mechanisms for rendering to an OpenGL context, not how to create or position a window or context, we have to use some other mechanism to do so. In C++, we used GLFW3. In Java, we used LWJGL. Here in Python, we use a library called Pygame (www.pygame.org). Pygame gives us access to the same functionality that we require for using the Oculus SDK: the ability to create a double-buffered OpenGL window of a given size, at a given desktop position, and without window decorations. The following listing shows the Python RiftApp class.

Listing 11.5   RiftApp.py

```python
import oculusvr as ovr
import numpy as np
import pygame
import pygame.locals as pgl

from OpenGL.GL import *
from cgkit.cgtypes import mat4, vec3, quat
from ctypes import *
from oculusvr import Hmd, ovrGLTexture, ovrPosef, ovrVector3f

class RiftApp():
  def __init__(self):
    ovr.Hmd.initialize()
    self.hmd = ovr.Hmd()

    self.hmdDesc = self.hmd.hmd.contents
    self.frame = 0

    # Workaround for a race condition bug in the SDK
    import time
    time.sleep(0.1)

    self.hmd.configure_tracking()
    self.fovPorts = (
      self.hmdDesc.DefaultEyeFov[0],
      self.hmdDesc.DefaultEyeFov[1]
    )
    projections = map(
      lambda fovPort:
        (ovr.Hmd.get_perspective(
          fovPort, 0.01, 1000, True)),
      self.fovPorts
    )
    self.projections = map(
      lambda pr:
        pr.toList(),
      projections)
    self.eyeTextures = [ ovrGLTexture(), ovrGLTexture() ]
    for eye in range(0, 2):
      size = self.hmd.get_fov_texture_size(
       eye, self.fovPorts[eye])
      eyeTexture = self.eyeTextures[eye]
      eyeTexture.API = ovr.ovrRenderAPI_OpenGL
      header = eyeTexture.Texture.Header;
      header.TextureSize = size
      vp = header.RenderViewport;
      vp.Size = size
      vp.Pos.x = 0
      vp.Pos.y = 0

  def close(self):
    glDeleteFramebuffers(2, self.fbo)
    glDeleteTextures(self.color)
    glDeleteRenderbuffers(2, self.depth)
```

Sets up as much internal state as possible without having an OpenGL context.

Releases Oculus SDK and OpenGL resources.

```
      self.hmd.destroy()
      self.hmd = None
      ovr.Hmd.shutdown()
                                          ┌─┐ Creates a window, passing
  def create_window(self):            ◁──┘   settings from the Oculus
      import os                                SDK to pygame.
      os.environ['SDL_VIDEO_WINDOW_POS'] = "%d,%d" % (
        self.hmdDesc.WindowsPos.x,
        self.hmdDesc.WindowsPos.y)
      pygame.init()
      pygame.display.set_mode(
        (
          self.hmdDesc.Resolution.w,
          self.hmdDesc.Resolution.h
        ),
        pgl.HWSURFACE | pgl.OPENGL | pgl.DOUBLEBUF | pgl.NOFRAME)
      window_info = pygame.display.get_wm_info()
      window = c_void_p(window_info['window'])
      ovr.ovrHmd_AttachToWindow(self.hmd.hmd, window, 0, 0)

  def init_gl(self):                  ◁─┐  Completes the
      self.fbo = glGenFramebuffers(2)   │  SDK setup.
      self.color = glGenTextures(2)
      self.depth = glGenRenderbuffers(2)

      for eye in range(0, 2):
        self.build_framebuffer(eye)
        self.eyeTextures[eye].OGL.TexId = np.asscalar(self.color[eye])

      rc = ovr.ovrRenderAPIConfig()
      header = rc.Header;
     ·header.API = ovr.ovrRenderAPI_OpenGL
      header.BackBufferSize = self.hmdDesc.Resolution
      header.Multisample = 1
      for i in range(0, 8):
        rc.PlatformData[i] = 0
      self.eyeRenderDescs = \
        self.hmd.configure_rendering(rc, self.fovPorts)

      self.eyeOffsets = [ ovrVector3f(), ovrVector3f() ]
      for eye in range(0, 2):
        self.eyeOffsets[eye] = self.eyeRenderDescs[eye].HmdToEyeViewOffset

      # Bug in the SDK leaves a program bound, so clear it
      glUseProgram(0)
                                                                   Builds the OpenGL
  def build_framebuffer(self, eye):                           ◁   offscreen rendering
      size = self.eyeTextures[eye].Texture.Header.TextureSize     targets for distortion
                                                                   rendering.
      # Set up the color attachement texture
      glBindTexture(GL_TEXTURE_2D, self.color[eye])
      glTexParameteri(GL_TEXTURE_2D,
        GL_TEXTURE_MIN_FILTER, GL_LINEAR)
      glTexImage2D(GL_TEXTURE_2D, 0, GL_RGBA8,
        size.w, size.h, 0, GL_RGB,
        GL_UNSIGNED_BYTE, None)
      glBindTexture(GL_TEXTURE_2D, 0)
```

```
    # Set up the depth attachment renderbuffer
    glBindRenderbuffer(GL_RENDERBUFFER, self.depth[eye])
    glRenderbufferStorage(GL_RENDERBUFFER, GL_DEPTH_COMPONENT,
      size.w, size.h)
    glBindRenderbuffer(GL_RENDERBUFFER, 0)

    # Set up the framebuffer proper
    glBindFramebuffer(GL_FRAMEBUFFER, self.fbo[eye])
    glFramebufferTexture2D(GL_FRAMEBUFFER,
      GL_COLOR_ATTACHMENT0, GL_TEXTURE_2D,
      self.color[eye], 0)
    glFramebufferRenderbuffer(GL_FRAMEBUFFER,
      GL_DEPTH_ATTACHMENT, GL_RENDERBUFFER,
      self.depth[eye])
    fboStatus = glCheckFramebufferStatus(GL_FRAMEBUFFER)
    if (GL_FRAMEBUFFER_COMPLETE != fboStatus):
      raise Exception("Bad framebuffer setup")
    glBindFramebuffer(GL_FRAMEBUFFER, 0)

  def render_frame(self):                         ◄─── Renders a left and right eye
    self.frame += 1                                    view to offscreen rendering
                                                       targets, then passes it to
    # Fetch the head pose                              the Oculus SDK.
    poses = self.hmd.get_eye_poses(self.frame, self.eyeOffsets)

    self.hmd.begin_frame(self.frame)
    for i in range(0, 2):
      eye = self.hmdDesc.EyeRenderOrder[i]

      glMatrixMode(GL_PROJECTION)
      glLoadMatrixf(self.projections[eye])

      self.eyeview = mat4(1.0)

      # Apply the head orientation
      rot = poses[eye].Orientation
      # Convert the OVR orientation (a quaternion
      # structure) to a cgkit quaternion class, and
      # from there to a mat4  Coordinates are camera
      # coordinates
      rot = quat(rot.toList())
      rot = rot.toMat4()

      # Apply the head position
      pos = poses[eye].Position
      # Convert the OVR position (a vector3 structure)
      # to a cgcit vector3 class. Position is in camera /
      # Rift coordinates
      pos = vec3(pos.toList())
      pos = mat4(1.0).translate(pos)

      pose = pos * rot

      # apply it to the eyeview matrix
      self.eyeview = pose;

      # The subclass is responsible for taking eyeview
      # and applying it to whatever camera or modelview
      # coordinate system it uses before rendering the
      # scene
```

```
      # Activate the offscreen framebuffer and render the scene
      glBindFramebuffer(GL_FRAMEBUFFER, self.fbo[eye])
      size = self.eyeTextures[eye].Texture.Header.RenderViewport.Size
      glViewport(0, 0, size.w, size.h)
      self.render_scene()
      glBindFramebuffer(GL_FRAMEBUFFER, 0)
    self.hmd.end_frame(poses, self.eyeTextures)
    glGetError()

  def update(self):
    for event in pygame.event.get():
      self.on_event(event)

  def on_event(self, event):
    if event.type == pgl.QUIT:
      self.running = False
      return True
    if event.type == pgl.KEYUP and event.key == pgl.K_ESCAPE:
      self.running = False
      return True
    return False

  def run(self):
    self.create_window()
    self.init_gl()
    self.running = True
    start = ovr.Hmd.get_time_in_seconds()
    last = start
    while self.running:
      self.update()
      self.render_frame()
      #pygame.display.flip()
      now = ovr.Hmd.get_time_in_seconds()
      if (now - last > 10):
        interval = now - start
        fps = self.frame / interval
        print "%f" % fps
        last = now
    self.close()
    pygame.quit()
```

> Calls the rendering mechanism, controls the program lifetime, and deals with user input.

This code is functionally very similar to the Java version presented earlier in this chapter and the C++ version included in our example repository. Let's take a closer look at the various components.

CONSTRUCTION

In the constructor we initialize the Oculus SDK as a whole using the static method initialize on the Hmd type:

```
  def __init__(self):
    ovr.Hmd.initialize()
    self.hmd = ovr.Hmd()
    self.hmdDesc = self.hmd.get_desc()
```

Next, we start the tracking sensors:

```
        self.hmd.configure_tracking()
```

We'll need to know about where the display is on the desktop and we'll need to know the fields of view supported for each eye:

```
self.fovPorts = (
  self.hmdDesc.DefaultEyeFov[0],
  self.hmdDesc.DefaultEyeFov[1]
)
```

The FOV ports are stored in a structure we'll use later during rendering configuration. But we also need to use them to construct the projection matrix for each eye:

```
projections = map(
  lambda fovPort:
    (ovr.Hmd.get_perspective(
        fovPort, 0.01, 1000, True)),
  self.fovPorts
)
self.projections = map(
  lambda pr:
    pr.toList(),
  projections)
```

The matrix as provided by the SDK is in a ctype structure. To pass it in to the OpenGL functions, we flatten it to a Python `tuple` type, which is an immutable list of objects, in this case floating-point values.

Next we need to set up information about the textures we'll use for offscreen rendering:

```
self.eyeTextures = [ ovrGLTexture(), ovrGLTexture() ]
for eye in range(0, 2):
  size = self.hmd.get_fov_texture_size(
    eye, self.fovPorts[eye])
  eyeTexture = self.eyeTextures[eye]
  eyeTexture.API = ovr.ovrRenderAPI_OpenGL
  header = eyeTexture.Texture.Header;
  header.TextureSize = size
  vp = header.RenderViewport;
  vp.Size = size
  vp.Pos.x = 0
  vp.Pos.y = 0
```

Here we allocate textures based on the size of the FOV. The exact details of the fields of view and the eye textures are covered in chapter 5.

CLEANING UP

Like Java, Python doesn't have the concept of a guaranteed destructor. Instead we've got a `close` method that we explicitly call when we're exiting the primary loop. In it we take care of cleaning up the OpenGL objects we've created:

```
def close(self):
  glDeleteFramebuffers(2, self.fbo)
  glDeleteTextures(self.color)
  glDeleteRenderbuffers(2, self.depth)
```

More critically, we need to shut down our use of the Oculus SDK. This includes destroying the Hmd instance, which stops the sensors, and then calling the overall SDK shutdown function. It should be done specifically in this order, which is the reverse of the order used to call the corresponding startup functions.

```
self.hmd.destroy()
self.hmd = None
ovr.Hmd.shutdown()
```

Let's move on now and look at how we get the output onto the Rift screen.

CREATING OUR OUTPUT WINDOW

Before we can see anything on the Rift screen (other than the desktop wallpaper, or some lost and lonely windows that have wandered to the wrong display somehow) we need to create a rendering surface.

As stated, we're using Pygame to create our display output. Interestingly, it seems to use the conventions of another cross-platform rendering library called SDL for positioning windows. Specifically it allows you to set the position of your rendering surface by setting an environment variable to the coordinates you want, like so:

```
def create_window(self):
  import os
  os.environ['SDL_VIDEO_WINDOW_POS'] = "%d,%d" % (
    self.hmdDesc.WindowsPos.x,
    self.hmdDesc.WindowsPos.y)
```

INITIALIZING PYGAME

Having set the required values, we call (yet another) library initialization function and then call the function that actually creates the window, in this case Pygame's somewhat confusingly named set_mode. We pass in both the resolution we want as well as a number of flags specifying that we want a hardware-accelerated OpenGL surface with double buffering and no window decorations:

```
pygame.init()
pygame.display.set_mode(
  (
    self.hmdDesc.Resolution.w,
    self.hmdDesc.Resolution.h
  ),
  pgl.HWSURFACE | pgl.OPENGL | pgl.DOUBLEBUF | pgl.NOFRAME)
```

We're taking a bit of a shortcut here. The resolution information provided by the SDK is the native resolution of the device, not *necessarily* the current resolution. The proper thing to do here is to iterate over all the displays available and find the one with a desktop position equivalent to the WindowPos member of the HMD description, and then query for its resolution. Doing this typically involves mechanisms that are platform-specific. For the sake of brevity, we've skipped this step here.

The last step in setting up is to retrieve its opened window and pass its reference back to the Oculus SDK, attaching the OVR instance to the created frame:

```
window_info = pygame.display.get_wm_info()
window = c_void_p(window_info['window'])
ovr.ovrHmd_AttachToWindow(self.hmd.hmd, window, 0, 0)
```

INITIALIZING OPENGL

Our `init_gl` method will be called almost immediately after the OpenGL surface has been created, allowing us to complete the Oculus SDK setup steps that rely on the presence of a rendering API.

Specifically this means creating the offscreen rendering targets (framebuffers in OpenGL) and calling the SDK-rendering configuration function, which creates a vertex mesh used for distortion.

We start off by allocating the OpenGL object names[5] required for the framebuffers:

```
def init_gl(self):
  self.fbo = glGenFramebuffers(2)
  self.color = glGenTextures(2)
  self.depth = glGenRenderbuffers(2)
```

For each eye we can now build the framebuffer proper. Additionally we can take the texture IDs and put them in the Oculus structure to let the SDK know from where it'll pull the rendered scenes during distortion:

```
for eye in range(0, 2):
  self.build_framebuffer(eye)
  self.eyeTextures[eye].OGL.TexId = np.asscalar(self.color[eye])
```

The call to `build_framebuffer` allows us to push out the OpenGL boilerplate for the framebuffer construction. We won't cover it in detail here, other than to say that you need to ensure that both the color and depth attachments should use the same size values as used in the `TextureSize` member of the per-eye texture structures.

Next we call the SDK method to configure the distortion:

```
rc = ovr.ovrRenderAPIConfig()
header = rc.Header;
header.API = ovr.ovrRenderAPI_OpenGL
header.BackBufferSize = self.hmdDesc.Resolution
header.Multisample = 1
for i in range(0, 8):
  rc.PlatformData[i] = 0
self.eyeRenderDescs = \
  self.hmd.configure_rendering(rc, self.fovPorts)
```

You may note that we're not passing in any of the OVR distortion capability flags to the `configure_rendering` call. Because Python supports default argument values (unlike

---

[5] Yes, they're only lowly integers. OpenGL refers to them as names.

Java), we've taken the opportunity to declare `configure_rendering` with reasonable defaults. If you examine the declaration you'll find it looks like this:

```
def configure_rendering(self, config, fovPorts,
                        distortion_caps =
                        ovrDistortionCap_TimeWarp |
                        ovrDistortionCap_Vignette):
```

This enables us to use much more terse syntax for the call to `configure_rendering`, assuming we're satisfied with the defaults given. Refer to chapters 4 and 5 for a more detailed discussion of the individual distortion capability flags and their meanings.

The last step of our OpenGL setup is to capture the per-eye offsets from the eye render descriptions retrieved from the Rift:

```
self.eyeOffsets = [ ovrVector3f(), ovrVector3f() ]
for eye in range(0, 2):
  self.eyeOffsets[eye] = \
    self.eyeRenderDescs[eye].HmdToEyeViewOffset
```

Our OpenGL initialization is now complete.

FRAME RENDERING

For all the setup and cleanup that we do, the core of the SDK functionality is contained in the rendering loop. This loop is responsible for iterating over both eyes, and for each of them rendering a scene from a given viewpoint.

Our very first step is to capture the user's current head pose for this frame. After that, for SDK distortion to function, we must bookend the frame rendering with the `begin_frame` and `end_frame` methods from our `Hmd` instance:

```
def render_frame(self):
  self.frame += 1

  poses = self.hmd.get_eye_poses(self.frame, self.eyeOffsets)

  self.hmd.begin_frame(self.frame)
  for i in range(0, 2):
    eye = self.hmdDesc.EyeRenderOrder[i]
    # ...
  self.hmd.end_frame(poses, self.eyeTextures)
```

The remainder of our code from this function happens within that ellipsis. Note that we don't iterate directly over the eyes. Instead we iterate over the range [0, 1], and for each value we fetch which eye should be rendered. Rendering the eyes in the proper order can improve the perceived latency on the device, because on hardware that refreshes the display from left to right or right to left instead of the much more common top to bottom, the SDK knows which eye will be illuminated first. It's therefore in your best interest to render the eyes in the expected order. See chapter 5 for more details.

Within the per-eye loop we're responsible for setting the appropriate projection and modelview matrices. The projection matrix is easy, because it's provided to us directly by the SDK and we stored it when we started up, so here we only need to load it:

```
glMatrixMode(GL_PROJECTION)
glLoadMatrixf(self.projections[eye])
```

Note that we're using Python's older, "classic" OpenGL matrix stacks support rather than a more modern implementation. It can be illustrative to provide the actual raw order of operations required.

We need to apply the position and orientation of the headset to the view of the scene. The begin_eye_render method used to let the SDK know we're starting rendering for the given eye provides us with a head pose value. Conveniently, this value will automatically incorporate prediction based on the timing values recorded by the SDK.

The OVR headpose structure has two distinct components: a position and an orientation. We'll convert each separately into matrices, and then concatenate the two matrices to pass them as a single transform to OpenGL.

First we'll find the head orientation:

```
rot = poses[eye].Orientation
rot = quat(rot.toList())
rot = rot.toMat4()
```

Next we'll find the head position:

```
pos = poses[eye].Position
pos = vec3(pos.toList())
pos = mat4(1.0).translate(pos)
```

The method quat() and the types vec3 and mat4 are from cgkit. As you can see, we've used cgkit to black-box the mechanics of working with OVR's quaternion and translation data.

Lastly we construct the cumulative pose matrix, concatenating the translation and rotation:

```
pose = pos * rot
self.eyeview = pose;
```

The variable self.eyeview communicates the head pose matrix back to the child class, which will read this value to calculate the actual camera matrix at rendering time. The subclass is responsible for taking eyeview and applying it to whatever camera or modelview coordinate system it uses before rendering the scene.

With the modelview and projection matrices fully set up, we can enable the framebuffer and render the scene itself to a texture:

```
# Activate the offscreen framebuffer and render the scene
glBindFramebuffer(GL_FRAMEBUFFER, self.fbo[eye])
size = self.eyeTextures[eye].Textures.Header \
  .RenderViewport.Size
glViewport(0, 0, size.w, size.h)
self.render_scene()
glBindFramebuffer(GL_FRAMEBUFFER, 0)
```

With the eye texture rendered, we complete the loop over the eyes. All that's left is to close our bookends with a final call:

```
self.hmd.end_frame(poses, self.eyeTextures)
```

This signals the SDK that the frame is complete and can be swapped to the display.

Now let's take a look at the main loop of our demo.

THE MAIN LOOP

Our `run` function is the only one (other than the implicit call to the constructor) that needs to be called from outside this class. It performs the setup, and then renders frames until it's told to quit. With the timing code removed, the loop is pretty straightforward:

```
def run(self):
  self.create_window()
  self.init_gl()
  self.running = True
  while self.running:
    self.update()
    self.render_frame()
    pygame.display.flip()
  self.close()
  pygame.quit()
```

And that's it—our main loop is in place and this `RiftApp` implementation is ready to fly. This base class provides a simple way to get up and running with Oculus Rift support in a Python application.

Of course, you need to have a subclass that will render something of interest to the user if you want to see `RiftApp` live in the Rift. So let's check out our `RiftDemo` class.

11.2.5 *The RiftDemo class*

Our demo class is short and sweet—all the shorter for not including the implementation of `draw_color_cube` or the keyboard-handling code (but you can find all that in the GitHub repository). Literally all this does is render a cube in space, nothing else, as shown in the following listing.

Listing 11.6 RiftDemo.py

```
#! /usr/bin/env python
import pygame
import pygame.locals as pgl
import oculusvr as ovr

from RiftApp import RiftApp
from cgkit.cgtypes import mat4, vec3
from OpenGL.GL import *                    ◁———  draw_color_cube
                                                 removed for brevity
def draw_color_cube:
  ...
```

RiftDemo extends RiftApp.

```python
class RiftDemo(RiftApp):
    def __init__(self):                              ◄─── Fetches the IPD, which we'll
        RiftApp.__init__(self)                            use to scale our cube.
        self.cube_size = self.hmd.get_float(
            ovr.OVR_KEY_IPD, ovr.OVR_DEFAULT_IPD)
        self.reset_camera()

    def init_gl(self):                        ◄─── Sets up OpenGL.
        RiftApp.init_gl(self)
        glEnable(GL_DEPTH_TEST)
        glClearColor(0.1, 0.1, 0.1, 1)        ┐ Keyboard-handling
                                              │ code also removed
    def update(self):                     ◄───┘ for brevity.
        ...
                                                  Renders the scene.
                                                  This will be called
    def render_scene(self):               ◄───   once for each eye.
        glClear(GL_COLOR_BUFFER_BIT | GL_DEPTH_BUFFER_BIT)

                                                       Loads the current camera
        cameraview = self.eyeview * self.camera   ◄─── position and headpose
        glMatrixMode(GL_MODELVIEW)                     view transform.
        glLoadMatrixf(cameraview.inverse().toList())
        glMultMatrixf(self.camera.inverse().toList())
                                              Renders the
                                          ◄── simple cube.
        draw_color_cube(self.cube_size)

RiftDemo().run();            ◄───  Serves as a
                                   main() function.
```

We extend the base class constructor so we can grab the user's interpupillary distance, because we scale the colored cube to match the IPD.

We also extend the base class's `init_gl` method to set a clear color that isn't quite black. This is useful because it makes it easy to distinguish the region of the screen where the distorted image has been rendered from the overall screen background that has nothing rendered to it at all.

Finally, we implement our `render_scene` method. Here we perform the standard clearing of the buffer and draw our colored cube. The cube, rendered at half a meter from the user with a width that's exactly the same as the distance between the eyes, is a valuable first test: it lets you tell at a glance if your matrix setup is correct. For more details on the usefulness of this test scene, see chapter 5.

The scene created should look like figure 11.3. A more complex example would also include (at least) a floor and a skybox in order to provide users with a greater sense of presence, as opposed to leaving them feeling like they're floating in a formless gray void. The details of making something fun is left as an exercise to the reader.

11.3   *Working with other languages*

If you're still looking to work with the Rift but Java, Python, and C/C++ aren't suitable for your work, you're not out of luck. We can't cover examples of every potential language you might want to use the Rift from, but bear in mind that to work with the Rift from *any* language, you only need a couple of basic things:

- A means of calling C functions
- A means of calling a rendering API like OpenGL or Direct3D

For OpenGL, where C bindings are available, the second requirement is essentially a reiteration of the first. In other words, if you can call C functions, you can produce a VR application for the Oculus Rift.

"Lisp in the Rift," anybody?

11.4 Summary

In this chapter you learned that

- You can develop for the Rift using Java or Python.
- Working with the Rift in Java or Python still requires the use of the Oculus SDK.
- For Python users, a library called PyOVR is available to interact with the Oculus SDK. PyOVR is available at github.com/jherico/python-ovrsdk.
- For Java users, the JOVR library is available to interact with the Oculus SDK. JOVR is available at github.com/jherico/jovr and via Maven.
- Both PyOVR and JOVR are open source libraries developed by the authors and made available to developers to ease integration of their applications with the Oculus SDK. Unlike the individual examples in this book, they're intended to be production ready.
- Each library provides both direct access to the Oculus SDK C API functions as well as a language-specific façade class to allow the use of the SDK functionality in a more object-oriented fashion.

Case study:
a VR shader editor

This chapter covers

- Creating a full-fledged VR application:
  a case study
- Putting what you've learned into practice
- Integrating Rift functionality with a third-party
  GUI framework

Up to this point, our demos have been toy applications. The samples you've seen so far are useful, but each has been designed to demonstrate a specific learning point or technical feature. In this chapter we present a larger, more complicated case study: we're going to create a complete end-to-end application, to serve as an example of the best practices that we've discussed so far and to illustrate the issues that can come up in more advanced programs.

To demonstrate the art of a fully formed VR app, we'll adapt an existing application into a VR context. We've chosen an application that's heavily graphical in nature but that runs on the web today and is strictly 2D. The application, Shadertoy (www.shadertoy.com), is a web-based tool for editing OpenGL fragment shaders. Shadertoy was created by Iñigo Quilez and Pol Jeremias.

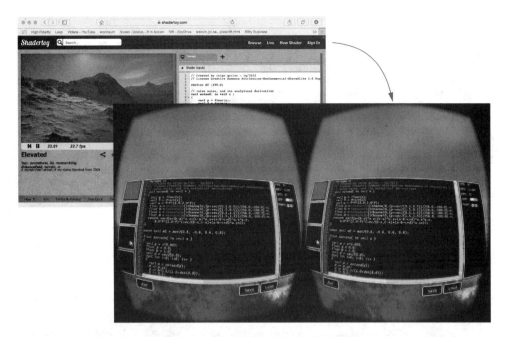

Figure 12.1   Shadertoy and ShadertoyVR. The shader visible on the screen is *Elevated* by Iñigo Quilez.

In this chapter we're giving that 2D app a new dimension: we're going to build ShadertoyVR (figure 12.1).

We've chosen to create ShadertoyVR because it's instructive, it's a chance to learn about some pretty nifty graphics stuff like raycasting, and its output looks awesome. Above and beyond that, it's a chance to build an app that lets you *edit code in virtual reality*. If you're a coder or if you've ever played one on TV, you know that writing code in a 2D text window locked to your monitor is the bread and butter of every day. How many times have you dreamed of having the code all around you? Now we're finally going to take coding into virtual reality. We're bringing the day of the infinite desktop that much closer.

12.1   The starting point: Shadertoy

Shadertoy is a rendering and programming site dedicated to graphics enthusiasts. The site hosts an online application where users can edit OpenGL Shading Language (GLSL) shader code (more on that later) and see their changes take immediate effect. Users edit GLSL code in a standard text form and can see the resulting output rendered, in real time, in another panel in the browser. Shadertoy uses the WebGL standard to run the shader code on the local GPU, so even though it's running in the browser it can leverage all the power of local accelerated hardware (figure 12.2).

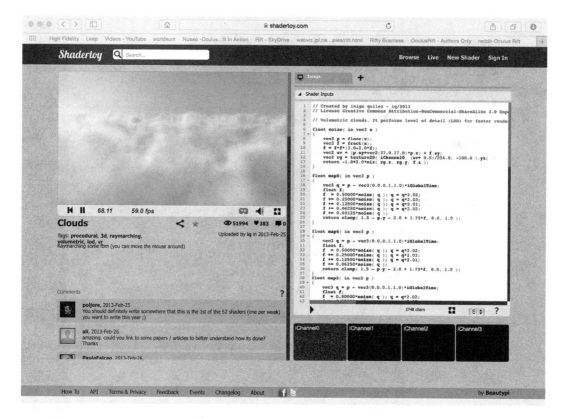

Figure 12.2   The Shadertoy interface, showing the shader *Clouds*

Shadertoy is driven by user-created content. Users can edit, save, upload and share small *fragment shaders,* which produce an astounding range of visual effects. Shaders can be driven by audio, video, and interactive inputs. Although some of the shaders on Shadertoy.com produce only 2D effects, a hefty number of them have been designed to render procedural 3D scenes, often animated.

On Shadertoy.com, each program is a fragment shader. These shaders are small programs written in the GLSL language. Most Shadertoy shaders use a technique called *raycasting* to create the illusion of 3D perspective. If you're interested in how these short (typically, under 100 lines) programs can create amazing visual panoramas, check out the last section of this chapter.

Programming with shaders: GLSL

Programmable shaders are the core of modern computer graphics. Shaders are small programs that are compiled and run on the GPU, capable of processing billions of pixel operations per second. Although we haven't called them out, each of our own examples has included demo code written in GLSL as an integral part of our rendering engine.

All of the user programs on Shadertoy.com are shader programs, written in GLSL. GLSL code tends to be succinct, to the point, and extremely focused on producing nifty graphics effects. You don't need to speak fluent GLSL to understand shaders—actually, the language looks a lot like old C code—so feel free to browse.

12.2 The destination: ShadertoyVR

We're going to adapt Shadertoy to a VR context. The goal is to go from figure 12.3a (the original web app) to figure 12.3b (the same shader, now sensitive to head motion and ready to render to the Rift). The two figures are stills from the same shader, but in figure 12.3b the image shows the familiar Rift oval distortions. Loading a shader into the Rift isn't the real challenge, though. Once we've got the basic building blocks in place, we're going to build what's shown in figure 12.4: a live text editor, completely contained inside the VR world, floating between the user and the shader output.

As we build this case study, you'll see how a Rift app can insert the user into homespun virtual scenes. We'll explore the issues that arise when rebuilding a two-dimensional interface inside a virtual space. The final result will be a VR application that runs in the Rift, in which the user will be able to edit their code on the fly and see the virtual worlds around them literally transform with the click of a button.

12.3 Making the jump from 2D to 3D

Now it's time to start planning. Let's begin with a few notes about how Shadertoy works in 2D, with a particular eye to its user interface: all of the visual gadgets and widgets that let users edit their shaders and select images and textures as inputs. Once the goal is clear, we'll cover the project-planning aspect of the task, and from there we'll dive into the real challenge: the technical implementation of the VR interface.

12.3.1 UI layout

The main workspace of Shadertoy.com presents users with a split-screen view of their shader. On the left, their current work is shown in a WebGL window, running live. This is where their virtual world appears, rendered entirely on the GPU by WebGL. On the right, the user has an editing window in which to write a fragment shader (figure 12.2).

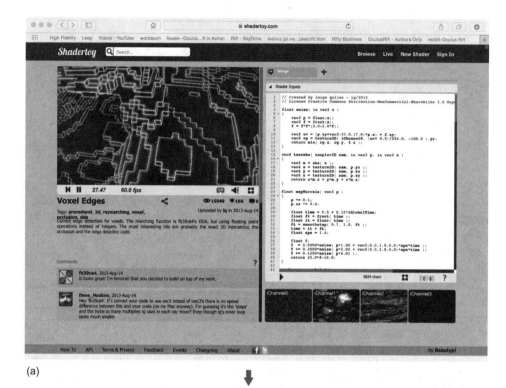

(a)

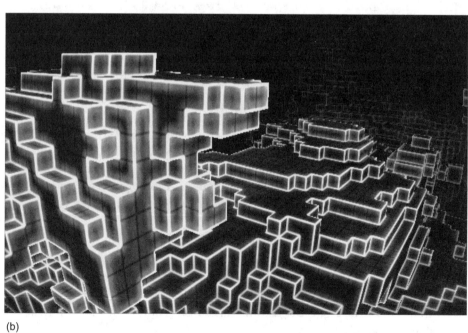

(b)

Figure 12.3   (a) Shadertoy; (b) ShadertoyVR

Figure 12.4 A VR shader with the editing window up, rendering the Voxel Edges shader as a VR environment

Users can modify the code in the text editor on the right, press the Run button, and immediately see the resulting output in the WebGL window. The website passes the geometry of a quadrilateral to WebGL and executes its built-in vertex shader, chaining into the user's handmade fragment shader.

The key to building a Shadertoy shader is that every pixel of the rectangle has a unique 2D coordinate, and you can choose color by coordinate. In computer graphics terms, this makes every shader a *procedural texture*. Your challenge is to find a way to produce an interesting texture, even an entire virtual world, using only your skill at assigning color to each pixel separately.

We encourage you to check out the site. It's easy to browse and play with the interface, experimenting and exploring what the code can do.

12.3.2 *User inputs*

In addition to the vertex shader and the basic inputs provided by OpenGL, the Shadertoy website provides a number of optional inputs that the fragment shader can use in creating the output. These include the time since the shader started running, the resolution of the output window, and a set of customizable input channels (figure 12.5).

Most of the inputs are nonconfigurable, their value determined by the web application alone. But each shader can have up to four *channel inputs*, the data for which is

```
◢ Shader Inputs

uniform vec3      iResolution;            // viewport resolution (in pixels)
uniform float     iGlobalTime;            // shader playback time (in seconds)
uniform float     iChannelTime[4];        // channel playback time (in seconds)
uniform vec3      iChannelResolution[4];  // channel resolution (in pixels)
uniform vec4      iMouse;                 // mouse pixel coords. xy: current (if MLB down), zw: click
uniform samplerXX iChannel0..3;           // input channel. XX = 2D/Cube
uniform vec4      iDate;                  // (year, month, day, time in seconds)
uniform float     iSampleRate;            // sound sample rate (i.e., 44100)
```

Figure 12.5   Shadertoy's available shader inputs

user configurable. Shadertoy supports five kinds of channel inputs: keyboard, 2D textures, cubemap textures, audio, and video.

The choice of channel inputs is made by clicking one of four buttons labeled iChannel beneath the code editor window. Selecting one of these channel buttons, the user is presented with a dialog (figure 12.6) from which they can select one of the

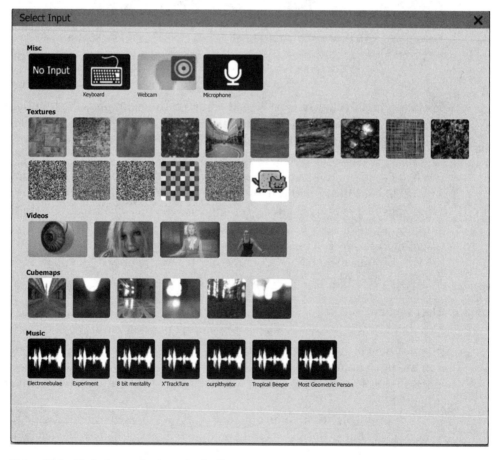

Figure 12.6   Shadertoy.com's channel selection screen

available channel inputs. The selected input becomes available to the running shader immediately. The shader's inputs will now include `iChannel` uniform values for the chosen channel, populated with content data. This gives shaders access to video inputs, backgrounds, textures, and even music.

12.3.3 Project planning

To create ShadertoyVR, we're going to have to meet a series of key milestones. At the end of the project, we'll have a standalone app that reproduces the core functionality of the Shadertoy website, in VR.

The milestones are

1 Picking a subset of features to implement
2 Understanding how to port existing shaders designed for the website so that they render properly in VR
3 Adapting the rendering mechanism from a 2D WebGL window to a VR environment
4 Creating a functional editing interface inside the VR environment
5 Coping with the performance constraints of VR

The core of the challenge we face will be to implement a smooth, usable two-dimensional user interface (the text-editing UI of the shader editor) in a virtual environment that can execute the user's shaders.

12.3.4 Picking our feature set

We begin by identifying the features of Shadertoy which we'll be re-creating.

CRITICAL FEATURES

There are several features that are essential to the ShadertoyVR app's function. These critical path features include

- Browsing preset shaders
- Loading and running shaders
- Saving new and modified shaders
- Editing shaders and being able to see the result
- Feedback on shader compilation success or failure
- Supporting cubemap and 2D textures as channel inputs
- Rendering the UI within the virtual environment

DESIRABLE FEATURES

Then we have the "nice-to-have" features. They're not critical path because you can use the application with or without them, but not having them can greatly diminish the usability of the app. Both are specific to the editor window for the fragment shader:

- Syntax highlighting
- Line numbers

If you're accustomed to writing code in an editor that does syntax highlighting, plain mono-colored text can make visually parsing a large block of code fairly tiresome.

When compiling and running the shaders, if there's an error it will be reported by the OpenGL driver with the associated line number. Being able to look at the editor and go directly to that line makes it much easier to debug the problem, and it sure beats scrolling down through the editor counting lines manually.

Fortunately, our choice of UI library ultimately makes adding both syntax highlighting and line numbers really simple. More on that in a moment.

DROPPED FEATURES

Shadertoy has additional features beyond these, which aren't necessarily suitable for adaptation to VR.

For instance, the Shadertoy website lets you create audio shaders, where the output is sound rather than a visual rendering. This is fairly cool and could perhaps even lead to interesting experimentation with spatialized sound, but the integration of audio into virtual reality is beyond the scope of this book.

Additionally, the Shadertoy website lets you use five kinds of channel inputs. Cubemaps and texture inputs are included in the application, as they're on the critical path (being used by many of the example shaders we've included as presets). But the remaining three channel input types (audio, video, and keyboard) were dropped.

12.3.5 UI design

Implementing a functional UI within a VR environment can be a tricky business. As we discussed in chapters 9 and 10, the less intrusive your UI, the more immersive your application.

In ShadertoyVR, our user will always be operating in one of three modes:

1 Editing their shader code
2 Working with (loading and saving) shader code and resources
3 Sitting back and looking around with a big grin as their virtual world unfolds around them

So, for modes 1 and 2, we're going to need an active UI. This calls for text panes, buttons, mouse interaction—the works. But for the third mode, we should heed the advice from chapter 9 and reduce the UI as much as possible—or eliminate it completely. This means that our UI elements will be appearing and disappearing interactively, as a function of the user's activity.

COMFORTABLE UI SCALE

How big should the user interface be?

Well, for one thing, the UI should be fairly simplistic and somewhat larger than life. A UI in VR isn't going to be nearly as legible as one on a conventional monitor, because the "screen door" effect of visible pixels in the Rift degrades legibility significantly. (Sorry, but it's the truth, at least in 2015.) To ensure that the elements are readable, you should target a *virtual* display resolution that's significantly smaller than the

Rift resolution. For ShadertoyVR, all of the UI dialogs are designed around a resolution of 1280 × 720, and even this is somewhat extravagant. The reason we chose a resolution of that size is that we wanted the texture thumbnails for the channel inputs to be discernible even when they're all displayed on a single screen, as part of the selection dialog.

Bear in mind that while the UI ends up being rendered offscreen at 1280 × 720, when it's finally rendered to the HMD display panel it's not covering anywhere near that many pixels, because it's being scaled and distorted, as well as being shown on each eye. For that reason we treat the UI design as we would if we were designing for someone with poor eyesight, a sort of large-print book equivalent.[1]

On the other hand, when writing a text editor, the larger the font the less text you can see at once, which can hurt the utility of the application. So whereas for the fixed elements like labels and buttons we've tended toward an almost cartoonish legibility, for the editing window itself we've opted for "slightly larger than normal" while ensuring that the user can customize this up or down to suit their particular desired balance of comfort and utility.

UI BEHAVIOR

Another critical factor in presenting user interface elements is the behavior of the UI window itself. It might be tempting to simply paste it in a fixed location relative to the observer, commonly known as *pinning*. In a pinned UI, no matter how you move or turn your head, the UI is always directly in front of you, so it can't be missed. The Oculus Health and Safety Warning (HSW) is a great example of a "pinned" UI.

Once you're past the HSW, though, UI pinning should be strenuously avoided. It's disconcerting and even oppressive to have something stuck in your field of view that doesn't respond properly when you move your head. This can lead to simulation sickness.

You'll note that even in conditions where it's critical to have UI elements that must be seen by the user, such as the HSW, the pinning is mitigated by making the element translucent so that the scene can be perceived behind the UI element itself. That helps retain head tracking and immersion as well.

Another reason to avoid UI pinning is for legibility:

- In a pinned UI, text at the edges of the field of view becomes difficult to read, because the head can't be turned to see it.
- Sometimes you might need to have text elements positioned in regions of the display that can hover on the edge of legibility due to pixels falling through the resolution of the display. If a UI element is pinned to the user's view, that text always ends up on exactly the same pixels with every frame.

---

[1] Alternatively, think of a program UI in the movies. Elements on the screen that are intended to be read by the *audience* (instead of by the characters in the movie) tend to be almost comically oversized.

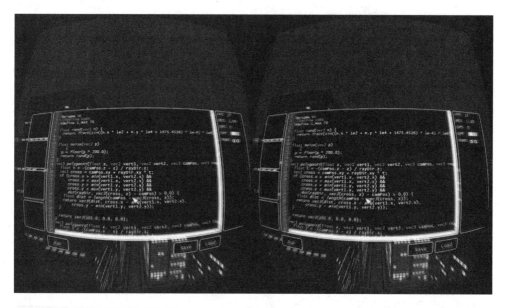

Figure 12.7   The code editor interface in action. The text window is 70 characters wide by 34 lines tall, with channel inputs on the left and feedback settings on the right. Control buttons—Play, Load, Save—are all slightly "cartoonishly" oversized for clarity.

Thankfully, the human visual system has a fantastic ability to re-create missing information over time. In an unpinned UI, if you're able to look at text and move your head slightly, changing the pixels and subpixels to which the text is rendered, it often becomes much easier to reconstruct the word shapes and comprehend what you're reading.[2]

After all's said and done, we've opted for a UI whose text field is 70 × 34, with oversized control widgets for clarity (figure 12.7). In the Rift, this feels like working on a 40-inch TV, positioned in space about a meter away.

12.3.6   *Windowing and UI libraries*

The next challenge we faced in this migration project was choosing a UI windowing toolkit that could give us the windowing features we need: the ability to open and close windows inside our OpenGL app, with text on clickable buttons, nifty draggable scrollbars, and so on. That's not a level of UI feature support that GLFW provides. Obviously we didn't want to write a new UI library from scratch,[3] so we needed to use something else that would support rendering the UI elements we needed, either to supplement GLFW or replace it altogether.

---

[2]   The VR mode of the game *Elite Dangerous* is an example of this. For a spaceship-based game, it involves quite a bit of reading through lines and lines of text, much of which would be much harder to read if it were pinned.

[3]   Well, maybe a little…

We had a few main requirements for our choice of UI library:

- We had to be able to create the kinds of UI elements we needed for our implementation. This mostly consisted of labels, images, and buttons, but we also needed a text editor window.
- We needed the UI library to be able to either natively target an OpenGL texture as its output, or at the very least allow us to convert the UI surface into a 2D image so that we could copy it to an OpenGL texture at will.
- We needed to be able to take mouse and keyboard input we would receive in the primary OpenGL output window (displaying a Rift distorted image) and inject that directly into our UI elements.
- The UI also needed to be responsive. It's no good if putting on the headset and interacting with the UI makes you feel like you're working with a PC from 1985.[4]

There's no lack of libraries for developing windowed UIs in an abstract fashion, and we looked at quite a few to accomplish what we needed.

The first point was pretty easy. It's hard to find a UI library that won't do labels, buttons, images, and text windows. If it doesn't it's not really a UI library.

The second two points were tougher. Most UI libraries focus on the windowing abstraction, on the assumption that the primary goal is to display a window or windows within the conventional desktop metaphor. They assume that their output will ultimately be some platform-native window, and that their input will be platform-native events, typically translated into some library-specific event wrapper. In other words, most UI libraries are intended to smooth out issues with developing cross-platform applications, not eject UI from the desktop metaphor altogether.

FINDING THE RIGHT UI LIBRARY

For C/C++ applications, the most popular and mature UI frameworks are probably Qt (qt-project.org), GTK+ (www.gtk.org), and wxWidgets (www.wxwidgets.org). We also considered writing the application in Java, in which case we could have used Swing, AWT, or SWT.

There are, alas, very few libraries that specifically target OpenGL as a "native" output option, though they do exist. libRocket (librocket.com) and CEGUI (cegui.org.uk) are two. Each lets you create a UI, interact with that interface by injecting mouse and keyboard input via well-documented functions, and render the resulting UI state to a variety of backend renderers. Both support OpenGL and Direct3D as renderers. libRocket aims to allow clients to create interfaces based on HTML/CSS. CEGUI allows clients to either create interfaces programmatically or use a layout tool to write custom XML files that can be inflated into UI objects at runtime.

Unfortunately, neither libRocket nor CEGUI has any mechanism for fetching input events from the underlying platforms. Rather, both rely on the application using them

---

[4] Unless that's what your virtual world is, of course—in which case, that's super cool. Can you port *Thexder*?

to intercept such events, translate them, and forward them on to the library via a set of methods designed for this purpose. Nor do these libraries deal with window creation or OpenGL context creation. Using either would have meant extending our GLFW application framework in order to take the GLFW keyboard and mouse events we receive, translate them into the corresponding library events, and call the library injection functions. This isn't necessarily bad, but it can be laborious.

Ultimately we chose to use Qt for our UI library.

CHOOSING QT

Qt meets our requirements pretty well:

- *Required UI elements*—Qt provides a vast array of UI components as well as programmatic and declarative mechanisms for designing UIs.
- *Offscreen rendering*—Qt supports offscreen rendering of UIs through a couple of mechanisms. For instance, you can convert any Qt QWidget (Qt's abstraction for both windows and controls) directly into a QImage, which can then be copied to an OpenGL texture.
- *Input injection*—QQuickRenderControl is specifically designed to allow it to receive forwarded input events from another Qt component. In this case, we use the OpenGL rendering window to receive events and forward them on to the offscreen UI.
- *Performance*—In our testing, Qt's UI behaves smoothly and well, even when rendered offscreen and overlaid into the Rift.

Aside from meeting our needs, Qt has a lot more going for it. It's extremely mature, widely used, well documented, and actively developed. It continues to add new features while for the most part maintaining compatibility with previously written applications (not really a concern from our point of view, but hey). And we liked that it supports CMake.

One caveat: Using Qt means *not* using GLFW. Both Qt and GLFW want to handle input from the native platform, so they can't be used concurrently in a given application. But this is more of a blessing than a curse, because it forces us to consider how the Rift might interact with additional underlying platforms and cope with some of the corresponding challenges.

12.4   *Implementation*

In this section, we'll cover the issues we faced implementing the application, and we'll focus on the key points that were the most challenging. We're not going to walk through the app line by line as we do for other demos in this book; even though we've scoped down the feature set, the hefty body of code of our ShadertoyVR app is far too much to list and annotate here, and besides, most of the code is specific to the framework we're using. If you'd like to browse the source code to ShadertoyVR, it's all on our GitHub repository. For this section, code snippets will be included where appropriate.

As we were doing our research for this chapter, we built several versions of Shader-toyVR, learning from each iteration as it evolved. We assumed that the toughest challenge would be the obvious one—running the shaders in VR, with distortion and binocular viewpoints. Very early in development, we already had a prototype app that could load a fragment shader and render it as a VR environment. We patted ourselves[5] on the back and thought we were most of the way there. Unfortunately, it turned out that replicating the basic rendering functionality of the original website was the easiest part of writing the application. The hardest part would be implementing the UI.

12.4.1 Supporting the Rift in Qt

Using Qt precluded the use of GLFW, so we needed to create a class that would allow us to do our Rift rendering in Qt. Because of the way we built up to the full `RiftApp` in chapters 3 through 5, it's built on top of `RiftGlfwApp` and `GlfwApp`, and therefore inextricably linked with GLFW. Rather than duplicate that kind of structure to create another class that was mostly the same code but inextricably linked to Qt, we wanted to extract everything that was "Rifty" from `RiftApp` and put it into a new class that was as free as possible from the notion of the underlying library tasked with creating the rendering context.

ABSTRACTING RIFT RENDERING AWAY FROM THE GLFW LIBRARY

Our new class, `RiftRenderingApp`, shown in the following listing, contains much of the same code that's in RiftApp, without the specifics of window creation and positioning. It focuses on the abstraction of Rift initialization and distortion using OpenGL, without delving into the implementation.

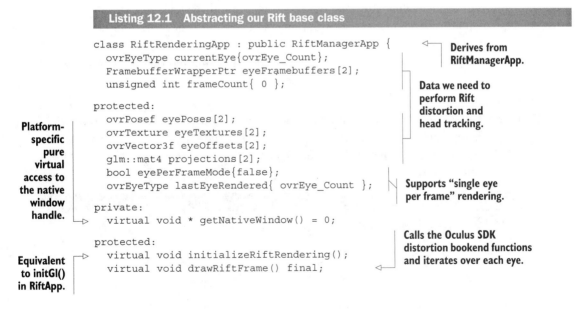

Listing 12.1 Abstracting our Rift base class

```
class RiftRenderingApp : public RiftManagerApp {          ⊲  Derives from
  ovrEyeType currentEye{ovrEye_Count};                        RiftManagerApp.
  FramebufferWrapperPtr eyeFramebuffers[2];
  unsigned int frameCount{ 0 };                             Data we need to
                                                            perform Rift
protected:                                                  distortion and
  ovrPosef eyePoses[2];                                     head tracking.
  ovrTexture eyeTextures[2];
  ovrVector3f eyeOffsets[2];
  glm::mat4 projections[2];
  bool eyePerFrameMode{false};
  ovrEyeType lastEyeRendered{ ovrEye_Count };              Supports "single eye
                                                            per frame" rendering.
private:
  virtual void * getNativeWindow() = 0;

protected:                                                  Calls the Oculus SDK
  virtual void initializeRiftRendering();                   distortion bookend functions
  virtual void drawRiftFrame() final;            ⊲          and iterates over each eye.
```

Platform-specific pure virtual access to the native window handle.

Equivalent to initGl() in RiftApp.

---

5 Brad, really. Mr. Davis did all the heavy lifting on the code for ShadertoyVR.

```
virtual void perEyeRender() {};
virtual void perFrameRender() {};
public:
  RiftRenderingApp();
  virtual ~RiftRenderingApp();
};
```

We've renamed renderScene() to perEyeRender().

Calls tasks once per frame.

The implementation of this class largely mirrors code from the `RiftApp` class. The difference is that although `RiftApp` relied on preexisting functionality in its `GlfwApp` base class to accomplish its task, `RiftRenderingApp` will expect classes deriving from it to know when to call the initialization and drawing functions.

The new breakdown of functions deserves some explanation. In our earlier examples, it was sufficient to simply encapsulate all our rendering into a `renderScene()` method. But in our Shadertoy application we have to do a bit of rendering work to composite the most recent UI view with the mouse cursor and composite it into a single texture. There's no reason to do this twice per frame, because the results should be the same. (In fact, we want to ensure that they are.) As we discovered while working on this app, it's valuable to have a method in which to update all of the resources that you might want to use during the rendering of each eye. In our case this is the UI texture, but it might easily be any sort of work that results in updating an offscreen texture that will then be used within the rendering cycle. So we've broken up `render-Scene()` into two functions:

- `perFrameRender()` is called once per frame as the name suggests. We still want any rendering work here to be accounted for in the Oculus timing mechanisms, so it's called after the SDK frame-begin method `ovrHmd_BeginFrame()`. The default implementation does nothing, so if you have no work you need to do once per frame you can ignore it.
- `perEyeRender()` replaces the old `renderScene()` method directly and is called inside the per-eye loop as in our previous examples.

We've added support for rendering only a single eye per frame, with the addition of the `eyePerFrameMode` Boolean member, which acts as a toggle, and the `lastEye-Rendered` member, which remembers the previously rendered eye, so that we alternate between them on each frame. Our main drawing function ends up looking like the following listing.

Listing 12.2 `drawRiftFrame()`, our core rendering-engine loop

```
void RiftRenderingApp::drawRiftFrame() {
  ++frameCount;
  ovrHmd_BeginFrame(hmd, frameCount);
  MatrixStack & mv = Stacks::modelview();
  MatrixStack & pr = Stacks::projection();

  perFrameRender();
  ovrPosef fetchPoses[2];
  ovrHmd_GetEyePoses(hmd, frameCount,
      eyeOffsets, fetchPoses, nullptr);
```

Performs all work that should only be done once per frame.

```
for (int i = 0; i < 2; ++i) {
  ovrEyeType eye = currentEye =
      hmd->EyeRenderOrder[i];               Skips if we're in
  if (eye == lastEyeRendered) {             eye-per-frame
    continue;                               mode.
  }
  lastEyeRendered = eye;
                                            Tracks the most recently
  eyePoses[eye] = fetchPoses[eye];          rendered eye.

  Stacks::withPush(pr, mv, [&] {            Updates current eye pose.
    pr.top() = projections[eye];
    glm::mat4 eyePose = ovr::toGlm(eyePoses[eye]);
    mv.preMultiply(glm::inverse(eyePose));

    eyeFramebuffers[eye]->Bind();
    perEyeRender();
  });

  if (eyePerFrameMode) {          If we're in eye-
    break;                        per-frame mode,
  }                               we're done.
}

if (endFrameLock) {
  endFrameLock->lock();
}
ovrHmd_EndFrame(hmd, eyePoses, eyeTextures);
}
```

Rendering only a single eye per frame is effective for performance enhancement and latency reduction, at the cost of smooth parallax VR. It can be very useful for debugging VR shader scenes.

Eye-per-frame mode isn't suitable for every application. It's particularly useful in applications that don't have a lot of motion relative to the viewer, or a lot of depth information. For instance, an astronomy program that lets you look at the sky and zoom in on regions of it would be an excellent candidate, because the scenery is essentially at an infinite distance. You don't (usually) get per-eye parallax with solar systems. The time-warping provided by the SDK can compensate for any changes in head rotation between the time a given eye was rendered and the time it was displayed.

In this application, because the scene might or might not contain something that equates to motion of the viewpoint, and might or might not have any depth, we provide the option for the user to toggle eye-per-frame mode on and off as appropriate for both the shader and their comfort level. For a shader that has no depth and no motion, there's very little benefit to rendering both eyes every frame, which allows the user to increase the amount of work their shader can do per frame.

But RiftRenderingApp is just a framework for interacting with the SDK with placeholders for rendering. It doesn't know how to deal with input or output, or how to create a window or OpenGL context. Because we're working with Qt in this example, let's examine how a class can integrate the Qt window with our framework class to create something more useful.

BINDING THE RIFT CODE TO A QT IMPLEMENTATION

Qt contains a variety of ways to represent some sort of onscreen window. Even for OpenGL windows, at least three classes are available: QGLWidget, QOpenGLWindow, and QWindow. Although the classes with GL directly in their name look inviting, they're tougher to work with for our purposes than QWindow.

Both QGLWidget and QOpenGLWindow are convenience classes, which are designed to take much of the burden of dealing with OpenGL away from the user. But they do so in ways that interfere with the way we want to interact with the Oculus SDK. It's possible to use a QGLWidget to act as a Rift output window, but only by overriding some of the event handler and manually disabling the buffer swapping. QOpenGL-Window is supposed to be a more modern replacement for QGLWidget, but it has even greater restrictions on how you can interact with GL, such as the inability to disable buffer swapping.

QWindow is the best choice for integrating Rift functionality with Qt, so that's what we've used. QWindow has no events for rendering to the window, instead leaving it up to the developer to directly control when and how anything is rendered to the window surface. Given that the Oculus SDK wants to control buffer swapping, and we want to do our rendering in a distinct thread, this is ideal for our example. Our resulting class looks like the following listing.

Listing 12.3 QRiftWindow, our QWindow GUI class

```
class QRiftWindow : public QWindow,
    protected RiftRenderingApp {
  Q_OBJECT

  QOpenGLContext * m_context;

  bool shuttingDown { false };
  LambdaThread renderThread;
  TaskQueueWrapper tasks;

public:
  QRiftWindow();
  virtual ~QRiftWindow();

  void start();
  void stop();
  void queueRenderThreadTask(Lambda task);

  void * getNativeWindow() {
    return (void*)winId();
  }

private:
  virtual void renderLoop();

protected:
  virtual void setup();
};
```

- **Derives from both QWindow and RiftRenderingApp**
- **Allows the class to use the Qt signals and slots functionality**
- **Qt's OpenGL context wrapper class**
- **Methods related to creating a rendering thread**
- **Provides access to the native window handle through the winId() method**
- **Rendering loop method**
- **Initialization method for setup**

One thing that's of particular note in listing 12.3 is all the code related to dealing with threads. For this you have to understand a bit about how Qt works. Every Qt-based application (that has some sort of UI) has a single object of type QGuiApplication or some type derived from it. This class doesn't represent any onscreen UI, but it's responsible for dealing with all the input events from the underlying OS as well as passing messages between Qt components. All of this happens on the thread on which the QGuiApplication instance was created and executed. Qt gets very cranky if you try to use objects on one thread from another without first calling a special function to move "ownership" of the object to the target thread.

To ensure the best rendering performance independent of what might occur on the main thread, our rendering loop needs to be on its own thread. LambdaThread encapsulates our rendering thread by calling renderLoop() on our instance. The start() and stop() methods allow the application code to control the lifetime of that thread.

When we write a new class derived from QRiftWindow and handle events such as a keyboard or mouse event, those events will be handled by the main thread, the one in which QGuiApplication is running its event-processing loop. In the example of changing the rendering resolution, we need to ensure that this happens between frames. Thus we have a container tasks for actions to be executed on the rendering thread, and a method queueRenderThreadTask for putting actions on that task queue from other threads (typically the main event-handling thread).

This is perhaps more complex than it needs to be; choosing a simple or advanced threading model is a function of the performance demands of your software. It's not strictly *required* that you perform rendering on its own thread. You could do so directly on the main thread in response to a given timer event, but this has potential downsides because other events being processed could potentially block your renders, causing you to miss your next frame, resulting in twitches and jumps within the headset. The last thing you want is for a particularly complicated software effect—something subtle, like a big explosion—to stagger your rendering rate because your renders and events are competing for the same thread.

Bear in mind that because you can't run a tight event loop on the main thread (the Qt application is already doing that) you have to deal with a different kind of complexity to ensure that you receive draw events frequently enough to meet your required frame rate while at the same time ensuring you don't starve the ordinary event processing. This is particularly true when using the Oculus SDK because the end frame call will wind up blocking until the swap buffer call has been made.

Now that you've seen the basic layout of the class, let's look at the most important parts of the implementation: the creation of the window and the render loop.

CREATING THE RIFT WINDOW

The creation of the window and its OpenGL context, then attaching the window to the Rift can all happen in the constructor, as you see in the next listing.

Listing 12.4 `QRiftWindow` constructor

```
QRiftWindow::QRiftWindow() {
  setSurfaceType(QSurface::OpenGLSurface);            ← Tells Qt we're going to use
                                                        OpenGL for rendering.

  QSurfaceFormat format;
  format.setDepthBufferSize(16);
  format.setStencilBufferSize(8);                     Sets up the OpenGL
  format.setVersion(3, 3);                            format including
  format.setProfile(                                  version and profile.
      QSurfaceFormat::OpenGLContextProfile::CoreProfile);
  setFormat(format);

  m_context = new QOpenGLContext;                      Creates the
  m_context->setFormat(format);                        OpenGL context.
  m_context->create();

  renderThread.setLambda([&] { renderLoop(); });

  bool directHmdMode = false;
  ON_WINDOWS([&] {
    directHmdMode = (0 ==                              Detects whether the
        (ovrHmdCap_ExtendDesktop & hmd->HmdCaps));     Rift is in direct mode.
  });

  setFlags(Qt::FramelessWindowHint);            ← Removes window
                                                  borders.
  show();

  if (directHmdMode) {
    QRect geometry = getSecondaryScreenGeometry(       If we're in direct mode, moves
        ovr::toGlm(hmd->Resolution));                  the window to a secondary
    setFramePosition(geometry.topLeft());              monitor (if possible).
  } else {
    setFramePosition(                                  If we're not in direct
        QPoint(hmd->WindowsPos.x, hmd->WindowsPos.y)); mode, puts the window
  }                                                    on the monitor
  resize(hmd->Resolution.w, hmd->Resolution.h);        corresponding to the Rift.

  if (directHmdMode) {
    void * nativeWindowHandle = (void*)(size_t)winId();
    if (nullptr != nativeWindowHandle) {               Calls the SDK function to
      ovrHmd_AttachToWindow(hmd, nativeWindowHandle,   attach the Rift display to
          nullptr, nullptr);                           the window.
    }
  }
}
```

Annotations (left margin):
- **Sets up the thread that will run the render loop. (Doesn't start the thread.)** → `renderThread.setLambda(...)`
- **Makes the window visible.** → `show();`
- **Sets the size of the window to the resolution of the Rift** → `resize(...)`

Most of this code is boilerplate Rift setup (just like the GLFW version) or boilerplate Qt prep. The getSecondaryScreenGeometry() function is a helper we've created to iterate over all the windows. It attempts to find a good nonprimary window on which to place the output (if we're in direct mode) and falls back on the primary monitor if no such window exists. As described in chapter 4, this is mostly handy for development so that the Rift window doesn't obscure your development environment.

Although in earlier applications the position of the onscreen window didn't really matter, in ShadertoyVR it definitely does. Eventually we'll be taking mouse events that are received by the onscreen window and forwarding them to our offscreen UI. That's why it's important that the entire onscreen window be physically on the screen. If the window is half-on and half-off the screen, you'll be able to see the whole thing in the Rift but you won't be able to use any of the virtual UI elements that correspond to half of the physical window that's offscreen, because your mouse can't get to those parts of the physical window.

One last item of note is the use of the `QWindow::winId()` member. The Oculus SDK needs native window handles for Direct mode to function, and most windowing abstraction libraries will have some kind of function that lets you get at the native identifier. With GLFW we had to use a special header and special preprocessor defines to enable it, but with Qt, it's a basic member on `QWindow`, which is handy.

There's not else much particularly new or interesting here. Everything else is either well covered in the Qt documentation or is something we've covered in chapters 4 or 5.

THE RENDERING LOOP

This brings us to the rendering loop and the functions used to control the rendering thread, shown in the following listing. The loop itself looks very similar to the `run()` method on our `GlfwApp` class.

Listing 12.5 ShadertoyVR's main rendering loop

```
void QRiftWindow::start() {
    m_context->doneCurrent();
    m_context->moveToThread(&renderThread);
    renderThread.start();
    renderThread.setPriority(QThread::HighestPriority);
}

void QRiftWindow::renderLoop() {
    m_context->makeCurrent(this);
    setup();
    while (!shuttingDown) {
        if (QCoreApplication::hasPendingEvents())
            QCoreApplication::processEvents();
        tasks.drainTaskQueue();
        m_context->makeCurrent(this);
        drawRiftFrame();
    }
    m_context->doneCurrent();
    m_context->moveToThread(QApplication::instance()->thread());
}
```

Annotations:

Called from the main thread to control the lifetime of the rendering loop

Initializes the Rift

Does any work that must be done on the rendering thread between frames

Moves our OpenGL context to the rendering thread, as mandated by Qt

Starts the thread and sets its priority

Sets the OpenGL context current for this thread

Processes events that have occurred on this thread

Calls our RiftRenderingApp parent class's frame rendering method

```
void QRiftWindow::stop() {
    if (!shuttingDown) {
        shuttingDown = true;
        renderThread.wait();
    }
}
```

Blocks for the renderloop to exit

Ensures that stop() is idempotent

Called from the main thread to control the lifetime of the rendering loop

12.4.2   Offscreen rendering and input processing

The two biggest challenges we face in our design are offscreen rendering and input processing:

- *Offscreen rendering is essential in our composited design.* The ability to create offscreen UI elements that respond to user input and can be efficiently rendered within the VR environment is a key part of building a quality application.

- *Input processing is critical to any app that interacts with the user.* ShadertoyVR is no exception. We need to guarantee that mouse and keyboard events are processed smoothly, without UI delay, to ensure an ongoing sense of immersion.

Our approach is one possible implementation for one framework, so we're not going to dive into the guts in too much detail. The fine points are closely tied to the specifics of Qt, as opposed to the Rift.

That said, we do want to cover a few more general concepts when dealing with rendering UI elements offscreen for use in a VR application.

RENDER UI IN A SEPARATE THREAD

We've probably all had to deal from time to time with an unresponsive UI. It can be frustrating. But in VR it can be more than frustrating; it can ruin the entire experience. As you'll recall from chapters 6 and 10, if the virtual environment suddenly freezes because the UI hit some kind of snag, it can be disconcerting or even nausea inducing.

If your UI ends up suffering from lag, you need to ensure that that lag remains confined to the UI within the VR scene, not the scene as a whole. So do all your UI rendering in a thread that's distinct from the VR rendering.

In our code, we've already punted the VR rendering to its own thread, so it's easy for us to follow this advice by keeping all the UI rendering work on the main thread. This is straightforward because all of the Qt events to refresh the UI already arrive on the main thread.

RENDER UI DIRECTLY TO YOUR RENDERING API

Our initial approach to offscreen UI was to render the UI to a buffer with Qt and then convert that to an image and copy the image down to the GPU. The plan was to use Qt's built-in ability to render any window to a QImage or QPixmap, which are Qt's abstractions for various kinds of 2D images. Then for each image we'd convert it into an OpenGL texture.

We discovered that this approach was barely functional. It meant that we were consuming a hefty fraction of the CPU-to-GPU bandwidth moving image data over the bus every frame. This was wasteful, but worse, it introduced stutters in the VR environment, because there's no way to schedule or prioritize the work of independent OpenGL contexts running on multiple threads.

We saw significantly better results with QQuickRenderControl. Based on its performance, we believe the rendering mechanism underlying QQuickRenderControl is either using OpenGL calls directly to create the UI elements or is extremely efficient about transferring only the dirty elements of a UI when a render occurs. The end result is that Qt provides an OpenGL texture that we can use directly, rather than a large 2D bitmap we have to inefficiently copy to the GPU.

The upshot is that we're using a shared OpenGL context (see the accompanying sidebar).

Shared OpenGL contexts

In OpenGL a *shared context* is one that's created with a previous context listed as a sibling. The two contexts each have their own state and their own default framebuffer, but they can share many of the other data that OpenGL processes, in particular textures. A texture created on one context can be rendered in the other. But it's still up to the developer of an application to ensure that objects are properly synchronized so that, for instance, one thread isn't writing to a texture while another thread is reading it.

OpenGL provides a variety of methods to enable developers to do this kind of synchronization, such as the ability to force commands to complete, or to set up a synchronization object that's signaled once all the commands executed before its creation are complete. We use both techniques in ShadertoyVR.

Some developers feel that using a shared context risks instability and extra code, but most modern OpenGL libraries (GLFW and Qt included) make creating a shared context no more difficult than creating a normal one. As for stability, with modern multithreaded rendering drivers, creating shared contexts within your application isn't much different from having multiple OpenGL applications running at once, which is no stability risk at all.

12.5 Dealing with performance issues

As we discussed in chapter 6, the performance of your application is critical for a good experience, and our Shadertoy application is no exception. Furthermore, because of the computational intensity of some of the shaders, there's little doubt that we'll be forced to use techniques from both chapters 6 and 10 to keep the app running smoothly.

Remember, the goal is *always* to hit or exceed your device's target framerates. On the dev kit models of the Rift, that's 60 Hz and 75 Hz for the DK1 and DK2, respectively.

FINDING YOUR TARGET AND REACTING WHEN YOU'RE NOT HITTING IT

In an ideal world you'd always hit your desired frame rate, and if you saw that it was dropping or was about to drop you'd take action. Unfortunately, even with the tools in the Oculus SDK it can be tricky to determine exactly *when* you need to respond to performance issues.

You'll be able to calculate the frame rate you're getting within your application, but because the SDK doesn't report at what refresh rate the Rift is currently being run, there's no easy way of knowing if the frame rate you're getting is the one you need.

It's not all gloom. In practice, there are only a few rates that it's likely to be, determined by the hardware capabilities of the Rift. Additionally, if you detect the user is running in Direct HMD mode, you know that they actually can't modify the refresh rate, so you need only a hardcoded mapping of the Rift model to native refresh rate.

Once you know your target frame rate, there comes the question of what to do when you find you're not hitting it. If, conceptually, you have only one dial then it's obvious what dial to turn. But if there are multiple things you can change to increase or decrease the rendering load, it's harder to determine what to do when your frame rate drops. For our application we've sidestepped the issue by exposing both the current performance (the actual frame rate) and the means for changing it directly to our users.

This isn't mere cowardice or laziness.[6] Because we're creating what amounts to a development tool for which the workload per frame can be literally *anything*, it's critical that we leave it up to the user to determine which of the available performance-tuning options provide the best experience for the shader they're developing.

EYE-PER-FRAME MODE AND TIMEWARP

If we see that the renderer isn't hitting the required performance (typically visible as jumping in the edges of objects as you turn your head), then one way to reduce the load is to only render a single eye on each frame, alternating between eyes. This instantly halves the overall rendering load. You can see in our previous code samples that we've built in support for rendering a single eye per frame.

As mentioned before, how effective and comfortable this is depends largely on the content you're rendering. For images that involve little or no binocular depth and that include limited angular motion, the technique works very well. If your shader gives the sensation of hovering over a mountain range in a hot air balloon, the visible difference between rendering one eye per frame and two eyes per frame is negligible. But if your shader immerses the viewer in the illusion of skiing down a forested mountain slope with trees whizzing past, then the shortcomings of eye-per-frame mode will be more than apparent.

Eye-per-frame mode can be particularly effective when used with the Rift's time-warp feature, which you saw in chapter 6. Timewarp will adjust positions of the textures

---

[6] OK, not *just* mere cowardice or laziness.

of each eye at render-time to keep their placement consistent with the user's head motion, even if what's being rendered to that eye is from a previous frame.

Because the rendered scene can vary so much, as can a particular user's comfort level with a given amount of depth cue disparity, the option to turn eye-per-frame mode on and off is left as an exercise for the user.

DYNAMIC FRAMEBUFFER SCALING

Dynamic framebuffer scaling, first explored in chapter 6, is superbly applicable to frame rate control in ShadertoyVR. We make quite a small number of draw calls per frame, with all of the complexity being in the fragment shader. The number of times the fragment shader is run per frame is directly proportional to the number of pixels being rendered, so reducing the offscreen framebuffer size almost always translates into a proportional increase in rendering performance.

In ShadertoyVR we've made the option to change the offscreen framebuffer size available to our users as keyboard shortcuts that will increase or decrease the percentage of the offscreen framebuffer used for rendering to any value between 1% and 100%.

That said, giving the user the ability to scale down the resolution of the rendered shader until it's a blurry mess presents us with a new issue.

SCALING TEXTURE IN THE VR SCENE, NOT THE UI

As we drive down the number of pixels we render, the quality of the scene goes down as well, blurring the image. But whereas reducing the sharpness of the VR scene rendered by the user's fragment shader is permissible, reducing the quality of the UI is not. Degrading the legibility of text is pretty much unacceptable.

The solution is to scale the VR scene without scaling the UI. In chapter 6, you learned how to render the entire scene to a subsection of the predistortion offscreen framebuffer and then tell the SDK to use that subsection rather than the whole texture. To apply the technique here, we need to tweak that process slightly. We still render the VR scene to a smaller area, but this time we do so to a second offscreen framebuffer.

Our `renderScene()` method is shown in the following listing.

Listing 12.6 Compositing the VR scene and the UI

```
void renderScene() {
  Context::Clear().DepthBuffer().ColorBuffer();

  shaderFramebuffer->Bound([&] {
    oria::viewport(renderSize());
    renderSkybox();
  });
  oria::viewport(textureSize());
```

Renders the VR scene to an offscreen buffer

Ensures we target the full SDK-specified offscreen texture size

```
    Stacks::withIdentity([&] {
      shaderFramebuffer->color.Bind(Texture::Target::_2D);
      oria::renderGeometry(plane, planeProgram, LambdaList({ [&] {
        Uniform<vec2>(*planeProgram,
          "UvMultiplier").Set(vec2(texRes));
      } }));
    });

    if (uiVisible) {
      GLuint currentUiTexture = ...
      if (currentUiTexture) {
        MatrixStack & mv = Stacks::modelview();
        mv.withPush([&] {
          mv.translate(vec3(0, 0, -1));
          Texture::Active(0);
          glBindTexture(GL_TEXTURE_2D, currentUiTexture);
          oria::renderGeometry(uiShape, uiProgram);
        });
      }
    }
    ...
  }
```

> Re-renders the VR scene to the full offscreen texture size

> Renders the UI

> Renders the UI to a floating rectangle one meter away from the user

Here we see the use of an additional offscreen framebuffer shaderFramebuffer, plus the use of the renderSize() and textureSize() methods. textureSize() reports the size of the texture that the SDK recommends for submitting rendered images to be distorted. renderSize() reports the same size after scaling by the texRes value.

Once we've rendered the VR scene to shaderFramebuffer, we grab the resulting texture and re-render it to the offscreen framebuffer where we're constructing the texture that will eventually be sent to the SDK. This original framebuffer isn't shown here but is implicitly set by the frame-drawing method that calls renderScene() once for each eye. The only caveat here is that you have to ensure that this framebuffer is preserved before shaderFramebuffer is bound and restored after it's unbound. In our example this is done implicitly by the FramebufferWrapper::Bound() method called on shaderFramebuffer.

Having rendered the VR shader at a potentially lower-than-full resolution, we now check if the UI is active and we have a valid UI texture, and if so draw the UI elements on top of the scene. The UI remains as sharp and crisp as if the GPU weren't overloaded. The cost of all these additional compositing and rendering operations is trivial compared to the cost of the intensive user shader.

This concludes our analysis of the design and implementation of ShadertoyVR. We hope you've found it educational and inspirational. Now let's shift gears and look at how the GPU can spin simple code into awesome worlds.

12.6 *Building virtual worlds on the GPU*

We've alluded to the virtual worlds that people have created on Shadertoy.com, and the VR environments we plan to wrap around our user in with ShadertoyVR. But where do these immersive 3D scenes come from? In this section we're going to set the Rift aside for a bit and discuss one of the oldest techniques in computer graphics, which remains one of the most exciting and current techniques today: raycasting.

12.6.1 *Raycasting: building 3D scenes one pixel at a time*

How can a complete 3D scene be created by a shader program, whose only output is the color of a given pixel? Well, every image is made of pixels. We only need to figure out what color a pixel *would* be, if the pixel were part of an image of a 3D scene. Compute that color and render it and voilà —you've got a 3D scene (or at least a picture of one).

To achieve this colorful effect, most of the 3D scene shaders on Shadertoy.com use a technique called *raycasting* (see the accompanying sidebar). In essence, the idea of raycasting is that at each pixel of the image, you're going to find a mathematical ray that starts at the camera eye and passes through the pixel. You'll then cast the ray forward, into the scene, and whatever it hits determines the color of the pixel (figure 12.8).

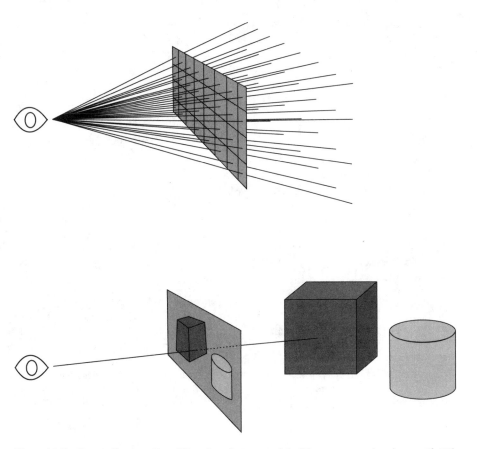

Figure 12.8 Raycasting in action. After choosing a ray origin (the camera eye) and computing the direction from the origin through the center of each pixel, we choose the color of the pixel based on the object in the scene hit by the ray. (Image © Neil Dodgson, University of Cambridge, England. Used with permission.)

DESCRIBING THE RAYCAST WORLD

Techniques for describing virtual scenes diverge radically, and we could easily devote an entire book to the subject. All such techniques, however, can be summarized as "figure out what the ray hits."

Broadly speaking, they usually break down into two types of techniques:

- *Ray tracing*—The shiny, reflective scenes where light and shadows try to be photo-realistic; scenes are often limited by the number of elements shown.
- *Ray marching*—The procedural or voxel worlds, often seemingly infinite, sometimes smooth, sometimes blocky; not so big on the reflective surfaces.

You'll find examples of both at Shadertoy.com. If you'd like to learn more, check out the following sidebar and the relevant reference sources in appendix C.

Raycasting, ray tracing, and ray marching

Raycasting is the general term for the technique where you start with a ray origin and direction, determine what object or objects in a scene the ray hits, and compute an output color from the intersection. How this determination is performed and how you define the scene objects are details of implementation, which vary based on the specific technique.

Ray tracing and ray marching are specific ways of implementing raycasting. Both are sometimes used in conjunction with algorithms that recursively generate more rays, such as for computing shadows, reflections, and transparencies.

Ray tracing is the term most commonly used for a broad class of implementations that represent rays as abstract mathematical models of partially infinite lines; mathematical expressions of primitives, written in computer code, are used to test for ray/primitive intersection. For instance, to test if a ray hits a sphere, you'd check (a) if the line of the ray passes within one radius of the center of the sphere, and (b) if it does so in the direction the ray has been fired. Ray tracing methods can be combined with other techniques to create extremely complicated models, such as Constructive Solid Geometry—a method that allows shapes to be added to or subtracted from each other.

Ray marching, on the other hand, uses an iterative approach: the ray is "marched" along its direction of travel until it hits something. This has the advantage that there's less demand for a purely mathematical model and more for discrete data structures. Ray marching is very well suited to rendering implicit surfaces, and many of the Shadertoy shaders are in this category. Most voxel renderers, such as Minecraft, use ray marching to quickly find which block is the first block per pixel hit by a ray. Ray marching tends to be less computationally expensive, but it can also produce less realistic output, depending on the fine-tuning of the size of each step of the march.

These algorithms depend on only two key inputs:

- The origin of the ray
- The direction of the ray

The origin of the ray is straightforward: it's the current position in 3D space of the camera, from which you'll render your scene. On Shadertoy.com, this is typically hard-coded in the fragment shader, for speed and clarity.

Computing the ray direction takes slightly more math, but not too much more.

12.6.2 *Finding the ray direction in 2D*

In a shader running on Shadertoy.com, locked into a single WebGL window, computing the ray origin and direction can be somewhat involved.

As part of the input parameters to the fragment shader, the shader will know the current pixel's 2D screen position, which is available in GLSL as the automatic variable `gl_FragCoord.xy`. In combination with the resolution of the window, you can compute the relative location of the pixel within the window; by combining the pixel's position with your knowledge of the chosen position of the camera eye and a fixed distance from the camera to the pixel plane, you can compute the origin and direction of each pixel's ray. Code that achieves this result can be found in the vast majority of the shaders on the Shadertoy site that create 3D scenes of some kind. Code in Shadertoy shaders that computes the view direction typically looks something like the following listing.

Listing 12.7 (GLSL) Finding ray direction from camera position and a point to look at

Converts the coordinates into range [-1, 1] →

Finds the coordinates of the pixel relative to the lower-left corner of the viewport ←

Corrects coordinates for window aspect ratio ←

```
vec2 q = gl_FragCoord.xy / iResolution.xy;
vec2 p = -1.0 + 2.0 * q;
p.x *= iResolution.x / iResolution.y;

const vec3 cameraOrigin = vec3(0, 1, 5);
const vec3 lookAt = vec3(0, 0, 0);
const vec3 cameraUp = vec3(0, 1, 0);

vec3 dir = normalize(lookAt - cameraOrigin);
vec3 xAxis = normalize(cross(cameraUp, dir));
vec3 yAxis = normalize(cross(dir, xAxis));
vec3 rayDirection =
    normalize(p.x * xAxis + p.y * yAxis + dir);
```

Chooses ray origin (eye position) and center of camera focus

X axis: extends to the right of the camera

View axis: the line from the camera to [0, 0] at the center of the screen ←

Y axis: extends above the camera

Finds the ray direction for this specific pixel

The key outputs here are two variables: `cameraOrigin`, which represents our ray origin, and `rayDirection`, which represents the vector from the eye toward the pixel.

In this snippet, `lookAt` represents the target we're looking at and `cameraUp` is the up direction. This code starts by finding the relative position of the pixel on the screen. We start with the location of the output fragment (in pixel coordinates) stored in `gl_FragCoord.xy` and the resolution of the window stored in `iResolution.xy`. Dividing one by the other gives us q, which is the relative position of the pixel on the screen, with (0, 0) in the lower-left corner and (1, 1) in the upper-right. This is then converted to p, using multiplication and addition to move the origin of the scene to the center of the rendering window. The upper-right is still (1, 1), but the lower-left is now (-1, -1), and (0, 0) is the exact center of the window. Finally, the X coordinate is modified to account for the aspect ratio of the screen.

The next step is to build the three columns of a basis matrix that'll represent a camera transformation. This transform is sometimes called the "world to camera" transform, or more colloquially, the "lookat" matrix. (Because it's what you tell the camera to…never mind, you get it.) A lookat matrix can be used to transform points in geometry so that they're in the correct location relative to your camera position and orientation; in other words, points move from world coordinates to camera coordinates. Lookat functions take three inputs: an eye position, a target or center, and a vector representing the up direction. The calculations of dir, xAxis, and yAxis produce three 3-dimensional vectors, which together make up the nine elements of a 3×3 orientation matrix.

We conclude by applying the camera orientation matrix to the 3D vector that represents this pixel. Here we take p, a 2D vector, and turn it into a 3D vector by appending the constant 1, the distance from the eye to the viewing place. So at the center of the screen, the resulting input vector is (0, 0, 1), on the positive Z axis.

The last line of listing 12.7 might not look like a matrix multiplication at first, but that's what it is: the product of the matrix whose columns are the three computed vectors, with the vector form of position p,

```
[ xAxis.x yAxis.x dir.x ]    [ p.x ]    [ p.x * xAxis.x + p.y * yAxis.x + dir.x ]
[ xAxis.y yAxis.y dir.y ] *  [ p.y ] =  [ p.x * xAxis.y + p.y * yAxis.y + dir.y ]
[ xAxis.z yAxis.y dir.y ]    [  1  ]    [ p.x * xAxis.z + p.y * yAxis.z + dir.z ]
```

…which simplifies to the GLSL expression:

```
rayDirection = normalize(p.x * xAxis + p.y * yAxis + dir)
```

This is the vector from the eye towards the pixel in world space.

12.6.3 *Finding the ray direction in VR*

The classic ray direction calculations demonstrated in listing 12.7 required baking in a fixed field of view and then computing the ray direction based on the position of the pixel on the screen. By contrast, when using the Rift, the field of view can change depending on the particular model of the headset you're using, and the projection matrix is typically asymmetrical, so we can't hardcode those constants into the GLSL code. Plus, of course, the user moves their head. All of this means that the simple hardcoded mathematics employed by the classic Shadertoy.com shaders must be adjusted.

This is where work we've already done for the Rift can be reused, leveraging a simple technique: the *skybox*.

The ray direction is actually the same direction value we'd use in creating a skybox effect. For a skybox, you typically draw a unit cube around the camera, with the center of the cube exactly at the viewpoint. The orientation of the viewpoint is taken from the camera orientation in the application, composed with the user's head pose (orientation only). The vertex shader then passes the vertices of the cube as inputs to the fragment shader. When the vertices are interpolated, each instance of the fragment shader receives as input a vector representing the direction from the camera to the pixel being rendered.

In a typical skybox, the interpolated direction vector is used as the lookup for fetching a color from a cubemap texture, but it also works perfectly as the ray direction we need for our shaders—so perfectly, in fact, that we're going to modify the existing set of standard inputs by adding two more fragment shader input variables, `iPos` and `iDir`, shown in the following listing. Then we're going to pass in the values of `iPos` and `iDir` from outside the fragment shader.

Listing 12.8   (GLSL) New standard inputs added to the code of the ShadertoyVR shaders

```
uniform vec3 iPos;
in vec3 iDir;
```

The per-eye head position, read directly from the Rift

The vertex position in the vertex shader.

The value of `iPos` is easily chosen: it's the user's head pose position for the current eye, as reported by the Rift. We'll update this uniform for each eye of every frame.

The value of `iDir` is slightly more subtle, but it's deliciously elegant. We want to compute a ray direction from the origin of a box centered on the user, to every pixel on the Rift's screen, rotated by the user's head orientation. The easiest way to do that is to let OpenGL do it for us! When the vertex shader outputs are interpolated across the polygons of our scene geometry—a skybox cube—the interpolated values of iDir will smoothly interpolate the position of every pixel in the view. The next listing shows our ShadertoyVR vertex shader.

Listing 12.9   (GLSL) default.vs, the ShadertoyVR vertex shader

```
uniform mat4 Projection = mat4(1);
uniform mat4 ModelView = mat4(1);

layout(location = 0) in vec3 Position;

out vec3 iDir;

void main() {
    iDir = Position;
    gl_Position = Projection
        * ModelView * vec4(Position, 1);
}
```

The classic orientation and camera matrices.

Vertex coordinates of our geometry (the corners of a unit cube).

Ray direction output.

iDir will interpolate every pixel of the cube's faces.

Outputs the 3D perspective-transformed position of the vertex.

The goal of this vertex shader is to generate ray directions for consumption by the current fragment shader. Just as in a classic 2D raycaster, where you'd interpolate the ray direction across all of the pixels of a plane (check out figure 12.8 again), here too we'll interpolate our ray direction. But where in 2D we interpolated across only a single rectangle, in 3D we'll render a cube centered on the origin; in doing so, the outputs of our vertex shader will be interpolated across every pixel of *the faces of a cube*. By orienting that cube as a function of head pose, we can ensure that no matter where you look, you'll always see a sweep of ray directions radiating straight out from your point of view. And the best part is we don't have to do any of the interpolation manually. Just like in the original WebGL app, we can let the rendering pipeline handle interpolating the vertex outputs into fragment inputs. The final result is that our new variable, iDir, will correctly interpolate the full set of ray directions to render our scene.

You may wonder, what about the camera projection? In listing 12.7 the distance from the camera to the plane of projection was defined to be 1. The aspect ratio was handled by directly multiplying the pixel coordinate p's X value with the aspect ratio of the window.

In our application the camera projection distance is implicit in the processing that generates iDir. As we render a skybox around the user's viewpoint, the GPU processes the projection matrix (provided by the Oculus SDK) and the camera orientation (built from the user's head pose) in the vertex shader. By the time we get to the user's fragment shader, the value it receives for iDir is already the ray direction. There's no longer any need for the fragment shader to handle camera projection or aspect ratios at all; the Rift effectively subsumes these concerns.

12.6.4 *Handling the ray origin: stereopsis and head tracking*

Because we're creating 3D scenes, we want to provide a stereoscopic view on the scene and provide head tracking, just as we would with any other VR application. No sweat! We're already using the orientation component of the head pose as part of the skybox-derived direction calculations. For the eye offset, we take the position component of the head pose (which when using the Oculus SDK will include the eye position offset) and provide it as iPos.

Note that this doesn't mean we need to discard any existing ray origin calculation inside the shader. This is important because many of the Shadertoy shaders animate the camera, causing it to move over time to, for instance, fly over a mountain range. Instead of just replacing the existing ray origin code, we add our head pose positional value to it. Literally—just add iPos to the camera position value.

One warning, though: now that we're using the Rift's eye offset parameters, we're assuming that we're working in meters. (Remember, the Rift's unit of choice is the meter.) If you set out to modify another author's Shadertoy shader, you may find that assumption doesn't hold in the other developer's code. In fact, most of the shaders we've encountered don't determine a length unit at all, but rather use hardcoded values intended to make the effect look good on the small WebGL output window.

The Rift's positional data can easily be scaled up or down to produce a desired effect. For instance, in one of our example shaders, Elevated, you appear to be moving across a mountain range. Adding the `iPos` value at its normal scale produces very little effect, because the scenery is all intended to look very distant, and thus would have minimal parallax.

But if we scale up the `iPos` value by a factor of 300,

```
ro += iPos * 300.0;
```

then instead of flying over mountains, it feels very much like you're hovering over a small scale model of a mountain range. Some of this effect comes from binocular parallax, but a significant part comes from the responsiveness of the viewpoint to small movements of your head. If you can lean forward to peek at a peak, the mountain feels very small in comparison to your sense of your own scale.

Modifying the ray origin by scaling `iPos` is strictly optional. If your intent is to make the user feel as if they're flying high above the earth, the difference between providing an offset between the eyes of less than 10 cm and providing no offset is negligible, so how you treat the `iPos` value is a matter of the effect you're trying to impart.

12.6.5 Adapting an existing Shadertoy shader to run in ShadertoyVR

We're now ready to adapt an existing shader to run in ShadertoyVR. All that will require is that we make appropriate use of `iDir` and `iPos`; the rest of the (virtual) world will take care of itself.

Here's the original camera code of Iñigo Quilez's demo *Elevated*, in which the viewpoint flies over a perpetual procedurally generated mountain range of rocky terrain.

Listing 12.10   (GLSL snippet) Original camera code for *Elevated*

```
// camera position
vec3 ro = camPath( time );
vec3 ta = camPath( time + 3.0 );
ro.y = terrain3( ro.xz ) + 11.0;
ta.y = ro.y - 20.0;
float cr = 0.2*cos(0.1*time);

// camera2world transform
mat3 cam = setCamera( ro, ta, cr );

// camera ray
vec3 rd = cam * normalize(vec3(s.xy,2.0));
```

Quilez computes `ro` and `rd`, his variables for ray origin and ray direction. The height value of `ro` is clamped to the height of his terrain map function.

The next listing shows our modified version of the same code, adapted to run in ShadertoyVR.

Listing 12.11   (GLSL snippet) Camera code for *Elevated*, adapted for ShadertoyVR

```
// camera position
vec3 ro = camPath(time) + iPos;
ro.y = max(terrain3(ro.xz) + 11.0, 150.0);

// camera ray
vec3 rd = normalize(iDir);
```

As you can see, we've replaced Quilez's code for finding `ro` and `rd` with the values of our own new inputs, `iPos` and `iDir`. And we've preserved the height map feature, where the camera never drops below the virtual terrain beneath it (figure 12.9).

Simple!

Figure 12.9   *Elevated* running in ShadertoyVR

12.7   *Summary*

In this chapter, we covered:

- Our case study of adapting a 2D WebGL app into a fully VR environment
- How to design a GUI UI for VR that meets the needs of a preexisting 2D UI
- How to integrate complex UI elements into a VR application
- The art of using framebuffer scaling to address performance constraints when GPU load exceeds the capabilities of your hardware
- Understanding raycasting and implementing it in a GLSL shader

Augmenting virtual reality

Augmented reality (AR) is the use of computers to digitally enhance your view of the real world. AR isn't science fiction; it's real today. Examples include the heads-up display overlaid on a fighter pilot's cockpit, glasses that project a map of your planned route on a tiny screen near your eye, or mobile phone games that show the room you're standing in with extra ghosts and goblins added on. AR is rapidly becoming one of the most active fields in the computing industry, because it's such an open-ended challenge with so much potential to improve day-to-day life. Especially as mobile phones become ubiquitous, the potential for digitally enhancing the everyday world seems limitless.

All of that said, this chapter is not about AR. This chapter is about VR, and how you can augment it with information from the real world.

Just as there's tremendous potential in allowing computing devices to mediate our views of the world, there's also tremendous potential—far more, in a sense—in allowing the real world to intrude into the necessarily isolated virtual space of the Rift. Virtual worlds divorced from our own have their place, but virtual worlds intermeshed with reality will play a vital role in the adoption of VR to come. A virtual space from which we can still interact with those left behind in the mundane world is far more compelling than an isolated bubble of high-polycount special effects. In this chapter we'll explore some (relatively simple) ways to bring the real world into VR.

To begin to get a sense of what's possible with augmented VR, let's list just a few of the digital inputs that are now available:

- Live audio and video streams from TV, media servers, video chats, and webcams
- Immersive photography, such as the panoramic shots and photo spheres captured by smartphones
- Live raw data feeds, such as public streams of airline flight trackers
- Local sensor hardware added to your environment, or even to the Rift itself, such as the Leap Motion
- Local GIS data, which can be used to build a virtual map of actual geography
- Location signals from the user (IP geocoding on desktops, GPS on mobile devices)

In this chapter we're going to do a deep dive into just a few of these technologies. We've chosen to explore immersive photography, live video streams, and the Leap Motion as our examples, because together they demonstrate the core principles of aligning external and internal data into a seamless whole in VR. As you explore these examples, pay special attention to the code at the interface between real and unreal; much of the challenge here will come from the mathematics and the interweaving of these multiple systems.

13.1 Real-world images for VR: panoramic photography

These days, high-resolution cameras in our pockets are commonplace; high-resolution cameras backed by processors more powerful than the entire American lunar landing program, no less. One of the rather neat things that we can do with these high-powered cameras is generate *panoramas* and *photo spheres*, advanced forms of digital images that are stitched together from a series of smaller, simpler images. These assembled pictures are tagged with metadata that describes how the image is to be rendered in cylindrical or spherical projection.

Panorama photos could almost have been designed with VR in mind. On a conventional screen, in a flat photo app, viewing these laterally expansive images can be difficult or unappealing. Head-tracking radically changes the experience. It's very natural, and naturally immersive, for our eyes to track over the same space that the camera originally traveled, looking to and fro to absorb a wider scene than a conventional monitor could display.

Figure 13.1 Panorama of the Piazza del Campo, Sienna, Italy

13.1.1 Panorama photos

Panorama is the name used for a relatively large class of stitched-together imagery, and panoramas can be generated in a number of ways. The most common by far is to use a camera to take a series of pictures while slowly rotating your point of view laterally by a short turn, typically from left to right (although that's not required). As the camera rotates it will capture a series of views sweeping a scene, much wider than a single photograph. The series of images is then stitched together by detecting overlapping image portions from one to the next. On mobile phones, the stitching is even easier, because the phone's accelerometer can be queried to detect the movement of the camera.

Panoramas can be rendered as a single wide frame, as in figure 13.1. Alternatively, in 3D they can be texture-mapped onto a cylinder, as in figure 13.2.

Most panorama image viewers scroll sideways along the image instead of using a cylindrical projection. Cylindrical projection would introduce distortion, as you can see, even though it shows the correct perspective effect for images captured by turning in place. You can see in figure 13.2 that the image distortion is visibly reduced—look at the road on the right, which runs straight along the front of the Piazza. In the unmodified horizontal panorama, the edge of the road bows in; in the cylindrical projection it's much closer to straight.

Figure 13.2 Cylindrical projection of the horizontal panorama. Note how the road (far right) has become straighter under projection.

13.1.2 *Photo spheres*

Photo spheres (developers.google.com/photo-sphere) are an image annotation format developed by Google for storing spherical images within conventional flat images. Photo spheres use the XMP (Extensible Metadata Platform) standard (www.adobe.com/devnet/xmp.html) to encode information within an image. XMP is an open standard that can be used to attach XML data to image files; XMP readers are available for most programming languages.

Photo spheres are ideally suited for the Rift because, unlike panoramas, the photo sphere is truly three-dimensional. The viewer can look up and down as well as side-to-side. Photo spheres support a rather nifty set of attributes that describe the orientation of the camera at the time of capture: you can specify Pose Heading, Pose Pitch, and Pose Roll attributes. These attributes indicate which way you were facing in compass degrees, how high up or down you were looking, and how tilted your camera was at the time of image capture. Cumulatively, this is sufficient to uniquely describe a 3D pose anywhere on earth except the North or South Pole.[1] This in turn means that later, when you're viewing a captured photo sphere, the display software can re-create the original setting and orientation.

When a photo sphere is captured, as with a panorama, multiple images are stitched together in software to produce a larger rectangle of pixel data. The stitching process, combined with the phone's own orientation sensors, allows the determination of the "footprint" that the image pixels occupy within the larger 360°×180° sphere of all possible headings. This is encoded as image metadata describing the left, right, top, and bottom extents of the image within the dimensions of the greater rectangle. Figure 13.3 shows an example of a photo sphere of the Piazza del Campo; compare it to the panoramic sample in figure 13.1, captured at the same site. The embedded image shows the characteristic distortion of a spherical projection, and contains numerical data indicating its embedding within the complete sphere.

These fields mean that the viewer can load an image and then embed it into a larger texture buffer, creating a texture that spans the full sphere and that only has pixels where pixels are valid, as shown in figure 13.4.

Code that renders photo spheres onto texture-mapped OpenGL spheres is relatively straightforward. Porting that code from a conventional display to the Rift is in many ways even simpler. All you need to do is place the wearer's viewpoint inside the sphere in the scene; the user turning their head will take care of the rest.

One caveat to bear in mind is that for once, parallax *isn't* your friend. A photo sphere is a single image captured from a single point in space; there is only one "eye" doing the capturing, even though the image itself was stitched from many separate frames. Picture a single eye, rotating in all directions: that means no binocular parallax. Instead, every pixel of the photo sphere is effectively at the same distance from the viewer. This means that you should treat a photo sphere as much more akin to an

---

[1] That's okay. We hear they're cold this time of year.

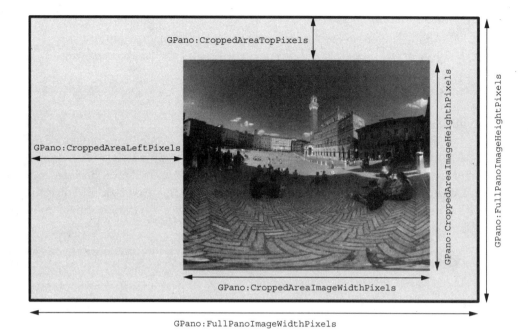

Figure 13.3   Metadata fields of the Google photo sphere image format

environmental cubemap than an actual sphere in space; infinitely large, infinitely clear, infinitely far away in all directions.

Practically speaking, this means that when rendering your photo sphere in the Rift, you either should make the sphere very large, or trim the translational component out of your eye pose matrices while you're rendering the photo sphere. If you preserve only the orientational component, then it won't swing around as the user moves their head.

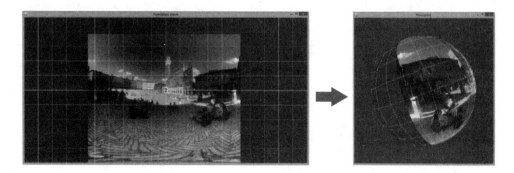

Figure 13.4   Wrapping a partial photo texture onto a sphere. The image used here is a photo sphere taken of the same plaza as the panorama shot in figure 13.1.

13.1.3 Photo spheres...in space!

Our photo sphere demo has three steps:

1   Loading the image and retrieving its XMP data
2   Embedding the image into the 360° × 180° panorama of the sphere
3   Rendering the actual sphere

Each step is pretty straightforward.

To begin, you need to parse out the metadata encoded into the image. A number of open source and for-pay products are available to do this, as well as numerous software libraries. In most cases their features boil down to "given an image, give me a key-value pair mapping that I can use to look up the fields I want." For example, the open source project Exiv2 (www.exiv2.org) produces the output shown in the following listing.

> **Listing 13.1   EXIF and XMP data retrieved from our sample image by Exiv2**

```
Exif.Image.Model                      Ascii        8  Nexus 5
Exif.Image.Orientation                Short        1  (0)
Exif.Image.DateTimeOriginal           Ascii       20  2014:06:20
    16:05:51
Exif.Image.MeteringMode               Short        1  (65535)
Exif.Image.ImageLength                Short        1  2563
Exif.Image.DateTime                   Ascii       20  2014:06:20
    16:05:51
Exif.Image.LightSource                Short        1  Unknown
Exif.Image.ImageWidth                 Short        1  3119
Exif.Image.Make                       Ascii        4  LGE
Exif.Image.GPSTag                     Long         1  226
Exif.GPSInfo.GPSTimeStamp             SRational    3  16:04:02
Exif.GPSInfo.GPSLatitudeRef           Ascii        2  North
Exif.GPSInfo.GPSLongitude             Rational     3  11deg 19' 52.237"
Exif.GPSInfo.GPSLongitudeRef          Ascii        2  East
Exif.GPSInfo.GPSDateStamp             Ascii       11  2014:06:20
Exif.GPSInfo.GPSProcessingMethod      Undefined    1  0
Exif.GPSInfo.GPSLatitude              Rational     3  43deg 19' 4.864"
Exif.GPSInfo.GPSAltitudeRef           Byte         1  Above sea level
Exif.Image.ExifTag                    Long         1  411
Xmp.GPano.UsePanoramaViewer           XmpText      4  True
Xmp.GPano.ProjectionType              XmpText     15  equirectangular
Xmp.GPano.CroppedAreaImageHeightPixels XmpText     4  2563
Xmp.GPano.CroppedAreaImageWidthPixels XmpText      4  3119
Xmp.GPano.FullPanoHeightPixels        XmpText      4  2900
Xmp.GPano.FullPanoWidthPixels         XmpText      4  5800
Xmp.GPano.CroppedAreaTopPixels        XmpText      3  334
Xmp.GPano.CroppedAreaLeftPixels       XmpText      4  1314
Xmp.GPano.FirstPhotoDate              XmpText     24  2014-06-
    20T14:03:56.173Z
Xmp.GPano.LastPhotoDate               XmpText     23  2014-06-
    20T14:05:24.13Z
Xmp.GPano.SourcePhotosCount           XmpText      2  25
Xmp.GPano.PoseHeadingDegrees          XmpText      5  317.0
```

❶ Google photo sphere fields

Xmp.GPano.LargestValidInteriorRectLeft	XmpText	1	0
Xmp.GPano.LargestValidInteriorRectTop	XmpText	1	0
Xmp.GPano.LargestValidInteriorRectWidth	XmpText	4	3119
Xmp.GPano.LargestValidInteriorRectHeight	XmpText	4	2563

The XMP data is structured XML, flattened here by the Exiv2 application. Reading this data is a simple matter of parsing the string output.

The Google photo sphere fields ❶ identify the size of the true image (3119 × 2563) inset into the larger total footprint of the panorama on a sphere (5800 × 2900) and where to place the image within the footprint (1314 pixels from the left edge, 334 from the top).

Once you've determined the dimensions of the image and the rectangular footprint of the total sphere, your next task is to read the pixels from the image file and build a larger texture map, whose dimensions are the total extent. Alternatively, instead of building a larger texture map, you could use a smaller texture map and careful assignment of texture coordinates to vertices—but using a larger rectangle is easier.

There are many ways to load an image and embed it into a texture map. The following listing shows one approach, using the OpenCV image library (opencv.org). We've trimmed out some of the extraneous parts, but the full code is on the book's GitHub repository.

Listing 13.2 Using OpenCV to load an image, and then embedding it into a texture

```
gl::TexturePtr loadAndPositionPhotoSphereImage(
    const std::string & pathToImage,
    glm::uvec2 &fullPanoSize,
    glm::uvec2 &croppedImageSize,
    glm::uvec2 &croppedImagePos) {
  cv::Mat mat = cv::imread(pathToImage.c_str());
  cv::cvtColor(mat, mat, CV_BGR2RGB);
  uchar *out = (uchar*)malloc(fullPanoSize.x * fullPanoSize.y * 3);

  memset(out, 84, fullPanoSize.x * fullPanoSize.y * 3);
  for (unsigned int y = 0; y < croppedImageSize.y; y++) {
    int srcRow = y * croppedImageSize.x * 3;
    int destRow = (croppedImagePos.y + y) * (fullPanoSize.x * 3);

    memcpy(
        out + destRow + croppedImagePos.x,
        mat.datastart + srcRow,
        croppedImageSize.x * 3);
  }

  texture = GlUtils::getImageAsTexture(fullPanoSize, out);
  free(out);
  return texture;
}
```

Annotations (left and right of listing):

- Retrieves the image data. OpenCV loads images into memory in BGR format.
- Retrieves the full panorama size, the cropped image size, and the cropped image position.
- Allocates 3 bytes per pixel times width times height.
- Converts from BGR memory ordering to RGB.
- Clears memory to a shade of light gray.
- Loops over the height of the inset image.
- Calculates the current source row.
- Writes to the current destination row, offset by the cropped image's vertical inset position.
- Copies all pixel data from source to destination.
- Releases the allocated buffer.
- Uses the GlUtils example framework to copy the RGB pixels into an OpenGL texture.

The output from `loadAndPositionPhotoSphereImage()` is an OpenGL texture buffer bound to a texture ID in our `GlUtils` example framework. The image will be uniformly gray (RGB 84, 84, 84) except where the pixels of the panorama image have been copied into place.

OpenCV always loads images into memory in BGR ordering (Blue, Green, Red). OpenGL uses an in-memory ordering of RGB (Red, Green, Blue), so we use the OpenCV routine `cv::cvtColor()` to reverse the ordering of the bytes of each pixel.

The last step is to render the photo sphere, which is stock OpenGL, shown next.

Listing 13.3   Rendering the photo sphere

```
void renderScene() {
  static gl::GeometryPtr geometry = GlUtils::getSphereGeometry();
  static gl::TexturePtr texture =
      loadAndPositionPhotoSphereImage(filepath, /* ... */);

  glClear(GL_DEPTH_BUFFER_BIT);
  gl::MatrixStack & mv = gl::Stacks::modelview();      Enlarges the sphere
  mv.withPush([&]{                                     to 50 meters across
    mv.scale(50.0f);
    texture->bind();                                   Binds our image texture,
    GlUtils::renderGeometry(geometry);                 renders a stock textured
    texture->unbind();                                 sphere, and unbinds
  });
}
```

The GlUtils example methods handle all the heavy lifting here. Using the built-in sphere geometry methods with their default texture mapping, you simply enlarge the sphere to far enough out that the user's head motion won't affect the image; the final result, shown in figure 13.5, is a Rift app that can take you to Sienna, or anywhere else in the world your camera can take you!

13.2   *Using live webcam video in the Rift*

Panoramas that enclose us are fine for static imagery, but for truly interactive content, nothing beats a live video stream. Be it from a video feed, remote videoconferencing, or a head-mounted webcam attached to the Rift, live video presents a unique set of challenges and opportunities. The potential for telepresence and augmented reality is striking.

Mounting a webcam on the Rift turns the Rift from an opaque, isolating black box into a pass-through video overlay that can integrate live computer graphics onto a real-time view of the world. With pass-through video, your computer can do live analysis of the scene around you and overlay that understanding in visual form onto the image you see. Live video also raises the possibility of scene recognition, gesture recognition, and contextual processing at unprecedented levels, as shown in figure 13.6.

In this section we'll walk through a demo of how to take video from a webcam mounted atop your Rift and bring that video feed into the headset, in VR. We'll be

Figure 13.5   The Piazza del Campo, Sienna, Italy, as seen through the Oculus Rift

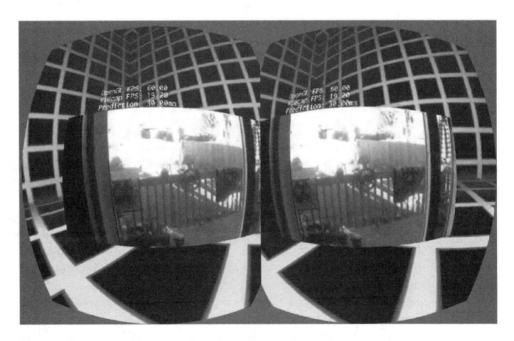

Figure 13.6   Live webcam imagery channeled into the Oculus Rift

using the OpenCV library again; it's a terrific library for smoothing out the varieties and vagaries of differing webcam standards. In brief, the steps for integrating live video into a webcam are as follows:

1 Design your app to be multithreaded so that capturing the video stream and rendering it can be as distinct as possible. This approach will help you avoid frame rate bottlenecks.
2 Connect to your webcam(s) on a background thread.
3 On your foreground (graphics) thread, pull frames off the video thread and convert them into OpenGL texture data.
4 Texture-map frame textures onto a target surface in the Rift, ideally a rectangle whose aspect ratio matches that of your webcam.
5 If your webcam is mounted on your Rift, then you'll want to apply *prediction* to improve image tracking for your user and reduce the risk of simulation sickness.

When integrating live video into the Rift, especially from a head-mounted webcam, you must be aware of a few factors that don't usually apply to video software:

- Your display device (the Rift) has a ridiculously low tolerance for latency. This will force design choices about when and how you capture video frames.
- Not all webcams are created equal. Most are designed to deliver quality images of central figures at a distance of a few feet; outside that range, image distortion may occur.
- If you stick a camera on your head, the image is going to jitter and move in ways that your real vision never has. Image stabilization is a lot more important in the Rift than outside it. You'll need to take extra steps to avoid unpleasant side effects.

13.2.1 *Threaded frame capture from a live image feed*

OpenCV makes the mechanics of capturing a stream of images from a webcam relatively straightforward, which takes a lot of the complexity out of integrating live video with the Rift. All the details of finding, opening, and pulling data from a webcam are taken care of for you.

It'll be tempting to try to do your webcam capture on your rendering thread, because that's where it's most convenient. Your rendering thread is going to be where your OpenGL context is set up, making assignment to GL textures straightforward. Unfortunately, most webcams operate at a default frame rate of 30 frames per second. This means that when you request a frame, OpenCV will typically block for about 0.03 seconds while the webcam captures the image and returns it to you.

Image retrieval therefore needs to be asynchronous, and pulling data from a webcam, or other high-latency source, should always be done on a separate thread from rendering.

With this in mind, we created the following listing, which shows one possible implementation of a background thread dedicated to webcam capture.

Listing 13.4 WebcamHandler, background-threaded webcam frame capture

```
struct CaptureData {
  cv::Mat image;
};

class WebcamHandler {

private:

  bool hasFrame{ false };
  bool stopped{ false };
  cv::VideoCapture videoCapture;
  CaptureData frame;
  std::thread captureThread;          Background thread and a mutex
  std::mutex mutex;                   for control synchronization.

public:

  void startCapture() {
    videoCapture.open(0);
    if (!videoCapture.isOpened() || !videoCapture.read(frame.image)) {
      FAIL("Could not open video source ");
    }
    captureThread = std::thread(      Forks our
        &WebcamHandler::captureLoop, this);   background thread...
  }

  void captureLoop() {
    CaptureData captured;
    while (!stopped) {
      videoCapture.read(captured.image);
      cv::flip(captured.image.clone(), captured.image, 0);
      setResult(captured);
    }
  }

  void setResult(const CaptureData & newFrame) {
    std::lock_guard<std::mutex> guard(mutex);
    frame = newFrame;
    hasFrame = true;
  }

  bool getResult(CaptureData & out) {
    if (!hasFrame) {
      return false;
    }
    std::lock_guard<std::mutex> guard(mutex);
    out = frame;
    hasFrame = false;
    return true;
  }
```

Opens the zeroeth webcam attached to the system.

...so long as stopped is not true.

Claims a lock on a mutex and holds it for as long as the instance is in scope.

Locks access to the stored frame variable.

Captures a single frame from the webcam. This is a blocking call, typically taking around 33 ms.

Stores image raster data bottom-to-top.

Records the captured frame.

Stores the captured frame and updates our state flag.

Returns false if a new frame is not yet available.

Copies the stored image into the out matrix, clears our state flag so that we don't apply the same update next render frame, and returns true.

```
void stopCapture() {
  stopped = true;
  captureThread.join();
  videoCapture.release();
}
};
```

> To stop the thread, we set our state flag and use Thread::join() to wait for the background thread to terminate.

The previous listing is a fairly standard implementation of a *single-buffered producer/consumer* model of multithreading. Here the capture thread is the *producer*, and it's tasked with filling its internal buffer with webcam images as frequently as possible. The methods startCapture() and stopCapture() use the standard C++ thread control mechanisms to fork and terminate a process thread. The method getResult(out) implements the producer pattern: if a new frame is available, it's returned in the passed output parameter.

In the event that the image buffer isn't consumed before another frame has been captured, the capture thread will replace its buffer with the most recent data.

Meanwhile, the rendering thread plays the role of *consumer*. Each time the rendering thread is ready to render a frame, it'll attempt to consume the available image buffer; if it does, it'll pass the texture image to OpenGL for display. The rendering thread will use its update() method, which is called once per frame, to attempt to retrieve image data from the capture thread and, if available, inform OpenGL, as shown next.

Listing 13.5   WebcamApp, a frame in space showing a live webcam feed

```
class WebcamApp : public RiftApp {

protected:

  gl::Texture2dPtr texture;
  gl::GeometryPtr videoGeometry;
  WebcamHandler captureHandler;
  CaptureData captureData;

public:

  virtual ~WebcamApp() {
    captureHandler.stopCapture();
  }

  void initGl() {
    RiftApp::initGl();

    texture = GlUtils::initTexture();              ←┐
    float aspectRatio = captureHandler.startCapture();  ←┐
    videoGeometry = GlUtils::getQuadGeometry(aspectRatio);  ←┘
  }

  virtual void update() {
    if (captureHandler.getResult(captureData)) {   ←┐
```

> Reserves an OpenGL texture. This will be the GPU buffer that stores the webcam images.

> Returns the aspect ratio of the webcam's resolution.

> Builds a quad with the set aspect ratio.

> If there's a new frame available, then...

```
      texture->bind();
      glTexImage2D(GL_TEXTURE_2D, 0, GL_RGBA8,
          captureData.cols, captureData.rows,
          0, GL_BGR, GL_UNSIGNED_BYTE,
          captureData.image.data);
      texture->unbind();
    }
  }

  virtual void renderScene() {
    glClear(GL_DEPTH_BUFFER_BIT);
    GlUtils::renderSkybox(Resource::IMAGES_SKY_CITY_XNEG_PNG);
    gl::MatrixStack & mv = gl::Stacks::modelview();

    mv.with_push([&]{
      mv.identity();
      mv.translate(glm::vec3(0, 0, -2));
      texture->bind();
      GlUtils::renderGeometry(videoGeometry);
      texture->unbind();
    });
  }
};

RUN_OVR_APP(WebcamApp);
```

> ...binds the texture buffer and updates it with glTexImage2D.

> Binds the current texture to render a frame in space, positioned 3 meters ahead of the viewer.

This Rift app renders a frame hanging in space before the viewer, illustrated in figure 13.7.

Figure 13.7   Webcam imagery textured into the Rift

13.2.2 *Image enhancement*

For all your augmented reality needs, you have a number of options. The OpenCV libraries stand out as a trove of easy-to-use, open source, computer vision algorithms. Here are just a few of the things you can do with OpenCV, usually in real time:

- Image smoothing, sharpening, and cleaning
  - Remove noisy fuzz from static images or live video
  - Boost image clarity
- Edge detection, straight-line detection
  - Highlight edges in view
  - Draw the user's attention to key image features
- Image similarity matching, feature detection
  - Track objects in view and target them for the user
  - Follow moving objects in video
  - Use template matching to identify previously seen objects in a scene
- Pattern recognition
  - Detect faces and highlight features
  - OCR (*Optical Character Recognition*—real-time image-to-text translation)

We could easily spend whole chapters on computer vision, but that would distract from the Rift, so we won't wax too eloquent about image analysis here. But if you're looking to experiment with image enhancement, OpenCV is a great place to start.

As a simple example, the following listing shows how to add edge detection to our Rift app. The code is quite short, and it runs in real time on the capture thread.

Listing 13.6 Implementing Canny edge detection with OpenCV

```
cv::blur(captured.image, captured.image, cv::Size(3, 3));
cv::cvtColor(captured.image, captured.image, CV_BGR2GRAY);
cv::Canny(captured.image, captured.image, a, b);
cv::cvtColor(captured.image, captured.image, CV_GRAY2BGR);
```

This example consists of four steps:

1. Reduce image noise by smoothing with a 3 × 3 local filter.
2. Downsample from 24-bit pixels to 8-bit pixels. OpenCV's edge detection operates best on 8-bit pixels.
3. Apply the Canny edge-filtering algorithm; a and b are constants defined by the user, defining edge-detection fidelity. (a = 10 and b = 100 would be reasonable sample values here.)
4. Upsample from 8-bit pixels to 24-bit pixels, shaded to shades of gray.

The end result is an image in which every pixel that differs strongly from its neighbors has been replaced with a bright shade of white, and all regions of the image that are similar to their immediate neighbors have been replaced with shades running to black. This identifies those pixels that are most likely to be on features of interest.

Figure 13.8   The Canny edge-detection algorithm, implemented with OpenCV and piped into the Rift.

Figure 13.8 shows edge detection in action. The image captured is the same view of the room as that in figure 13.7 (except that the cat moved).

The OpenCV website has a number of demos of cool tricks, like text recognition, facial recognition, image differencing, and stitching. Give yourself a treat and spend some time exploring what you can do with computer vision today.

13.2.3 Proper scaling: webcam aspect ratio

You may have noticed that the rectangular images shown in figures 13.6 and 13.7 weren't square. Webcam images rarely are. Most webcams capture images in rectangular aspect ratios—typically wider than high, and nowadays, typically in HD resolutions. That means that the geometry we're texture-mapping—the quadrilateral that's showing our captured frames—needs to be rectangular as well. Because we're already checking our connection to the webcam by capturing a first frame in startCapture(), we can enhance startCapture() a smidgen to return the aspect ratio of the webcam. That will let us choose the right dimensions for our target geometry when it's time to render. We'll modify startCapture() as follows (new lines are shown in bold):

```
float startCapture() {
  videoCapture.open(0);
  if (!videoCapture.isOpened() || !videoCapture.read(frame)) {
    FAIL("Could not open video source to capture first frame");
  }
  float aspectRatio = (float)frame.cols / (float)frame.rows;
  captureThread = std::thread(&WebcamHandler::captureLoop, this);
  return aspectRatio;
}
```

This way, we're confident that the webcam's image dimensions are available as we launch the background thread.

13.2.4 *Proper ranging: field of view*

Another very nice optimization will be to position the textured quad at a distance from the viewer, chosen such that it fills a field of view of the user that exactly matches the field of view of the webcam. Every webcam has a field of view (FOV); they typically vary from 45 to 70 degrees, but they can be much wider, especially if you're using a fisheye lens.

To approximate your webcam's FOV, level it horizontally and point it at an object of known width at a known distance. Line your webcam up so that the object exactly fills the view of the camera, with both ends equidistant from the lens, as in figure 13.9.

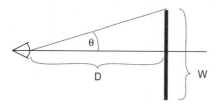

Figure 13.9   Calculating θ, the FOV of your webcam. D = Distance to known object, chosen so that it exactly fills the webcam's view. W = Width of known object.

If you know the distance from the lens to the object and the width of the object as it exactly fills your camera's field of view, then trigonometry defines that θ is equal to the tangent of half your object's width over the distance: $θ - \tan(W/2)/D$. Doubling θ yields the horizontal field of view of the webcam.

The same logic holds in our virtual scene. Given a chosen distance at which we want to display our captured webcam imagery, we can use this equation to determine the optimal width of the texture quad in virtual meters.

Let's say we want to position the texture quad at a distance of 10 meters from the viewer, and our webcam has an FOV of 45°, or $π/8$. An FOV of $π/8$ means $θ - π/16$. Then the equation for the width of the quadrilateral would be $W = 2\,D\,a\tan(θ) = 3.8$ meters wide.

13.2.5 *Image stabilization*

Now let's look at some of the problems that arise specifically when you strap a webcam to your head. (What? It happens more often than you'd think.)

The greatest challenge to immersive throughput of live, head-mounted video is latency, but it can affect you in more ways than you might think. Raw camera-to-Rift update latency is critical, obviously, but if you use the background-threaded approach we've already covered, you should be able to minimize that, at least to within the limits of the webcam itself. The other significant issue is going to come when you start to move your head: *image stabilization*.

To solve the image stability problem, we benefit from the sensors already at hand (or rather, at head). The Rift is constantly capturing its own position and orientation at a significantly higher rate than the webcam is capturing images. So it's not too hard to capture that pose information as we capture each frame. Doing so requires only four changes (shown in bold) to our existing demo class:

1. Extend `CaptureData` to include an extra HMD pose field:

```
struct CaptureData {
  ovrPosef pose;
  cv::Mat image;
};
```

2. Add a reference to the HMD in the `WebcamHandler`:

```
class WebcamHandler {
  // ...
  CaptureData frame;
  ovrHmd hmd;
  // ...

  WebcamHandler(ovrHmd & hmd) : hmd(hmd) { }
```

3. Capture the current head pose in each call to `captureLoop()`:

```
void captureLoop() {
  CaptureData captured;
  while (!stopped) {
    float captureTime = ovr_GetTimeInSeconds();
    ovrTrackingState tracking =
        ovrHmd_GetTrackingState(hmd, captureTime);
    captured.pose = tracking.HeadPose.ThePose;

    videoCapture.read(captured.image);
    cv::flip(captured.image.clone(), captured.image, 0);
    set(captured);
  }
}
```

4. Compute the differential latency matrix and apply it to the modelview stack:

```
glm::quat eyePose = Rift::fromOvr(getEyePose().Orientation);
glm::quat webcamPose = Rift::fromOvr(captureData.pose.Orientation);
glm::mat4 webcamDelta =
    glm::mat4_cast(glm::inverse(eyePose) * webcamPose);

mv.identity();
mv.preMultiply(webcamDelta);
mv.translate(glm::vec3(0, 0, -2));
```

Step 4 is where the interesting stuff happens. That's where we compute the difference between the current eye pose orientation and the head pose that we captured alongside the webcam frame. Pushing the product of ($eyePose^{-1}$ × webcamPose) onto the modelview matrix stack is mathematically akin to subtracting the `eyePose` from the `webcamPose`, and adding the difference to the modelview.

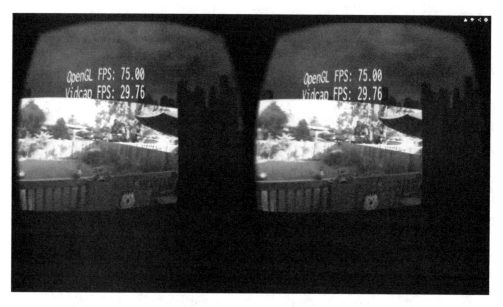

Figure 13.10   This image was captured from live video in the Rift as an author's head was turning quickly to the right. To preserve persistence of the image in the user's eyes, as the head turns, the video frame slides in the opposite direction, holding the image pointing at the same place in the real world; then as the webcam stream catches up to the user's head motion, the frame will "catch up" and settle in the center of the view again.

In other words, even though your head has moved, the picture stays in the same place relative to the real world. As your head turns one way, the frame bumps a bit the other way, so the pass-through image of the room around you, as seen through the webcam, hangs more steadily in the virtual space in front of you. As your head turns more quickly, the difference between the pose captured a few milliseconds earlier and the pose captured on the instant grows; that larger difference swings the rendered position of the textured quadrilateral further away from the direction of head travel, but as head motion slows, the image returns to stable in front of the eyes. The perceived stability of the image is dramatically improved (figure 13.10).

13.3   *Stereo vision*

A natural upgrade from sticking a webcam on your head is, well, sticking two webcams on your head. Two webcams means you can show a unique view to each eye; you can have stereo vision, inside the stereo view of the Rift. A number of developers have experimented with using stereo webcams with the Rift, and a quick web search will turn up everything from cheerful hobbyists to inventors who've attached stereo cameras to flying quadcopter drones.

One word of caution: the more stuff you attach to your Rift, the more you risk occluding some of the IR LEDs, the built-in tracking lights that help the Rift's infrared webcam track the headset. Blocking one or two IR LEDs isn't the end of the world; the Rift software can do remarkably well if a few are covered or blocked. But the more LEDs you cover, the poorer the position capture and the rougher your VR experience. So, for example, don't use some big anchoring plate to cover the whole front of your DK2; you'll completely destroy positional tracking. If you have to anchor to the front of the Rift, keep the anchor point small, and use a small webcam. If you have a larger camera, set the webcam atop the Rift, where there are fewer LEDs and you'll only risk reducing fidelity when you're looking down (a less common gesture).

13.3.1 *Stereo vision in our example code*

The code changes in our demo framework to switch from mono to stereo inputs are, to be entirely honest, pretty trivial; we've listed them here, with the new code in bold. Basically, instead of writing

```
gl::Texture2dPtr texture;
gl::GeometryPtr videoGeometry;
WebcamHandler captureHandler;
CaptureData captureData;
```

you write

```
gl::Texture2dPtr texture[2];
gl::GeometryPtr videoGeometry[2];
WebcamHandler captureHandler[2];
CaptureData captureData[2];
```

and add loops as appropriate to the setup, cleanup, and update methods.

Setup:

```
void initGl() {
  RiftApp::initGl();

  for (int i = 0; i < 2; i++) {
    texture[i] = GlUtils::initTexture();
    float aspectRatio = captureHandler[i].startCapture(hmd,
        CAMERA_FOR_EYE[i]);
    videoGeometry[i] = GlUtils::getQuadGeometry(aspectRatio);
  }
}
```

Cleanup:

```
virtual ~WebcamApp() {
  for (int i = 0; i < 2; i++) {
    captureHandler[i].stopCapture();
  }
}
```

Update:

```
virtual void update() {
  for (int i = 0; i < 2; i++) {
    if (captureHandler[i].get(captureData[i])) {
```

```
texture[i]->bind();
glTexImage2D(GL_TEXTURE_2D, 0, GL_RGBA8,
    captureData[i].image.cols, captureData[i].image.rows,
    0, GL_BGR, GL_UNSIGNED_BYTE,
    captureData[i].image.data);
texture[i]->unbind();
      }
    }
  }
```

Those loops take care of the lion's share of the upgrade to stereo vision. All that remains is to select the correct view for the correct eye in our rendering method:

```
texture[getCurrentEye()]->bind();
GlUtils::renderGeometry(videoGeometry[getCurrentEye()]);
texture[getCurrentEye()]->unbind();
```

One of the quirks of this demo that we can't code in a portable manner is the fact that everybody's PC is different, particularly the order in which USB devices are plugged in (especially if you've got multiple USB cameras attached). Happily, OpenCV handles multithreaded requests to multiple webcams almost seamlessly. To simplify addressing multiple cameras, we've introduced an extra array, which we used during setup in initGl(); for one author's home PC setup; that array looks like this:

```
int CAMERA_FOR_EYE[2] = { 2, 1 };
```

That is to say, the left eye will be shown the output from the third webcam connected to the PC, and the right eye will be shown the output from the second.[2]

13.3.2 *Quirks of stereo video from inside the Rift*

Unfortunately, adding stereo input to the Rift isn't necessarily the best thing to do.

For one thing, if you glue a pair of webcams to your head, it's going to be a lot like looking at the world through a laggy periscope. As you swing your head, your point of view will move as though your eyes were much further from your neck than usual. That can be a disorienting experience, not dissimilar to looking along the length of a rocking boat, so you're going to be much more vulnerable to motion sickness and simulation sickness. That can get pretty rough! Don't try to power through it, either, because with sim sickness that can end pretty colorfully—if you're experimenting with live 3D stereo and you feel yourself becoming ill, ease out of VR and take a break immediately.

For another thing, our image stabilization code starts to get a little suspect at this point. As written, we're individually stabilizing each eye. That will give each eye a nice, stable image without jitter or shakiness, which is great. But the two eyes will be seeing images stabilized with head poses captured at *two different times*. So while the images will be stable, the quads that display them will be moving independently, shaking in

---

[2] The first webcam (index zero) is built into the laptop screen.

different directions. It's not entirely clear what effect this is going to have on users, but it's probably not good.

13.4 *The Leap Motion hand sensor*

The *Leap Motion* (www.leapmotion.com) is a stereo depth-sensing device designed to capture hand positions and gestures. The Leap was pioneered in 2008 by David Holz and developed for production in 2010 by Holz and Michael Buckwald, in the hopes of bringing the sci-fi future of gesture-controlled UIs into the real world. Holz and Buckwald had a vision of being able to sculpt 3D surfaces and control interactive software in 3D, just like in the movies (see chapter 9).

The Leap was originally intended to be placed on your desk, face up to the space above your keyboard. You'd then move your hands through the air above your keyboard, gesturing to trigger behaviors on the PC. For example, waving your hand from right to left could be configured as clicking the Back button on a web browser or closing the current application. Holding up a hand, index finger extended, and "tapping" the air in the plane above the Leap would be interpreted as a mouse click. Essentially, picture the gesture functionality of a laptop's touchpad or a tablet's touchscreen, but without the pad or screen—all the interaction is in the space above your keyboard (figure 13.11).

The Leap is a very cool PC peripheral with a lot of potential that's still being explored. Leap Motion supports an App Store designed to encourage innovative uses of their device, and there's talk of embedding the sensor into laptops and tablets for airborne control. But it wasn't until the Oculus Rift came along that the VR applications of the Leap really opened up.

Originally the Leap was meant to point straight up off the desk, but a simple removable bracket (available by mail from Leap Motion, or you can 3D print your own) attaches the Leap to the front of the Oculus Rift, pointing forward. By mounting this lightweight hand sensor on the front of the Rift, you can now detect hand positions and gestures from within VR apps (figure 13.12).

Figure 13.11 The Leap Motion Controller's view of your hands (source: Leap API documentation)

Figure 13.12   An Oculus Rift DK2 with the Leap Motion mounted on a removable bracket attached to the faceplate. The Leap can be popped out of the bracket holder and doesn't block the Rift's IR LEDs.

The potential here is striking. One of the biggest problems with the Rift has always been that it's hard to reach the controls after you've strapped a big opaque square of plastic to your noggin. But if you can see your real hands in virtual space, then that's a game-changer (figure 13.13).

Through our innate sense of proprioception, seeing our real hands in a virtual space dramatically reinforces the sense of immersion and presence. It's also a major leap forward (no pun intended) for the capability, flexibility, and intuitiveness of VR interface design. As we covered in chapter 9, gestural interfaces have the potential to be the most natural, instinctive, easy-to-learn, and easy-to-use interfaces ever developed for human-computer interaction.

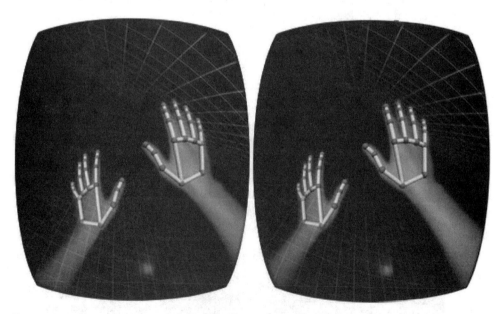

Figure 13.13   The Leap supports pass-through video, blending your hands with virtual overlay and 3D stereo imagery. The video is IR only, so this is "night vision" of your hands. (Source: LeapMotion.com.)

13.4.1 Developing software for the Leap Motion and the Rift

The Leap Motion has been designed for indie developers from day one, and its SDK is one of the most well documented and clearly designed that it's been our pleasure to work with. It's also constantly being enhanced and developed as the Leap Motion team improves and expands on its ability to recognize an airborne human hand. With that in mind, we're going to present sample code here for a very simple interactive application combining the Leap and the Rift.

It should be emphasized that the code shown here (and on our GitHub repository) was written against the Leap SDK 2.1.6. Leap's SDK support for the Rift is still in active beta, so anything committed to print today is unlikely to work without update in, say, a year's time.

Let's begin with the basics. The Leap consists of a pair of IR cameras and an IR LED. The IR LED shines brightly out of the top of the Leap, and the IR light bounces off objects near the Leap to be captured by the cameras. The cameras use conventional depth-estimation algorithms based on feature-matching to estimate the distance from the Rift to features in the scene.

Lighting conditions and the Leap

The Leap's reliance on IR light for its image capture is a mixed blessing. On the one hand, it means that the Leap can be used effectively in low light. On the other hand, it means that the Rift and the Leap collide a bit in that both rely on IR light for their data, and it means that the Leap is vulnerable to unusually bright lighting conditions. If you're working on integrating the two, you may find that optimal lighting conditions are hard to achieve.

The Leap's approach to depth-sensing is different from that of, for example, the Microsoft Kinect, which projects an active grid of IR data into the scene and then detects the distortion of the grid on objects in the near view. The use of an IR lamp instead of a more expensive projector means that the Leap can be manufactured at lower cost, but it also means that it'll sometimes suffer greater issues with accuracy.

Interestingly this also means that the Leap can be used as a pretty good night-vision camera!

Based on the depth estimates formed by comparing the images from the Leap's two cameras, the Leap uses built-in software that has been highly optimized to try to detect the hands in the space in front of it. As a general rule, there aren't many things that are shaped like hands that aren't hands, so the Leap usually does a pretty good job. By assuming that a hand has five fingers[3] and the conventional arrangement of ligaments and tendons, the Leap can often even estimate the position of digits that it can't see.

---

[3] Not necessarily a safe assumption, as evidenced by the 1987 landmark case *Montoya vs. Rugen*.

The Leap SDK reports hand data in terms of the position of the palm of the hand and the bones of each finger. Each finger is defined as having four bones, each of which can then be described independently in terms of position, orientation, and length. (For simplicity's sake, the thumb is considered a finger with four bones, even though most real human thumbs lack the metacarpal bone found in the other four fingers. The thumb's "metacarpal" is reported as a zero-length bone.)

The Leap also offers limited support for detecting the arm above the wrist, combining camera imaging with medical reasoning based on the visible portions of the hands. Hands are far easier to detect with the Leap's depth-sensing technology than arms are, because arms are comparatively devoid of distinguishing features.

The Leap's head-mounted display mode

When using the Leap with the Rift, the Leap SDK recommends that you "hint" to the Leap that it's oriented vertically, on your face, instead of horizontally, on your desk. This tells the Leap to choose hand-detection heuristics more predisposed to detecting the back of the hand than the front, because it'll be seeing the hand from behind instead of below.

The C++ command to pass the appropriate hint to the Leap is as follows:

```
controller.setPolicy(Leap::Controller::PolicyFlag::POLICY_OPTIMIZE_HMD);
```

The Leap SDK contains numerous examples of how to make best use of the anatomical and mathematical data made available through the Leap API.

13.4.2 *The Leap, the Rift, and their respective coordinate systems*

The Leap's coordinate system was originally designed for a device sitting face-up on your desk. That coordinate system won't change when the Leap is attached to the faceplate of the Rift, but the device itself will be rotated forward 90° (figure 13.14).

The challenge is to map from the Leap's rotated coordinate system into the Rift's own basis. In the Rift, the flexibility of OpenGL means that your coordinate system is

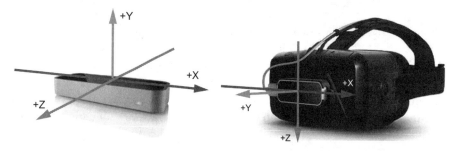

Figure 13.14   The Leap's coordinate system, as reported when the Leap is on a desk (left) and when it's on the Rift (right)

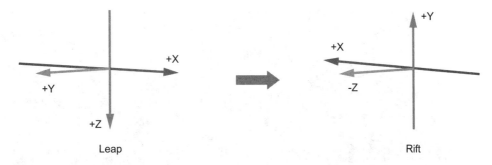

Figure 13.15   Transformation from Leap coordinates to Rift coordinates

up to you, but most commonly we choose to place the camera looking down the negative Z axis, with positive X to the right and positive Y proceeding vertically upward. Using these axes, we need to execute the following basis transform (figure 13.15):

```
Leap +X → Rift -X       [1 0 0] → [-1 0 0]
Leap +Y → Rift -Z       [0 1 0] → [0 0 -1]
Leap +Z → Rift -Y       [0 0 1] → [0 -1 0]
```

We'll implement this basis rotation with the following code, which will convert the Leap's `Vector` type into the GLM `vec3` type:

```
glm::vec3 leapToRift(Leap::Vector & vec) {
  return glm::vec3(-vec.x, -vec.z, -vec.y);
}
```

We also need to consider the units of the two devices, and the position of the Leap on the front of the Rift. OpenGL units are traditionally meters, and as we apply Rift concepts like the IPD and the player height, the choice of meters becomes fixed. The Leap, on the other hand, reports its values in millimeters. The Leap's origin is the Leap peripheral itself, which is positioned about 7 centimeters ahead of the viewer. In the Rift's frame of reference, those 7 centimeters are along the negative Z axis. So to convert from Leap to Rift, we must divide all Leap positions by 1000 and then subtract 0.07 meters,

```
glm::vec3 leapToRiftPosition(Leap::Vector & vec) {
  return leapToRift(vec) / 1000.0f + glm::vec3(0, 0, -0.070);
}
```

taking us from millimeters to meters, and from the center of the Leap to the center of the Rift.

13.4.3   Demo: integrating Leap and Rift

In this demo we're going to build a simple interactive scene in which the user can drag a sphere from place to place on the XY plane by waving their hand (figure 13.16). When the wearer extends their index finger, the sphere becomes interactive; when touched, it follows the tip of the finger.

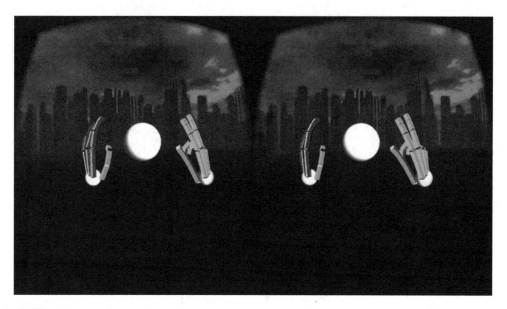

Figure 13.16   The user's hands can interact with the scene.

Clearly this could be a more complex and interactive application, but our focus here is on the synergy between Leap and Rift, not on the many potential uses of the pairing. The Leap website contains a host of more advanced and fascinating demos.

The Leap supports both event-driven and threaded data access models, making it very accessible to different styles of software development. We're going to use the threaded API, and as you'll see this means that our access to the Leap is virtually identical to our access to webcam data in the previous examples in this chapter.

For clarity, we've split the code for our Leap demo into three parts, listings 13.6, 13.7, and 13.8:[4]

- Listing 13.7 shows the `LeapHandler` class, which implements the producer/consumer pattern we used earlier.
- Listing 13.8 shows the `LeapApp` class, which captures Leap and Rift data and implements the drag operation.
- Listing 13.9 shows the rendering and graphics support methods that use Leap frame data to model the pose of a human hand.

---

[4] In reading these code listings, take them with a grain of salt. The Leap SDK is in beta and under active development, so the code we present here may (and probably will) cease to be accurate after printing. Be sure to check out developer.leapmotion.com and our GitHub repository for the latest updates.

Listing 13.7 LeapDemo, part one: `LeapHandler`, the producer/consumer model

```
struct CaptureData {
  glm::mat4 leapPose;                  Holds a Leap::Frame
  Leap::Frame frame;                   object
};

class LeapHandler : public Leap::Listener {      ◁——  Inherits handlers to
                                                       capture Controller
private:                                               and Frame state

  bool hasFrame{ false };
  std::thread captureThread;           Most thread logic
  std::mutex mutex;                    and state remains
  CaptureData frame;                   unchanged
  ovrHmd hmd;
  Leap::Controller controller;         ◁——  Entry point to Leap
                                             state and callbacks
public:

  LeapHandler(ovrHmd & hmd) : hmd(hmd) {
  }                                          ❶  Registers this Listener with the
  void startCapture() {                         Leap::Controller to receive
    controller.addListener(*this);     ◁——       onConnect() and onFrame events
  }
                                       ❷  On shutdown, removes this
  void stopCapture() {                    Listener from the Leap::Controller
    controller.removeListener(*this);  ◁——
  }

  void set(const CaptureData & newFrame) {
    std::lock_guard<std::mutex> guard(mutex);    Locks the mutex, and
    frame = newFrame;                            captures a copy of
    hasFrame = true;                             the frame state
  }

  bool get(CaptureData & out) {
    std::lock_guard<std::mutex> guard(mutex);
    if (!hasFrame) {
      return false;                              Locks the mutex, returns
    }                                            a copy of the frame state,
    out = frame;                                 and clears local state
    hasFrame = false;
    return true;                         ❸  Hints to the Leap
  }                                          SDK that it should
                                             expect to see the
  void onConnect(const Leap::Controller & controller) {   backs of hands
    controller.setPolicy(                                  more often than
        Leap::Controller::PolicyFlag::POLICY_OPTIMIZE_HMD);  the front
  }

  void onFrame(const Leap::Controller & controller) {     Captures current
    CaptureData frame;                                    state: the Leap's
                                                          hand position(s)
    frame.frame = controller.frame();                     and the Rift's
    frame.leapPose = Rift::fromOvr(                        head pose
        ovrHmd_GetTrackingState(hmd, 0.0).HeadPose.ThePose);
```

```
        set(frame);
    }
};
```

We begin by modifying our `CaptureData` class to contain a `Frame` of data from the Leap and a head pose captured from the Rift. A `Frame` is the principal data class in the Leap SDK, and its methods give access to hand position and orientation and all finger data.

```
struct CaptureData {
  glm::mat4 leapPose;
  Leap::Frame frame;
};
```

"But wait," you say. "Why bother with the Rift's head pose?" (the `glm::mat4 leapPose`). It would be great if things were as simple as this:

1 The Leap tells you where your hands are.
2 The Rift renders your virtual hands.

Alas, life's not that easy, because here's what really happens:

1 The Leap tells you where your hands are, from its point of view.
2 Your head moves and turns, moving and turning the Rift.
3 The Leap doesn't know it's moved, because it has no accelerometers, so it thinks your *hands* have moved.
4 The Rift renders the world, from its point of view—which isn't the same as the Leap's.
5 Hilarity ensues.

In short, we have to transform incoming hand position and orientation data from the Leap's frame of reference to the Rift's. Because we capture hand data at a specific instant in time, we need to correlate that with the matching head pose of the Rift. `CaptureData` becomes the binding of frame data to basis transform.

This way, if you hold your hand up before your face and rotate your head, keeping your hand fixed in space, the virtual hand will remain at the same point in virtual space as well. The Leap will see the hand swinging away, but the updated transform on the Rift will cancel that out. We'll read this data in the method `renderScene()`, in listing 13.9.

Most of the rest of the code in listing 13.7 should look familiar from earlier in this chapter; we've built the same scaffolding of producer/consumer model, using a mutex to ensure that no race conditions corrupt our data. The differences between this listing and the earlier webcam versions come in where we handle our connection to the Leap.

When we start the handler up or shut it down, we need to connect to and disconnect from the Leap with calls to `controller.addListener` ❶ and `controller.removeListener()` ❷. When the Leap SDK finds the Leap hardware, it will call our callback method, `onConnect()`.

In onConnect() we give the Leap an important hint ❸:

```
controller.setPolicy(Leap::Controller::PolicyFlag::POLICY_OPTIMIZE_HMD);
```

This line tells the Leap SDK to expect to see the *backs* of hands more often than the *fronts*.

That may sound like a pretty spurious thing to say, but it's critical for effective function in the Leap. The Leap uses heavily heuristic algorithms to improve its processing speed. Sometimes that can mean sacrificing accuracy, but speed of capture is critical. There's a fair analog to the technical challenges of the Rift here, in miniature: through proprioception, we have a strong sense of where our hands are, how our fingers are flexed, and so on. Our fingers are extremely deft and we can position them with great precision, so the challenge of the Leap is not only to detect the hands and fingers but to do so fast enough that there's never a visible disconnect between real motion and virtual position.

(Hey, at least there's no risk of making the user nauseous if you don't read their hand position correctly.)

> **NOTE** A *heuristic algorithm* is one that trades precision and accuracy for fast, flexible results, typically by solving problems through contextually guided experimentation and adaption rather than strict procedural analysis. Heuristic algorithms are less dependable than classic computing, but are often capable of producing answers to "softer" problems more quickly than would be possible through a rigorous insistence on correctness and precision.
>
> In the case of the Leap, specifying the current context ("we expect to see the back of the user's hand") helps the Leap to choose image analysis parameters to most quickly interpret its stereo camera imagery. For example, it will know that the fingers are most likely to curl away from its point of view, not toward it.

Once we've set up our connection to the Leap SDK, the actual capture is easy. We override their API method onFrame():

```
void onFrame(const Leap::Controller & controller) {
  CaptureData frame;
  frame.frame = controller.frame();
  frame.leapPose = Rift::fromOvr(
      ovrHmd_GetTrackingState(hmd, 0.0).HeadPose.ThePose);
  set(frame);
}
```

The method onFrame() is called from the Leap's listening thread each time a new hand pose is available. When onFrame() is called, we capture a complete copy of the current hand settings. Then we capture the current pose of the Rift, storing them in our CaptureData structure.

It would be elegant if we could take advantage of timewarp here. We know that there's going to be a brief lag between the instant when we capture the frame, here, and the instant when we render the positioned hand in listing 13.8. We could pass in a positive time delta in our call to ovrHmd_GetTrackingState(); the Rift would return its predicted head pose a few milliseconds from now. Unfortunately, the Leap SDK doesn't (currently) offer such a predictive feature, so there'd be no way to make a similar request to the Leap. For our demo, we opted to keep the two devices in lockstep without prediction.

One interesting possibility for the future is that by analyzing the past several frames of the Leap's motion, it may be possible to build a coarse prediction function for finger and palm positions. We are far, far more sensitive to our own head pose than to hand pose, and it's possible that even a limited extrapolation from recent velocity could be an effective predictor of hand pose a frame or two in advance. Future research topic, anybody?

This covers connecting to the Leap. Next up is reading back the data we've captured and putting it to good use, shown here.

Listing 13.8   LeapDemo, part two: LeapApp data capture and interaction

```
class LeapApp : public RiftApp {

  const float BALL_RADIUS = 0.05f;

protected:

  LeapHandler captureHandler;
  ShapeWrapperPtr sphere;
  ProgramPtr program;
  CaptureData latestFrame;
  glm::vec3 ballCenter;

public:

  LeapApp() : captureHandler(hmd) {                ❶ Begins Leap and
    captureHandler.startCapture();                    Rift pose capture
    ballCenter = glm::vec3(0, 0, -0.25);
  }

  virtual ~LeapApp() {              ❷ Ends pose
    captureHandler.stopCapture();      capture
  }

  void initGl() {
    RiftApp::initGl();
    program = oria::loadProgram(              ❸ initializes OpenGL, loads
        Resource::SHADERS_LIT_VS,                our standard lit shader
        Resource::SHADERS_LITCOLORED_FS);        and geometry, and disables
    sphere = oria::loadSphere(                   the HSW pop-up
        {"Position", "Normal"}, program);
    ovrhmd_EnableHSWDisplaySDKRender(hmd, false);  #C
  }                                              ❹ If new frame data is available
                                                    from the Leap, then captures it...
  virtual void update() {
    if (captureHandler.get(latestFrame)) {          ...and examines it to see
      Leap::HandList hands = latestFrame.frame.hands();   if it contains a valid hand
      for (int iHand = 0; iHand < hands.count(); iHand++) {  with index finger extended
```

```
        Leap::Hand hand = hands[iHand];                    #F
        Leap::Finger finger = hand.fingers()[1];           #F
        if (hand.isValid() && finger.isExtended()) {       #F
          moveBall(finger);
        }
      }
    }
  }
}
void moveBall(Leap::Finger finger) {
  glm::vec3 riftCoords =
      leapToRiftPosition(finger.tipPosition());
  riftCoords = glm::vec3(
      latestFrame.leapPose * glm::vec4(riftCoords, 1));
  if (glm::length(riftCoords - ballCenter) <= BALL_RADIUS) {
    ballCenter.x += (riftCoords.x - ballCenter.x) / 4;
    ballCenter.y += (riftCoords.y - ballCenter.y) / 4;
  }
}
```

If so, moves the ball toward the tip of the finger

⑤ Converts the fingertip's position to world coordinates

Compares the position of the fingertip to the center of the sphere

As you can see, the Leap's Hand and Finger APIs are very clean and easy to follow. After we've done the standard setup **❶**, **❷**, **❸**, the interesting data processing happens in update(). If the capture thread has delivered a new frame **❹**, we loop over the Hands in the frame, checking each for an extended index finger. The index finger is finger [1] in the Hand's Finger array.

If we find an extended index finger, then it's time to get our E.T. on. The method moveBall() converts from Leap coordinates to world coordinates **⑤** by transforming into Rift coordinates, then to the world basis. The method leapToRiftPosition() exchanges basis axes and converts from millimeters to meters, adding the offset necessary to compensate for the Leap stuck 7 cm ahead of the center of the user's eyes when wearing the Rift. We then multiply by the Rift head pose that we captured alongside the Leap hand data. This transforms from coordinates that are relative to the current heading of the Rift, to world coordinates.

Now we can test the distance in world coordinates from the fingertip position to the sphere. If the two points are close enough (less than BALL_RADIUS), then we update the ball's position by adding a fraction of the intervening distance to its current position. The ball will now follow the user's fingertip until the user moves too quickly, or closes their hand.

This covers our update loop and using sensor data to move the ball; all that remains is the actual rendering, shown in the following listing.

Listing 13.9 LeapDemo, part three: rendering

```
virtual void renderScene() {
  glClear(GL_DEPTH_BUFFER_BIT);
  GlUtils::renderSkybox(Resource::IMAGES_SKY_CITY_XNEG_PNG);
  gl::MatrixStack & mv = gl::Stacks::modelview();

  mv.with_push([&]{
    mv.transform(latestFrame.leapPose);
```

Clears the screen and renders a skybox.

Rendering of hands and fingers takes place with the Rift-to-world transform on the modelview stack.

```
        Leap::HandList hands = latestFrame.frame.hands();
        for (int iHand = 0; iHand < hands.count(); iHand++) {
          if (hands[iHand].isValid()) {
            drawHand(mv, hands[iHand]);
          }
        }
      });
```

Loops over and renders each valid Hand.

```
      GlUtils::draw3dLine(
          glm::vec3(ballCenter.x, -1000, ballCenter.z),
          glm::vec3(ballCenter.x, 1000, ballCenter.z));
      GlUtils::draw3dLine(
          glm::vec3(-1000, ballCenter.y, ballCenter.z),
          glm::vec3(1000, ballCenter.y, ballCenter.z));
      drawSphere(ballCenter, BALL_RADIUS);
    }
```

Renders our manipulation target, a ball floating in virtual space.

Renders a sphere at the wrist joint.

```
    void drawHand(const Leap::Hand & hand) {
      drawSphere(leapToRiftPosition(hand.wristPosition()), 0.02f);
      for (int f = 0; f < hand.fingers().count(); f++) {
        Leap::Finger finger = hand.fingers()[f];
        if (finger.isValid()) {
          drawFinger(finger, hand.isLeft());
        }
      }
    }
```

Loops over all Fingers.

Each finger's basis is independent of the others.

Renders each valid Finger. We need to know whether this is a left or right hand.

```
    void drawFinger(const Leap::Finger & finger, bool isLeft) {
      MatrixStack & mv = Stacks::modelview();
      for (int b = 0; b < 4; b++) {
        mv.withPush([&] {
          Leap::Bone bone = finger.bone((Leap::Bone::Type) b);
          glm::vec3 riftCoords = leapToRiftPosition(bone.center());
          float length = bone.length() / 1000;

          mv.translate(riftCoords);
          mv.transform(leapBasisToRiftBasis(bone.basis(), isLeft));
          mv.scale(glm::vec3(0.01, 0.01, length));
          oria::renderColorCube();
        });
      }
    }
```

finger.bone(i) retrieves the *i*th bone in the finger.

Models the fingers and thumb of the hand as an array of four bones.

Converts the finger bone's center to Rift coordinates.

Converts bone length from millimeters to meters.

Translates to the center of the bone.

The finger bone model is a scaled and stretched cube.

Uses the bone's basis transform to orient the cube.

Renders the cube.

```
    void drawSphere(glm::vec3 & pos, float radius) {
      MatrixStack & mv = Stacks::modelview();
      mv.withPush([&]{
        mv.translate(pos);
        mv.scale(radius);
        oria::renderGeometry(sphere, program);
      });
    }
```

drawSphere() encapsulates rendering a simple sphere at a given point and radius.

leapBasisToRiftBasis() converts a Leap::Matrix to a glm::Matrix.

```
    glm::mat4 leapBasisToRiftBasis(
        Leap::Matrix & mat, bool isLeft) {
```

```
    glm::vec3 x = leapToRift(mat.transformDirection(
        Leap::Vector(isLeft ? -1 : 1, 0, 0)));
    glm::vec3 y = leapToRift(mat.transformDirection(
        Leap::Vector(0, 1, 0)));
    glm::vec3 z = leapToRift(mat.transformDirection(
        Leap::Vector(0, 0, 1)));
    return glm::mat4x4(glm::mat3x3(x, y, z));
  }

  glm::vec3 leapToRift(Leap::Vector & vec) {
    return glm::vec3(-vec.x, -vec.z, -vec.y);
  }

  glm::vec3 leapToRiftPosition(Leap::Vector & vec) {
    return leapToRift(vec) / 1000.0f + glm::vec3(0, 0, -0.070);
  }
};
```

> **Converts both hands to a right-handed coordinate system.**

```
RUN_OVR_APP(LeapApp);
```

We begin with what's become our standard rendering preamble: clearing the display and rendering a skybox around our scene. Even in such a simple example as this, where our scene is a sphere floating in nothingness, the skybox is important for a Rift app because it gives context for head tracking. Without the skybox responding to head motion, it's hard to gauge the position and size of the floating interactive sphere.

We'll render the skybox and the sphere in world coordinates; no hidden complexities there. But we do need to be slightly more careful when we render the hands, because remember: they're being captured and framed from the point of view of the Leap, which is attached to your face. So before we can render hands, we need to change our current working basis from world coordinates to Rift coordinates; that way, when we render Rift-coordinate hand positions, they'll appear (to our point of view) in world positions.

To do so, we push the latest captured Rift head pose onto the modelview stack:

```
mv.transform(latestFrame.leapPose);
```

We capture and update this pose at every update to the Leap frame data. Each hand is rendered as a sphere set at the wrist, attached to five chains of stretched cubes to form the fingers. We use our support methods to convert from the Leap's basis to the Rift's, and to rotate and position each wrist and each bone of the hands.

The fingers of the hand are stored in a Leap `Frame` as a chain of four bones. Each bone has its own center and rotational basis. The method `bone.basis()` returns the basis for each bone, which we can convert into a rotation-only basis by applying it to the three orthonormal basis vectors, X [1, 0, 0], Y [0, 1, 0], and Z [0, 0, 1]. Conveniently, the `Leap::Matrix` class has a simple method for applying a basis transform to a direction: `transformDirection()`. So building our local rotation matrix expressing the Leap's rotations in Rift coordinates is a simple matter of building the matrix:

```
glm::vec3 x = leapToRift(mat.transformDirection(Leap::Vector(1, 0, 0)));
glm::vec3 y = leapToRift(mat.transformDirection(Leap::Vector(0, 1, 0)));
glm::vec3 z = leapToRift(mat.transformDirection(Leap::Vector(0, 0, 1)));
// Resulting 3x3 matrix: glm::mat3x3(x, y, z))
```

There's one interesting gotcha, though. It appears that the Leap reports the frame of the left hand in a left-handed basis but the right hand in a right-handed basis. To compensate for this, when building the Rift-space matrix that describes the orientation of each bone of each finger, we negate the X axis of the Leap source basis. So we change the first line of the previous code snippet to

```
glm::vec3 x = leapToRift(mat.transformDirection(
    Leap::Vector(isLeft ? -1 : 1, 0, 0)));
```

which ensures that all Rift-space matrices are in the same handedness.

The last methods of this snippet are code you've already seen:

```
glm::vec3 leapToRift(Leap::Vector & vec) {
  return glm::vec3(-vec.x, -vec.z, -vec.y);
}
```

which exchanges axes to convert from Leap space to Rift space, and

```
glm::vec3 leapToRiftPosition(Leap::Vector & vec) {
  return leapToRift(vec) / 1000.0f + glm::vec3(0, 0, -0.070);
}
```

which scales input coordinates from millimeters to meters and offsets the Leap value to account for the Leap itself being anchored 7 cm ahead of the center of the user's eyes in the Rift.

13.5 *Summary*

In this chapter you learned how to

- Load, examine, and display panoramic and photo sphere images, to create a wraparound virtual scene from photos of the real world
- Blend live webcam video into your virtual world
- Use two webcams to create stereo reality in the Rift
- Virtually model your hands using the Leap Motion stereo sensing peripheral
- Use basis transforms to migrate data from the Leap to the Rift

appendix A
Setting up the Rift in a development environment

This appendix covers

- Selecting a display mode
- Configuring the displays in your OS
- Configuring the Rift for your use
- Verifying your setup and troubleshooting
- Working without a Rift

Getting the Rift set up for use is well documented in the *Oculus Rift Development Kit Instruction Manual* that comes with the kit, and if you follow those instructions, you should be able to get the Rift up and running as a user. But if you're planning on using the Rift in a development environment, you may find that the setup you want to use while you develop for the Rift isn't the same as it would be for simply using the Rift. For example, while using the Rift, you'll probably prioritize performance over ease of switching between applications. For development, it may be better to take a performance hit in exchange for being able to see both the output and the debugger at the same time. What works best for you depends on your needs and preferences.

When it comes to setting up your development environment, we expect that you may need to make the most choices around selecting the display mode you want to use.

A.1   Selecting a display mode: Direct HMD Access or Extended Desktop mode

Prior to SDK 0.4, the Rift was seen by your computer as simply another monitor and setting up the Rift required configuring the Rift display in your OS. With the release of the DK2 and the 0.4.x version of the software, Oculus introduced a runtime component that runs on your computer as a service. This service allowed applications to be displayed directly on the Rift without the Rift display becoming part of the desktop (eliminating the need to configure the Rift display in your OS). Unfortunately, as of this writing, this direct display mechanism is unstable and not available on all platforms. Fortunately, Oculus provides an easy way to continue to use the Rift as if it were simply another monitor.

To select your display mode, with the Rift connected to your computer and turned on, run the OculusConfigUtil that was installed with the runtime and select Tools > Rift Display Mode. You should then see the Rift Display Mode selection panel (figure A.1).

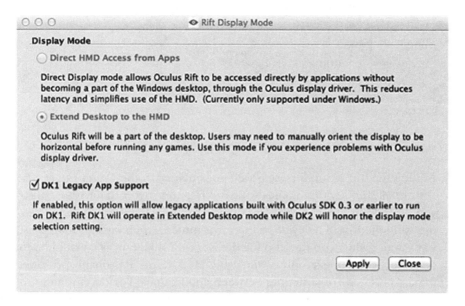

Figure A.1   The Rift Display Mode selection panel

If you plan on running applications built with Oculus SDK 0.3 or earlier on a DK1, you should select DK1 Legacy App Support, but otherwise, this option isn't too vital. For applications built on 0.4 or later, you have the choice between two display modes: Direct HMD Access from Apps and Extend the Desktop to the HMD. Table A.1 shows the pros and cons of each mode.

Table A.1 Rift display modes: pros and cons

Display mode	Advantages	Disadvantages
Direct HMD Access from Apps	Better performance Provides an option to mirror the Rift display on your desktop so that you can see what's on the Rift without wearing the Rift No need to configure displays in your OS	Not currently supported for Mac OS or Linux. Unstable.
Extend Desktop to the HMD	Only option for Mac OS, Linux Stable	Requires display configuration. There's a portion of the desktop where you can "lose" windows or your mouse. You can't normally see what's displayed on the Rift without wearing the Rift.

If it's available to you and it works on your hardware, we recommend the Direct HMD Access mode. But because of the instability of Direct HMD mode, particularly on OpenGL, for our examples you may need to use Extended Desktop mode. To use Extended Desktop mode, your next step is to configure your displays in your OS.

A.2 Configuring the displays in your OS for Extended Desktop mode

If you're using Extended Desktop mode, with the Rift connected to your computer and powered on, it should be automatically recognized as an additional monitor. By default most operating systems will end up creating an additional screen for output to that monitor.

Clarifying the terminology: "display" is an overloaded term

Before we get into the various setups, we should clarify terminology. "Display" is a pretty overloaded term, so let's avoid it and talk about *screens* and *monitors*. For our purposes, a *monitor* is a physical device that you connect to your computer and that's capable of displaying an image. Monitors have a physical size and, in the case of LCD displays, a native resolution measured in pixels horizontally by pixels vertically. Your computer almost certainly has one or more monitors physically connected to it. The Rift headset is, or rather contains, a monitor. A *screen*, on the other hand, is an abstraction by your OS, and is (one of) the area(s) to which it will render windows. Because a modern OS can render the same screen to multiple monitors, the relationship between the two can be fuzzy. You could have two monitors, but only one screen. Probably the most common use of this is connecting laptops to external display devices such as projectors so that you can give a presentation, but this kind of setup is also valuable if you're developing for specialized display hardware, such as the Rift.

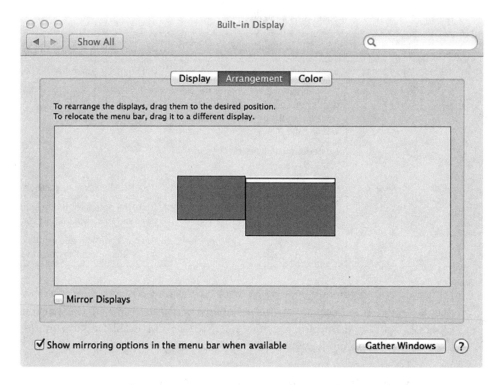

Figure A.2 Display configuration panel with the Rift configured to extend your display

To configure your displays and decide how to map screens to your available monitors, use your OS's display configuration panels:

- *Windows*—In Control Panel, select Displays, or in Windows 8, start typing `Display` in the Start screen until the Display Settings item appears and select it.
- *Mac OS*—Under the Apple menu, select System Preferences > Displays.
- *Linux*—Use the display panel for your chosen desktop environment or use the `xrandr` command-line tool.[1]

When you connect the Rift, you'll have two physical monitors and two virtual screens, as seen in figure A.2.

This is termed *extending* your display, because you're effectively extending the borders within which your OS can display output. In most cases the Rift should be set as the extended portion of the display and the main monitor as the primary display.

---

[1] Linux has an interesting advantage here. Its display settings are much more configurable and flexible than the other desktop OSes, allowing you to place one monitor inside the output window of another, meaning you get the benefits of cloning (seeing the Rift output both on the device and a conventional monitor) without the drawback of having your normal monitor locked to the same display resolution as the Rift. The performance impact of this isn't well explored, but it's certainly handy for development and debugging.

Using the Rift as the primary display?

Using the Rift *as your primary display* isn't a realistic option. Looking through the Rift presents each eye with an image of a different portion of the desktop. Selecting anything or even figuring out on which half the mouse pointer is located is nigh impossible.

But it's important to note that some Unity applications will only run on the primary display. For those applications to run, you'll need to set the Rift as the primary display before running the application. You can configure the primary display in your operating system's Display configuration panel.

Because working with the desktop isn't really possible when looking through the Rift, you should first make sure the Display configuration panel and the application you want to launch are situated such that they'll be at least partially on the extended portion of the display. That way, you'll still have easy access to them after switching the Rift to be the main display.

Your other option is to clone (or mirror) your display, where the output of one screen gets sent to both the Rift and your monitor. In this setup, you still have two monitors but only one screen, as seen in figure A.3.

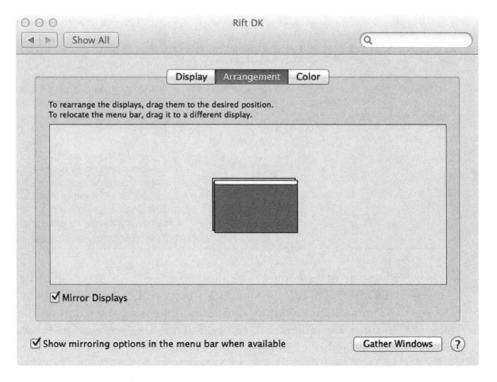

Figure A.3 Display configuration panel with the Rift configured to clone (mirror) another monitor

For both configurations, whether you're cloning a display or extending your desktop, the resolution of the display should be set to that of the Rift. Which configuration you choose is a matter of taste; there are advantages and disadvantages to both.

A.2.1   Extending or cloning (mirroring): which should you choose?

To help you decide which configuration is right for you, table A.2 summarizes the pros and cons of configuring the Rift as an extended display or as a cloned (mirrored) display.

Table A.2   Extended vs. cloned: pros and cons

Display configuration	Advantages	Disadvantages
Extended	Better performance Resolution can be optimized for the Rift without affecting your primary display.	There's a portion of the desktop where you can "lose" windows or your mouse. On some systems, when you extend the desktop to the Rift, the Rift is set by default as the primary display, making your system almost impossible to use.
Cloned (Mirrored)	You can see your entire desktop. There's no portion of the desktop where you can "lose" windows or your mouse. You can preview Rift graphics and show them to others, in the iconic "two ovals" view.	Performance can suffer. *Screen tearing* (visual artifacts in the display caused by showing information from two or more frames in a single screen draw) may occur. You may see significant twitches or jumps in animation, particularly if the frame rate falls below 70 fps. You can set the refresh rate to 60 Hz to minimize this issue, but you'll see blurring. Depending on your display driver, you may not be able to clone the Rift DK2 monitor, because it reports the resolution as 1080 × 1920 rather than 1920 × 1080. Some systems aren't able to clone a monitor that's rotated with one that's not.

The big advantage of extending your desktop is performance. Using the latency testing hardware available from Oculus VR on a DK1, we found that the latency between rendering a frame on the computer and having the pixels on the display panel change in response was about 20 ms when running in extended mode versus 50 ms when running in cloned mode. If you're measuring performance to speed up your game or fight motion sickness, that kind of latency differential can have a significant impact.

There are two downsides to extending your desktop, both of which can be quite bothersome:

- Your computer treats the additional area as potential space on which to display non-Rift content (other windows). Non-Rift-specific content displayed on the Rift and nowhere else is extremely difficult to interact with, by the very nature of the Rift display. Each eye only sees half of the overall display and some portions of the display aren't visible at all as long as the Rift lenses are in place.
- You can't see what's being displayed when you run your application unless you put on the headset. It can be helpful to you, as a developer, to see what's being displayed on the Rift while someone else is user-testing your software.

Using a cloned (mirrored) display means that there's no portion of your desktop where you can lose your mouse or windows, and it allows you to see what's being displayed on the Rift without having the Rift on yourself. Cloning has some downsides as well:

- As we mentioned earlier, performance suffers.
- The OS can only assign a screen a single resolution. The native resolutions of the Rift headsets (at least for the DK1 and DK2) aren't typical for modern monitors, so you'll have to make a choice between sacrificing some of your non-Rift monitor's resolution to target the native resolution of the Rift monitor, or using the non-Rift monitor's native resolution and allowing the Rift to scale the image to fit its display panel. Attempting to clone or split with another monitor that has lower resolution than the Rift is definitely not recommended.
- A screen can have only a single refresh rate. The *refresh rate* is the frequency with which the screen can be updated to show a new image; when two displays are cloning each other, we'd like them to be updated in rigid lockstep. Unfortunately, in many cases, even with a common refresh rate the two monitors won't be in perfect sync. This can be problematic because rendering systems such as OpenGL and Direct3D use the period after a monitor has finished updating one frame but before it begins the next, a period known as the *vertical blanking interval*, to change the image. This ensures that you never see the top of one image and the bottom of another at the same time (a display artifact known as *tearing*). But with cloned monitors, the vertical blanking interval isn't necessarily going to occur at exactly the same time, so on one of the screens tearing is likely to occur, and it's often difficult or impossible to control which one.

A.3 Improving your development environment

Whether you clone the display or you extend the display, you won't be able to see your development environment and your output at the same time. As developers, we prefer to use two monitors in addition to the Rift because it allows us to see our development environment and our output at the same time. The downside of this setup is that it's not necessarily easy to achieve. The foremost issue is that not every video card will drive three monitors. Although triple monitor support is becoming more common, it's by no means ubiquitous and it's almost unheard of in laptops. If your hardware limits you to only two monitors, there are a number of approaches you can take to add another monitor.

A.3.1   Fix it

If you have the budget and the space in your PC, you can always upgrade your video card. Both AMD and NVIDIA have entry-level graphics cards supporting triple-monitor output, so you should be able to solve the problem for less than $150.

A.3.2   Fix it cheaply

If a new video card isn't in your budget, or your hardware doesn't support it (such as on a laptop), there's another approach to adding support for another monitor: the USB video adapter. These currently run in the $50 range and are suitable for use with most laptops. If your laptop has a USB3 port, give that adapter some extra bandwidth. USB video adapters love extra bandwidth.

Regrettably, USB video adapters aren't typically suitable for 3D graphics, at least not the kind employed in working with the Rift. What they *are* suitable for is displaying your desktop and/or development environment. By making a monitor connected to a USB adapter your primary display and displaying Visual Studio or Xcode or Eclipse on it, you can leave your more powerful video card and its connected monitors (presumably including the Rift) free to render the graphically intense output you create.

Using a USB video adapter leaves you free to choose between cloning and extending your displays, with the caveat that you should probably clone only those displays connected to the same underlying video card. So in the case of a laptop development environment, you'd want to clone a screen to the laptop monitor and connect the Rift through the laptop's built-in external display port.

One caveat: As of this writing the most popular external USB video adapter chipset, manufactured by DisplayLink (www.displaylink.com), works well with Extended Desktop mode but has conflicts with Direct HMD mode. If you're experiencing issues running in Direct HMD mode on a system that has the DisplayLink drivers installed, try switching to Extended mode. In testing, that worked well for us.

A.3.3   Clone it with a gadget

There's another approach to cloning the display: a signal splitter. Due to the convergence of TV and computer monitor connectors, HDMI splitters are readily available and can be used to clone a single signal from your computer to both a conventional monitor and the Rift. As far as your computer is concerned, there's only a single monitor to deal with, but the signal goes to both pieces of hardware.

NOTE Depending on your display driver the Rift DK2 monitor may report its resolution as 1080 × 1920 rather than 1920 × 1080. We aren't aware of any consumer-level HDMI splitters that are able to clone a monitor that's rotated with one that's not. For this reason, cloning may only be useful for DK1 owners.

Fortunately, because their primary market is AV equipment owners, HDMI splitters are commodity hardware and therefore cheaply available. Unfortunately, using an HDMI splitter has a huge drawback: it interferes with the EDID information coming from the connected displays. All modern TVs, projectors, and computer monitors alike have a data structure known as Extended Display Identification Data (EDID). EDID encodes certain information about the device, chiefly the resolutions it supports, but also information about the model and manufacturer of the device. The EDID information is read by other devices that these displays are connected to over HDMI or DVI.

The Oculus SDK uses the EDID information from the Rift monitor to identify which of the various monitors attached to the system is actually a Rift. Splitters, on the other hand, usually either report the EDID of only one of the displays or the other. Or, and this is even worse, sometimes they'll construct an entirely new EDID out of some combination of the elements from the connected devices. Trying to find documentation on what a given splitter will do before you buy it is usually futile, and devices that either provide good documentation or configurability in this regard end up costing as much as, if not more than, a new video card.

HDMI splitters face the same disadvantages related to resolution and refresh rate as described in the section on cloning your display.

A.3.4 Remote development

A fourth option is to dedicate an entire PC to the Rift. It's quite reasonable to develop on one computer, deploy code or compiled binaries to another, and run there. This will naturally introduce latency around network file transfers and seamless transitions from developing to testing, but if you have a spare PC lying around and its GPU is up to the job, go for it.

The biggest downside to a two-computer development rig is that a lot of little elements of the software development process are going to get more complicated. Debugging, for one: you're going to need to learn to connect your IDE debugger to a remote process on a second system. In some contexts that can be straightforward (in Linux, it's practically the default), but not all operating systems are so forgiving of having remote processes hooking into an executing binary. We're not saying that it can't be done—we're just saying it's not trivial.

A.4 Configuring the Rift for your use

Before you begin using the Rift, it's well worth your time to take a moment to configure the Rift for your personal use. To configure the Rift, you should adjust the headset for a perfect fit and create a user profile. Both will contribute to a much more comfortable Rift experience.

ADJUSTING THE HEADSET FOR A PROPER FIT

The Rift is reasonably comfortable to wear, but it's worth taking a few minutes to adjust the headset for a proper fit. A proper fit will reduce fatigue and will help prevent motion sickness.

- *Select and install the correct lenses for your eyesight*—You can wear the Rift with glasses, but it decreases your field of view and most people find it more comfortable not to wear them. In addition, it's possible to scratch the Rift lenses with your glasses, so this is something to avoid if you can. The Rift DK2 comes with two pairs of lenses, referred to as A and B lenses. Use the A lenses if you're farsighted or don't require any vision correction, and use the B lenses if you're nearsighted. The Rift DK1 comes with three pairs of lenses, referred to as A, B, and C lenses. Use the A lenses if you're farsighted or don't require any vision correction, the B lenses if you're moderately nearsighted, and the C lenses if you're very nearsighted. See the *Oculus Rift Development Kit Instruction Manual* that comes with the kits for information on how to change out the lenses.

- *Adjust the distance between the lenses and your eyes*—Use a coin to turn the adjustment wheels on the side of the headset to set the distance of the lenses as close to your eyes as possible, but not so close your eyelashes hit them. To adjust the distance, turn the adjustment wheel toward the lenses to bring the lens closer to your eye and turn the adjustment wheel toward the display to move the lens farther away. Both lenses must be adjusted to the same distance.

- *Adjust the straps for a snug fit*—The straps should fit snugly around your head but not be too tight. Also, try not to have barrettes or hair bands in between the straps and your head.

The next step is to create a user profile. Your profile will take into account which lenses you're using and where you have set the lens adjustment wheel.

A.4.1 Create a user profile

The Rift takes into account certain physical characteristics of the user, such as height and the distance between the eyes, when rendering content. Although the default settings provide a reasonable experience, we recommend that you create a profile with your own information for the best possible experience. To create a profile, with the Rift connected and powered on, run the Oculus Configuration Utility, as seen in figure A.4.

To create a profile, click the + next to the user name pull-down list. Select the lenses you're using, specify where you have the lens adjustment wheel, and enter your gender and height. You can also click Advanced to enter additional information.

With the headset ready and a profile created, the next step is to make sure your setup is working correctly.

A.5 Verifying your setup and troubleshooting

To verify your setup, there are two demo applications we suggest running: first is the demo scene that can be accessed from the Oculus Configuration Utility (the *Desk Demo*) and second, the *OculusWorldDemo* (also known as *Tuscany*) that comes with the

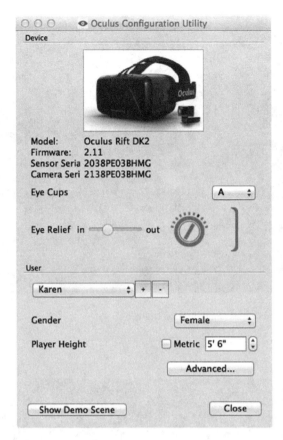

Figure A.4 The Oculus
Configuration Utility user
profile setup

Oculus SDK. The *Desk Demo* shows off the positional tracking and provides a view that can help you make sure that you have the positional camera in a good location. The downside to this demo is that you can't move about in the scene. The *Tuscany* demo gives you an opportunity to see what it's like to navigate in a VR world.

To run the *Desk Demo*, run the Oculus Configuration Utility and select Show Demo Scene. You'll be presented with the Oculus Health and Safety Warning, which after reading, you can dismiss by pressing any key. You can then begin the demo by clicking Start. You're then presented with a desk scene (figure A.5).

You may need to select Recenter from the menu panel in front of the desk to be at the desk. If you don't see the menu panel, press the spacebar or turn around until you see it. At this point, we recommend that you turn camera bounds on to make sure that you're located within the camera's tracking bounds (figure A.6).

Getting the camera into the right spot may take a bit of fiddling. But once the camera is in the right place, we suggest you try a navigable scene (*OculusWorldDemo*), to get a feel for what it's like to move around. A link to the *OculusWorldDemo* executable file can be found in the root of the Oculus SDK installation. This demo puts you

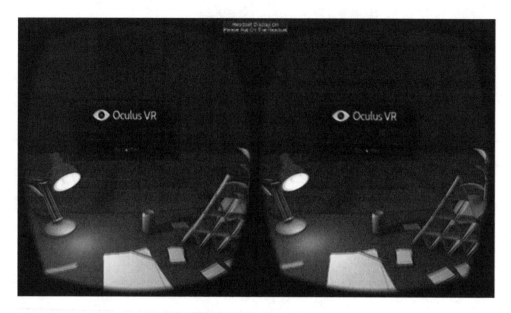

Figure A.5   The *Desk Demo* run from the Oculus Configuration Utility

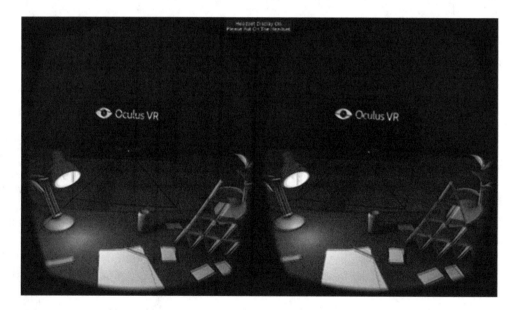

Figure A.6   The desk scene with camera bounds turned on

Figure A.7 *OculusWorldDemo (Tuscany)* **screen shot**

inside an old Tuscan villa, as shown in figure A.7. You can move around and explore the environment using the A, S, W, D keys (on a QWERTY keyboard) and mouse controls, or a connected game controller such as an Xbox gamepad.

Make sure you see the demo running on the Rift display and on any additional displays cloning the Rift. With the headset on, move your head and look around to ensure that head tracking is being correctly registered.

For either demo, if you aren't seeing the display and/or the demo isn't head tracking, here are some things to check:

- Make sure you have powered on the Rift. For the DK2, use the power button on the headset and check that the power indicator light is blue. The indicator light glows blue when the headset is powered on and receiving a video signal and orange when the headset is on but not receiving a video signal. For the DK1, use the power button on the control box and check for the blue light in the Oculus eye logo.

- Check all of the Rift's cables. It's easy to forget to plug one of them in. You can look at the Oculus Configuration Utility to see if the Rift and positional camera have been detected.

- If only one eye is displaying, or you see a white square for one of the eyes, check to see that you're running the Rift using the correct resolution. This can also happen if you're in windowed mode and some other pop-up is covering the other eye.

If this is your first time using the Rift, you may experience some motion sickness. For advice on dealing with motion sickness—and especially, for our advice that you *not* try to just "power through" the queasiness—please refer to section 1.6.

A.6   *Developing without a Rift*

One concern we often hear is that the Rift is still a work in progress and the DevKits can be hard to come by. If you're interested in building your game or app for the Rift but don't want to wait for your development kit from Oculus (or pay the 200% markup that some resellers are asking for kits on eBay!), then you may be working without a headset. Never fear: you can do it.

Remember, the Rift is really two discrete devices in one: the tracker and the display. Both are accessed through the Oculus Rift SDK. The tracker will send streams of packets as messages, instances of OVR::Message, that you'd normally read directly from the device via the SDK. We discuss the mechanics of this in detail in chapter 2. The display is also identified through the SDK, and once you've targeted the preferred video device, you'll need to render images to that device with exactly the correct aspect ratio and optical distortion. Chapter 4 delves into those optical details.

Without a Rift, you can still use the SDK. You can build and link your code against the SDK's libraries without an actual headset at the other end of the wires. You won't get any packets and you won't find the display (of course), but the SDK libraries will still load and run. For that matter, you don't need to have found a Rift display to show video; as discussed earlier, any screen will do while you're developing. If you're doing it right, you'll see the Rift's split-screen rounded images on your normal monitor.

Another approach is recording a Rift for offline use. If you're a small development team and you've only got one DK among a few of you, a useful trick is to record the packets streaming from the Rift while one user wears it, and then "play back" those packets from disk for other developers. You can simulate how your software will respond to the quaternions indicating a user looking up, down, and around by feeding the packets back into your app as though they'd just come in fresh off the wire, without actually having the wire. In essence you simulate having a Rift.

Another option is to use Unity, a popular game engine. Unity's support for the Rift continues to evolve, and it can easily be used to develop for the Rift, even when you don't have a headset. See chapters 7 and 8 for more on Unity.

appendix B
Mathematics and
software patterns
for 3D graphics

This appendix covers

- Coordinate systems, what they mean, and how they're best expressed in code and matrix form
- Fundamentals of matrix linear algebra, with a focus on concepts that are key to 3D computer graphics
- Methods for representing rotations
- Examples of software design patterns common in 3D graphics: scene graphs, matrix stacks, and the modelview matrix stack

This appendix isn't a mathematics textbook; there's a vast field out there dedicated to linear algebra and matrices, which these few pages couldn't possibly hope to contain. Here we'll touch only on concepts directly related to computer graphics and the Rift, and we'll do so fleetingly. For more depth, please check out the references in appendix C, online, or at your local library.

B.1   Coordinate systems

Within any virtual environment, somewhere there's a position [0, 0, 0]. We refer to this as the *origin* and all other frames of reference are defined relative to this point. The origin may be anywhere—anchored to the user's screen or at the virtual center of a virtual world. In a virtual environment, there's really no "there" there, so the origin can be literally anywhere you want.

If an object is defined in coordinates that are relative to the origin, then we say that it's defined in *world coordinates*.

Frequently, we want to be able to describe the relative positions of vertices in an object without relying on their absolute position in world coordinates. In such cases it's common to use a frame of reference that's specific to the object, which we call *local coordinates* (see figure B.1). Local coordinates are defined in terms of world coordinates by an orientation and a position (and sometimes more), which are bound to the object. In local coordinates, the vertices are defined relative to a local center and a local trio of X, Y, and Z axes; these form the local frame of reference. The position and orientation of the local frame of reference can now be changed freely without ever changing the [X, Y, Z] values of the vertices defined within that frame.

To define the conversion from local coordinates to world coordinates, it's common to capture the orientation and position together as a four-by-four matrix, which is called the *transform* of the object. When each vertex defined in local coordinates is multiplied by the object's transform, the resulting point is the position of that vertex in world coordinates.

In computer graphics it's common to refer to other standard frames of reference beyond world and local, such as camera coordinates, in which all geometry is defined

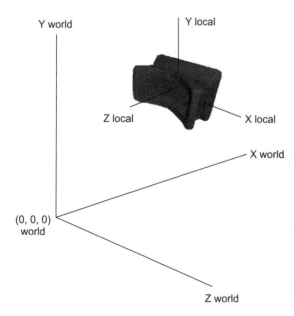

Figure B.1 A model of the Rift with local axes, positioned at the origin of a local coordinate system, in the context of the world coordinate system

relative to the camera, and screen coordinates, in which all geometry has been transformed into perspective projection for rendering to the screen.

B.2 Introduction to matrices

A *matrix*[1] in 3D computer graphics today is a rectangular array of real numbers, typically a two-dimensional 4×4 grid.[2] Matrices are one of the core concepts in modern graphics and are used by virtually every 3D platform on the market. The term *matrix* has many uses and many meanings, across mathematics and beyond, but this appendix will focus explicitly on the mainstream, contemporary, computer graphics usage of matrices. So, for our limited purposes, matrices are 4×4 arrays of floats or doubles.

Here's an example of a matrix:

```
[1 0 0 0]
[0 1 0 0]
[0 0 1 0]
[0 0 0 1]
```

This is what we call the *identity matrix*: a 4×4 grid of numbers that has much the same effect in matrix math as the number 1 does in conventional math. (If we multiply any other matrix by the identity matrix, the result will always be the other matrix.)

The mathematical properties of matrices include the following:

- Matrices support many of the same operations as real numbers:
  - Addition
  - Subtraction
  - Multiplication with another matrix
  - Multiplication with a vector
  - Inversion $(1 / x)$
- Matrix multiplication is *associative*:

  ```
  (A • B) • C = A • (B • C)
  ```
- Matrix multiplication is *not commutative*:

  ```
  A • B ≠ B • A
  ```
- The formula for matrix-vector multiplication is as follows:[3]

  ```
  [A B C D]   [ Q ]   [ AQ + BR + CS + DT ]
  [E F G H] • [ R ] = [ EQ + FR + GS + HT ]
  [I J K L]   [ S ]   [ IQ + JR + KS + LT ]
  [M N O P]   [ T ]   [ MQ + NR + OS + PT ]
  ```

---

[1] "Unfortunately, no one can be told what the Matrix is. You have to see it for yourself."

[2] ...wait, we just did.

[3] In GLSL, the OpenGL shader language, these lines of additions and multiplications could simply be written as

```
vec4 V;             // GLSL vector, length 4
mat4 M;             // GLSL matrix, 4x4
vec4 W = M * V;     // W is set to M times V
```

which demonstrates that GLSL's primitive vec4 and mat4 types for vectors and matrices take a lot of the hard work out of matrix mathematics!

B.3   Matrix transforms

A *transform* is a recipe for converting locations in space from one frame of reference to another, usually expressed in a 4 × 4 matrix. Computer graphics is home to many such transforms, such as perspective and projection.

When you're building a scene out of 3D geometry, three transforms are especially useful:

- *Translation*—Motion in space. A translation will linearly add to the X, Y, and Z coordinates of a point.
- *Rotation*—A change in orientation that preserves the location of the origin.
- *Scale*—A change in size on one or more of the three axes. You can scale an object on any of the three axes independently, which is convenient for transforming primitives into more advanced shapes, such as stretching a sphere into an ellipsoid.

Each of the core transforms is easily expressed by a 4 × 4 matrix, as shown in table B.1.

Table B.1   Common matrix transforms

`[1 0 0 x]`
`[0 1 0 y]`
`[0 0 1 z]`
`[0 0 0 1]`
Translation by vector [x, y, z]
	`[x 0 0 0]`
	`[0 y 0 0]`
	`[0 0 z 0]`
	`[0 0 0 1]`
	Scale by vector [x, y, z]

`[1    0      0    0]`
`[0  cos θ -sin θ  0]`
`[0  sin θ  cos θ  0]`
`[0    0      0    1]`
Rotation by θ around X
	`[ cos θ 0 sin θ  0]`
	`[   0    1   0    0]`
	`[-sin θ 0 cos θ  0]`
	`[   0    0   0    1]`
	Rotation by θ around Y
		`[cos θ -sin θ 0  0]`
		`[sin θ  cos θ 0  0]`
		`[  0      0   1  0]`
		`[  0      0   0  1]`
		Rotation by θ around Z

`[  (cos θ)+x²(1-cos θ)`	`y(1-cos θ)-z(sin θ)`	`xz(1-cos θ)+y(sin θ) 0 ]`	
`[ xy(1-cos θ)+z(sin θ)`	`(cos θ)+y²(1-cos θ)`	`yz(1-cos θ)-x(sin θ) 0 ]`	
`[ xz(1-cos θ)-y(sin θ)`	`yz(1-cos θ)+x(sin θ)`	`(cos θ)+z²(1-cos θ) 0 ]`	
`[          0`	`0`	`0           1 ]`	
Rotation by θ around arbitrary unit axis [x, y, z]			

B.4   Representing rotation

In addition to matrix transforms, mathematicians and software developers have developed several other methods of representing orientation. Although a 4 × 4 matrix representation is convenient because it can be concatenated with other transforms, it doesn't lend itself to easy inspection or interpolation.

- If the primary interaction with an orientation is direct user control, such as in an airplane, then orientation is typically stored in *Euler angles*.
- If the primary interaction with an orientation is smooth transition from one orientation to another, such as by traveling a great circle arc around a sphere, then orientation is typically stored in *quaternions*.

- If the goal is to interpolate from one point on the unit sphere to another point on the unit sphere, then the technique of *spherical linear interpolation ("slerp")* may be used without an explicit rotation representation.

B.4.1 Euler angles

Euler angles represent an orientation as the combination of *roll*, *pitch*, and *yaw* (figure B.2). These values are defined relative to a stable initial orientation—that is, local coordinates:

- Roll is rotation about the local Z axis.
- Pitch is rotation about the local Y axis.
- Yaw is rotation about the local X axis.

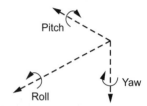

Euler angles are excellent for representing orientation in a way that's easy to understand. They're also handy for writing code that converts from one coordinate system to another, which might have a different "handedness" or which might swap the purpose of the Y and Z axes. Many systems that are grounded more in cartography than graphics will represent vertical translations with the Z axis rather than the Y axis.

Figure B.2 The classic Euler angles: roll, pitch, and yaw

To convert from Euler angles to a matrix, the three scalar values are converted to rotations about their respective axes. The rotation matrices are then concatenated together with matrix multiplication. When calculating the matrix form, bear in mind that all three angles are defined in local coordinates. Each rotation changes the axes of the other two.

There are six possible orderings of the three rotation matrices; the ordering roll-pitch-yaw is common. Using the matrices given in table B.1,

```
roll = (rotation about Z);
pitch = (rotation about (Roll • Y));
yaw = (rotation about (Pitch • Raw • Z));
Cumulative orientation matrix = yaw • pitch • roll;
```

B.4.2 Quaternions

Quaternions[4] are four-dimensional mathematical constructs that use a combination of real and imaginary floating-point numbers to express an oriented frame of reference. Quaternions are handy for storing and expressing rotation transformations in a basis-independent, handedness-independent manner, and lend themselves well to interpolation.

---

[4] This appendix speaks specifically to *unit quaternions*, quaternions of unit length. In computer graphics, when working with quaternions, it's extremely common to assume unit length.

A quaternion is typically written as

```
Q = w + x i + y j + z k
```

where i, j, and k are independent imaginary vectors. The parameter w is a real scalar, and so the quaternion itself is a four-dimensional entity.

The rotation by angle θ around unit vector (x, y, z) can be written as a quaternion:

```
Q = cos (θ/2) + sin (θ/2) (x i + y j + z k)
```

The unit quaternion Q = w + x i + y j + z k can be written as a 4 × 4 rotation matrix:

```
[ 1-2y2-2z2  2xy-2zw   2xz+2yw  0 ]
[   2xy+2zw  1-2x2-2z2  2yz-2xw  0 ]
[   2xz-2yw  2yz+2xw   1-2x2-2y2 0 ]
[     0         0          0    1 ]
```

Quaternions have interesting mathematical properties, such as the fact that unlike normal 3D vectors, you can multiply two quaternions to get a third. But the multiplication operation on quaternions isn't commutative—that is, AB ≠ BA. (This makes sense: matrices have the same trait.) But where a matrix is stored in 9 or 16 floats, a quaternion uses only 4 and is always invertible.

B.4.3   *Spherical linear interpolation ("slerp")*

Spherical linear interpolation, sometimes written more succinctly as "slerp," is a method for achieving constant-speed linear interpolation between two points on the unit sphere. Slerp is useful for operations such as swinging a virtual camera around a fixed point in space.

Given two points P1, P2, both on the unit sphere, find the angle θ between the vectors from the origin to P1 and P2. The operation slerp(P1, P2, t) is then defined to be

$$slerp(P1,\ P2,\ t) = \frac{sin((1-t)\theta)}{sin(\theta)}P1 + \frac{sin(t\theta)}{sin(\theta)}P2$$

As t goes from 0 to 1, this will smoothly linearly interpolate a point around the unit sphere, following the shortest path.

Note that slerp can't be used if the two points P1 and P2 are exactly opposite each other across the unit sphere (P1 = –P2) because this will yield θ = 0. If θ is zero, $sin(0) = 0$ will yield a divide by zero in the slerp expression.

Slerp can also be used for interpolating between quaternions. If interpolating quaternions, slerp will return a smooth linear rotation from one quaternion to another. This can be very effective for camera transition effects, such as smoothly reorienting from one fixed camera position to another.

B.5 *The scene graph software design pattern*

Every virtual environment is founded in the world basis, but most objects have their own local coordinate systems. In many scenes, objects are positioned and oriented relative to other objects, not to the world at large. This introduces the concept of coordinate systems that are defined relative to other coordinate systems, which are in turn themselves relative to yet more coordinate systems.[5]

The *scene graph* design pattern is a common software design pattern often found in 3D applications that display scenes of nested objects. A scene graph stores and accesses all objects in the scene through a directed tree data structure, in which each node is associated with a matrix transform. When rendering an object at a node, its vertices are transformed by the concatenated multiplication of all of the transforms of all of the nodes above it in the tree.

For example, if the geometry of a hand is defined by its transformation relative to the arm, and the arm in turn is described relative to the body, then the assembly of all elements in the scene could be expressed in a scene graph. Figure B.3 shows the hand, arm, and torso of a robot.

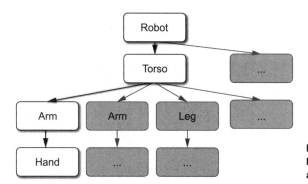

Figure B.3 A scene graph. Each node can store geometry and a 4 × 4 matrix transform.

The cumulative transform of a leaf node is the concatenation by matrix multiplication of its transform with the ordered concatenation of each previous parent in the tree:

$$T_{\text{handToWorld}} = T_{\text{robot}} \bullet T_{\text{torso}} \bullet T_{\text{arm}} \bullet T_{\text{hand}}$$

Recalling that matrix multiplication is associative, this means that the vector product of applying the cumulative transform to geometry defined at the level of a leaf node (such as to find V, the world coordinates representation of vertex coordinate V_{hand}) can be expanded as follows:

$$
\begin{aligned}
V &= T_{\text{handToWorld}} \bullet V_{\text{hand}} \\
&= T_{\text{robot}} \bullet T_{\text{torso}} \bullet T_{\text{arm}} \bullet T_{\text{hand}} \bullet V_{\text{hand}} \\
&= T_{\text{robot}} \bullet (T_{\text{torso}} \bullet (T_{\text{arm}} \bullet (T_{\text{hand}} \bullet V_{\text{hand}})))
\end{aligned}
$$

---

[5] "It's turtles, all the way down."

where

V_{hand} is in hand local coordinates;

$T_{hand} \bullet V_{hand}$ is in arm local coordinates;

$T_{arm} \bullet (T_{hand} \bullet V_{hand})$ is in torso local coordinates;

$T_{torso} \bullet (T_{arm} \bullet (T_{hand} \bullet V_{hand}))$ is in robot local coordinates; and

$T_{robot} \bullet (T_{torso} \bullet (T_{arm} \bullet (T_{hand} \bullet V_{hand})))$ is in world coordinates.

B.6   *The matrix stack software design pattern*

A common software design pattern associated with implementations of scene graphs is the *matrix stack*. A matrix stack is a data structure whose behavior is modeled on that of a classic stack, modified to simplify the most common use cases of matrix math.

The API of a matrix stack typically consists of the following methods:

- `void push(Matrix)`—Pushes a new matrix onto the top of the stack, setting its value to be equal to the matrix product of the current top of the stack times the new entry.
- `Matrix pop()`—Removes the topmost element of the stack.
- `Matrix peek()`—Returns the current topmost element of the stack or the identity matrix if the stack is empty.

The matrix stack differs from a conventional stack in its `push()` operation. Where a conventional stack's `push()` operation will insert a new value verbatim at the top of the data structure, the `push()` operation of the matrix stack computes the product of the current top of the stack times the new parameter received and inserts the product of the two at the top of the data structure.

Matrix stacks are an especially useful design pattern when geometry is defined relative to other scene elements, and they're frequently used in conjunction with scene graphs.

The real selling point of the matrix stack design pattern is that it caches the products of matrices that will be used more than once. In the robot example given earlier, if the robot had four arms, the product of ($T_{robot} \bullet T_{torso}$) would only need to be computed once.

```
push(Trobot);        // Stack = Trobot
push(Ttorso);        // Stack = Trobot • Ttorso
for each arm do
   push(Tarm);       // Stack = Trobot • Ttorso • Tarm
   render arm;
   pop();            // Stack = Trobot • Ttorso
pop(Ttorso);
push...
```

B.7   *The modelview software design pattern*

You can consider your camera—the viewpoint from which you'll be rendering your virtual scene—as though it were an element in your scene, just like any other scene object. You can store a local-to-world transform for the camera, which if applied to [0, 0, 0] (the local center of the camera, from its own point of view) returns the camera's position in world coordinates.

A common design pattern among those who've chosen scene graphs and matrix stacks is to redefine the ultimate origin of the world from global coordinates to coordinates that are relative to the camera by redefining the world as being centered on the camera instead of the world origin. In this approach, all geometry, all positions, and all spatial relationships are entirely defined from the point of view of the viewer; the universe centers on the user. In other words, the world really *does* revolve around you.

In a matrix stack framework, this is quite simple to implement: instead of the bottommost matrix on the stack being an identity matrix, it can be a world-to-camera transformation that transforms from the world basis to the camera basis. This isn't actually the transform of the camera itself but rather its inverse. You don't want your camera in your scene; you want to shift the whole world around as if the camera were the origin (without the constraint of keeping the camera always at the actual origin). The use of a matrix to hold both the (inverse) transformation of the view as well as the transformations of all the models stacked above it in the scene is the origin of the term *modelview* matrix. In this pattern you'll often see references to the *current modelview matrix*, which refers to the particular matrix that's currently at the top of the stack.

Until the release of version 3.3, OpenGL provided an API for maintaining and manipulating matrix stacks, including a stack explicitly dedicated to the role of modelview stack. This stack approach was deprecated in 3.3 and removed entirely in 4.3, once the standardization of shaders meant that the implementation of local-to-world-to-camera transformations had become the responsibility of the individual software author. Today many applications reproduce the old matrix stack functionality or use a library that does so, because it was a marvelously convenient way of working with nested models and frames of reference. This book is no exception; our example code uses the GLM library to store and manipulate matrices, and our `Stacks` class includes the method `Stacks::modelview()`, which returns a static singleton modelview matrix instance.

appendix C
Suggested books
and resources

There is a tremendous wealth of resources available today, online and on paper, about virtual reality, 3D graphics, user interface design, and the host of other topics we've touched on in this book. In this appendix we've listed just a few of the sources that we found educational and inspiring. We've also included a shortlist of some of the earliest and most influential Rift demos.

Books, research papers, and websites

3D graphics programming

- *Fundamentals of Computer Graphics,* by P. Shirley, M. Ashikhmin, and S. Marschner (A. K. Peters/CRC Press, 2009)
- *Computer Graphics: Principles and Practice,* by J. D. Foley, A. van Dam, S. K. Feiner, and J. F. Hughes (Addison-Wesley Professional, 2013)

OpenGL

- *The OpenGL Programming Guide: The Official Guide to Learning OpenGL, Version 4.3,* by D. Shreiner, G. Sellers, J. M. Kessenich, and B. M. Licea-Kane (Addison-Wesley Professional, 2013)
- *OpenGL SuperBible,* by G. Sellers, R. S. Wright, and N. Haemel (Addison-Wesley Professional, 2013)
- *OpenGL Insights,* by P. Cozzi and C. Riccio (A. K. Peters/CRC Press, 2012)
- *Shadertoy*—shadertoy.com

- *Anton's OpenGL 4 Tutorials*—antongerdelan.net/opengl
- The *GPU Gems* series, by various authors (Addison Wesley)

Developing for the Rift

- *Oculus Best Practices Guide*—developer.oculus.com/documentation

Motion sickness/simulator sickness

- *Textbook of Maritime Medicine*, by the Norwegian Centre for Maritime Medicine (2013). See chapter 20, "Motion Sickness" (textbook.ncmm.no).
- *Validating an Efficient Method to Quantify Motion Sickness*, by B. Keshavarz and H. Hecht (2011). *Human Factors: The Journal of the Human Factors and Ergonomics Society* 53.4: 415–26.
- *Simulator Sickness Questionnaire*, by R. S. Kennedy, N. E. Lane, K. S. Berbaum, and M. G. Lilienthal (1993). *The International Journal of Aviation Psychology* 3(3): 203–20.
- Motion Sickness Susceptibility Questionnaire Revised and Its Relationship to Other Forms of Sickness, by J. F. Golding (1998). *Brain Research Bulletin*, 47(5): 507–16.

UI design for VR

- 3D User Interfaces: New Directions and Perspectives, by D. A. Bowman, S. Coquillart, B. Froehlich, M. Hirose...and W. Stuerzlinger. (2008). *IEEE Computer Graphics and Applications* 28(6): 20–36.
- Design and Evaluation of Mouse Cursors in a Stereoscopic Desktop Environment, by L. Schemali and E. Eisemann (2014). *3D User Interfaces (3DUI), 2014 IEEE Symposium* (pp. 67-70). IEEE. Recorded talk is available at vimeo.com/91489021.
- Developing Virtual Reality Games and Experiences—www.gdcvault.com/play/1020714. Presented at GDC 2014.
- Egocentric Object Manipulation in Virtual Environments: Empirical Evaluation of Interaction Techniques, by I. Poupyrev, S. Weghorst, M. Billinghurst, and T. Ichikawa (1998). *Computer Graphics Forum*, 17(3): 41–52.
- Kinect Hand Detection, by G. Gallagher—video.mit.edu/watch/kinect-hand-detection-12073
- *Make It So: Interaction Design Lessons from Science Fiction*, by N. Shedroff and C. Noessel (Rosenfeld Media, 2012)
- Lessons learned porting *Team Fortress 2* to virtual reality—media.steampowered.com/apps/valve/2013/Team_Fortress_in_VR_GDC.pdf

- Pointing at 3D Target Projections with One-Eyed and Stereo Cursors, by R. J. Teather and W. Stuerzlinger. (2013). *ACM Conference on Human Factors in Computing Systems*: 159–68.
- Pointing to the future of UI, by J. Underkoffler (2010). Talk given at TED, www.ted.com/talks/john_underkoffler_drive_3d_data_with_a_gesture.
- Selection Using a One-Eyed Cursor in a Fish Tank VR Environment, by C. Ware and K. Lowther. (1997). *ACM Transactions on Computer-Human Interaction Journal*, 4(4): 309–22.
- *Usability Engineering*, by J. Nielsen (Morgan Kaufmann, 1993)
- *VR Lessons Learned: A Post-mortem published by Marauder Interactive about Enemy StarFighter*—enemystarfighter.com/blog/2013/9/5/vr-lessons-learned
- Marvel's Agents of S.H.I.E.L.D – T.R.A.C.K.S. (season 1, episode 13). The clip with the holotable is available at www.youtube.com/watch?v=SeiJ2jHyy7U.
- World Builder, by B. Branit (2007)—www.youtube.com/watch?v=VzFpg271sm8

Unity

- Unity official site: unity3d.com
- Unity documentation, tutorials, and training: unity3d.com/learn
- *Unity in Action*, by J. Hocking (Manning, 2015)

Demos, games, and apps

VR demos, games, and applications *worth a view*

- *Tuscany*, by Oculus—share.oculusvr.com/app/oculus-tuscany-demo
- *Team Fortress 2*—www.teamfortress.com
- *EVE Online*—www.eveonline.com
- *Don't Let Go!*, by Skydome Studios—share.oculus.com/app/dont-let-go
- *Chicken Walk*, by Mechabit Ltd.—share.oculusvr.com/app/chicken-walk
- *GiganotosaurusVR*, by Meld Media—share.oculusvr.com/app/meld-media—giganotosaurusvr
- *Jerry's Place*, by Greg Miller—jerrysplacevr.com
- *Private Eye*—privateeyevr.com/
- *Shadow Projection*—globalgamejam.org/2014/games/shadow-projection-oculus-rift
- *Spaceflight VR*—share.oculusvr.com/app/space-flight-vr
- *Strike Suit Zero*—strikesuitzero.com/
- *Technolust*, by Iris Productions—irisproductions.ca/technolust/
- *Titans of Space*, by DrashVR—www.crunchywood.com
- *Trial of the Rift Drifter*, by Aldin Dynamics—share.oculusvr.com/app/trial-of-the-rift-drifter

Oculus Share

A number of demos can be found on Oculus Share (share.oculusvr.com). Oculus Share is the official Oculus developer portal where you can upload games, tech demos, and experiments. It's well worth keeping an eye on this site; new content is added regularly.

appendix D
Glossary

This appendix contains a glossary of terms common to virtual reality development.

6DOF   A common abbreviation for "six degrees of freedom," referring to devices able to move and sense position on the three rotation axes (yaw, pitch, roll) and the three spatial axes (X, Y, Z).

AUGMENTED REALITY   The nascent field of using computing devices to extend and enhance data about the real world around us. Glasses that overlay information about what the user is looking at, or Tony Stark's heads-up display in the movie *Iron Man*, are typical examples.

AUGMENTED VIRTUAL REALITY   The use of the visual motifs of augmented reality in a virtual reality context, such as a HUD inside a video game. Well suited to the blending of real-world video and other streaming content into a Rift application.

BARREL DISTORTION   The mathematical inverse of a pincushion distortion. In a barrel distortion, lines that are normally straight curve outward.

CHROMATIC ABERRATION   A type of distortion caused by lenses that fail to bend light of different frequencies by the same amount. Blue light will be bent at a greater angle than green light, and green at a greater angle than red. This is the property that gives a prism the ability to split a white beam of light into a spectrum.

COLLIMATED LIGHT   Light whose rays have been aligned in parallel, such as in a laser. Because it doesn't converge, collimated light is described as "converging at infinity." The Oculus Rift uses high-quality lenses to collimate the light from its screen.

COORDINATE SYSTEM   In a three-dimensional coordinate system, three coordinates [X, Y, Z] locate a point by its distance from an origin [0,0,0] where three orthogonal axes meet. In the initial frame of reference of the Rift and in OpenGL graphics, the X axis typically measures left-to-right, the Y axis typically measures height or elevation, and the Z axis typically measures back-to-front.

CUTSCENE   A long-standing device used in games to convey story without direct interaction from the player. In cut scenes the player stops playing and watches a little movie inside the game—maybe a snippet of film with real actors, or a rendered CGI animation, or even prerecorded animations in the engine of the game itself; there are many styles.

EULER ANGLES   A trio of angles representing roll, pitch, and yaw. In conjunction with a fixed ordering of evaluation, these values describe the orientation of a frame of reference.

HEAD POSE   In VR applications, the head pose is a combination of the orientation and position of the head relative to some fixed coordinate system.

HMD   Head-mounted display.

IMMERSION   The art and technology of surrounding the user with a virtual context, such that there's world all around you.

INTERPUPILLARY DISTANCE (IPD)   The distance between the pupils of the eyes.

LATENCY   An interval in time between two correlated events. In the Oculus Rift, latency is the interval between the time when a user moves their head and the time when the view is updated to reflect the change. The term *motion-to-photons* is also used.

LOCAL COORDINATES   Coordinates that are relative to the origin and frame of reference of the current object.

MATRIX   In computer graphics, a matrix is a rectangular array of numbers, most commonly 4×4.

MATRIX STACK   A data structure whose behavior is modeled on that of a classic stack, modified to simplify the most common use cases of matrix math. Commonly used in the context of a scene graph or hierarchical model.

MODELVIEW MATRIX   A matrix that determines the position and orientation of the virtual camera in 3D space. It can also be used to position individual items within the scene relative to the camera.

MOTION SICKNESS   The symptoms of discomfort people feel when experiencing a mismatch between actual motion and what their body expects. In traditional motion sickness, such as you might get from riding in a car or boat, motion is felt but not seen.

ORIGIN The position at coordinates [0, 0, 0]. All other positions are defined relative to this point. Every frame of reference has an origin.

PARALLAX The apparent change in an object's position when viewed from two different angles (such as when the object, or the viewer, is in motion).

PINCUSHION DISTORTION The distortion that happens when you magnify an image using a lens. In a pincushion distortion, lines that are normally straight curve inward.

PITCH Rotation on the X axis. When using the Rift, this is when you tilt your head forward (look toward the ground) or back (look to the sky).

PRESENCE The visceral reaction to a convincing immersion experience: when immersion is so good that the body reacts instinctively to the virtual world as though it's the real one.

PROJECTION MATRIX A matrix that's responsible for mapping points in 3D space into perspective, such that they can then be projected onto a plane (the display panel) to produce a 2D image that appears 3D. A projection matrix implicitly defines a view frustum with a given field of view, as well as the aspect ratio of the output display panel.

PROPRIOCEPTION The sense of the relative position of parts of the body, as well as the strength of effort currently being exerted.

QUATERNION A four-dimensional mathematical construct that can be used to represent a three-dimensional rotation transformation. Quaternions can be difficult to work with, but they're a more efficient means of storing an arbitrary rotation than a rotation matrix; a quaternion needs four floating-point values whereas the matrix needs nine or sixteen.

ROLL Rotation on the Z axis. When using the Rift, this is when you tilt your head to the left or right, toward one shoulder.

ROTATION MATRIX A 3×3 or 4×4 matrix that describes a change of orientation, without altering position or scale, which preserves the relative angles between vectors.

SCALE MATRIX A 3×3 or 4×4 matrix that describes a change of size, without altering position or orientation. If the scale is uniform—that is, all three axes are scaled to the same degree—then the scale will preserve the relative angles between vectors; alternatively you can scale an object on any of the three axes independently.

SCENE GRAPH A software design pattern often found in 3D applications that display scenes of nested objects. A scene graph stores and accesses all objects in the scene through a directed tree data structure, in which each node is associated with a matrix transform and may be associated with scene element geometry.

SIMULATOR SICKNESS   Another name for motion sickness specifically triggered by being in a simulated or VR environment.

STEREOSCOPY   A method of provoking the illusion of depth in a binocular view by transmitting different images to each eye.

STRABISMUS   A disorder in which your eyes don't line up. This misalignment can result in stereoblindness (the inability to see in 3D using stereo vision) or double vision. This disorder is also known colloquially as being cross-eyed or wall-eyed.

TRANSFORM   A recipe for converting locations in space from one frame of reference to another, usually expressed in a 4×4 matrix.

TRANSLATION MATRIX   A 4×4 matrix that expresses motion in space. A translation will add to the X, Y, and Z coordinates of a point, while preserving the relative angles between vectors.

VECTION   A type of self-movement illusion that can occur if a moving object takes up the majority of a user's view, and the user interprets the situation as self-movement that they didn't initiate. A classic example of vection is when someone is at a train station and a nearby train moves. They see the train move and interpret that as though they're moving.

VERGENCE   The simultaneous movement of both eyes to achieve binocular vision.

VIEW FRUSTUM   The region of space in the modeled world that may appear on the screen; this is the field of view of the notional camera. Typically shaped like a truncated pyramid.

VIRTUAL REALITY (VR)   A computer-generated environment that can simulate physical presence in places in the real world or imagined worlds.

VR SICKNESS   Another name for motion sickness specifically triggered by being in a VR environment.

WORLD COORDINATES   A frame of reference defined relative to the global origin.

YAW   Rotation on the Y axis. When using the Rift, this is when you turn your head to your left or right.

index

RELATED MANNING TITLES

Unity in Action
Multiplatform game development in C# with Unity 5
by Joseph Hocking

> ISBN: 9781617292323
> 352 pages, $44.99
> June 2015

C# in Depth, Third Edition
by Jon Skeet

> ISBN: 9781617291340
> 616 pages, $49.99
> September 2013

D3.js in Action
by Elijah Meeks

> ISBN: 9781617292118
> 352 pages, $44.99
> February 2015

Arduino in Action
by Martin Evans, Joshua Noble,
  and Jordan Hochenbaum

> ISBN: 9781617290244
> 368 pages, $39.99
> May 2013

For ordering information go to www.manning.com